AF361613

Land and Liberty

Hagley Library Studies in Business, Technology, and Politics

Richard R. John, *Series Editor*

LAND AND LIBERTY

Henry George and the Crafting
of Modern Liberalism

Christopher William England

Johns Hopkins University Press
Baltimore

Johns Hopkins University Press
2715 North Charles Street
Baltimore, Maryland 21218
www.press.jhu.edu

Library of Congress Cataloging-in-Publication Data

Names: England, Christopher William, 1984– author.
Title: Land and liberty : Henry George and the crafting
of modern liberalism / Christopher William England.
Description: Baltimore : Johns Hopkins University Press, [2023] |
Series: Hagley Library studies in business, technology, and politics |
Includes bibliographical references and index.
Identifiers: LCCN 2022007839 | ISBN 9781421445403 (hardcover) |
ISBN 9781421445410 (ebook)
Subjects: LCSH: George, Henry, 1839–1897. | Single tax—United States—
History. | Land tenure—United States—History. |
Liberalism—United States—History.
Classification: LCC HD1313 .E44 2023 | DDC 336.22—dc23/eng/20220218
LC record available at https://lccn.loc.gov/2022007839

A catalog record for this book is available from the British Library.

*Special discounts are available for bulk purchases of this book. For more
information, please contact Special Sales at specialsales@jh.edu.*

For Tameka and Theo

CONTENTS

Introduction

In 1869 Henry George, a self-educated San Francisco newspaper editor, traveled to New York to break the Associated Press's news monopoly.[1] He failed. Popular lore, however, was that he did something more significant. While walking through the city's slums, he was struck by the squalor and had an epiphany. His son in later years recounted that George wandered the city, "thinking how here, at the center of civilization, should be realized the dream of the pioneer—the hard conditions of life softened, and society, preserving the general relations of equality, raised as a mass from the bottom into a state of peace and plenty. How different the view that met his gaze! On every hand he beheld evidences of advancing civilization, but of a civilization that was one-sided; that piled up riches for the few and huddled the many in filth and poverty."[2]

In the 1830s, Alexis de Tocqueville had traveled the United States and found a country so enraptured with "a popular and universal faith" in progress that even steamboats were not built to be "durable," because people looked to the future, rather than holding on to the past.[3] New York City cast a pall over this optimism. George's experience mirrored that of other provincial utopians, such as Charles Fourier and Friedrich Engels, who were disillusioned by the future they witnessed in the metropole and searched for their own solutions to the paradox of progress and poverty.[4] After years of searching, George concluded that rent grew steadily with the progress of society, redistributing wealth from producers to idle landholders. George dedicated his life to socializing rent and securing the fruits of progress for all.

After the Russian Revolution shook the world in 1917, Karl Marx looked like the inevitable heir of this utopian moment. But until then, when Georgists crossed paths with socialists, they generally did so as senior partners. A decade before the Bolsheviks seized control of Russia, they had squandered the month of May 1907 in London, unable to win over their fellow socialists and lacking the money to either complete the Fifth Congress of the Russian Social Democratic Labor Party or return to Russia. The globe-trotting businessman Joseph Fels was happy to strike a blow at Russian feudalism and rescued the conference with a loan of £1,700. Vladimir Lenin symbolically acknowledged Fels by sitting next to him as the conference closed. Lenin, however, could not manage a formal thanks to his bourgeois benefactor, instead mustering "a few brusquely spoken acknowledgements in German" and disregarding the Georgist pamphlet Fels handed him as he departed.[5] Lenin's bemused response was mirrored by an encounter in Cleveland's city hall, where Emma Goldman stormed in, demanding the right to speak on the public square and expecting to be arrested for preaching anarchism.[6] Instead, George's friend Mayor Tom L. Johnson informed Goldman he had built the public square for such discussions. He even expressed his appreciation for the anarchist Peter Kropotkin. According to Frederic C. Howe, "Goldman looked nonplused . . . hesitated, found no answer. Then she turned and left the room."[7] The responses of Goldman and Lenin illustrate how revolutionary rhetoric was deflated by cooperation with bourgeois society. Consequently, Georgists, who had no qualms with liberal democracy, were far more likely to wield political and economic resources in the years before the Russian Revolution.[8]

George proved adept at recruiting elites who ought to have been his most avid opponents. Besides the mayor and streetcar monopolist Tom Johnson, there were A. B. du Pont, scion of one of the country's oldest business dynasties, and Fels, business manager for a commercially successful detergent. George persuaded each of these men that their fortunes had been unfairly acquired. Each chose to allocate this ill-gotten wealth to destroying the system by which they had obtained it. They were joined by an adept group of middle-class intellectuals, professionals, and self-identified "bohemians"—artists and writers of a more genteel stripe than is now associated with that term. The cultural, social, and political sway of this group, which included some of the brightest propagandists, legal minds, and technocrats of the age, accounts for most of George's impact. He also secured a popular base in the "radical middle class" of skilled workers who longed to be self-employed, often transitioning back and forth between wage labor and proprietorship.[9] Farmers eager for land redistribution, tenants upset with high rents, and urbanites demanding municipal services joined coalitions with Georgists. However, the true faithful were generally skilled, mostly independent, urban artisans who prioritized individual autonomy and resented the landlords, monopolists, and taxmen who robbed them of the full value of their labor.

George imagined that a modern social welfare state could be erected with a confiscatory tax on the full value of land and natural resources. His supporters would call this the "single tax" to draw on anti-tax sentiment, though George had originally described it as "land nationalization," which was more apt. Because land and natural resources were finite, taxes on them would not reduce their supply and thus would not be passed to the consumer. Rather, as the cost of holding land increased, its usefulness to the owner—and therefore its price—would drop proportionally. A tax on the full rental value would cause land to lose all value, creating a situation analogous to government leasing.[10] In an economy without rent or taxes, producers would keep what they made, and the growing value of land would subsidize free public transit and higher education, opening opportunity to all.

By placing all taxes on land—something liberals had often doubted could ever justly be considered property—George promised the benefits of a welfare state without violating his audience's faith in the right to keep the fruits of their labor. There was an outpouring of popular support. Americans bought Henry George Cigars, which were democratically priced (i.e., cheap) and advertised with huge murals depicting the working-class hero. When he visited Australia, George was hailed as "a man of the Century" by the *Daily Telegraph*.[11] Many prominent figures of the period would describe reading George's *Progress and Poverty* in their biographies as if it were a major event, or even a turning point, in their lives. One credible estimate suggested that by the turn of the century, five million of his books had been distributed, enough to make George perhaps the most widely read American of the nineteenth century. George's reach only grew afterward, as Joseph Fels endowed a transnational organization to propagate his ideas. Brand Whitlock estimated that after the endowment of the Fels Fund, "every third man in those countries covered by the postal treaties receives every morning a circular letter on the Singletax."[12]

Georgism became a global movement because it appealed to issues that were broadly relevant: land and liberty. Georgism was intended to salvage liberalism at a time when it appeared increasingly difficult to reconcile an ideal of liberty rooted in free labor with the power that large corporations wielded. It was also a response to substantive changes in the economic power of land. Merchant capitalism had expanded across the globe in a sprawling quest for resources, trade, and waterpower. However, in the nineteenth century, a new reliance on fossil fuels concentrated economic activity on coal mines, factories, railroads, and commercial hubs. Large workforces managed the unprecedented productive power harnessed by burning through centuries of stored carbon energy. As workers huddled (often within walking distance) around these new hubs, they struggled for space.[13] This ushered in growing concerns about rent and the power of landlords, some of whom monopolized whole towns and managed the lives of their workers. Conflict with the landlord was as modern as conflict with the employer; what had changed most with industrialization was arguably not the relationship between man and man but that between man and earth.[14]

Land was important not just because of its impact on economic inequality but also because it was the foundation on which democratic communities rested. Georgism belonged to a tradition of working-class movements that hoped to reshape social geography, ensuring that communities were no longer built simply to gratify landlords' quests for speculative gain.[15] Sometimes supporters imagined that big cities would crumble without the thirst for rising land values, but usually they understood that as owners became more like renters, they would economize on space, spurring density. By encouraging owners to develop or abandon land, land value taxation would thread the needle between density and overcrowding, creating more built space for people to live comfortably in the city. George imagined that the American countryside, which sprawled with large, underutilized farms, would be centralized into small towns (perhaps with large encircling agricultural commons) that could offer the social and educational perks of urban life. On the other hand, he promised New Yorkers that his tax would allow them to buy their own homes as speculators sold off empty lots. In a time when most middle-class Americans imagined that cities corrupted the republic, George promoted a vision of the city as a bulwark of democracy that facilitated the open exchange of ideas.[16]

The belief that land nationalization would safeguard liberty gave the movement a sense of millennial conviction that often bordered on religious faith. William Lloyd Garrison II once wrote George to say that, while he was sympathetic, he did not believe the taxation of land was a panacea. George's response was, "Nor I, but I am sure freedom is." "Since then," Garrison observed, "my faith has grown. . . . It is the handmaiden of freedom and must unlock the bolts and bars."[17] George promised that the single tax would salvage liberal democracy and liberate progress from the constraints of aristocratic society.

George's language of equal rights, democracy, and social welfare seem well-worn today, but they were exceptional at a time when the meaning of liberalism was in flux. In the seventeenth century, when philosophes advocated for a free society, they often imagined that a constitutional monarchy might better protect rights than an unruly republic.[18] Before the Revolution, colonialists had generally associated "liberty" with the grant of a special privilege that was not only exclusive but often entailed authority over others: "the rights of Englishmen" or "the liberty to own slaves."[19] The Declaration of Independence and Thomas Paine's *Common Sense* introduced an egalitarian republicanism into the liberal tradition, but they were hardly universally embraced. Although Paine was venerated by the nation's radical artisans, the well-to-do often dismissed him as, in Theodore Roosevelt's words, "a dirty little atheist." In a nation of slave owners, even the Declaration of Independence's paean to universal rights was often neglected, if not explicitly rejected—most famously by Alexander Stephens, vice president of the Confederacy.[20] Abolitionists popularized the Declaration as a founding document that embodied their faith in equal rights and universal suffrage. But in the years after the Civil War that vision seemed largely discredited, as emancipation gave way to growing inequality and popular unrest that suggested democracy was incompatible with the free labor system of abolitionism. In the years when George wrote, ex-abolitionists and self-identified liberals often repudiated universal suffrage. By offering a blueprint for equality consistent with the ideal of free labor, George won abolitionists like William Lloyd Garrison II to welfare policies that had been seen as inconsonant with their ideals. In the process, George salvaged their vision of natural rights for all and allowed their expansive, optimistic liberalism a path forward into the twentieth century.

Although Georgism has struck many commentators as a historical dead end, much of modern liberalism owes a debt to it. Georgists were on the cutting edge of the fight for such reforms as direct legislation, public ownership of utilities, the Australian ballot, municipal home rule, leasing of the public domain, judicial reform, and Progressive taxation. In fact, Georgists did manage to institute moderate forms of land value taxation in municipalities across the country. Nowhere did the severity of these taxes ever approach what George had imagined, though they played an important role in the partisan politics of the age, drawing urban voters to the Democratic Party and helping to secure Woodrow Wilson's New Freedom its place in history even as they shaped it in their image. When the United States emerged from World War II as a liberal behemoth, it did so under a system that resembled George's vision of widespread property ownership bolstered by heavy public interventions in housing, utility, and natural resource policy. The midcentury American social state would, as George hoped, grow to ensure that citizens could participate in a capitalist economy while also drawing increasingly sharp boundaries between public and private spheres.

George was, however, less a catalyst for change than he was a link in a chain. He personified a strand of liberalism that predated him by a century. Although he helped reshape liberalism, there were others waiting in the wings to give life to a set of ideas whose time had come. Even had this new liberalism never taken shape, the crony capitalism of the Gilded Age was crumbling. George's historical function was in a sense conservative; he provided a set of ideas that allowed this system to unravel along liberal, rather than socialist or authoritarian, lines. Many others were looking to eugenics and German authoritarianism for answers. The real battle would not be between reform and the status quo—defenders of which had all but entirely departed the field by the time this story ended—but whether the new America would be liberal or illiberal.

While Georgists sometimes made common cause with turn-of-the-century American Progressives, it is not clear how readily they can be classed with them. The dominant strands of Progressivism are now seen as opposed to individualism, committed to regulating social behavior, and deeply indebted to illiberal German political economy. Georgists, in contrast, were classically liberal, individualistic, and even libertarian on questions like vice enforcement and regulation. Whereas academic Progressives used eugenics to extend expert control to the most intimate aspects of citizens' lives, Georgists believed that people were tabulae rasae and embraced racial liberalism.[21] The case against Georgists as Progressives is not unambiguous; they sometimes called themselves Progressives. However, they more frequently referred to themselves as liberals or radicals—a term that at the time referred to the leftmost branch of liberalism. They identified not with their fin-de-siècle American contemporaries but with abolitionists, English liberals, and fellow Georgists in China or Latin America. Like Marxists, they were partisans of an ideology that was embedded in its place and time but whose self-identification was transnational and transhistorical. Most significant, Georgists doubted that progress would follow inevitably from scientific development, though it was this belief in the power of technical experts to manage society that gave *progressivism* its salience.[22]

Georgist's Progressive antagonists helped modernize the United States, introducing public sanitation, safety regulations, and statistical analysis of public policy. However, their vision of modernity was not always one we would find appealing today. When intellectuals looked abroad, they saw European powers expanding throughout the globe, establishing systems of racial caste, and developing global power under undemocratic regimes. Progressive intellectuals set aside traditional faiths in democracy and rights to join the current of respectable international opinion and, in so doing, anticipated many of the worst elements of the wave of authoritarian nationalism that would crest in the twentieth century. Liberalism has often been faulted for failing to live up to its promises of universal freedom and equal rights, but it was the Progressive era—a period when an unprecedented number of Americans were willing to openly break with these faiths—that historians of the African American experience have marked as the "nadir" of postbellum Black history. Progressives have not received sufficient blame for this because the period was a moment of contradictory movements toward and away from democracy. But, as this book shows, much of this progress toward democracy occurred due to the efforts of liberal Georgists with a lineage and philosophy diametrically opposed to that of academic progressives.[23]

While Progressive academics did much of the yeoman's work of constructing the modern administrative state, it was Georgists who better anticipated modern liberalism. Progressive were, according to Eldon Eisenach, "nationalists to the core . . . in direct opposition to an abstract 'rights-based' discourse."[24] Whereas Progressives believed that the nation-state should have untrammeled authority over the individual in questions of the public good, George worked to reconcile individual rights with the growing importance of cooperation and government in modern life.[25] According to many accounts, liberalism rose from the grave after World War I reignited doubts about the benevolence of state action and then flowered in midcentury into a full-fledged rights revolution. The sense that liberalism had disappeared from the Progressive era is not unwarranted—even the Democratic Party, which stood firmly behind constitutionalism, did so largely to defend the power of states to deprive African Americans of their rights. However, Georgists preserved a current of liberal thought that, despite major differences with the New Deal, laid the groundwork for a modern liberalism that balanced individual rights with state action. When the New Deal re-embraced rights rhetoric and delineated boundaries between public and private sectors, it built on precedents Georgists had established.[26]

In this story, I follow a cohort of activists that formed around Henry George and grew in the years after his death. George's audience was too large to track how most readers responded to him, and any attempt to weigh his influence by this measure would be impossibly nebulous. No definitive organization demarcated the formal boundaries of the movement, and so an overemphasis on organization would lead—and has led—historians to deny the existence of the movement. But there was a well-connected network of activists with a clear and comprehensive idea of what Georgism meant, sanctioned by George himself. Of course, any movement has layers, and allies flicker into this story, whose orthodoxy can be hard to evaluate. Any litmus test for the movement would necessarily be arbitrary, so instead of drawing a hard boundary around the movement, I provide substantive accounts of how individuals related to its ideas and institutions with an emphasis on what they did on its behalf. In this book I use "single tax" and "Georgism" interchangeably, though the former emphasizes Georgists' remedy, while the latter encompasses their philosophy more generally. Both of these terms, however, have their problems: George saw "single tax" as reductive, and "Georgism" is largely a modern term that stands in for awkward or anarchic phrases like "Georgeite," "Henry George men," or "George movement."

My goal in this book is to rescue Georgism from the condescension of posterity, not to write a legal brief for the single tax. In recovering a forgotten and oft-misrepresented movement, I have felt a responsibility to identify why its believers once dedicated themselves to a vision of the good society that might appear incomprehensible to us. Georgism, if properly understood, can productively challenge many modern assumptions. However, in treating Georgism as credible, my goal is not to argue for its adoption; whether the single tax is good policy is largely tangential to this project. By opposing the private ownership of land, a resource that George identified as the most stable and enduring source of wealth, Georgists reenvisioned classical liberalism for a new age by highlighting its promise of constant dynamism and competition, bereft of inherited privilege. That vision deserves its place among the poles around which we organize our thought, because without it our political imagination is smaller. Personally, I do find that dream of social mobility enchanting and the plucky, irascible single taxers endearing. I am not, however, confident society would thrive under such instability.

CHAPTER 1

Progress and Poverty

Land and Inequality in the Liberal Tradition

> The earth, in its natural, uncultivated state, was, and ever would have
> continued to be, the COMMON PROPERTY OF THE HUMAN RACE.
>
> Thomas Paine, *Agrarian Justice* (1796)

Michael Davitt was a little-known Irish nationalist who had scarcely caught the attention of the British authorities when he was discovered smuggling guns into Ireland and sentenced to fifteen years of penal servitude. By the time of his second conviction, in 1881, he had become a national hero. The "father of the Land League," Davitt had mobilized the Irish against the eviction of tenants during the lean year of 1879. It was during this second stint of penal servitude that Davitt reread the works of Henry George, an obscure American radical to whom he had been introduced by Patrick Ford, the editor of the *Irish World*. When British authorities released Davitt in 1882, his agitation had secured Irish tenants protection from eviction and rent increases, but he left Portland prison believing that this had not been nearly enough. In prison, Davitt was won over to George's vision and catapulted the obscure writer to international fame.[1] Unlike so much of American reform pioneered by the well-heeled moralism of the sons of Puritan New England, George would find his base in a hardscrabble cosmopolitanism.[2]

For Davitt, the land issue was deeply personal. His extended family had shared a twenty-one-acre farm during the potato famine. Without income, the family was evicted in 1850. Though not yet five years old at the time, he would always remember the image of "the remnant of our household furniture flung about the road; the roof of the house falling in and the thatch taking fire; my mother and father looking on with four young children, the youngest only two months old."[3] After their eviction, Davitt's family migrated to Haslingden, England. Davitt took a job at a mill and, at eleven years old, was asked to perform the work of an absent machine minder. When Davitt objected that he was too small to reach the machinery, the foreman kicked him and threatened to fire him. The machine stalled. Davitt, standing on his toes, reached in to remove an obstruction and lost his balance. His arm was smashed in the cogs of the machine. Davitt insisted that he would rather die than have his arm amputated, but his mother had her own opinions. He was chloroformed and awoke to find his right arm missing. The collapse of the Irish peasantry had made Davitt into fodder for England's "satanic mills."

But it was not just personal experience that prepared Davitt to popularize George; both men spoke a common language with shared presumptions about land informed by a century of liberal critiques of rent. This chapter highlights classical liberalism's analysis of landed property. Liberal economists argued that land was the root of poverty, both because it imposed natural limits on growth and because rent grew steadily so that tenants secured few, if any, benefits, from economic growth. Thomas Malthus's thesis that the produce of land could not feed the world's growing population earned economics the moniker of the "dismal science." This idea, however, coexisted with Ricardian rent theory, which suggested that landed wealth redistributed the proceeds of progress to the idle wealthy. Malthusian political economy justified economic and political inequality as inevitable; Ricardian rent theory implied that a democratic public might be able to create a more equal society. These two threads splintered in the 1870s, as Herbert Spencer built on Malthus to remake liberalism into a justification for oppression, and Henry George, introducing American republicanism into the discourse, imagined a future without Malthusian constraints on prosperity.

Land and Classical Liberalism

When George argued that taxing land was the only way that most of the world's population could ever climb out of poverty, he built on ideas about the relationship between progress and land that dated to the dawn of the Enlightenment. The appointment in 1774 of Anne Robert Jacques Turgot as controller-general of finances signaled the Enlightenment's rise to respectability in France's ancien régime. Turgot embodied the Enlightenment faith that advances in knowledge and science would make mankind progressively "better and happier."[4] He devoted himself to the study of economics and, like others in the French Enlightenment, embraced the taxation of land. Turgot believed that neither the laborer nor the businessmen could bear taxes without reducing their production, thereby slowing the nation's progress. Like the physiocrat economists François Quesnay and Pierre Samuel du Pont de Nemours, Turgot believed that because the supply of land was finite, it was the only form of wealth that earned a surplus that could be taxed without the burden being shifted elsewhere through higher prices. Physiocrats believed that a free market, free trade, and an *impôt unique*—a "single tax" on land—were key to realizing economic progress.[5] Thus, a century later when A. B. du Pont, a descendant of the physiocrat Pierre du Pont, approached Henry George to offer his support, George hesitated to accept him as a disciple, because "his ancestor had the philosophy before I was born."[6]

In eighteenth-century France and England, philosophers who spoke on behalf of a new class of self-made men challenged landed property in language that evoked class conflict with traditional, landed elites. Liberals saw state power as intimately interwoven with the economic power of the landed aristocracy, and sometimes prioritized breaking up landed wealth over defanging the state. Victor de Riqueti, Marquis de Mirabeau, argued in *Théorie de l'impôt* (1760) that the monarch rescinded his right to rule if he established taxes that were "exorbitant and destructive" and that the only tax which did not fit that description was a tax on the *produit net* of land.[7] While the tract did not go over well with public authorities—he spent a week in prison, followed by exile from Paris—Mirabeau had consented to monarchy if the burden of funding the state rested on the landed aristocracy. Similarly, the father of English liberalism, John Locke, argued that land taxes were the only ones that could not be shifted; in this way he cautioned aristocrats that burdensome taxes on labor or capital would also fall on them.[8] Adam Smith stoked class conflict in *The Wealth of Nations* (1776), suggesting that England's tax system had been designed to exempt the nobility and impose the whole burden on the working people, whom aristocrats loathed as mere "emancipated bondsmen."[9]

Smith questioned whether liberals should even consider land property. Smith rejected the code of gentility, which idealized aristocrats as refined and cultured because they did not engage in manual labor. Instead, Smith emphasized the value of labor, rooting his ideas in John Locke, who attributed property rights to one's ownership of their persons and, by proxy, of what they produced. This justification for property applied at best imperfectly to land, which was, according to Locke, a gift of God.[10] For Smith, Lockean property theory meant that rent was theft: "The produce of labour constitutes the natural recompense or wages of labour. In the original state of things, which precedes both the appropriation of land and the accumulation of stock, the whole produce of labour belongs to the labourer. . . . As soon as the land becomes private property, the landlord demands a share of almost all the produce which the labourer can either raise or collect from it."[11] Land taxation appealed to an emergent middle class that prized mastery of craft and smarted at the condescension of an aristocracy that idealized idle refinement.[12] Smith was famously an admirer of competition, but he believed "the rent of land . . . was naturally a monopoly price."[13] Because a finite amount of land existed, supply could not rise to meet demand. Landed property was not a part of a competitive marketplace; its function had always been to stifle political and economic freedom.

English workers embraced land taxation by mounting similar, though usually more radical, attacks on the landed aristocracy. In 1775, Thomas Spence presented a lecture to the Newcastle Philosophical Society in which he proposed that land be owned in common and that rents serve as the only source of public revenue. Spence would inspire many members of the Chartist movement, which fought to secure the British working classes the right to vote. By 1802, it was reported to the prime minster that most of London had been decorated with the graffiti "Spence's Plan and Full Bellies."[14]

In the 1810s, David Ricardo, Thomas Malthus, Sir Edward West, and Robert Torrens each independently posited a theory of rent that gave substance to Smith's concept of monopoly price. Recent studies of grain price movements had revealed that as population grew, more land was placed under cultivation, and the price of grain rose. This was counterintuitive: an expanding supply of grain meant that prices should go down. Economists concluded that agriculture was subject to diminishing returns. Farmers met demand by resorting to less advantageous land, and commodity prices grew to support the least efficient producers. The result was that the holder of land with better soil or location reaped a windfall in rising commodity and land prices: rent. Economists noted that this rent was directly proportional to the average yield of the land. In short, because land was finite, its value and that of the food or fuel collected from it were determined not by supply and demand but by scarcity and relative advantage. As population grew, producers would meet supply by making recourse to progressively more marginal land, and the disparity in grades of land under cultivation—as well as the rent this disparity produced—would increase.[15]

Land rent was something that could be redistributed, but other economists now argued that the plight of Davitt and his ilk was an inevitable outgrowth of nature. Thomas Malthus argued that the discovery of diminishing marginal returns in agriculture demonstrated that progress would be reserved for a small class of elites. In 1789, Malthus, who was born into the English gentry, published *An Essay on the Principle of Population*. He sought to discredit the ideal of progress by showing that poverty was insurmountable. Good arable land was in short supply, so agricultural production grew by resorting to more marginal land. Population, however, grew geometrically, and therefore the demand for food would constantly outstrip the supply. The poor could earn only enough to sustain themselves, and often not even that; starvation was a natural and inevitable remedy to population outgrowing the earth's ability to support it. This philosophy would lead Sir Charles Trevelyan, assistant secretary of Her Majesty's Treasury, to label the Irish Potato Famine "an effective remedy for reducing surplus population." Later, when Malthus wrote his *Principles of Political Economy* (1820), he concluded that rent was essential because it was the only way to create a class of "unproductive consumers." Workers could afford only bare necessities, so the idle aristocracy served the important social function of creating consumer demand. Therefore, Malthus supported policies, such as tariffs on imported grain, that would increase the rent landowners accrued.[16]

David Ricardo, in contrast, argued that rent impeded the progress of society. Ricardo was a stockbroker who had been disinherited by his Jewish father for marrying a Quaker. As a member of the rising middle class, he lacked Malthus's affection for the landed gentry. According to Ricardo, growing population required agriculture to resort to progressively less advantageous land, increasing the marginal utility of better-situated land and the rent it earned. Rent, therefore, would constantly grow with progress, redirecting wealth from the productive functions of labor and capital; "the interest of the landlord is always opposed to that of the consumer or manufacturer."[17] The taxation of land and the free importation of grain would reduce the share of wealth reserved for idle landlords. While Ricardo accepted Malthus's arguments about the insufficiency of nature, he rejected Malthus's fatalistic determination that progress was impossible.[18]

The consensus was that the roots of poverty were in land; the question was whether this was because of the rapaciousness of landlords or the stinginess of nature. George and Davitt found sufficient support in the tenets of liberal political economy to blame rent for inequality. In his *Principles of Political Economy* (1848), the leading philosopher of liberalism, John Stuart Mill, coined the term "unearned increment" to describe how idle landlords profited from the rising value of land.[19] Mill seemed to make land the model for monopoly, which he defined as "a natural or artificial limitation of quantity."[20] He formed the Land Tenure Reform Association in 1873, which, among other things, promoted a tax on all increases in the value of land.[21] Davitt often referenced Mill's arguments that landownership in Ireland had "never to this day been recognized by the moral sentiments of the people" and that private property in land should be eliminated when it was inexpedient or unpopular.[22] George corresponded with Mill, cited his support for land taxation, and adopted "unearned increment" as a motto for his movement. The nascent capitalism of the nineteenth century has often been understood as a reflection, if not a product, of the liberal philosophies of Smith and Mill; George, however, would use their ideas to challenge that system.

Land and Democracy in America

George would be deeply influenced by European liberal thought, but also by an American tradition contending that successful republics rested on the equal distribution of landed wealth.[23] Most people believed Rome had fallen because the growth of large estates drove the yeoman farmer off the land. Roman history taught that republics would fall from the inside as the wealthy obtained power and the dispossessed poor were forced either to beg the elite for a living or rally to demagogues. Caesar had been able to seize power, and his successors to maintain it, because Roman citizens depended upon wealthy benefactors. An equal distribution of landed property would ensure the independence of the yeoman farmer essential to a stable republic.

Based on these presumptions, several leading figures in the Revolutionary era entertained the physiocrats' land tax to prevent the centralization of landed wealth. Both Benjamin Franklin and Thomas Jefferson were intimately associated with the physiocrats and spoke highly of their principles.[24] In *Agrarian Justice*, Thomas Paine, the leading propagandist of the artisan class, declared land "the common property of the human race" and proposed that "ground-rent" be confiscated and returned to the citizenry as "compensation, in part, for the loss of his or her natural inheritance, by the introduction of the system of landed property."[25] By providing citizens upon reaching the age of twenty-one with a lump-sum payment to compensate for their loss of the share of the common stock of land, the republic would preserve a relative equality of wealth that mitigated against elite usurpation of power.

But these early Americans believed the taxation of land was necessary only in more settled communities, not in the United States, where the western land available for conquest made redistribution unnecessary. Paine, during his long career in American politics, never argued for land nationalization, waiting instead for his moment in the French Revolution to strike at Old World aristocracy. Benjamin Franklin wrote to his physiocrat correspondents in

France that, though he supported their ideas, "our legislators are all land-owners, and they are not yet persuaded that all taxes are paid by the land."[26] Jefferson was most explicit that it might be advisable for the government to collect land rents and break up speculation when the poor were barred access to land but not when there was still open land to claim:

> Whenever there are in any country uncultivated lands and unemployed poor, it is clear that the laws of property have been so far extended as to violate natural right. The earth is given as common stock for men to labour and live on. . . . It is too soon yet in our country to say that every man who cannot find employment, but who can find uncultivated land, shall be at liberty to cultivate it, paying a moderate rent. But it is not too soon to provide by every possible means that as few as possible shall be without a little portion of land. The small landholders are the most precious part of the state.[27]

Classical republican theory dictated that such a condition of inequality would eventually arise, but Jefferson worked assiduously to postpone it with western land policies like the Northwest Ordinance and Louisiana Purchase.

In the 1830s, this idealization of the yeoman farmer became a focal point of American working-class radicalism. In those years, the Workingmen's parties of New York and Philadelphia were formed to demand free land and free education so workers could be independent citizens rather than dependent wage earners. In 1843, the movement to lobby the federal government for free land coalesced under the National Reform Association (NRA). Its leader, George Henry Evans, claimed that the free land would allow the worker to "redeem himself from the slavery of wages."[28] Horace Greeley, the iconic editor of the *New York Tribune*, seared the cause into American memory with his famous exhortation to "Go West young man, go west and grow up with the country."[29] The promise of bountiful land made the notion of taxing or redistributing land anathema; America's most famous antebellum economist, Henry C. Carey, was also one of the leading opponents of Ricardian rent theory and its contention that landed property would ultimately foster inequality.[30] Higher rates of profit awaited those willing to strike out and compete in the urban market, yet, except for a small contingent of rebellious sons and daughters, the majority of Americans stayed on the farm to pursue dreams of independence, stability, virtue, and competence.[31]

Perpetuating the yeomanry required a constant supply of new land. Without laborers, the yeoman farmer relied heavily on his children to perform the backbreaking work of running a farm. In return for years of hard work, the farmer, as the patriarch, was expected to provide a farm to each of his male children. The conflation of property ownership with citizenship was too strong for the patriarch not to meet his obligations even as open land was devoured by population growth. The English novelist Anthony Trollope identified the type of citizenry small proprietorship was thought to encourage when he observed of a Wisconsin patriarch: "He astonishes you by the extent of his knowledge. . . . To me I confess that the manliness of such a man is very charming. He is dirty and perhaps squalid. . . . But over and above it all there is an independence which sits gracefully on their shoulders and teaches you at first glance that the man has a right to assume himself to be your equal."[32] For Americans still trying to prove that common people could rule themselves, allowing one's children to fall into the dependence and subordination of wage labor was anathema.[33]

These expectations for an expanding empire of yeoman citizens put northern farmers on a collision course with the southern planter class. It was widely understood that the yeomanry had been run out of operation wherever slavery had taken root. The planter class had its own rival interest in expansion because new territory meant more plantation agriculture and hence increased demand for slaves. The high cost of human chattel to work western land bolstered plantations with profits from the domestic slave trade and speculations in slave mortgages. Confining slavery to the South and opening the public domain to the yeomanry were cemented into a single cause with the formation of the Free Soil Party in 1848. Six years later, this movement was solidified when Alvan Earl Bovay, former secretary of the NRA, presided over the meeting in a schoolhouse in Ripon, Wisconsin, where the Republican Party was born. When popular sovereignty was established in Kansas and Nebraska, potentially opening the territories up to slavery, northern farmers shifted their allegiance to the new Republican Party, which promised to bar the expansion of slavery and distribute western land to yeoman farmers.[34]

After slaves were emancipated during the Civil War, the plight of freedmen, propertyless in a sea of landowning whites, promised a sort of peonage incompatible with visions of republican equality. George W. Julian, a Republican congressman from Indiana, told Congress that, if "land monopoly" remained in place, ex-slaves would be forced into a "system of wages slavery . . . more galling than slavery itself."[35] Julian was supported by Henry George, then an up-and-coming newspaperman; Julian, a former Free Soil vice-presidential candidate, would return the favor and credit George with "an exalted place among the heroes of humanity."[36]

During the period of Reconstruction in the wake of the Civil War, Black voters and legislators in the South turned to property taxation to both fund state governments and force the forfeiture of plantations. Abraham Galloway, a state senator from North Carolina, declared that he wanted "to see the man who owns one or two thousand acres of land, taxed a dollar on the acre, and if they can't pay the taxes, sell their property to the highest bidder . . . and then the negroes shall become land holders."[37] Frank Moss, a Black delegate at Virginia's constitutional convention in 1868, argued that "if we do not tax the land, we might as well not have come here to make a Constitution."[38] Reconstruction-era state governments used revenue from property taxes to fund the first public school systems in most southern states. Legislators in South Carolina purchased land and resold it with low-interest, long-term loans, thereby providing one-seventh of the state's Black population with homesteads. In Mississippi alone, more than six million acres of land were forfeited by planters unable to pay their property taxes. In most cases, though, Black proprietorship was forestalled when southern whites "redeemed" state governments from Black suffrage and returned forfeited land to its original owners.

When northern liberals rejected Reconstruction-era property taxes, they laid the groundwork for a national movement against democracy. E. L. Godkin's *The Nation* led liberal opinion in arguing that Black legislators were "rapacious rogues who rob and rule a people helpless and utterly exhausted"—though this assertion was ironically juxtaposed to statistics showing that of the ten states with the highest per capita tax rates, only one was in the South.[39] Popular demand for the appropriation of southern land suggested to many northern liberals that their faiths in private property and universal suffrage were irreconcilable. *The Nation* mused that "whenever poor or dependent men have votes, and social conditions are unequal, there is that kind of subserviency in voting which we call 'intimidation' at the South."[40] When free labor failed to produce the general prosperity liberals had imagined, periodicals like the *Atlantic Monthly* blamed the racial inferiority of African Americans, evoking the natural hierarchies of traditional conservatism. As mounting labor unrest raised the threat of expropriation in the North, liberals often argued for importing southern strategies of disenfranchisement. Rejecting equal suffrage and the right of workingmen to assemble, liberalism was distilled to a single liberty: "freedom of contract." British liberals had speculated that landed property undermined democracy; Americans like Godkin proved that a liberalism that treated landed property as sacrosanct could blur into feudalism.[41]

Faith in universal white male suffrage had taken root during the 1820s and 1830s when the ownership of productive property was so widespread that few worried about the ballot box becoming a site of class conflict. But, after the Civil War, Abraham Lincoln's promise that anyone could become a proprietor in a free labor economy looked increasingly remote. As settlers found the available land progressively less fertile, the Homestead Act (1862) was revised in 1877 to allow claims of as much as 640 acres for desert land that had proven difficult to squeeze a living from. Railroads had received land grants from state and federal governments that, combined, amounted to about 9 percent of the total acreage of the U.S. public domain. In granting land adjacent to the track to railroad corporations, the federal government ensured that the most valuable properties, with the best access to agricultural markets, were taken out of the public domain for homesteaders. Thus, despite the promise of "free" land, farmers who could afford it purchased land from railroad corporations, and about 60 percent of homesteaders, driven to the margins, failed to secure their claims to government land. Between 1862 and 1890, approximately two million Americans migrated to the West, but the nation's population grew by 32 million as a flood of European immigrants arrived and took low-wage jobs.[42] Urban rents grew with industrialization. From 1885 to 1900 the value of land in Boston, excluding improvements, grew by nearly 85 percent.[43] The total value of real property in the United States tripled between 1860 and 1890 as the urban population grew from 25 percent of the nation in 1870 to nearly 40 percent in 1900. With more workers crowded in unsanitary urban conditions, Americans were on average shorter and sicker, with lower life expectancies that belied the promises of industrial progress.[44]

There was plenty of land in the West that would never be claimed, but most industrial workers could even not afford streetcar fare, so vast tracts of open land did little to relieve demand for space in the dense settlements that sprouted up within walking distance of factories. To house their workers, large factories relied on crowded tenements with as little as two square yards per resident. Without ventilation, approximately seven out of every thousand tenement residents in lower Manhattan died of tuberculosis; in at least one instance the local fishmonger washed his wares in the same sink that all the other residents used as a urinal.[45] Sometimes employers decided to house their workers directly, but these scenarios were hardly any less corrosive to republican equality. By 1916, some 3 percent of American workers lived in employer-provided housing. Often this was in so-called company towns, where the employer owned most, if not all, of the housing and retail businesses. Generally unincorporated, company towns routinely lacked elected local government and were run by the employer, who might also determine what goods were sold and what religion was practiced in the community. Because workers in a coal town in Harlan County, Kentucky could not own property, they could not serve on juries. In Huerfano County, guards employed by Colorado Fuel and Iron barred workers suspected of sympathies with labor unions from entering voting precincts on company land.[46] Company towns troubled social critics who feared they heralded a new feudalism hostile to civil rights; to drive the point home, they penned scathing critiques of the industrialists' restrictive practices with titles like "A Modern Lear" and *King Coal*.[47]

Condemning company towns as feudalistic embodied a form of liberalism that had seen the power of landed wealth as no different than the power of the state. Malthus's rival tradition of justifying inequality received powerful new support in the British philosopher Herbert Spencer. In his *Social Statics* (1851), Spencer turned Malthus's predictions of persistent poverty into a recipe for progress, made possible because "humanity is being pressed against the inexorable necessities of its new position . . . molded into harmony with them and has to bear the resulting unhappiness as best as it can."[48] According to Spencer (who, ironically, was sickly, cloistered, and likely a lifelong virgin), the inability of the earth to feed the weakest members of the species would spur progress by eliminating those least adapted to civilization. The publication of Charles Darwin's *On the Origin of Species* eight years later lent credence to Spencer's evolutionary ideas.[49] It is a testament to the extent of liberal antipathy against landed wealth that even Spencer initially argued that "equity . . . does not permit property in land."[50] However, progress for Spencer was a process of slow, natural evolution, so he objected to land nationalization, except as a remote hypothetical.

Spencer secured international fame by rationalizing growing inequality as necessary for civilizational progress.[51] He noted that in biology, evolution gave undifferentiated species, such as single-cell organisms, progressively more complex and differentiated parts. This "physiological division of labor" was analogous to the way individuals in society had risen from an undifferentiated mass of subsistence farmers to specialists with progressively more defined functions in society.[52] The component parts of the organism, like individuals in society, were structured hierarchically, with a nervous system responsible for organizing the system.[53] The evolution of the "social organism," therefore, required growing inequality, often reinforced by public policy. According to Spencer, authorities overstepped when they engaged in benevolent policies like public education, but they should be more active in prosecuting criminals and protecting property. The problem with politicians was not that they were too active but that they "impede adaption of human nature to the social state, both by what they do and what they leave alone."[54]

Spencer embodied a liberalism that was splintering away from its faith in democratic equality. Like Godkin, he excused the inequality of industrial capitalism. He even made nice with the old enemies of liberalism—slavery and feudalism—by arguing that oppression was necessary to discipline the race as it progressed through the stages of civilization.[55] Spencer's leading American supporter, Yale professor William Graham Sumner, labeled democracy "the pet superstition of the age."[56] The steel magnate Andrew Carnegie tried to reconcile his Spencerianism with democracy but understood the inherent difficulties. At one time in human history, he observed, "there was, substantially, social equality, and even political equality." But the development of the race required the concentration of wealth into the hands of the most capable executives, producing "rigid castes."[57] Carnegie hoped that, if the wealthy donated their earnings to the public, class conflict could be abated, but the days when every citizen could have an independent competence were gone. Monopolies governed by the evolutionary elite were optimal because "wealth, passing through the hands of the few, can be made a much more potent force for the elevation of our race than if distributed in small sums to the people themselves."[58] George, rejecting Malthusianism, would draw on Ricardian rent theory to argue that this new inequality was the result not of natural development but of an economic system designed to benefit rentiers. In the process, he salvaged a liberal tradition that was so far into decline that it had become indistinguishable from traditional, authoritarian conservatism.

The Emergence of Land Nationalization

As expanding social and economic hierarchies eroded the homogenous republic of yeoman farmers in postbellum America, classical republican anxiety about the stability of democratic institutions experienced a resurgence. Thinkers such as Edward Bellamy and Henry Demarest Lloyd drew comparisons to the yawning social divisions that tore the Roman republic apart in its final years.[59] Theodore Roosevelt, in *The Winning of the West*, saw the "end of the frontier" as presaging a day when Americans would lose their independence, equality, and appreciation for liberty.[60] Most famously, when Frederick Jackson Turner presented "The Significance of the Frontier in American History" at the World's Columbia Exhibition in 1893, he argued that the disappearance of free land in the West would undermine the traditional foundations of American democracy.

As free soil was exhausted, Americans increasingly returned to taxation to ensure an equitable distribution of landed property. In *The Gilded Age* (1873), Mark Twain and Charles Dudley Warner told the story of the Hawkins family, whose patriarch, Silas Hawkins, discovered a large deposit of mineral resources and bought seventy-five thousand acres in the mountains of East Tennessee. Because "all that is necessary to hold the land and keep it in the family" was "to pay the trifling taxes on it yearly," Silas held onto the land with the expectation that expanding transportation infrastructure—canals and railroads—would cause it to grow in value.[61] Silas's children came to disdain work and the family relocated to Washington, D.C., to lobby for federal infrastructure funds. The family embarked on a path of political and moral corruption until Washington Hawkins came to realize that the land was a "curse" and that he had "depended on it all through my boyhood and never tried to do an honest stroke of work for my living."[62] Immediately, after this epiphany, however, Washington received a high property tax bill, whereupon he tore up the bill and announced, "The spell is broken."[63] He would abandon the property along with his family's quest to make a fortune in speculation. Land taxation hit the corruption of the Gilded Age at its root.

Enough thinkers were gravitating toward land nationalization in the years prior to George's rise to fame that many understood him less as the author of a movement than its anointed leader. To emphasize this idea, in the years immediately prior to the publication of *Progress and Poverty*, his supporters republished as pamphlets a handful of short works arguing for land taxation.[64] Alfred Russell Wallace, who famously theorized natural selection contemporaneously with Charles Darwin, was wrapping up the final chapters of *Land Nationalisation and Its Aim* when he happened upon *Progress and Poverty* and realized he had once again been beaten to the punch.[65] Similarly, in 1878 Charles Frederick Adams published an article arguing that land was "the natural gift of God" and that the "rent of it" should be "applied for the benefit of the entire people." A year later, George published *Progress and Poverty*. Adams would then become one of the leading presenters for the Henry George Lecture Association.[66] Although Adams choose to march under George's banner, he, like many others, understood that the idea had a future with or without George.

This new current of land nationalization would draw on Smith, Ricardo, and Mill to rebut Malthus and Spencer, but it would also move beyond Ricardo's conflation of land with agriculture. George observed that urban rents were rising and built on Ricardo's differential theory of rent to argue that all social progress was embedded in space and was therefore subject to rent. J. Stitt Wilson, elected mayor of Berkeley, California, in 1911, explained that the city is our "Social Mother, in whose household we all live." It was the city that served as the foundation for civilization: the site of economic, social, and cultural life. With the progress of the community, the land on which it was built grew in value. Underneath the hustle and bustle of a busy city, the land sat as a representation of that community—its value a quantifiable assessment of every advantage and amenity that its denizens created. The value of this land had been produced by the whole community and yet was assessed upon its tenants as the price of belonging. Thus, it was the most natural thing in the world that "the social body, the city or state, should pay its own bills out of that wealth which it has itself socially created. Let the values she herself socially creates fall into her own treasury, and from this, her own treasure, let her pay her own bills [using] taxation on land values."[67]

Although land had always been crucial to the way liberals understood poverty, this new way of seeing rent—as the sum of all the values created by the advance of civilization—more firmly identified hopes for progress with the abolition of landed inequality. Either mankind would embrace land nationalization and realize the fruits of progress, or land would remain private, inequality would grow, and republican civilization would decay. According to this school of thought, individual rights and society were not in conflict; it was only through recognizing the values that society had created collectively that individual rights could be secure. Liberalism would now entail both individual and communal rights.

CHAPTER 2

The Prophet of San Francisco

Confronting the Modern Metropolis

> George himself, while decidedly an "intellectual" of the highest order so
> far as capacity to reason on the theoretical plane went, was yet, by virtue
> of his personal experience and of prolonged continued contact with the
> life of that great American "producing class," the most representative
> ideologist that class has ever had.
>
> Selig Perlman, *The Theory of the Labor Movement* (1928)

Henry George was born on September 2, 1839, in a respectable row house less than half a mile from Philadelphia's Independence Hall. Born in the shadow of the Declaration of Independence, he was reared in the tradition of working-class reform. Within a few years of Henry's birth, the growth of his family—he was the sixth of fourteen children—pushed his father to resettle in the Southwark District, a more affordable, working-class neighborhood. Two years before George's birth the neighborhood had been the location of labor riots. A decade before that it had served as a birthing ground for Philadelphia's Workingmen's Party. Echoes of its platform, including free public education, land reform, and an end to state-chartered monopolies, would find their way into George's work.[1]

In Philadelphia, the tension between American ideals and practice was inescapable. George later recalled that as a young boy he had "seen the shackled slave under the shadow of Independence Hall carried by federal arms back to his master."[2] America was thus a work in progress. George would later write: "I love the American Republic not for what it is but for what it was intended to be, and for what in fullest measure it yet may be made."[3] George would be instrumental in the formation of a "new liberalism," but he was also steeped in the liberalism of the eighteenth century.

George has been described as growing up somewhere between the "genteel" middle class and the better-to-do working class, but, at the time, success was defined not by lucrative, consistent employment but ownership and independence. By the time of George's birth, the local slave population was dwindling rapidly, but it remained uppermost in the minds of workers, who rejected the traditional term for an employer—"master"—because it evoked the servitude of the slaves they sometimes worked alongside. Groups like the Workingmen's Party demanded "free soil" because they aspired to be independent proprietors, free from this stain of dependence. A small but growing number of Philadelphia's workers were becoming permanent wage laborers, but many of these were journeymen who had sacrificed their childhood to apprenticeships in a moral economy that promised them a future as self-employed artisans.[4]

Henry's father, Richard, like many others seeking self-employment, often risked his financial stability for independence. His campaign work for the Democratic Party earned him a cushy patronage job at the U.S. Custom House in Philadelphia. But once he had raised enough money, Richard, a strict Episcopalian, put his savings into a religious bookstore. The business was not self-sustaining, and Richard was forced to return to the custom house. Despite the promise of higher income and greater stability, he resented the return to the position, complaining that he was given too "much to do" and "consequentially [had] too little time to study."[5]

The city of Philadelphia served as Henry's alma mater. He received little formal education, but with a strict Episcopalian bookseller as a father, he was urged into a life of private study. Henry relied on the Franklin Institute and the Quaker Apprentice Library for new books and educational lecturers. The Franklin Institute had been founded by Benjamin Franklin—himself a self-educated printer—as a resource for popular education. As Henry absorbed the readings of transcendentalists like Ralph Waldo Emerson, he acquired a faith in the public institutions and urban life that made his education possible. This experience made George atypical for his time. The census found that even in 1860 fewer than one in five Americans lived in cities. Many saw urban life as a corruption that would erode republican institutions. In contrast, George's experiences in the city of Philadelphia prepared him to see urban community as a source of edification that could bolster democracy.[6]

George was a student of American intellectual traditions, but he was also a rebel, eager to reinterpret them. He imbibed the populism of the Democratic Party, so that when he became a writer in his adulthood, his father would share his writings with "some good old Jackson Democrats" to prove that "I have a son so bold and firm and consistent for the old Democratic principles."[7] On some particularly divisive issues, however, George split with "the Democracy." He believed in the abolition of slavery at a time when proponents of restricting slavery were being driven from the party.[8] Furthermore, like many an overchurched child before and after, he grew distant from the traditional faith of his parents. He abandoned religion temporarily and then experimented with unorthodox spiritualist doctrines, such as Swedenborgianism. Associated with transcendentalism, this "New Church" promised a direct connection to God through communion with nature.

Before turning fourteen, George left school to become a sailor. Henry George Jr. would later claim that his father had threatened to run away if he was not permitted to indulge his sense for adventure. The Reverend Ignatius Horstman remembered his classmate differently:

> His parents did not allow him to play with boys on the street. I can recall Henry George going to church every Sunday, walking between his two elder sisters, followed by his father and mother—all of them so neat, trim, and reserved. Henry was then a delicate boy, almost girlish in appearance and manner. When he was thirteen years old, the doctor informed his father, that if he expected Henry to live, it was absolutely necessary to remove him from his present surroundings; that he should send him to sea for a long cruise.[9]

George Jr. was a reliable narrator, but Horstman's account seems consistent with the parenting style of Christian booksellers. Probably there was some truth to both narratives. If so, Henry grew up a sheltered student whose youthful rebellion drove him to join the unruliest class of workers. Later in life, in crafting his origin story, he decided to emphasize his rebelliousness over his bookishness. George was an intellectual who choose to join the ranks of the American producing class.

Young Henry joined the crew of the *Hindoo*, making a fourteen-month voyage to Calcutta and Melbourne. The merchant marine, as an epicenter of cross-culture exchange, helped shape his worldview. One of his shipmates, upon seeing a Brazilian man dressed in the height of fashion without any shoes, informed him that black men were naturally unfit to wear footwear. George realized that the man was dressed according to local fashion and concluded that theories of "hereditary transmission have really no more bearing than this of our forecastle Darwinian."[10] The foremast had also served as the birthplace of modern labor protest; the term "strike" derives from the act of lowering a ship's sails.[11] George experienced such a work stoppage on the *Hindoo*. When the ship docked in Australia, several members of the crew asked to be discharged and, after the captain refused, vowed not to work. They were sentenced to a month of forced labor. On his trip, George developed a sympathy for not only striking workers but also the global poor.[12] He had been drawn to India with fantasies of an exotic, ancient civilization. His curiosity survived the journey; in India he purchased a monkey who slept on his head every night on the voyage back to Philadelphia. But in his letters, George lingered less on the exoticism of Calcutta than on the contrast between "the handsome country residences of the wealthy English" and "the number of dead bodies floating down in all stages of decomposition, covered by crows who were actively engaged in picking them to pieces."[13] Later in life, George would often reference Hindu parables on the immorality of poverty. In his cosmopolitan sympathies, George could not have been more different from his rival Herbert Spencer, who built his philosophy on essentialist racial claims, though he did not so much as set eyes on an ocean before he turned twenty-one.[14]

After returning to Philadelphia, George wandered through a series of jobs, mostly in printing. This was naturally a literary trade, and its members were often intellectuals, generally with a radical tinge. It was in the printing trades that Benjamin Franklin first encountered Enlightenment thought, and the profession probably had a similar influence on George. If George had not heard free soil ideas in his Jacksonian household, he almost certainly did now; Philadelphia's printing trades had helped birth the National Reform Association.[15] This "hard-fisted mechanic," as he described himself, found the discipline imposed on a wage laborer unbecoming and on at least one occasion had an altercation with a foreman whose "domineering insolence" he found unbearable.[16] Like many Americans, George was lured west by stories of opportunity on the frontier. At nineteen, he took a job as ship steward on the *Shubrick*, traveling to California by way of St. Thomas, Barbados, Pernambuco, Monte Video, and Rio de Janeiro. He arrived at San Francisco in May 1858. Though drawn west by the promise of Oregon, he found it offered less opportunity than he had hoped. After a brief spell in Victoria, British Columbia, he trekked back to San Francisco.

There, George's career was as erratic and unsettled as it had been in Philadelphia, but he fit into the culture of the young frontier metropolis. He saw San Francisco as the sort of classless, meritocratic paradise that Jacksonian democracy idealized. George's latter-day reforms could be seen as an effort to re-create a San Francisco where "all had started from the same level—where the banker had been a year or two before a journeyman carpenter; the merchant a foremast hand; the restaurant waiter had perhaps been educated for the bar or the church, and the laborer once counted his 'pile.'" There "the wheel of fortune had been constantly revolving in other places unknown, social lines could not be sharply drawn, nor a reverse dispirit."[17] Although sometimes described as idiosyncratic in dress, George generally adopted the persona of the archetypical western male. His early penchant for whiskey and gambling faded later in life. He would, however, remain attached to his vice of choice: cigars. Whereas Rousseau practiced his critique of landed property in the salons of Paris, George sharpened his in San Francisco's saloons. After he became a newspaper editor, he once brawled in his office with a reader upset about his editorials. When investigating charges of brutality at the local prison, he pushed aside an armed warden to enter the premises.[18] The rowdy George could never be labeled "a socialist of the chair."

After Matthew McCloskey, a wealthy Irish Catholic, forbade the unemployed George from courting his niece, the defiant suitor pulled a coin from his pocket and asked Annie Corsina Fox, "This is all the money I have in the world, will you marry me?"[19] In 1862, when interfaith marriages were still rare, Henry married Annie. But the pressure of providing for a family made George's periodic lapses in employment more painful. By 1865, when the second of George's four children was born malnourished, the family told the milkman that they could no longer pay him. Desperate, George accosted the first well-dressed stranger he met on the street and begged him for five dollars lest his family starve. George remembered, "I think I was desperate enough to have killed him" had the benevolent stranger not agreed.[20] This frank admission would underline for George, and many of his supporters, crime's roots in poverty.

George cobbled together a meager living printing, soliciting newspaper subscriptions door-to-door in Alameda County, and selling his wife's sewing, but he aspired to independent proprietorship. In the early republic, newspapers were generally owned by the artisans who set their type, but with the commercialization of the press, capitalists and professional editors assumed control of news businesses, and typesetters were reimagined as mere mechanics, unqualified for literary pursuits.[21] George aspired to be part of the shrinking group of printers who crossed the threshold out of manual labor. To that end, he submitted a short contribution to the *Journal of the Trades and Working Man*, distinguished as the first labor periodical on the West Coast. In this piece, he bemoaned the elitism underlying "talk of the 'work people' and 'farm servants' of this coast."[22] It was a crude start to a meteoric writing career. A week later, he published his second article, in the literary journal *Californian*, home to the local luminaries Mark Twain and Bret Harte.

In his early journalistic career, George was invested less in the cause of land reform than in an expansive vision of liberal equality. In articles, some under the pen name "Proletarian," he wrote an ode to Lincoln and supported Radical

Republicans, then fighting for racial equality in the South. His devotion to republican ideals took an ill-conceived international turn when he joined a group of filibusterers who chartered the *Brontes* for a military campaign to overthrow Emperor Maximilian and reestablish the Republic of Mexico. Federal authorities intervened and halted the departure of the *Brontes* as it prepared to set sail. After he became famous, George was accused of piracy for his role in the expedition, and, in fact, a small group among the filibusterers had drawn up plans to seize a French gold transport. George, on the other hand, had sworn an oath over the flag of the Mexican Republic and saw the expedition as an opportunity to atone for his failure to fight for equality during the Civil War. As a sailor during a time when the cry of equality was reaching a crescendo, George's sense of liberty was less bounded by nation or race than it had traditionally been for most of his countrymen.[23]

George climbed the ladder of the newspaper business under the mentorship of old-time advocates of free homesteading. James McClatchy hired George to write for the *San Francisco Times*, of which George became the managing editor in June 1867. The Belfast-born McClatchy had befriended Horace Greeley and joined the Land Reform Association upon arriving in the United States.[24] McClatchy had written for Greeley's *Tribune* in New York before heading west to lead a campaign to invalidate Spanish land grants and secure the state's territory—often violently—for white squatters.[25] McClatchy used the *Times* as an echo chamber for the *Tribune*'s twin pillars of land reform and abolition. He recognized George's talent and quickly promoted him, making him coeditor in 1867. George thus grew to intellectual maturity under the mentorship of the free soil movement.[26]

California was particularly ripe for new ideas about communal landownership because disputes over land titles granted by the Mexican government left the ownership of much of the state unclear, often leading to violent conflicts between squatters and property owners. In 1866, the city of San Francisco evicted squatters who had claimed seven thousand acres of beachfront property. Under George's direction, the *Times* advocated that the land be distributed into small homesteads with large plots reserved for the public to support colleges, charitable organizations, and parks. The case encouraged George to consider how the public ownership of land could benefit citizens. It also allowed George to cut his teeth in practical politics. Although the city ultimately distributed most of the land privately, Mayor Frank McCoppin retained a large tract that would become Golden Gate Park. McCoppin wrote George twice to thank him for his support on the issue.[27]

With a growing public profile, George followed in his father's footsteps and tried proprietorship. After leaving the *Times*, George served a stint as managing editor of the new *San Francisco Chronicle*, which he converted from a small theatrical publication to a full-sized newspaper. His first try at ownership, however, was with the *San Francisco Herald*. George moved to Philadelphia and then New York in order to wire news from the East Coast and circumvent the Associated Press. The AP held a monopoly on up-to-date telegraphic news and, to limit competition, allowed its members to prevent publications in their local markets from joining. When George tried to build an alternative telegraphic service, the AP colluded with Western Union, which doubled the cost of his messages and priced him out of operation. When he complained that the two corporations had combined to stifle competition, the president of Western Union told George he should build his own telegraph system.[28] Because Western Union contracted with railroads to string its network along their rights-of-way and even shared staff with railroad corporations, the nation's news, communications, and transportation systems were all merging into an integrated monopoly.[29] It was this behemoth that broke the *Herald* and sent George home penniless, with a growing sense that the pathway to independence had been blocked by monopoly.

Upon returning to California, George worked odd jobs for two years before making another try at publishing in 1871 with the *San Francisco Daily Evening Post*. Here he matured as a journalist. In search of justice, George now took up the familiar cause of sailors. In 1873, the merchant ship *Sunrise* arrived in San Francisco after a voyage marred by so much brutality that three crew members had flung themselves to their watery deaths. George discovered these abuses and demanded prosecution. When the captain and first mate fled, the *Post* offered a reward for their apprehension. The two were ultimately caught, tried, and convicted. Hard-hitting journalism was a dangerous enterprise in San Francisco, where editors were frequently targeted for assassination or killed in duels.[30] George experienced this violence personally when his criticisms of the chief of police inspired an irate detective to accost him at the Mint Saloon. In the ensuing altercation, the detective first threatened him, then grabbed him by the neck and began hitting him. When George struck back, the detective pulled a gun, only to be interrupted by bystanders. When he was not swashbuckling, George took on more prosaic causes like graft in the school system and wage cuts for teachers.[31]

At the *Evening Post*, George would begin to flesh out his big idea: a theory to explain poverty. Shortly before beginning at the paper, George had a revelation.

On a hike in the foothills of Oakland, he asked a passerby, out of curiosity, the price of land in the area. He was astounded when the man responded that it was likely one thousand dollars an acre. George remembered, "Like a flash it came upon me that there was the reason for advancing poverty with advancing wealth. With the growth of population, land grows in value, and the men who work it must pay for the privilege." When George was young, the most common path unskilled workers took to the middle class was buying a farm on the edge of the city; even residents of what would become Central Park in Manhattan made ends meet by foraging, gardening, and keeping pigs. Now, hills on the remote periphery of San Francisco were too expensive for the poor to rest their heads on. George's epiphany did not strike ex nihilo, but it "crystallized" his "brooding thoughts into coherency." George had already discovered the idea of land value taxation in the works of John Stuart Mill. He remembered this moment in the Oakland foothills as his seminal epiphany because it solidified the idea that rising land values were the root cause of inequality. George had not yet discovered his "single tax," but he had discovered the paradox of progress and poverty.[32]

George espoused his new ideas about progress and urban rent in an article titled "What the Railroad Will Bring Us," the prescience of which made him famous. In the article, he discussed the city's hopes that the completion of the transcontinental railroad would bring prosperity and turn San Francisco into a great metropolis. George was confident that the last of these two propositions would be true, even predicting that it might become the "first city of the continent." He took pleasure in the thought that San Francisco's connections to the world would turn it into a cultural mecca: "We shall have our noble charities, great museums, libraries and universities; a class of men who have leisure for thought and culture; magnificent theaters and opera houses, parks and pleasure gardens. We shall develop a literature of our own, issue books which will be read wherever the English language is spoken." At this point, however, George departed from the long tradition of boosters who predicted that new cities would bring wealth to their inhabitants.[33] He pessimistically concluded that the railroad "will not benefit all of us, but only a portion." Progress would mean rising rents and inequality. The concentration of wealth in railroad corporations would spark corruption, turning the government against its people.[34] In subsequent years, George's predictions seemed to play out, defying the ingrained faiths of settlers and earning George a reputation as a prophet.

During the 1870s, George became involved in a less savory cause: anti-Chinese nativism. In 1869, he published an article in the *New York Tribune* calling the Chinese in San Francisco "long-tailed barbarians . . . making princes of our capitalists . . . and crushing workers into the dust."[35] He argued that immigration reduced wages by increasing labor competition and depicted the Chinese as culturally backward and unassimilable. He forwarded the article to John Stuart Mill, who was skeptical of George's racist undertones but endorsed his economics. George published Mill's letter, sparking excitement that the world's leading philosopher dabbled in the provincial affairs of San Francisco. In corresponding with the most prominent English liberal about an article in the leading publication of the free soil movement, George demonstrated his deep roots in those traditions.[36]

George's mixture of nativism and labor politics reflected prevailing white opinion in Gilded Age San Francisco, but as George witnessed the movement unfold, he distanced himself from prejudices that he could no longer reconcile with his philosophy. In 1878, Dennis Kearney came to prominence as the leader of California's nativist Workingmen's Party. Kearney interspersed his tirades against the Chinese with attacks on the "land pirates" and argued that "the land question is the future great question of this country."[37] The Workingmen's Party won enough offices in local elections in 1878 to control the state's constitutional convention. George was offered the party's nomination as a delegate, but he was hissed out of the nominating convention when he expressed his concerns about the movement.[38]

In an article for *Popular Science Monthly*, George broke with the movement for Chinese exclusion. The Chinese had become a "scapegoat . . . for all political demoralization and corruption." George repudiated as "infantile" his earlier argument that immigration would bring down wages.[39] Acknowledging that his *Tribune* article was "crude," he explained that he "had not then come to clear economic views."[40] Although George soured on nativist prejudices, he still believed it was necessary to halt Chinese immigration. He rarely discussed immigration after reaching intellectual maturity, but when he did, he claimed Chinese culture was both too different and too advanced for immigrants to set it aside and embrace American culture. This viewpoint contrasted with his position on the vast waves of immigration from southern and eastern Europe, which George welcomed despite the misgivings of many other native-born Americans. George's growing faith that the maldistribution of wealth accounted for social differences eroded his racial essentialism but left a belief in cultural differences that prevented him from fully embracing the egalitarianism many others would see in his philosophy.[41]

When George published his first book, *Our Land and Land Policy*, in 1871, he was still straddling the politics of free land and land taxation. The book's first paragraph bemoaned how little arable land remained in the public domain. While George discussed land value taxation, he gave equal attention to railroad land grants, which were consuming what remained of the public domain. He argued that these grants had increased the price of land and incentivized inefficient routes designed to claim land rather than transport goods.[42] While it only sold about a thousand copies upon release, *Our Land and Land Policy* marked the beginning of Georgism as a movement. It served as the foundational text for the Land Reform League of California, formed in 1878. James McGuire, a future congressman and gubernatorial nominee, was active in the group; the preservationist John Muir stopped by for at least one meeting.[43] As a mark of his growing prestige, George was invited to lecture on political economy at the University of California at Berkeley. He treated the speech as a job talk, though no position was offered. His son later claimed that the faculty was offended when George implied academic economists were unduly influenced by financial self-interest and class biases.[44]

The *San Francisco Evening Post* ceased publication in 1875, but George had helped elect Democrat William Irvin as governor of California, and, in return, he asked Irvin "to give me a place where there was little work to do and something to get, so that I might devote myself to some important writing."[45] In January 1876, Governor Irwin appointed George state inspector of gas meters, which secured George a reasonable living with minimal time commitment. This political patronage acted like a research grant. With his sinecure, George stepped back from the immediacy of the newspaper business to focus on writing that would be timeless, rather than timely. The Land Reform League of California served as his sounding board.

On September 18, 1877, George wrote a short note in his diary: "Commenced 'Progress and Poverty.'" This piece, which he envisioned as a short article, grew under the encouragement of his friends. Henry George Jr. later remembered his father during this time as only half present. He paced the floor smoking cigars; his countenance showed "tense thought in the brow and a gleam in the deep-blue eyes that looked straight through and beyond you, as if to rest on the world of visions of the pure in heart."[46] He would suddenly disengage from conversations or make unplanned jaunts to the bay, where he would sit and think.[47]

It is hard to imagine now how an artisan with a middle school education could write a book that challenged the world's leading thinkers with the literary mastery and intellectual breadth of *Progress and Poverty*. By the time he wrote it, George had accumulated nearly eight hundred books in his home library overlooking the San Francisco Bay. He also made generous usage of the public libraries and interspersed his readings in political economy and philosophy with poetry-reading breaks to further cultivate his style. George Jr. noted that his father was more of a "browser" than a "deep reader" and that he "read 'at' most books, not through them: Yet in his dipping he had the art of culling the particular parts that were useful to the purposes of his mind."[48] Some of his followers would claim that their real education began after his ideology had given structure to the disconnected facts they had acquired in college, even giving them new powers of extemporaneous speech.[49] It was this same ideological thinking that allowed George to construct a book of remarkable breadth, relating everything from British imperialism to the fall of the Roman Republic back to land. George's rise to literary fame was novel and inspiring because he had acquired his erudition by tapping the public resources of a democracy rather than the luxury of an Old World inheritance. Aside from that, though, George was like most other men who had contributed to the history of ideas up to that point: an autodidact heedless of disciplinary boundaries. The rising class of credentialed, specialized academics represented a new and untried approach to the formation of knowledge that, in economics, would find its first major challenge in George's classical humanism.[50]

It was the very improbability of George's accomplishment that nurtured his charismatic aura. Charismatic authority is based on the paradoxical impression that a leader is both relatable and yet born with an exceptional, even divinely granted power. José Martí, himself one of the great charismatic figures of the century, described George in terms that emphasized these traits of talent and empathetic attachment: "He is a man born to be the father of men. When he sees an unhappy man, he feels a slap on his own cheek!"[51] Since George wrote for people like himself—an aspirational middle class—he would draw on wells of charismatic authority, inspiring lieutenants with similarly relatable, yet exceptional narratives. The sociologist Max Weber, who popularized the concept of charisma, saw it as naturally in conflict with the other great source of authority in the modern era: bureaucracy. Bureaucracy, which would become the vehicle for many of George's antagonists, was a part of capitalism's modernization process—a tool through which business established an efficient and predictable national economy. Although a natural outgrowth of liberal democracy, bureaucracy was also a threat to it in that it wrested power from elected officials. Whereas bureaucratic authority was stable and conservative, charismatic authority was revolutionary, bending the development of the state to individual will. The granting of extraordinary influence to charismatic individuals endangered democratic norms, and yet was also the means through which democracy was attained, as nations turned to heroes like George Washington or Simón Bolívar to humanize the republic. George lent his charismatic authority to the cause of democracy, combatting a nascent faith that professional bureaucracy could steward capitalism into the future better than the electorate.[52]

George finished his book manuscript in March 1879. Upon writing the last word, he fell to his knees and wept, overcome by the feeling that his fate now rested in the "Master's hands." That sense of divine destiny became to him "a religion strong and deep, though vague."[53] This faith that he was performing the work of some higher power hardly demonstrated humility, but George's confidence was not so much in himself as in the inevitability of a cause that he believed preceded and transcended him.[54] The completion of *Progress and Poverty* would be the defining moment of George's life; his philosophy had reached maturity and he had taken his first steps toward the world stage. It is impossible to determine with certainty the book's circulation after it first appeared, because it was republished in innumerable unauthorized auditions, serialized in newspapers, and abbreviated in short pamphlets. Clearly, though, *Progress and Poverty* became a global phenomenon.[55]

While *Progress and Poverty* was important, to measure George by this one book undercuts and misinterprets him. At nearly six hundred pages, many loaded with dense economic terminology, the book became required reading for the initiated. It was hardly, however, the tip of the spear. Supporters preferred his shorter, less dense works for propaganda.[56] During various periods, *The Irish Land Question* and *Protection or Free Trade*—possibly even *Social Problems*—eclipsed *Progress and Poverty* in sales, serving as the reading public's introduction to George's philosophy. These texts considered how land intersected with colonialism, free trade, labor unionism, and economic concentration. In contrast, *Progress and Poverty* was an exhaustive argument for taxing land; overemphasizing it obscures the broader ideology George espoused. It was his *Das Kapital*, not his *Communist Manifesto*.

As I show in later chapters, *Progress and Poverty* was less important for George's movement than commonly imagined, but more important for liberalism than is usually appreciated. It was a juncture that represented both continuity and change. Henry George was raised in several intersecting currents of reform, but he was willing to buck them all. *Progress and Poverty* would draw on classical liberalism, free soil ideology, and republicanism but also break from them in meaningful ways. George's aspiration to reach the whole "brotherhood of man" encouraged him to draw on Hinduism and Judaism. His assertion that society had its own claims to collective property would incorporate a sort of socialism into a liberal tradition that had often been associated, fairly or not, with unchecked individualism.

CHAPTER 3

The Truths of Smith and Proudhon

Crafting a New Liberalism

> What I have done in this book, if I have correctly solved the great problem
> I have sought to investigate, is, to unite the truth perceived by the schools
> of Smith and Ricardo to the truth perceived by the schools of Proudhon
> and Lassalle; to show that *laissez faire* (in its full true meaning) opens the
> way to a realization of the noble dreams of socialism.
>
> Henry George, *Progress and Poverty* (1879)

When Henry George completed *Progress and Poverty* in 1879, one of the world's leading philosophers, Herbert Spencer, was already on record in favor of land nationalization. In writing *Progress and Poverty*, George happily cited Spencer's support for the principle, and yet his references to Spencer were generally critical. *Progress and Poverty* was written with the hope of delivering mankind from the poverty George had witnessed in his life, but to the extent that it engaged in philosophical discourse, it was as an attack on Spencer. The book's major focus on civilizational decline was not native to George or his movement—for which declension tropes would grow less significant over time—but instead were a direct assault on the period's reigning Spencerian philosophy: the idea that biological, scientific, and technological progress would elevate civilization to a higher plane without state intervention. As George pushed *Progress and Poverty* out to publication, he expressed his desire to confront the world's most famous advocate of land nationalization more directly in another book, which he did in 1893 with *A Perplexed Philosopher*.[1]

It made little sense for George to target Spencer if his only goal was to promote land nationalization, a cause that, as far as he knew, they both still shared. But George had a larger mission: to salvage an egalitarian and democratic strand of liberalism. The popularity of Spencerianism represented a manifest truth: capitalist society was becoming more hierarchical, and private entities were gaining power commensurate with, if not greater than, that of governments. Industrialization was eclipsing the yeoman republic. Spencer sought to justify and legitimate these changes within the progressive framework of the Enlightenment. George sought to reverse them and foster a more egalitarian republic. He would square Adam Smith with Pierre-Joseph Proudhon and, by integrating elements of socialism into the liberal tradition, provide a way for liberals to reconcile their faith in property with the social services necessary to promote a stable, egalitarian democracy.

Land and Inequality

George rejected the Malthusian idea that the mass of mankind was destined to be poor because of the scarcity of natural wealth. This was the argument that underwrote inequality and the struggle for survival in Spencer's thought, and even more optimistic liberals like Mill and Ricardo had offered, at best, slight revisions to Malthus's predictions. George easily dispensed with Malthusianism: "The richest countries are not those where nature is most prolific. . . . The countries where population is densest and presses harder upon the capacities of nature, are, all other things being equal, the countries where the largest proportion of the produce can be devoted to luxury and the support of non-producers."[2] George argued that larger and denser populations should be more efficient and that more laborers would produce more wealth. The problem was "the injustice of society, not the niggardness of nature."[3]

Scarce resources were a problem—as Ricardo had suggested—only because the boon they offered was unequally distributed. While it might seem that people were moving away from their dependence on the land, George argued that modernization only increased demand for natural resources, and hence rent. Ricardian rent theory stated that demand for natural resources would increase proportionally with population, but this proposition assumed that people consumed an equal quantity of natural resources. George, conversely, noted that, while a French monarch "could not hold or digest more than the stomach of a French peasant . . . while a few rods of ground would supply the black bread and herbs which constituted the subsistence of the peasant, it took hundreds of thousands of acres to supply the demands of the king" for more land-intensive crops and livestock, large estates, and horses. "Improvements in the arts" and more efficient ways of organizing business were creating a new class of industrial barons who lived better than ancient kings, and thus "every increase in the power of producing wealth must result in an increased demand for land and the direct products of land."[4] This growing demand for land would drive up rent, thereby increasing inequality with material progress. Here was the answer to the riddle of progress and poverty.

George predicted that all material progress would produce a proportional increase in the demand for land. Thus, reforms aimed at distributional justice would also be undermined by rent. In *Protection or Free Trade*, George argued that the producer was robbed by the protective tariff, patents, banks, corrupt government, and standing armies, but "they are the lesser robbers, and to drive them off is only to leave more for the great robber to take."[5] Land nationalization was not a panacea but a "fundamental" reform, necessary for social progress:

> If all monopolies, save the monopoly of land were abolished; if, even, by means of cooperative societies . . . the profits of exchange were saved, . . . nothing whatsoever would be done toward the equalization of wealth. I do not say that in the recognition of the equal and unalienable right of each human being to the natural elements . . . lies the solution of all social problems. I fully recognize the fact that even after we do this, much will remain to do. But whatever else we do, so long as we fail to recognize the equal right to the elements of nature, nothing will avail to remedy that unnatural inequality of the distribution of wealth which is fraught with so much evil and danger.[6]

George perceived railroads and telegraphs as monopolistic because there were natural limits to their reproduction; they required unique rights-of-way or, in effect, large conglomerations of uniquely situated landed property. These natural monopolies should be socialized like land.[7] Monopolistic privileges permeated the economy, but since land was the "residual claimant" that consumed the excess profits of society, nationalizing its value was the prerequisite for all meaningful economic reform.

The dangers of this inequality were evident in the financial panics that routinely paralyzed post–Civil War America, causing labor strife and mass violence. George was one of the first political economists to argue that these recessions were caused by the maldistribution of wealth. The reigning economic theories of the era, including the Wage Fund Theory and Say's Law, indicated that without government intervention the supply and demand of goods should be correlated. Thus, there should never be more goods than consumers could manage to purchase. George believed that this formula neglected a third factor: rent. Real estate prices would rise with prosperity, slowing growth and ultimately reaching levels that the economy could not sustain. Thus, rent would produce "a cessation of demand, which would again check production there, and thus the paralysis would communicate itself through all the interlacings of industry and commerce."[8]

Drawing on the history of Rome, George argued that these conditions would undermine the republican institutions that had formed the foundation of social progress. He wrote that "given a community with Republican institutions, in which one class is too rich to be shorn of its luxuries . . . and another so poor that a few dollars on election day will seem more than any abstract consideration . . . power must pass into the hands of the jobbers who will sell it as the Praetorians sold the Roman purple."[9] While Spencer had hailed the concentration of economic power as evolutionary progress toward the natural rule of the competitive elite, George argued that monopolistic privileges had fostered a ruling class that stood above democratic institutions: "Is there not growing up among us a class who have all the power without any of the virtues of an aristocracy? We have simple citizens who control thousands of miles of railroad, millions of acres of land . . . who choose the governors of sovereign states as they name their clerks . . . and whose will is as supreme with the legislatures as that of a French king sitting in bed of justice." These conditions were enlarging the institution of wage labor, which "threatens to compel every worker to seek a master, as the insecurity which followed the break-up of the Roman Empire compelled every freeman to seek a lord."[10]

Yet George broke with republicans who equated civic virtue with rural life. Having received his education from the city of Philadelphia, he described in almost mythical terms the city's ability to lift the public intelligence: "Here intellectual activity is gathered into a focus, and here springs the stimulus which is caused by collision of mind with mind. Here are the great libraries, the storehouses and granaries of knowledge, the learned professors, the famous specialists. Here are art galleries, collections of philosophical apparatus, and all things rare, valuable, and best of their kind."[11] In contrast, George described rural Americans, whose large speculative investments in land required sprawl that undermined community, as "half-savage cowboys, whose social life is confined to the excitement of the 'round-up' or a periodical 'drunk' in a railroad town."[12] Notably, what George prized about the city was the "collision of mind with mind." In contrast to contemporaries who believed modernization should be led by the intellectual elite, George emphasized the role of social discourse in preparing the democratic public to govern itself. Taxing sprawl out of existence would foster integrated urban communities. George embraced the progressive forces of urbanization and technical specialization but lamented that rising land values and speculation limited access to both by pricing citizens out of the communities that could foster social and intellectual development.

The Social Value of the City

It was George's explanation of rising urban rents that constituted his most significant contribution to liberalism. Drawing on his experience with urban growth during the boom years of San Francisco, he told the parable of a lone settler who started a community that grew into a great metropolis. During its early days, the settler "must be his own blacksmith, wagonmaker, carpenter, and cobbler"; he "cannot have his children schooled" and, "though nature is prolific, the man is poor." Once a settlement was established, "there are gratifications for the social and intellectual nature—for the part of the man that rises above the animal. The power of sympathy, the sense of companionship, the emulation of comparison and contrast, open a wider, and fuller and more varied life."[13] The city fostered economies of agglomeration and opportunities for specialization unknown to the primitive community.[14] This concentration of population "brings out a superior power in labor, which is localized on land . . . [and] which thus inheres in the land as much as any qualities of soil."[15] "All these advantages attach to the land," and thus lots "are worth more than would suffice to pave them with gold coin."[16] All the progress of the community thus became the property of the landlords: "Our settler . . . is now a millionaire. Like another Rip Van Winkle, he may have laid down and slept; still he is rich—not from anything he has done."[17]

George's parable expanded on existing concerns about land in Ricardian political economy. Adam Smith had argued that prices should be proportional to the value of labor employed in production, but since land could not be reproduced, the landlord had monopoly power. Ricardo posited that any advantage in productivity that a given parcel of land had over the most marginal land under cultivation would be assessed as rent. In Mill's words, "The superiority of the instrument is in exact proportion to the rent paid for it."[18] Ricardo associated land's value with its agricultural and extractive yields, but George observed that the "sandy waste" on which San Francisco was built was more valuable than the most productive agricultural land in the world.[19] The advantages of the city—specialization of labor, high culture, economies of scale, faster distribution, retail potential, and broader social life—were all factored into rental value. George's readers often assumed that his discussions of "land" were about agricultural reform, but in fact he was shifting the focus of classical political economy away from the rents of agricultural land. In *The*

Science of Political Economy, George observed that "space" would have better conveyed his meaning because his primary insight was to explain the rising value of small urban lots.[20]

Although liberals had always contended that rights to landed property were at best provisional, George's parable of urban development suggests something even more radical: that the community had its own proprietary rights. John Locke had laid the foundation for liberal property theory by arguing that individuals had a natural right to themselves and, by extension, to what they produced. This applied imperfectly to land because it was a gift of God. Thus, Mill wrote, "when the sacredness of property is talked about it should always be remembered that this sacredness does not belong in the same degree to landed property."[21] In contrast, George's parable meant that land rent was the creation of the entire community. Everything citizens built was embodied in the value of the land. Just as the labor of the individual gave them title to what they produced, the labor of the community gave it title to what it produced: land values.

John Locke's theory of property rights had justified the expansion of a commercial economy; now George's argument about social value recast individual rights into social rights. When Spencer seemed to abandon the cause of land nationalization, George chided him, writing that "to deprive others of their rights to the use of the earth is to commit a crime inferior only to taking away their lives or personal liberties."[22] George retained Locke's faith in the natural right to retain what one produced, because "that which a man makes or produces is his own, against all the world—to enjoy or to destroy, to use, to exchange, or to give."[23] Yet he also contended that the community had a right to an ever-expanding fund of social wealth that could be redistributed to ensure that "no one need fear poverty" and that "mental activities now devoted to scrapping together riches would be translated into far higher spheres of usefulness."[24] George had grafted the welfare state onto classical liberalism.

George promised equal opportunity, not equality, but he doubted that there was much difference. He asked, "How many men are there who fairly earn a million dollars?"[25] He doubted that wealth inequality was rooted in natural inequalities, noting "how little have the best of us . . . that may be credited entirely to ourselves; how much to the influences that have molded us."[26] He argued that in a society where the necessities of life were easy to come by, people would look askance at those who worked relentlessly to acquire wealth. Noting that Olympic athletes once fought over a "wreath of wild olive," he argued that, "for a ribbon," people have "performed services no money could have bought."[27] Without the fear of poverty, people would seek acclaim in "the management of public affairs" and work that "extends knowledge . . . enriches literature, and elevates thought."[28] The emergence of an economic elite reflected not natural inequality but social dysfunction. The equality that had animated American democracy was still obtainable under a truly liberal political equality.

Poverty and the Decadence of Republican Civilization

The nineteenth century had witnessed more social changes than the whole millennium that preceded it. The telegraph annihilated distance. The railroad made it possible to trade when rivers froze and purchase fruit and vegetables out of season. Time and space had been disrupted. Humanity was within living memory of an age when most people were employed in the cultivation of land and satisfied many of their needs on their own. Now, increasingly sophisticated machinery and business organizations meant that the majority could hardly conceive of how those needs were met. They put their faith in society to provide for them, and their ability to comprehend the processes by which it did so became more remote with every passing year.[29] Particularly startling was the fact that this modern age had been born without any conscious plan. Instead, it had taken root exactly as state management had given way to the open field of competition. Herbert Spencer had become a renowned philosopher by noting the parallel to natural selection; absent any intelligent design, a system of increasing complexity and differentiation had developed in the contest for individual gain. The railroads and the telegraphs, like butterflies and flowers, were, many thought, the product of a system of unbridled competition.

George's theory of history challenged this growing faith in biological evolution and contended that it was democratic equality that spurred progress. George charted the collapse of historical republics to show that progress would not proceed inevitably from the evolution of the species. Spencer had argued that with social evolution came greater complexity and the development of a "regulative class" that used disciplinary regimes like slavery and serfdom to train the race to be industrious and socially compliant.[30] George, in contrast, argued that this inequality undermined the free institutions that were a precondition for progress. He rejected the idea that progress was a function of racial evolution, arguing that if modern man stands higher than his ancestors it is because "we stand on a pyramid, not that we are taller."[31] Whereas Spencer debated "the benefits of extirpating inferior races," George cited evidence that black children performed better than their white peers until the effects of racial discrimination set in. Thus, even the most entrenched hierarchy in American life was a function of political design, not genetic essentialism.[32]

To men like Andrew Carnegie who read Spencer to mean that they were an evolutionary elite destined to rule, George argued that the benefits of a free market were not rooted in the organizational talent of profound intellects but the "unconscious cooperation" of society. To illustrate his point, George cited the example of shipbuilding: "Consider the timbers, the planks, the spars . . . the canvass of various textures; the blocks and winches and windlass; the pumps, the boats, the sextants, the chronometers, the spy-glass and patent logs . . . and all the various things, which it would be tiresome to fully specify, that go to the construction and furnishing of a first-class sailing-ship of modern type. . . . Directed cooperation never did, and I do not think in the nature of things it ever could, make and assemble such a variety of products."[33] In this liberal theory of intelligence, freedom was a precondition for diverse social groups to engage with one another and produce innovations that a single intelligence—whether it be that of a Prussian bureaucrat or Darwinian entrepreneur—could never manage alone. To George and his followers, this "conscious cooperation" of elite management was objectionable regardless of whether it was spearheaded by the state or by the private sector. Louis Post, George's most important spokesman, argued that there were two paths toward socialism: either "the absorption of industries by the government, or . . . the absorption of government by industrial agencies."[34] Even advocates of centralization often recognized that there was a thin line between monopoly capitalism and socialism. George Perkins, who helped organize the merger of giant monopolies such as US Steel and International Harvester, saw himself as creating "a form of socialism" by creating an economy controlled and managed by large business interests.[35] Conversely, the perennial socialist candidate Eugene V. Debs observed that the monopolistic trust "is the most enlightened method of production. . . . When we gain the public power then we can by law transfer this trust from private hands of eight or ten or a dozen individuals to the collective people. It is already co-operative."[36]

George opposed this top-down centralization and hoped instead to foster the unconscious cooperation of small producers. He understood that society had progressed past a Jeffersonian republic of yeoman farmers but believed that taxing landed wealth could provide workers with the leverage to become economically independent. Removing taxes on production would increase employment, improving labor's bargaining power. Taxing undeveloped land would force speculators to put it on the market. This would spur construction, creating jobs and lowering rents. With vacant land open and free, even poor workers would be able to gather the capital to stake out a living on the earth. Thus, George believed that "instead of laborers competing with one another for employment . . . employers would everywhere be competing for laborers. . . . The employers of labor would not have merely to bid against other employers . . . but against the ability of laborers to become their own employers upon the natural opportunities freely opened to them by the tax which prevented monopolization."[37] The division between capital and labor would crumble. George promised a "cooperative commonwealth," arguing that breaking up monopoly would give the masses the means to form voluntary cooperatives and the "more equal distribution of wealth would unite capitalist and laborer in the same person."[38]

George recognized that industrialization and urbanization augured an increasingly complex society, but he believed that progress hinged on providing the democratic public the means to manage that complexity, rather ceding more authority to Spencer's elite "regulative class." George noted that "as society develops, a higher and higher degree of social intelligence is required, for the relations of individuals to each other becomes more intimate and important, and the increasing complexity of the social organization brings liability to new dangers."[39] Land rents would constantly grow with the progress of society, offering ever-larger resources with which to provide citizens with the intellectual tools to engage constructively in shaping public policy. The expropriation of rent would allow the state to encourage the lifelong education necessary for a vital republic, supporting "museums, libraries, gardens, lecture rooms, music and dancing halls, theaters, universities, technical schools, shooting galleries, playgrounds, gymnasiums."[40]

George argued for splitting up not just private but also public power. Government's coercive powers would become superfluous under conditions in which society was healthy and self-regulating. Although it would grow in wealth with the expropriation of land rents, government would have most of its disciplinary powers gradually stripped away until it became little more than a trustee of the public's wealth. George divided society into private and public functions that he believed were a matter of natural law: "Realizing as I do the correlative truth of both principles [I] can no more call myself an individualist or a socialist than one who considers the forces by which the planets are held to their orbits could call himself a centrifugalist or a centripetalist."[41] Adhering to Jacksonian tradition, he refused to allow these two spheres to intersect with public-private contracts or the regulation of private business. The prohibition of alcohol illustrated the dangers regulation posed to honest government: "Where it is prohibited, illicit sales, it risks nothing to predict, would still go on. These illicit sellers would all the more need the favor and connivance of officials owing their positions to politics and must therefore use their influence and spend their money."[42]

Stripped of its regulatory and coercive powers, government would use its benevolence as the trustee of public wealth to create a more moral society. As it accrued the resources to fund old-age pensions, free public transportation, free health care, and free higher education, mankind would grow more peaceful and prosperous, so that the coercive functions of the state would wither away. Law enforcement, the judicial system, and standing armies would dwindle. Both Spencer and George aspired to a morally perfect future in which the state would be unnecessary; however, Spencer believed it could be created only through centuries of oppression weeding out those unsuited to modern civilization, whereas George placed his faith in the modern welfare state.[43]

This state of social peace and morality would have an additional benefit: the salvation of the soul. Christians had long aspired to purify America, but earlier religious reformers like the abolitionists had hoped to exhort individuals to adopt moral ways. George's environmentalist interpretation of vice, in contrast, suggested that the commonwealth should be fixed so that it allowed individuals to live more moral lives. This idea was most evident in the conclusion of *Progress and Poverty*, which positioned religious salvation as the end goal of reform. George's book reached its crescendo with the conclusion that Manichean archetypes embodied an ultimate struggle to liberate human virtue:

> Here, now, in our civilized society, the old allegories yet have meaning. . . .
> Ormuzd still fights with Ahriman—the Prince of Light with the Powers of
> Darkness. He who will hear, to him the clarions of the battle call. . . . Strong
> soul and high endeavor, the world needs them now. Beauty still lies imprisoned, the iron wheels go over the good and true and beautiful that might
> spring from human lives. And they who fight with Ormuzd, though they may
> not know each other—somewhere, sometime, will the muster roll be called.[44]

Near the end of the nineteenth century, many Christians adopted a "social gospel" that prioritized economic reform. Important proponents of this idea, including George Herron and Herbert Bigelow, were devotees of George. From George, these individuals derived the faith that paradise was not merely something to be hoped for after death but a goal that the faithful should try to realize on earth.[45] Walter Rauschenbusch, the most prominent of the social gospelers, would credit the origin of his social consciousness to "the agitation of Henry George," noting I "wish . . . to record my lifelong debt to this single-minded apostle of a great truth."[46] In fact, the term "social gospel" was probably coined in 1886 by a Congregationalist minister from Dubuque, Iowa, who used the term to describe *Progress and Poverty*.[47]

George's religious language, however, was partly a way to expand the appeal of his ideas. When one follower exhorted him to emphasize Christianity, he retorted that he preferred not to discuss religion but knew that it had been important to securing his support.[48] George's most influential religious argument was, in fact, not rooted in his Christian faith at all. Originally delivered to the Young Men's Hebrew Association of San Francisco in 1878, his speech "Moses" highlighted the Jubilee, when, every fifty years, the landed property of Israel was redistributed. George argued that this proved the Jewish faith was incompatible with private property in land. Drawing on his theories about progress and social organization, he argued: "From the free spirit of the Mosaic Law sprang that intensity of family life that amid all dispersions and persecutions has preserved the individuality of the Hebrew race; that love of independence that under the most adverse circumstances has characterized the Jew. . . . It kindled that fire that has made the strains of Hebrew seers and poets phrase for us the highest exaltations of thought; that intellectual vigor that has over and over again made the dry staff bud and blossom."[49] The great Scottish advocate of land nationalization, Thomas Spence, had—unbeknownst to George—also cited the Jubilee as evidence of the immorality of landed property. However, Spence portrayed Mosaic law as part of the Christian tradition, whereas George characterized the Jubilee as distinctly Jewish. Regrettably, he opined, Christianity's focus on the afterlife had eclipsed Judaism's designs to improve life on earth.[50]

George was so comfortable appealing to other religious traditions because of his ecumenical natural law philosophy. He described his own religious faith as a "feeling" that struck him after finishing *Progress and Poverty* and became "a religion strong and deep, though vague—a religion of which I never like to speak or make any outward manifestations, but yet that I try to follow."[51] In *Progress and* Poverty, he cited the Hindu epic *Ramayana* as evidence of the immorality of poverty.[52] Beneath these types of appeals was a sense that all religions were expressions of some underlying truth: "The Scriptures of the men who have been and gone—the Bibles, the Zend Avestas, the Vedas, the Dhammapadas, and the Korans; the esoteric doctrines of old philosophies, the inner meaning of grotesque religions, the dogmatic constitutions of Ecumenical Councils, the preachings of Foxes, and Wesleys, and Savonarola, the traditions of red Indians, and beliefs of black savages, have a heart and a core in which they agree—a something which seems like the variously distorted apprehensions of a primary truth."[53] Like the transcendentalists he read as a boy, George believed that religions presented "myths and symbols in which men have tried to display their deepest perceptions."[54] Unlike Locke, George did not search for natural law in a state of nature. Instead, he believed mankind had embedded its innate sense of morality in cultural traditions, so that moral truth was singular and absolute, but best identified through an investigation of the commonalities that united diverse cultures.[55] This pluralistic natural law philosophy facilitated authentic appeals to diverse normative values. Building arguments on his audiences' moral premises allowed him to make unlikely converts from a broad array of backgrounds. This cultural pluralism was important enough to the movement's sense of itself that Anna George de Mille would highlight it in the title of her father's biography: *Henry George: Citizen of the World* (1950).

Whereas Spencer scoured the globe for evidence of natural inequality, George did the opposite. "The Hindoos and the Chinese," he noted, "were civilized when we were savages."[56] Those civilizations became petrified by customs designed to reinforce inequality. The fractured character of European civilization had allowed it to progress under a condition of relative equality and associational cooperation: "the growth of larger and denser communities," "the increase of commerce," "individual liberty," and "democratic government" had "set free the mental power which has rolled back the veil of ignorance . . . which has harnessed in our service physical forces besides which man's efforts are puny; and increased productive power by a thousand great inventions."[57] Whereas the liberalism of Spencer and Godkin increasingly justified inequality as the fruit of progress, George argued that progress would reverse itself when inequality became entrenched.

The Professional Critique of George

George's contention that Lockean philosophy necessitated a sort of socialism was nearly unassailable within the existing framework of classical liberalism. The liberal giant John Stuart Mill had argued that rent acted like an "elastic and extensible band" to hold back progress, though it was not a "wall" that would block all development.[58] George's observations about the impact of urbanization and scientific improvements on demand for resources were clear additions to classical theory that made rent look much more like a wall than a band. The economist Francis A. Walker argued that George failed to account for the way innovations in transportation would effectively expand the supply of land, but otherwise did little to challenge George's refinements of Ricardian theory. Walker sought to complicate George's argument about industrialization by contending that some innovations in production would be "land saving" in that they allowed for more efficient use of land and resources, though the research of William Stanley Jevons had long since demonstrated that inventions that seemed to save resources often further increased demand for them.[59] In a series of three lectures critiquing George, the economist Alfred Marshall ceded classical economics to George, noting that he successfully employed "phrases, which were used by the last generation of economists, but which the rising generation almost to a man have abandoned, not as false, but as liable to misrepresentation or misleading."[60] In his speeches, Marshall argued that the law of diminishing returns in agriculture proved that farm profits would fall.[61] This had no relation to George's argument about resource and urban rents; diminishing returns were actually the foundation on which Ricardian rent theory was based. Marshall acknowledged that he "failed utterly" to turn classical economics against George.[62] But, as Marshall suggested, economists were setting aside the doctrines of Smith, Ricardo, and Mill. By arguing that the consumer, rather than labor, set the value of commodities, a new wave of neoclassical economists shifted the discipline away from a focus on earned and unearned values.[63]

George's critics contended that political economy should be reserved for credentialed professionals who would leverage their expertise to create a more orderly society. Two years after Walker published his attack on George, he became the first president of the American Economic Association (AEA). In his inaugural address, Walker laid out a vision that would inspire the AEA. Economists, he argued, were disinterested experts who must staff an expansive new administrative state and overcome the irrationalities of laissez-faire through the power of technical expertise.[64] Walker was a ruthless practitioner of this new bureaucratic management; as commissioner of Indian affairs, he had pushed the agency to adopt a policy of "rigid reformatory control" of indigenous people, forcing them to adopt industrial labor and barring them from leaving reservations lest they engage in wanton race mixing.[65]

Progressives in the AEA often railed against the "atomistic individualism" of liberalism.[66] George denied that individualism and collectivism were useful ways of thinking about society, because every social system had to balance both principles. Instead he distinguished between the "conscious cooperation" of a society controlled by a single intelligence and the "unconscious cooperation" of individuals working together freely, pooling their collective intelligence and distinct skills. The phrase "unconscious cooperation" encompassed the dreams of the liberal tradition better than the caricatures of "atomistic individualism" leveled by its critics. Adam Smith had written of the wealth of "nations," not individuals. John Stuart Mill supported cooperatives and adopted many of the insights of thinkers like Hegel and Humboldt.[67] Spencer, described by one recent biographer as "anti-individualist," emphasized the "social organism" that would progress toward a state of collective freedom by imposing "social discipline" until individuals evolved a "social self-consciousness."[68] Spencer, who suffered from insomnia, insisted, for example, that "the liberty of all" required the strict regulation of urban life to prevent noise pollution, until, presumably, evolution relegated the despotism of street musicians, church bells, and railway whistles to their place among the barbarisms of the past.[69] Progressives, many of whom embraced Spencer's motif of the "social organism," differed far less from him than they sometimes liked to imagine.

Progressive economists would seek not to overturn the Spencerian faith in biologically determined hierarchy but rather to shift the chairs at the table so they sat at the head. In his seminal book *Social Control*, the sociologist Edward A. Ross frequently referenced Spencer and his core dilemma: how to make the race fit into the constructs of civilized society.[70] Ross emphasized the role of evolution in shaping the behavior of races but disagreed with Spencer that natural selection was the best way to weed out unsociable characters. The superior race, he noted, was particularly individualistic: "The restless, striving, doing Aryan, with his personal ambition, his lust for power . . . is under no easy discipline."[71] Without the hereditary constitution suited for civilization, people needed an "elite" who were the natural "leaders of society" and were responsible for establishing social control.[72] Ross argued that the monopolist had misused that power and it was time for the professional administrator to assume it: "In order to protect ourselves against the lawlessness . . . of overgrown private interests, we shall have to develop the state, especially on its administrative side. . . . As higher education, claiming more and more years of one's life, widens the space between those who have it and those who do not, and as the Enlightenment of the public wanes relative to the superior enlightenment of the learned classes and the professions, the mandarinate will inevitably draw to itself a greater and greater share of social power."[73] This was Spencer's regulative class growing with the complexity of society, only in Ross's account educated experts should supplant the businessman. Ross's "social control" would become a rallying cry for the sort of Progressive whom Georgists were often in conflict with.[74]

This statist vision of social evolution also had roots in the philosophy of Auguste Comte, who had anticipated many of Spencer's ideas about a social organism evolving toward greater differentiation and inequality. Comte, however, imagined that a new priesthood of scientists would assume responsibility for managing society in coordination with captains of industry. Comte insisted that liberalism and its faith in "equality" were a historical phase whose time had passed. David Croly had his first major brush with history when he coined the term "miscegenation" as part of a hoax to discredit Abraham Lincoln. Then, after becoming the leading American apostle of Comte's positivism, Croly denounced government "by the people," deemed it "immoral" to preach social mobility, and became an early supporter of large corporations.[75] His son, Herbert Croly, carried much of his father's faith into the mainstream of Progressive politics when he founded the *New Republic*. Croly built on Comte's vision of a scientifically managed society to argue that "natural selection" should be supplanted by "artificial selection" and that the state could "improve the means whereby men and women are bred."[76]

Challenging expert authority—even expertise in racist pseudo-science—can be construed as populism, but that label fit George imperfectly. George's sense of knowledge formation was traditionally liberal: rooted in the idea that the free exchange of ideas fostered a collective knowledge greater than that of even the best-trained individual. While the language of freedom of expression can be leveraged to give epistemological preference to the claims of socioeconomic or racial groups that claim to be the real "people," George did not indulge in that reasoning. He respected expertise and built his arguments not on the ramblings of hayseeds but on the principles of leading British economists. While George sometimes referenced a producerist sense of class similar to that employed by American populists, he was always careful to include intellectuals among America's producers. Furthermore, he always believed too much in individual freedom to adopt a deterministic sense that class predicted the value or content of one's opinions. Rather than expressing distrust of status, George was usually solicitous—possibly to a fault—of elites.

The Precarious Future of Liberalism

Neither the ideas of George nor those of his professional rivals would precipitate the age of reform that would follow, but the two groups would struggle over the form it would take. Progressivism was less a unified movement than a period of structural failure in which financial panics, labor unrest, and economic chaos underscored the bankruptcy of industrial capitalism. Professionals, concerned about unsavory competition undermining their markets by raising doubts about the safety of their products, were often at the forefront of calls to regulate their own industries.[77] The movement to establish a central bank, for example, began with a meeting of bankers and archconservative senator Nelson Aldrich in the luxury hunting resort of Jekyll Island. Hardly converts to socialism, they were inspired by a catastrophic financial panic in 1907 and investigations of international banking practices demonstrating that the industry required reorganization to be globally competitive. The Federal Reserve system, therefore, developed out of crisis, not ideology. However, the ideas circulating during the period would have vast consequences for the shape such institutions took. Aldrich planned to put American finance under the control of a private association of federated bankers. Georgists instead advocated for a Federal Reserve Board nominated by the US president, a policy that Woodrow Wilson, whom they rallied around, persuaded Congress to enact. Thus, the centralization of American finance took a democratic form, though it could have evolved into corporatist economic management by bankers.[78]

George salvaged liberalism by modernizing it. Under his guidance, a tradition of land reform designed to promote yeoman farmers became the redistribution of rent to fund a modern welfare state. Urban areas were reimagined not as hindrances to but as epicenters of republican virtue. Religion became a loose evangelical passion for uplifting humanity and liberating its potential. The semimythical salience assigned to land in the American civil religion was transmuted into an argument about monopoly that also called for the social ownership of utilities. In the time of the American Revolution, an easy alliance had been struck between the liberal doctrine of property rights and republican concern for the community's civic virtue.[79] That union was no longer so self-evident in the late nineteenth century, when railroads girdled the country and made the prosperity of the entire nation subject to the whims of a handful of executives. George, however, demonstrated how, even according to the strictures of classical liberalism, these corporations could be construed as less than private and that, by socializing natural monopolies, property rights could be strengthened. Thus, a strict, classically liberal theory of property could be harmonized with the sort of equality necessary to support a republic.

CHAPTER 4

Labor Omnia Vincit

Crafting the Movement

It is not possible for any sort of men to collect together incongruous
elements of discontent and by compromising differences and pooling
demands create a live party. The initiative must be a movement of
thought. . . . When some fundamental issue, that involves large principles
and includes smaller questions . . . begins to come to the front in thought
and discussion, then a new party . . . must begin to form, . . . though . . . [it]
may retain old names and develop from old organizations.

Henry George, "The New Party" (1887)

Progress and Poverty might well have gone unnoticed without George's now-lesser-known third book. *The Irish Land Question*, published in 1881, tied land nationalization to the cause of Irish nationalism and thereby garnered George mass acclaim. George soon drew support from conservationists, ex-abolitionists, socialists, and even monopolists. He was able to construct a broad coalition because of his skillful and intentional efforts to frame the issue of land as foundational to an array of reforms and ethical systems. George believed land nationalization was not just the solution to poverty but also the only question large enough to provide common ground for the nation's "incongruous elements of discontent." This coalition, rooted in labor and Irish nationalism, would begin to give way by the end of the 1880s, but by then George's concept of social value had expanded his base to more affluent Americans committed to liberal ideals.

Incongruous Elements of Discontent and a Movement of Thought

Upon its initial publication, *Progress and Poverty* earned some muted praise from esteemed intellectuals, including a friendly letter from Horace White, editor of *The Nation*. White's response was characteristic of early reactions to George, which treated land nationalization as a theoretical issue. White wrote that "it is a very impressive work," but if George's ideas had their virtues, they were not of practical significance for their age: "The taxing power of the state may eventually, I think, confiscate rent, but it will be a long time."[1] The

Sacramento Bee, then edited by George's mentor James McClatchy, was one of the few publications to promote the book.

In 1880, George moved to New York, without his family and with few resources, in hopes of promoting his philosophy. He struggled to find work writing and speaking and spent much of his time meeting local authors and politicians. George accepted a smaller cut in royalties to reduce the price of the book, which helped improve its circulation, though not his standard of living. In its first year, *Progress and Poverty* sold a thousand copies, unimpressive by the standards of its future success, but more than was typical for a book on political economy.

But George quickly found that land nationalization was, White's contention notwithstanding, a very timely issue. In Ireland, Michael Davitt had organized the Irish Land League to protect Irish tenants, and the land question emerged as the focal point of Irish nationalism, which had energetic supporters on both sides of the Atlantic. George met and befriended Patrick Ford, a former writer for William Lloyd Garrison's *Liberator* who had founded the *Irish World,* the leading Irish American newspaper in the United States. When Davitt traveled to New York to raise money, Ford introduced him to George. Davitt, though not immediately won over to George's ideas, promised to promote *Progress and Poverty.*[2]

In 1881 George published *The Irish Land Question* to weave together the cause of Irish home rule and land nationalization: "The cry has indeed gone up that the land of Ireland belongs to the people of Ireland, but there the recognition of the principle has stopped." George took the principle further: "If . . . the land of Ireland rightfully belongs to the people . . . it must be resumed by the whole people."[3] If the idea of the nation was defined by the homeland, it followed that collective ownership of land would be a key component of nationalism. Yet it was also a step, George believed, toward transnationalism, providing common ground for the oppressed around the world. By emphasizing "land nationalization," George believed the Irish could build a coalition with their "natural allies," the "English working classes."[4] George contextualized the Irish cause in a broader anti-colonialism, comparing Ireland to India, which he characterized as "a great estate owned by an absentee and alien landlord."[5]

Later that year, Patrick Ford hired George to travel to Ireland as a correspondent for the *Irish World,* an assignment that would give him intimate experience with the transnational struggles of the landless poor and a platform for international fame. George's first speech in Dublin was so well received that the crowd attempted to unhitch his carriage and pull it themselves, though he rejected the display, which seemed too evocative of the servile status of the Irish. Annie George was invited to preside over a meeting of the Ladies' Land League while rumors swirled that its members would be arrested as the putative heads of a movement whose male leaders had already been apprehended.[6] The highlight of George's trip was his arrest in 1882 as a "suspicious stranger." Traveling with Davitt after his release from Portland prison, George went to three shops in search of a collar stud. Unbeknownst to him, he was followed by constables, who considered each of these shopkeepers suspicious characters and therefore interpreted the trip as a conspiracy. The constables waited to arrest George until after he had purchased a train ticket out of town, so they could apprehend him in front of a crowd. George, undeterred, passed out copies of *The Irish Land Question* in the courtroom. The case was dismissed as groundless. When George returned to the United States, he found the incident had made him a famous freedom fighter. Louis Post organized a banquet at Delmonico's to celebrate his return, and much of New York's high society, including Henry Ward Beecher, judges, and Tammany officials, attended. George had little interest in this sort of elite soiree; he forgot about the event and arrived late, though, to Post's pleasant surprise, appropriately dressed.[7]

Davitt emerged from Portland prison a pronounced disciple of George. He moderated his nationalism to focus more on economic change. Like George, he now advocated home rule rather than compete independence. He used the issue of land nationalization to build bridges with the English working class and became a conspicuous force in the emergence of England's nascent Labour Party. His position became broadly anti-colonial, embracing the movement for Indian independence. Davitt departed from George only in that he advocated that the state compensate landowners for their investments prior to nationalization. George disapproved but acquiesced: "I don't care what plan anyone purposes, so that he goes on the right line."[8]

Davitt found his influence in Ireland diminished, however, by the growing cult of personality surrounding Charles Parnell, a wealthy landowner. Irish nationalists alleged that Davitt had been "captured" by George and was now less devoted to Irish independence than land nationalization. Davitt worked to balance the contentious politics of Irish nationalism with land nationalization. In 1882 he invited the Irish American priest Edward McGlynn to speak alongside him during his American tour, giving the cause an important new ally, whom George deemed a one-man "army with banners."[9] By combining a millennial, religious anti-poverty doctrine with Irish national-ism, McGlynn reached a mass audience that at times exceeded George's.

George also began to attract a growing audience among ex-abolitionists, for whom he provided a new hope that an expansive liberalism of equal rights could be reconciled with private property. After the Civil War, Francis Shaw had become "hopeless on social questions" amid growing inequality and the failure to liberalize the South. Then, Shaw read *Progress and Poverty* and the "'light broke on him.'"[10] With a newfound confidence that liberty had failed to realize progress only because it had not gone far enough, Shaw threw himself behind George. Shaw bolstered sales of *Progress and Poverty* by paying to have a thousand copies sent to libraries around the country and printing a cheap copy of the book that workers could afford.

For George, Shaw's money was less important than the endorsement that tied his cause to the abolitionist tradition. George claimed it was the "highest compliment and best advertisement of the book and the knowledge of it can spread as many copies as the donation." Shaw, a famous abolitionist in his own right, had obtained notoriety during the Civil War as the father of Colonel Robert Gould Shaw. Shaw's son had perished leading the first regiment of Black troops to fight in the war, making him a legend long before his depiction in the 1989 film *Glory*.[11]

Shaw was not the only middle-class liberal to bolster George's movement in its early days. Louis Post was a diminutive, bearded lawyer and editor of the *New York Truth*, a one-cent labor paper with a circulation of 75,000 to 100,000 mostly working-class readers.[12] Post syndicated *Progress and Poverty*, giving it a "big circulation among the very class" that George claimed to "want most to reach."[13] The paper was the de facto organ of New York's Central Labor Union, the organization that would nominate George for mayor.[14] Post would become, next to George himself, the most important writer of the movement. Post was hardly a ready convert, but he was swayed by George's appeals to the liberal tradition. He quickly read *Progress and Poverty* and at first dismissed it. The revolution George proposed clearly made him a "crank" or a "long hair." Post himself was already a reformer, but of the respectable variety. A de-cade earlier he had joined the effort to "reconstruct" the post–Civil War South by means of the Freedmen's Bureau. So, when Post read *The Irish Land Question*, he was struck to see George compare land monopoly to slavery. The young editor's mind began to turn: "The appeal stirred me deeply. Revising within me my anti-slavery spirit of Civil War times, then less than twenty years behind us, it made me realize that the struggle for relative human rights had not triumphed at Appomattox, as enthusiastic patriots of the period like myself had confidently believed."[15]

As George's working-class readership grew, his writings obtained a wider circulation than was evident in his robust book sales. His audience was short on funds, but high on zeal for spreading the good word. Reading George became a communal phenomenon. The Wisconsin Progressive Robert La Follette wrote in his biography that he encountered George as a boy in an "intellectual activity and awakening" where be both "heard and felt . . . the movement" of agrarian dissent developing around him. It was in the context that "a dog-eared copy of one of Henry George's early books got into our neighborhood. It was owned by a blacksmith . . . a big powerful fellow, who was a good deal of a reader and thinker." Although La Follette had not yet developed an interest in politics, the blacksmith compelled him to read the book, which was visibly well used, presumably from having been much passed around.[16]

George's books evoked such collective enthusiasm that the very act of reading them was like a social movement. The Chicago Painters Assembly of the Knights of Labor devoted twenty minutes of every meeting to reciting passages from *Progress and Poverty*.[17] During this period of popular religiosity, the parallel to a sermon would have escaped no one. Similarly, Samuel Gompers recalled that the workers in his cigar shop kept a library stocked with George's writings. Workers would alternate reading aloud to the shop during breaks. In this way his union read *Progress and Poverty* and George's articles in the *Irish World*.[18]

It is remarkable that a long, often theoretical work like *Progress and Poverty* was so avidly consumed by humble mechanics, blacksmiths, and cigar rollers, but George understood working people. Simplifying his writing would have been at odds with his faith that common people had the intelligence to manage an increasingly complex world. Thus, when told that he was speaking over the heads of his audience, he objected: "Working men are men and are susceptible of lofty aspirations. I never will consent to appeal to them on anything but high grounds."[19] But as a "working man," George's writing veered toward practical illustrations—stories of shipbuilding and urban development that were part of the lived experience of people like himself. These stories reflected both George's authentic connection to his audience and his belief that economics was something that the average person could—and must—understand to be an independent, voting citizen.[20]

The appeal that these "lofty aspirations" had for workers was evident in how many people not only read George but dedicated themselves to spreading his ideas. One pamphleteer in Birmingham, England, claimed to have distributed 2,300 copies of *Progress and Poverty*.[21] The circulation of George's periodical and pamphlet literature likely dwarfed that of his full-length books. George's publishing operation distributed pamphlets, some reportedly obtaining a circulation in the millions, at a price of $8.50 per stack of 5,000.[22] These were passed out by the faithful, such as one Chicago workingman who in the early days of the movement found he "could not make speeches, nor carry on a public debate, and he had little money to contribute." So, "week after week he stood behind his little stock of books, tracts, and pamphlets. . . . Years have passed, the man's hair has turned white, yet still he attends every meeting of the club, eager to supply the stranger with food for his soul."[23]

With a growing audience, George built a transnational movement with a series of international speaking tours through the United States, England, Scotland, Ireland, and Australia. He assembled a global network of supporters who advised him on local conditions and helped him adapt his message to his audience. His speeches were generally extemporaneous and emotive. Armed with only a handful of notes, he improvised on a general theme. The cadence of his speeches was slow, thoughtful, deliberate, and melodic. George suffered from stage fright and would appear nervous as his speeches began. Gradually, he would be carried away by the force of his argument, and his self-consciousness evaporated as he approached a rhetorical crescendo. Even his opponents conceded his eloquence. When George first spoke in Glasgow, 1,940 attendees signed up for the new Scottish Land Restoration League. George's rhetorical prowess was not the only reason he was so successful here; this was the country that a century earlier had given the world Thomas Spence's plan for communal land ownership.[24]

The early 1880s were a period of rapid growth and dynamism for George's nascent movement, though it was often still seen as a part of the larger drift toward socialism. One radical Portland, Oregon, paper called George's tax "communism in land," which, the author added, was "the most revolutionary change that can possibly be proposed."[25] After returning from his trip to Ireland, George published a series of articles that were collected and published in 1883 as *Social Problems*, an accessible book that considered how land value taxation related to other reforms, such as paper currency and government ownership of utilities. While not one of his most significant books, *Social Problems* would be the introductory text for perhaps George's most important supporter, Tom L. Johnson.

Johnson's conversion testified to George's remarkable ability to reach across the class divide into the citadel of capital. Johnson was a Cleveland businessman who had made a fortune in the streetcar business. One day a "train boy" tried to sell Johnson *Social Problems*. He refused it. The conductor chimed in and offered to pay for the book if Johnson did not enjoy it. Johnson took him up on the offer but was troubled by what he read. He subsequently purchased *Progress and Poverty*. Another reluctant convert, Johnson was initially upset by the way George had turned upside down the logic of liberalism. He employed his company's lawyers to find a hole in George's argument. They failed. Johnson could not deny that George's logic followed naturally from the liberal Lockean property theory that was gospel to businessmen like himself.

What struck Johnson was how George inverted the ethic of the business proprietor to show that monopoly rent was created by and owed to the community. Johnson realized his own "street railway fortune was due not so much to his enterprise as to the natural growth of the cities in which he operated. He didn't make the town; the town made him." Johnson experienced this revelation in 1883 and met George in 1885. In their first meeting, George suggested that Johnson might even be a candidate for elected office; Johnson brushed aside the idea because his pointed and direct mode of speech was ill-suited for long, effusive campaign orations.[26] Time would show that George had a better sense of Johnson's potential than he himself did.

George also attracted early conservationists. In October 1890, Daniel Beard, a leader in the scouting movement, sent George a copy of one of his books about the benefits of nature for children's development. Beard claimed that it showed "how a mind running on practical subjects was still unconsciously preparing itself to receive your grand ideas when you sent them to the world."[27] George wrote back expressing support for the positive "mental effects" of nature on youth, and the two subsequently became close friends.[28] Beard brought his ideas to fruition when he founded the Sons of Daniel Boone, which, after merging with other scouting organizations, became the Boy Scouts of America.

Beard exaggerated the extent to which his own ideas had anticipated George's, but they both felt that private property in land was undermining republican virtue. Beard explained: "The time will come when the exclusion of trespassers from all private lands will be so universal that unless there is some public place belonging to the people, there will be no playground for them but the public roads and the health and morals of our population absolutely depend upon their possessing the opportunity for outdoor recreation."[29] Beard believed a tax on speculative landholdings would open rural land for common use, allowing children to grow with nature. The western experience that many felt had been essential to American identity would thus be preserved. When Hamlin Garland first met Beard at a "Henry George meeting," they bonded over a "desire to perpetuate the traditions" of the western frontier.[30]

The most adamant challenge to George came from the academy. On March 7, 1884, toward the end of the second of his five tours of England, George spoke at Oxford University. George adjusted his message to his audience; he spent most of the lecture discussing the privilege that being a student at Oxford entailed. He encouraged his audience to use their advantages to uplift the less fortunate not through charity but through structural change. At the end of the lecture, he briefly sketched out his land tax. George was greeted by so many jeers and boos from the crowd of "unruly young aristocrats," as he called them, that he struggled to complete the speech.[31] The economist Alfred Marshall was the first to rise and speak, claiming that George misunderstood all the economists he criticized, but that this was to be expected since he did not have professional training. Marshall chided George for not discussing the importance of thrift in preventing poverty and offered statistics purporting to show that the conditions of the working class were improving. The aura of value-neutral science was broken shortly thereafter when a member of the crowd yelled that land nationalization was "scandalously immoral." George declared that this was the most disorderly meeting he had ever addressed and left the stage to chants of "land robbery." Students subsequently printed a satirical "Socialist Alphabet," with entrees such as "G is for George . . . / H is for the household word he became / O are the orphans and widows whose right / P Pounds one hundred will amply requite." Not long thereafter, Davitt was scheduled to speak on campus but was locked inside his hotel room by a group of angry students.[32]

A month later, one of Scotland's most powerful aristocrats, George Douglas Campbell, the duke of Argyll, published an attack on George. George had sent the duke a copy of *Progress and Poverty* out of appreciation for his work toward the abolition of slavery, but the peer would not tolerate attacks on his own wealth. In "The Prophet of San Francisco," published in *Nineteenth Century*, the duke mocked the pretensions of a frontier intellectual. Campbell compared George to a flat-earther because he rejected the science of economics, particularly the Malthusian doctrine that poverty was an inevitable result of agricultural scarcity.[33] The duke attacked George as "immoral" since he repudiated "public and private honor" in calling for property rights to be over-turned. In a probable reference to Spencer, Campbell concluded that George rejected the "scientific . . . laws which govern the social developments of our race."[34] The Scottish Land Restoration League counseled George that a successful response to the duke would earn him considerable fame.[35] In "The Reduction to Iniquity," George compared Campbell, who defended ancient land titles rooted in conquest as a question of honor, to those who, "declaring the slave trade piracy, still legalize the slavery of those already enslaved."[36]

The hauteur of these attacks, which paradoxically combined claims of scientific objectivity with an aristocratic moral code, only advanced George's cause. George's supporters appropriated the duke's term of derision and took to calling him the "Prophet of San Francisco." The dispute would also garner George a supporter of symbolic significance. William Lloyd Garrison II read the exchange with a disposition toward Campbell, whom he held in high regard because of his support for abolition. Like his famous father, the younger Garrison believed the free market was the moral alternative to the coercion of slavery. Thus, he dismissed George as a "professional labor reformer," part of a "fluent but work-shunning brotherhood." Once Garrison read the exchange, however, "the native dignity of the humble printer was in marked contrast to the scarcely veiled contempt of his Grace and the true nobleman stood revealed."[37]

Garrison's surname tied Georgism symbolically to the abolitionist tradition. Like Johnson, Garrison was a reluctant convert who would struggle for years with George's ideas before he was willing to accept them. Finally, he was publicly "baptized" in the cause and promoted it as the "New Abolition." Garrison dropped the "II" from his name in most of his writings, making him indistinguishable from his legendary father. "We do not deny that the law considers land property," he noted, "but thirty years ago it also recognized the ownership of human flesh."[38] Georgism, like abolitionism, sought to protect property rights while ensuring that ill-gotten wealth, acquired through expropriation rather than labor, was abolished.[39] Many sons and daughters of abolitionists, including Clarence Darrow, Brand Whitlock, and Elizabeth Magie, joined the movement believing it was the heir to abolitionism, sometimes with an assent from their forebears.[40]

Irish nationalists remained George's largest and most important constituency, but his liberal universalism left him skeptical of them. Patrick Ford and his *Irish World* kept the US wing of the movement aligned with him, but in Ireland the leadership of Charles Parnell had shifted the movement away from Davitt. George doubted that nationalism divorced from economic reform meant anything other than a superficial exchange of political elites: "The only class in my opinion worth considering in any country is the class which these proposed measures totally ignore—the laborers. Not that they are the only class worth thinking about, but until they are affected nothing general or paramount can be attained . . . and while I have sympathy with the Irish people . . . I cannot think that any mere political change could do anything to improve the condition of those classes of the Irish people who most desire our sympathy and most need our aid."[41] George had little faith in national identity as a force for change. The natural base for his movement was the transnational "producing" class.

George and the Producing Class

George turned to the politics of class. Between 1884 and 1886, he wrote *Protection of Free Trade* with the explicit purpose of winning wage earners over to free trade.[42] Although George often spoke of working men, his understanding of class was rooted in liberalism and producerism, not Marxism. "Producers" included industrial workers, white-collar professionals, small farmers, and small proprietors. On one hand were "aristocrats" who, like the barons, of old lived idly on rent. George tolerated strikes as an expedient for redistributing rents but expected divisions between capital and labor to disappear after land had been nationalized.[43] The purpose of organized labor was to unite voters around democratic reforms and mobilize producers against rent-seeking landlords and monopolists. These views reflected a bundle of typical beliefs about labor's role in a republic.

The largest labor organization of the 1880s was the Noble and Holy Order of the Knights of Labor, and it shared with George a remarkably similar set of beliefs. Founded in 1869 as a secret society, the Knights, as the honorifics in their title suggested, intended to elevate the status of the laborer. While politically diverse, they were inclined toward the brand of labor republicanism that sought to reverse the advance of wage labor. In one public statement the Knights of Labor (K. of L.) affirmed that its members believed, "as Thomas Jefferson did, that dependence, by its subservience and venality, suffocates the germ of virtue and prepares fit tools for the designing and ambitious; and, also, that corruption of morals in the mass of cultivators of the soil is a phenomenon of which no age or nation has ever furnished one example."[44] The Knights hoped to supplant wage labor with a "cooperative commonwealth" of voluntary, independent workers' cooperatives. Leadership disliked the strike as an instrument for change and saw class conflict as a type of factionalism anti-thetical to republican government. The Knights drew on the free soil tradition and called for "reserving of the public lands—the heritage of the people—for the actual settler; not another acre for railroads or speculators." The historian John L. Thomas described the K. of L. as "the institutional embodiment of George's economic views and faith in educational politics."[45]

In 1883 the grand master workman of the K. of L., Terence Powderly, issued a circular urging members to read *Progress and Poverty*.[46] That same year, while serving as mayor of Scranton, Pennsylvania, Powderly issued a public declaration against land speculation. He claimed that the current system thrust "all, or nearly all, the burdens of taxation upon the houses and improve-ments of the working men, the stores and dwellings of the businessmen and the shops and mills of the manufacturer." He proposed that the city establish a crude system of land value taxation. The measure made no progress in the city council, but Powderly pushed through more objective methods of assessment that increased property tax returns from approximately $9 million to nearly $12 million.[47]

Within a couple of weeks, George heard of Powderly's actions and wrote him, elated. He disclosed that he had joined the Knights recently and called it the "standard that [could] lead to victory." George was concerned, though, that its *Journal of United Labor* lacked "definite purpose, commensurate with the greatness of the organization. . . . Small measures may, as you say, be good enough in their way, but you cannot upon them build up a great organization or arouse that enthusiasm which will enable it to hold its membership and drive its power to a common end."[48] Piecemeal reform, George believed, was unable to unite a coalition. A big idea could foster unified action among di-verse interest groups.

In 1885, at the annual meeting of the Knights of Labor in Hamilton, Ontario, Powderly pushed the order's land plank closer toward Georgism and tied the land question directly to the goal of eliminating wage labor. Powderly de-claimed that because of land monopoly, "the man who goes to the West to-day and is willing to toil must toil for another, and the fruit of the soil which his labor produces must be given to the stranger."[49] He recommended the elimina-tion of alien landownership, confiscation of all land used for speculative pur-poses, and a cap of one hundred acres on land holdings. These proposals evoked the old free soil ideal. Powderly also proposed "boards of industry," staffed by workingmen to observe city councils and push for better taxation, particularly higher assessments on unused property.[50] Thus the Knights were transitioning, as George himself had, from the politics of free soil to the taxation of land. Free-born Lewis, a railroad clerk from Omaha, Nebraska, proposed that the Knights endorse exemptions on improvements of up to $1,000, pushing the burden of taxes onto land. Lewis's local later rebranded itself the "Henry George Assembly," a name it shared with a local of Black female cooks and domestic workers in New York City.[51]

The Knights' interest in land reform reached a crescendo in 1886. The organization was on the cusp of what would be known as the Great Upheaval. A strike wave in the preceding year had raised the organization's profile and sent the order's membership soaring to an all-time high of over 700,000. Members of the K. of L. ran for office across the country. Coping with this tremendous expansion, the organization held a special meeting. The Legislative Committee now recommended that large landholdings be taxed at full rental value.[52] J. P. McGaughey, secretary general of the Co-operative Board, argued that access to free land was essential to ending wage labor, because it would open land for agricultural cooperatives. He proclaimed: "Give us the land, and we will give you back the fruits of the land in the form of strong-limbed, strong-hearted, well-educated and honest workmen and women, independent citizens and intelligent voters."[53]

In New York, the strikes of the Great Upheaval impressed upon labor the need for political power and precipitated Henry George's electoral career. In 1885 the Central Labor Union (CLU) struck against the streetcar company. The city sent the police to work the streetcars and keep the lines running. This response made it evident that labor could be crushed by the state if its agents were hostile.[54] On September 23, a convention was held at Clarendon Hall of 175 labor organizations representing 60,000 workers. Frank Ferrell, a Black K. of L. leader, compared George to John Brown and promised that George would bring "industrial emancipation." Afterward, 360 out of 409 CLU delegates voted to nominate George for mayor of New York City under the banner of the new United Labor Party (ULP).[55]

George had, over several years, developed a close relationship with the CLU. He had spoken to the organization, which was closely tied to the Irish Land League, on several occasions. His lieutenant, Louis Post, served as the organization's legal counsel.[56] When the CLU organized the nation's first Labor Day parade in 1882, it invited George to speak. George, who was touring England at the time, declined, but William McCabe, a half-Irish, half-Maori agitator who was part of George's inner circle, took the leading role. Appointed the parade's grand marshal, McCabe arrived to find no crowd, with Labor Day apparently dead on arrival. Undeterred, McCabe marched through the city, haranguing workingmen into a parade that snowballed into an institution.[57] At subsequent parades, George was given a seat of honor for reviewing the procession.[58]

The Mayor of New York

George had little interest in being mayor. He believed that a poor showing, which had greeted New York's previous labor candidates, would hurt his reputation. He declined the nomination. When the CLU insisted, George relented and promised he would stand for election if 30,000 citizens signed a petition demanding it. To acquire the signatures, the CLU organized a massive volunteer campaign. This proved a brilliant strategy on George's part. If George was compelled to join the race, he would have momentum and a ready-made campaign machine. The CLU eagerly secured the necessary signatures; Henry George would be the United Labor Party's candidate for mayor of New York.

George was reticent to govern, but eager to campaign. Under the New York state constitution, George would not have the power to implement tax or utility reforms, and a victory would leave him an ineffectual figurehead, bound for failure. He believed the race, however, would "bring the land question into practical politics."[59] Agents of New York's Tammany Hall political machine offered George a seat in Congress if he dropped out of the race. He was told that he would lose, and the campaign would only cause trouble. George, elated, responded: "You have relieved me of an embarrassment. I do not want the responsibility and the work of the office of the Mayor of New York, but I do want to raise hell!"[60]

Throughout the campaign, George argued that land nationalization would directly benefit working-class New Yorkers. A confiscatory land tax promised something like a modern welfare state. If the city were its own landlord it could afford to build "public accommodations, playgrounds, schools, and facilities for education and recreation." Speaking at Cooper Union, a free institution of higher education, George said that the city should build "twenty such institutions as this." He proposed that streetcars be owned by the people and operated free of charge. If land values were captured, George promised, free public transit would pay for itself as it drove up the value of adjacent real estate.[61] After speculators sold off their excess land, everyone would be able to own "a house and home."[62] One satirical cartoon drawn by Joseph Keppler depicted George enticing a workingman with demands slipping out of his "horn of promises." These promises included "no taxes," "free land," "free lunch," "free cigars," "free rides," "free theater," "free boycotts," "no police," and "no boss."[63] Most broadly, George asked whether the city should belong to the people. At a meeting in Chickering Hall, George bemoaned the fact that "the land belongs in usufruct to the living, and yet Stuyvesant Square has to be closed at 6 P.M., because Peter Stuyvesant, who went to heaven many years ago, said so."[64] By investing most of its resources in Central Park, New York had prioritized lifting uptown real estate values over accessibility for working-class urbanites. George, in contrast, imagined a city that provided space to all its residents.[65]

As the campaign picked up steam, George's ideas permeated the city's intellectual life. George spoke seven times a day at open-air meetings outside factories, by train stops, and on street corners. The United Labor Party established a campaign paper, the *Leader*, with a circulation of 50,000. Tammany Hall nominated Abraham Hewitt, an iron manufacturer and former congressman not associated with the machine's corrupt regime, because it understood one of its own men was liable to lose to George. Hewitt himself had reached out to George when he first arrived in New York, expressed admiration for *Progress and Poverty*, and employed George to write a report on labor for his congressional office.[66] Hewitt refused to debate George in public, but he consented to a series of written exchanges. These letters were printed in the local newspapers so that, according to Samuel Gompers, they were "read and discussed in practically every home and public meeting in New York."[67] A charismatic political hopeful making his case to the people, as familiar as it is today, was remarkable during this period, when voters were about as likely to be drawn to the polls by beers from the local saloonkeeper as by the issues of a presidential race.[68]

The debates between Hewitt and George hinged on a labor party's implications for democracy. Hewitt called George a socialist and anarchist. He argued that "an attempt is being made to organize one class of our citizens against all other classes, and to place the Government of the city in the hands of men willing to represent the special interests of this class."[69] This was a damaging charge. Ever since James Madison had attacked partisanship in his *Federalist* essays, faction had been seen as deadly to a republic; even future labor leader Samuel Gompers paid special attention to refuting the charge, arguing in his speeches that the ULP represented "true republicanism and universal democracy."[70] George shared Hewitt's conception of republican politics but saw working-class politics through a different lens. He famously countered the argument that he was for workingmen by responding, "I am for men." This was not a repudiation of his class leadership; George proudly declared himself the "candidate of organized labor."[71] Instead, George denied that workers were a special interest, because the interests of the working people were the public interest: "The men who earn their bread by manual labor are," he claimed, "in this as in every community, the vast majority. Their interests must be the interests of the community at large." He would represent all producers: "editors, reporters, teachers, clergymen, artists, authors, physicians, store-keepers, merchants—in short, representatives of all classes of men who earn their living by exertion of hand or head." He refused only to represent "that class who live by appropriating the proceeds of the toil of others."[72]

George was initially ambivalent about becoming mayor, but as he observed the coalition assembling at his feet, he began to embrace the possibility.[73] The local Catholic Church hierarchy had begun to show signs of opposition, but Father McGlynn built a nascent Catholic social justice movement behind George. Patrick Ford rallied Irish nationalists. Many Germans and Jews sided with George out of sympathy for unions and socialism. On October 2, George received a second nomination from a group of middle-class supporters including the future leader of the Socialist Labor Party, Daniel De Leon.[74] He also won the support of future NAACP founder Charles Edward Russell; novelist William Dean Howells; Karl Marx's daughter, Eleanor; and famed religious skeptic Robert Ingersoll.[75] Several African American campaign clubs were formed to support George, and the leading Black journal in New York, the *Freeman*, declared that "colored men do not hesitate to say that Henry George's party is the party of the colored man."[76] George wrote for the *Freemen*, condemning the murder of Black labor organizers in South Carolina and declaring that "the land belongs to all the people . . . the black as well as the white."[77] The academy was less friendly. The president of Columbia University, F. A. P. Barnard, asked the trustees to dismiss De Leon from his lectureship after he spoke on behalf of George.[78]

There was enough continuity between Georgism and the earlier tradition of free land that many former National Reform Association members found themselves in Henry George's camp.[79] Some of the old guard claimed George had appropriated their ideas, but most had opposed land taxes because it would undermine individual ownership. W. F. Evans, the brother of George Henry Evans, understood George as representing the reform movement's natural evolution. In a personal letter, he encouraged George to "take hold of it as, 30 years ago we took hold of things. We got the freedom of the public lands—'voted ourselves a farm'—abolished imprisonment for debt; secured the rights of women to a good degree; . . . abolished chattel slavery." Now Evans encouraged George to push on and "abolish land monopoly and wages slavery." Despite a shared spirt, substantive differences between the two remained. George aspired to make the city fit for democracy, but Evans still hoped to resurrect the yeomanry, suggesting that George "pass a land limitation law" that would "double the freeholders in 10 years."[80]

George's campaign was a national event. It became the epicenter of the Great Upheaval's electoral front. In nearly two hundred municipalities the Knights of Labor ran candidates for office, often under the auspices of the United Labor Party, usually with real or symbolic relationships to the New York campaign. In Newark, a devoted follower, Hugh O. Pentecost, ran for mayor on the ULP ticket. In a symbolic ritual, George was nominated for mayor of New York in Newark's Labor Day parade. According to Louis Post, this strange procedure meant that "the proposed nomination lost all local significance in the national interest and sympathy it attracted."[81] George traveled to Kansas City the night of that city's elections to speak for the local labor candidates.[82] In Rutland, Vermont, ULP candidates secured most local offices, increased tax assessments, and established a special tax on unoccupied land. In Chicago, the ULP elected seven assemblymen and five judges and came only sixty-eight votes short of electing a congressman. As in New York, the platform called for public ownership of utilities and equitable taxation, including "taxation to the full limit of the law of unoccupied land."[83] Chicago's Democratic machine scrambled to incorporate the dissidents, thereby cementing an enduring electoral alliance with labor in the windy city.[84] Powderly, grand master workman of the Knights, shied away from George's campaign because of growing tensions with the Catholic Church, but when rumor spread that he opposed George, he traveled to New York and gave a rousing speech. He told the crowd: "Let it be known that there are things besides strikes . . . and that these other things are a proper regulation of the land system which will guarantee to every man that which is justly his, and no more."[85]

On Election Day, November 2, 1886, George traveled around New York in a carriage with Father McGlynn and Terence Powderly. At the end of the day, Hewitt won with 90,552 votes. George came in second with 68,110 votes. Theodore Roosevelt carried the standard of Lincoln to a third-place showing with 60,435 votes. George had transformed the independent labor ticket into the city's second party.

Some have claimed that George would have won the election without fraud, which was endemic to US elections at the time.[86] The ULP lacked Tammany Hall's party machinery, which, according to many accounts, was used to intimidate voters and stuff ballot boxes. George gave the accusations a subtle nod when he argued in his concession speech that the secret ballot was the key to future victory and suggested the results would have been different given "a fair vote."[87] Even on the other side of the Atlantic, Friedrich Engels understood the stories coming out of New York to mean that the election was won by "a colossal mass of fraud."[88]

George believed he had secured a victory. Michael Davitt wrote to congratulate him: "Some of your worst enemies out here hoped you would be [elected]. The votes polled for you demonstrate your influence with the Labor Party and you have gained a great victory without experiencing the terrible risk you would have to run in the hopeless task of clearing out the City Hall."[89] George had avoided the damage to his reputation of a flawed mayoralty while still, as he had hoped, raising hell. Evoking the specter of the George campaign, the governor of New York, David B. Hill, soon pushed through labor legislation. The state established regulations on child and female labor, abolished prison contract labor, passed the ten-hour day for workers, and banned so-called ironclad contracts, in which workers signed away their right to unionize. Labor Day became a state holiday.[90] Voter fraud worked to George's benefit, making his defeat purely "nominal."[91] In his concession speech on November 2, George proudly claimed, "I would rather have one such glorious defeat as this than ten thousand elections in the ordinary way."[92]

The magnitude of George's electoral returns attracted the attention of international commentators who saw in them a radical new horizon for American politics. While Friedrich Engels believed George and Powderly were theoretically antiquated, he found the ULP's rapid gains to be "absolutely unheard of." He warned that "if we in Europe do not hurry up the Americans will soon be ahead of us."[93] On the opposite end of the spectrum, London's *Saturday Review* contended that George's success presaged a frightening time when the "socialist vote" would "become as important a factor in American politics as the Irish vote." Concluding that Roosevelt's anemic performance was intentional, the author claimed the Republican Party had supported the "Socialist Candidate" to win over Irish voters.[94] This theory built on rumors circulating in the press, including *Puck*, that Roosevelt had been set up to lose. While no Republican candidate could have won in New York City, coming in "several lengths behind a tramp apostle of Labor from the boundless West" was an embarrassment that "ruined . . . his political chances."[95]

It is tempting to see George and Roosevelt as the "progressives" challenging the democratic machine, though the two could hardly have been less alike. In 1877 Roosevelt had helped organize a mass meeting at Steinway

Hall to establish limits on the right of non–property owners to vote on municipal affairs. Before the *Irish World* became the vehicle of George's rise to prominence, it was one of the leading voices in the fight to save the suffrage for its primarily working-class readership.[96] Ten years later, when Roosevelt and George were arrayed against each other, the scion of the state's Dutch aristocracy retained his antipathy toward popular politics. Excluded from the epistolary debate between Hewitt and George, Roosevelt published "Machine Politics in New York City" in the highbrow *Century Magazine*. In that article he explained that the city was ill-governed because the wealthy "neglect their political duties" and leave politics to the "densely ignorant," particularly "the laboring men, mostly of foreign birth or parentage."[97] Roosevelt lumped Tammany Hall together with labor politicians. Both were "demagogues . . . who promise if elected they will try to pass laws to better their condition; they are hardly prepared to understand or approve the American doctrine of government, which is that the state has no business . . . to better the condition of a man or set of men."[98] Later in his career, Roosevelt realized that he needed to appeal to workers' emotions, painting "circus posters" for his audiences. When Roosevelt reached out to workers, they often reached back at him, but what emerged from that dialogue was only a more benevolent crusade to impose his Knickerbocker moralism and nationalism. In 1908, he wrote the Georgist muckraker Lincoln Steffens: "Curious enough, events have forced me to make my chief fights in public life against privilege, but I know from actual experience . . . that what is needed is the fundamental fight for morality."[99]

The Collapse of Producerism

George's mayoral loss was less troubling than his nascent conflict with the Catholic Church. On November 17 and 18, Michael Corrigan, the archbishop of New York, warned against "certain unsound principles and theories which assail the rights of property."[100] Father McGlynn, already suspended by the Church for supporting George, was called to Rome on December 4. When McGlynn refused to go, the Church excommunicated him. McGlynn was indignant and continued evangelizing without his pulpit. As president of the Anti-Poverty Society, he preached the gospel of George infused with millennial religion. On January 20, 1889, Corrigan made attendance at McGlynn's meetings a reserved case, a sin that could not be absolved without a bishop.[101] The conflict between McGlynn and Corrigan was a microcosm of the struggle within American Catholicism between liberalism and conservatism. McGlynn, who encouraged his flock to attend public schools and embrace secular government, wanted Catholics to assimilate. Conversely, Corrigan still resented Italy for dethroning the Catholic Church after the country was unified into a secular, democratic nation. At a rally marking the twenty-fifth anniversary of the dissolution of the papal states, Corrigan demanded the restoration of the "Pope-King."[102] Broadly skeptical of the rising liberal philosophy that had deposed his Holy Father, Corrigan observed in one sermon that "providence has made this [equality] impossible. . . . Why then should we attempt to keep up the fiction that all men have equal rights?"[103] Corrigan used McGlynn's radicalism to frighten the American clergy into subordination to conservative Rome.[104]

Many of George's Irish supporters, including Patrick Ford, split with the movement as the Church classed it a heresy. The Catholic onslaught on George became a liability for Grand Master Workman Terence Powderly and his organization. Powderly, like many members of the order, was Catholic and had worked assiduously to protect the K. of L. against a Church hierarchy that distrusted it. The Church had officially condemned the Canadian branch of the K. of L. A meeting of archbishops in October 1886 failed to reach a consensus on whether to condemn the US branch. The question of the K. of L.'s status was referred to Rome even as the papacy considered McGlynn's case.

The Knights' relationship with George was a threat to its standing with the Catholic Church and working-class Irish Americans. Moreover, the 1886 bombing at a labor protest in Chicago's Haymarket Square in Chicago produced a backlash against radicalism that had the K. of L. retreating toward conservativism. At the 1887 convention, Powderly asked for a formal declaration that the order was opposed to anarchism. M. J. Butler, a ULP candidate in Chicago, rebutted accusations that he was an anarchist and turned the question around: "If anything could increase the respect and esteem I have always had for our General Master Workman, it is the stand he took in support of Henry George, in New York; yet permit me to state, that by doing so he left himself open to the charge of being an anarchist just as much as some of his less gifted brethren in Chicago did."[105] When an amendment for the taxation of land values was proposed in 1888, the organization deemed the question "inexpedient to legislate."[106]

The Catholic Church worked to rebuke the Knights of Labor, Henry George, and Father McGlynn in a way that would be nuanced enough not to incite backlash. In September 1888, Powderly was informed that the Church would tolerate the K. of L. if it revised its constitution. Many in the Church feared that direct criticism of George would only increase his exposure, much as the duke of Argyll's attack had. Therefore, the archbishop of Cincinnati recommended a statement that would condemn George implicitly without referencing him or his books directly.[107] On February 6, 1889, the Church condemned George's books *sub secreto*. Then, on May 15, 1891, it released *Rerum Novarum*, the definitive encyclical on Catholic social justice. *Rerum Novarum* condemned "new ideas" that denied property rights in land and capital. The initial draft of the encyclical had, in accordance with the traditional doctrines of Thomas Aquinas, declared landed property just but not sacrosanct. In general, the encyclical grew out of a long-smoldering desire on the part of social Catholics for a definitive statement on Church economic policy, but the decision to revise doctrine and declare land rights sacrosanct was likely intended as an attack on George specifically.[108] Rather than wealth redistribution, *Rerum Novarum* posited its own corporatist vision of social welfare. It acknowledged the inevitably of class differences and required the wealthy to care for the poor, following a tradition of paternalism and reciprocity rooted in the Church's feudal past. On December 23, 1892, Reverend McGlynn was permitted to return to the Church on the condition that he accept the new encyclical, which he did, though he continued to support land taxation, arguing that it did not violate *Rerum Novarum*.

Although the Catholic Church had rejected the confiscation of land, it had not explicitly repudiated George. George was unwilling to reframe his ideas as "merely a reform of taxation," but many of his supporters were, thereby "avoiding the objections" from their church that it violated a sacred right to property.[109] Powderly, now cleared by the Church, brought the K. of L. more firmly into the fold of Georgism than before. In a *Baltimore Sun* interview he recommended land taxation, provoking him and George to resume their correspondence.[110] At the annual meeting of the K. of L. in 1889, Powderly pushed for a plank endorsing land value taxation. The preamble to the organization's constitution was amended to represent an orthodox Georgist position: "The land, including all the natural resources of wealth, is the heritage of all the people, and should not be subject to speculative traffic. Occupancy and use should be the only title to the possession of land. The taxes upon land should be levied upon its full value for use, exclusive of improvements, and should be sufficient to take for the community all unearned increment."[111] The K. of L. had long been partners with George, evolving along parallel lines, but this change essentially made them disciples. George announced that it was the "most important event . . . the *Standard* has been able to record."[112] He quietly understood, however, that the organization was no longer what it had been and encouraged Powderly to work with the Farmers' Alliance. Thus began an effort to introduce a Georgist land plank in the platform of the new Farmers' Alliance political party, the Populist Party.[113]

The Knights were in decline. From 1886 to 1888 membership plummeted from 700,000 to 259,578. The K. of L. had encountered an array of difficulties. Failed strikes exposed weaknesses in its organization, employer organizations shut out unions, and many unskilled locals formed at the height of the Great Upheaval found that they did not have the funding to sustain a union over the long term. The collapse was most distinctly felt in the urban centers where Catholics predominated; in 1886 urban workers made up 44 percent of the K. of L., whereas by 1888 they composed only 31 percent.[114] Briefly, it appeared that rural Black workers in the South would constitute a new core of support for the Knights, but white supremacists violently put down their organizations.[115]

With the collapse of the K. of L., a new style of unionism emerged that was less amenable to George's philosophy and program. The American Federation of Labor (AFL) formed in 1886 under the guidance of Samuel Gompers. Gompers had opposed the formation of the ULP, though he rallied to the cause, managing the campaign's speakers bureau when it became clear labor was on George's side.[116] After the campaign, he attacked George's tax for promising neither "present reform, nor an ultimate solution."[117] Whereas George believed labor should be organized to amplify the workers' political power, Gompers argued that partisan politics divided and weakened labor. Instead, Gompers emphasized the use of strikes to increase wages for skilled white male workers. Georgists postulated that Gompers's rejection of electoral politics was in direct response to the 1886 ULP campaign, and some harangued the AFL as a special interest group.[118] Gompers and Georgists, though, were still sometimes aligned as democratically minded liberals. In a sense, Gompers was a more conventional liberal whose gripe was that government interfered with his workers' right of contract by barring them from bargaining collectively with their employers. Furthermore, Gompers, whose workers would soon be harassed by clipboard-carrying college graduates with dreams of scientifically managing their every move, was no more impressed by the rising cult of expertise than Georgists were.

Although the nascent split with labor cast a pall over the movement, George's political instincts were substantiated. Land nationalization fit naturally within the philosophy of the nation's largest labor union. It had drawn a diverse array of supporters. The 1880s justified George's claim that land nationalization could foster a coalition more powerful than a group of disconnected interest groups.[119] The decline of the Knights of Labor would be a major setback for George's movement, but support for land nationalization would persist in the American Federation of Labor, and even Gompers would find occasion to revise his opinion on land value taxation. While the late 1880s would be a dark time for the movement, land nationalization had brighter days ahead.

The Democracy of Henry George

Joining the Democratic Mainstream

> We both need and want the assistance of these people.
> John Altgeld to William Jennings Bryan, 1897

After 1886, George's movement changed drastically. As its working-class support dwindled, it was reinvented as the "single tax" movement, using anti-tax sentiment to appeal to the liberal middle class. It abandoned independent politics for the Democratic Party. Even land value taxation was thrust aside—temporarily—as supporters concluded that politics must be reconstructed before the nationalization of land could be established. George urged a reluctant movement into the mainstream of US politics and, in the end, sacrificed his life to incorporate his movement into the Democratic Party. From the outside, these changes looked like decline, as his cause ceased to resemble the sort of mass, working-class phenomenon evoked by the term "movement." But, as a middle-class movement, Georgism would be better positioned to insinuate itself into power.

Inching toward Incrementalism

In August 1887, Louis Post mounted a platform in Syracuse, New York, to deliver a speech supporting Henry George's candidacy for New York secretary of state. He issued a vigorous appeal for cross-party unity: "The aristocrats of the Democratic Party and the aristocrats of the Republican Party have got to come together," because "when we get both of their heads on one pair of shoulders it will only take one blow to cut off two heads." Continuing his harangue, Post added, "We will make one of these old parties feel it—one of them, I say; I don't know which one. (a voice 'Tammany Hall!') I don't know which one, and, between you and me, I don't care which one."[1] No one in the crowd that day could have imagined that two decades later the speaker would serve in the administration of a Democratic president. But the movement's integration into the Democratic Party—or "the Democracy," as the parlance of the day dictated—was already beginning.

George took the first step toward mainstream politics immediately following his defeat in the 1886 New York mayoral election. He had first proposed the secret ballot in the 1870s but reemphasized it on November 6, when he conceded the election at Cooper Union. He promised that allowing citizens to vote privately would prevent the type of voter intimidation used to steal the election.[2] At this final meeting of the campaign, the attendees established a group to promote ballot reform.[3]

Two years later, in 1888, Louisville, Kentucky, became the first city to enact the secret ballot. Arthur Wallace, who had proposed the ordinance, said he discovered the idea in one of George's articles.[4] The experiment spread rapidly; five states enacted the secret ballot the following year. The reform garnered support from across the political spectrum, but Georgists formed the vanguard. The *New York Times* reported that in Brooklyn the cause was "started by Georgeites, nourished by prohibitionists, aided by Democrats, and abetted by Republicans."[5] Similarly, the bill that established the secret ballot in Missouri had been drafted by that state's Single Tax League before being introduced by future Speaker of the US House of Representatives Champ Clark.[6] Thus, in their 1886 defeat, Georgists learned that land nationalization might be out of reach but that, by working within mainstream parties, they could win reforms that would democratize the nation and undermine the corrupt machines that stood in their way.[7]

The success of the secret ballot was in stark contrast to George's dismal ventures in independent politics. His 1887 campaign to be New York's secretary of state on the ULP ticket had ended in a stunning defeat. He garnered 72,281 votes across the state—barely more than what he had polled just in New York City the previous year. Within the city, his vote had been cut nearly in half.[8] The ULP had undergone a schism. Members of the Socialist Labor Party (SLP) used parliamentary tricks to capture the party publication, *The Leader*, and seemed intent on seizing the party.[9] The party consequently expelled members of the SLP, a contentious decision that prompted some activists to leave the ULP and form the splinter Progressive Labor Party. While sympathetic to the socialists, the Progressive Labor Party comprised a diverse assembly of statist radicals; the party's nominee for state attorney general, T. B. Wakeman, was a positivist who demanded "the substitution of bureaucratic administration for politics," eliminating all civil organizations until a government dominated by scientific experts prevailed as "the true church."[10] Given that this fringe party secured fewer than 6,000 votes across the state, however, its departure from the ULP hardly accounts for the 31,000 votes George lost in the city.[11] Most likely, it was the Catholic Church's attacks on the movement that caused George's mass support to crater. Patrick Ford, whose *Irish World* had been instrumental in his rise, now attacked George as anti-Catholic, undermining his support among Irish nationalists.[12]

Father Edward McGlynn struggled to keep the United Labor Party alive, but George wanted nothing to do with third-party politics. Aside from his embarrassing defeat, George feared his relationship with the ULP could expose him to charges of impropriety. The Republican senator Thomas C. Platt had reportedly given money to the manager of the ULP, Gaybert Barnes, to bankroll a George presidential campaign that would split the Democratic vote in key swing states, such as New York. George rejected the scheme and ended his association with the party, though some of his supporters, including McGlynn, bitterly resented his departure.[13]

The evaporation of Irish support meant that the movement needed to rebrand and attract new constituencies. George found a more influential base of support in the native-born, urban middle class. Post framed this moment as a transition from the "Labor phase" to the "Singletax phase," in which "class contests and class interests" were shuffled aside.[14] Thomas Shearman, a lawyer renowned for his defense of Henry Ward Beecher, had coined the phrase "single tax" in 1887. George used the phrase once in *Progress and Poverty* but disliked it as a slogan because "it only suggests the fiscal side of our aims." However, with this anti-tax bent, the movement attracted more middle-class and even upper-class constituents. In principle, George was troubled by Shearman's approach, but he concluded that "the very fact that he approaches the matter in another way enables him to reach a class of people whom men like myself could not affect."[15] Supporters of the reconstituted "single tax" movement tended to be more like George in their socioeconomic background. Its leaders were generally urban, self-made businessmen who prioritized economic mobility. They fought to protect the fruits of their labor from both rent and taxation.[16] While a handful of very wealthy men like George Foster Peabody and Tom Johnson made their way into the movement, they came from modest backgrounds and resented the way wealth inequality in the new urban economy had obstructed their success.

George's fear that Shearman's approach overemphasized the "fiscal" side of his argument was well founded. Some businessmen joined the movement in the hope of cutting their taxes and had little interest in causes like public ownership of railways and telegraphs. Shearman provoked division in the ranks when he argued that his single tax should tax land only enough to fund a limited state. The idea struck at the heart of George's vision of a welfare state that would expand constantly with the ever-growing value of land. George called Shearman's plan the "single tax limited" and contrasted it with his own plan for a "single tax unlimited." Debates over the "single tax limited" faded after the 1880s, but a persistent, often uneasy divide lingered. Thirty years later, Clarence Darrow still observed: "There are two kinds of Single Taxers . . . one class who believes that all taxation should be placed upon land values because it is the simplest and easiest and the fairest way to collect taxes" and the other, "who really believe[s] in the common ownership of the land" and thinks "it should be a part of the public wealth, should be used for public improvements, for pensions, and belong to the people who create the wealth."[17]

In 1887 President Grover Cleveland proposed tariff reductions in his message to Congress.[18] In the wake of the ULP's collapse, this move posed an enticing opportunity for the movement to establish an alliance with the Democratic Party. George believed tariffs fostered monopoly. But he also saw free trade as a practical way to raise the question of the single tax. Cutting the tariff would reduce government revenues, necessitating new sources of funds and creating an opportunity to push for the single tax.[19] In *Protection and Free Trade*, George explained: "The political art, like the military art, consists in massing the greatest force against the point of least resistance; and to bring a principle most quickly and effectively into practical politics, the measure which presents it should be so moderate as (while involving the principle) to secure the largest support and excite the least resistance." George concluded, "We have, ready to our hand, in the tariff question, a means of bringing the whole subject of taxation and, through it, the whole social question into the fullest discussion."[20] Post wrote that at first the single tax "seemed easy to popularize and therefore the obvious first step. Since then, however, experience has demonstrated the necessity for making the first step a shorter stride."[21] Thus, single taxers rallied to tariff reform as a step toward land nationalization.

During the tariff debates of the Cleveland years, George argued for incremental changes in public revenue designed to bring the United States closer to the single tax. While he suggested that a land value tax could be effected at the time, he also offered a variety of alternatives to regressive tariffs on consumer goods. In *Protection and Free Trade*, he proposed printing paper money to fund the government. He discussed income and inheritance taxes. Believing that the public and private sectors should never intersect, he argued that if liquor were to be a controlled source of public revenue, it should be with the establishment of a public monopoly of its sale, rather than through regulation and taxation.[22]

When Cleveland lost his reelection campaign in 1888, George chose to remain with the Democratic Party and fight to keep the tariff issue alive. As Georgists won congressional elections, a "coterie of Single Taxers," including Tom Johnson and the populist Jerry Simpson, coalesced in Washington, DC. According to Simpson's biographer, this group met regularly and "joked, philosophized, and planned together."[23] The leader of this group was Johnson, whom George sensed had a "destiny."[24] The two were close and, after bicycles were introduced into the urban ecosystem, enjoyed going on rides together. As George watched Johnson's rise, he became content "that my best usefulness is outside of politics" because Johnson carried his mantle.[25] Aside from this tight-knit group, there was perhaps a wider circle of sympathetic representatives in the Fiftieth Congress. According to Johnson, there were approximately twenty representatives who thought the single-tax argument "unanswerable" but were reluctant to publicly associate with it.[26]

In the months before Cleveland's 1892 presidential campaign, Johnson conceived of a dramatic way to ensure that free trade dominated the election. After consulting with George, Johnson convinced five other congressmen to read George's *Protection or Free Trade* into the *Congressional Record*. As part of the *Congressional Record*, representatives could use their franking privilege to mail the book to their constituents free of charge. Thus, 1,024,000 copies of the book were distributed via frank in the months before the election.[27] The *New York Times* expressed "emphatic disapproval and disgust" at this enormous abuse of the franking privilege.[28]

The stunt succeeded in seizing the nation's attention during the campaign season. According to the *Chicago Tribune*, single taxers made *Protection or Free Trade* the "principal [document] of the campaign."[29] Because Democrats refused to disavow Johnson's antics, Republican congressman Bowers claimed that it was "essentially the Democratic platform as adopted by this house." Hence, "the Democratic Doctrine," he claimed, was "opposed to private property in land." Future president William McKinley claimed the plan signaled that Democrats had "given up their old theories of taxation and are ready to accept the land-tax scheme of Henry George."[30] George privately took more pleasure in the public's association of the Democratic Party with his ideas than in the wide distribution of his book.[31]

With a national profile, Johnson redoubled his efforts to make free trade the primary issue of the 1892 election. At the Democratic National Convention, Johnson convinced Lawrence T. Neal of the Resolution Committee to add to the agenda a resolution calling not just for tariff reductions but also for unfettered free trade. Johnson canvassed the convention for support and was one of three individuals to speak on its behalf. Despite apparently tepid support, the resolution passed 564 to 324.[32] Rumor had it that the plank was a test vote for Cleveland's opponents and had little to do with the proposal's merits.[33] However, the distribution of a million copies of *Protection or Free Trade* doubtless gave Johnson clout at the convention among congressmen who were bombarded by constituent requests for the book. Cleveland was so concerned about the plank that, after the convention, he invited George, Johnson, and Post to his home to discuss it. While the plank was only symbolic, Johnson used it as a weapon to batter Democrats with the charge of being unfaithful to their pledges when they opposed tariff cuts in the ensuing revenue debates.[34]

The election of 1892 was a major victory for Henry George. Cleveland won the presidency on a platform George had helped design, and a host of single-tax congressmen were swept in with the Democratic landslide. Tariff revision, as George predicted, precipitated conversations about new sources of revenue. In the debates over the Wilson-Gorman tariff bill, five representatives voted for a federal land value tax. Georgists fueled calls for progressive taxation. Tom Johnson proposed an income tax amendment drafted by Thomas Shearman. Shearman's analysis of the maldistribution of wealth was cited constantly in the floor debates over the income tax, though ultimately Congress approved a different income tax bill, one that, unlike Johnson's, taxed individuals as well as corporations. Georgists had played a prominent role in the debates that established the first, short-lived, peacetime income tax in the United States.[35] Henry George was even spotted observing the debate from the gallery, and several congressmen reportedly left the floor to introduce themselves.

Johnson emerged as a major political force, and behind him stood George. A successful congressional career suggested to George that "politically, Johnson is steadily coming to the front. He has now got out over three million of the January speeches, and scattered as they are, all over the United States they are having a *very* great effect. I think his position as a '96 possibility is becoming more and more clear."[36] For Georgists to have distributed more than three million copies of Johnson's speeches in the 1890s suggests that their propaganda operations dwarfed those of even major parties, which, when they formed professional publicity bureaus a decade later, were still distributing candidate's speeches in the hundreds of thousands.[37] George's suspicion that Johnson might be a Democratic presidential candidate was echoed by such major papers as the *Chicago Tribune*.[38] Aside from his role in the tariff debate, Johnson had presented a bill for interconvertible bonds that earned the acclaim of the midwestern press by promising to spur inflation and relieve indebted farmers.[39] Behind the scenes, George had actually drafted the bill. Johnson later called George his "private tutor" because of their close collaboration during his congressional career.[40]

With his focus on mainstream politics, George eschewed attempts to form utopian communities. The nation's long history of failed communal experiments suggested that these communities would discredit his cause. Nevertheless, several communities were formed, and some have thrived to the present day. Fairhope, Alabama, founded in 1894, and Arden, Delaware, founded in 1900, survive as private corporations that own the land and charge rent to fund public projects and cover the personal taxes of their members. They inspired famous visitors like Upton Sinclair (a longtime resident of Arden), Sherwood Anderson, Elizabeth Mead, Wharton Escherick, Clarence Darrow, and John Dewey.[41] Harold Ickes visited Fairhope and served on the advisory council to the local Organic School; fellow New Dealer Arthur Morgan enrolled his son at the school.[42] When, in 1911, a hostile neighbor alerted authorities that Ardenites were playing baseball and tennis on the Sabbath, the eminent intellectuals Scott Nearing and Upton Sinclair were among those the police apprehended.[43] The roll of notable visitors tended toward the artistic, reflecting the bohemian orientation of these communities. This was particularly the case for Arden, with its cottage-style architecture and open spaces inspired by William Morris's Arts and Crafts movement and Ebenezer Howard's greenbelt communities.[44]

At the Single Tax Conference of 1893, single taxers who resented the movement's drift toward broader reformism won a Pyrrhic victory. George had written into the charter of the Single Tax League a provision in favor of public ownership of natural monopiles, including telegraphs, railroads, and gas utilities. A majority at this conference, swayed by what George characterized as "a strong tendency to anarchism," voted to strike this clause, thereby prioritizing tax cuts. "There was pathos," observed Post, "in the picture as I saw [George] marching demurely up the aisle at the tail-end of the minority procession of the negative voters."[45]

The somber drama of George's alienation from his own movement reinforced his bias against organization, solidifying its individualistic structure. According to Post, George "was never sympathetic with attempts at permanent organization. He believed that such organizations had a tendency to prejudice the public mind."[46] In *Social Problems*, George had espoused the theory that ideology, not organization, should structure collective action: "Social reform is not to be secured . . . by the formation of parties. . . . Until there be correct thought, there cannot be right action; and where there is correct thought, right action *will* follow."[47] This sentiment against organization hardened after the single tax conference. The following year, when the movement was struggling over whether to endorse the Populist Party, George argued against collective action because "organization had always, so far as the single tax was concerned, been a failure." Instead, he recommended that Georgists "work . . . as individuals." This absence of organization would define the movement.[48]

During the 1890s the utopianism of land nationalization also took a back seat to property tax reform. At the Union Square office of *The Standard* in 1888, George met with Thomas Shearman, William T. Crosdale, and William McCabe. Shearman proposed a group that would organize business support for local option in taxation. In 1901 twenty-five out of thirty-three state constitutions had uniformity clauses that required all types of property to be taxed at the same rate.[49] Permitting municipalities to determine their own rates of taxation might liberate businessmen from the cumbersome personal property tax while facilitating local experiments with land value taxation. Shearman's plan to lobby for local option was initially dismissed. Choosing instead to focus on direct agitation for land value taxation, George's followers soon gathered 115,502 signatures for a land value tax petition presented to Congress in 1892. But even the faithful believed that this effort was nothing but an "opportunity . . . for finding our friends and bringing them together."[50]

The importance of home rule was proved in 1892 when Jackson Ralston led a fight to successfully institute land value taxation in Hyattsville, Maryland. The Maryland Court of Appeals revoked the tax, declaring it a violation of the state uniformity clause.[51] The Hyattsville case proved that state constitutions needed to be revised to allow land value taxation. Shearman's home rule idea then coalesced with the formation of the New York Tax Reform Association, which proved so successful at attracting businessmen that the single tax element was eventually muscled out of the organization.[52] However, through the first few years of the twentieth century, it made considerable progress under the leadership of the single taxer Lawson Purdy, who parlayed his work into a decade-long assignment as New York City's tax assessor.

The last independent single tax party contrasted sharply with the budding progress of incremental tax reform. In 1896, single taxers from across the country flocked to Delaware to campaign for the short-lived Single Tax Party. Activists hoped to have more impact by concentrating resources on a small state. Canvassers went door to door, speakers from around the nation traveled to the state, and a local campaign publication, *Justice,* was formed to promote the party. However, a discouragingly small 3 percent of the electorate voted for the Single Tax Party. Even George paid little attention to the race, instead traveling across the country to report on William Jennings Bryan's presidential campaign.

A Nation Afire

As the single tax transitioned into the mainstream of American political life, it found itself in competition with an array of new doctrines struggling to reconstruct an economy that failed to deliver on its promise of independence. It is tempting to lump together the forces of change and reaction, but, in fact, relations between these groups were complex, shifting, and provisional. Single taxers were better able to make common cause with both the laissez-faire of Grover Cleveland and the socialism of Eugene V. Debs than the nascent discourse of academic Progressivism.

A new faith in government regulation would find its first great prophet in the scion of one the most established and conservative families in the nation. Fairly or not, Presidents John Adams and John Quincy Adams have been seen as the great antagonists to democracy in the American tradition, and when Charles Francis Adams was born in 1835, he was destined to a spot at Harvard University and a seat among the Boston Brahmins. However, he found that these plums no longer mattered in a world that had come to worship the new god of scientific progress. His brother, Henry, recorded in his autobiography that they "had discovered the worthlessness of a so-called education" and "so-called connections," and that now "Boston meant business. The Bostonians were building railways. Adams would have like to help in building railways, but had no education."[53] In 1869 Charles struck back with "A Chapter in Erie," published in the *North America Review.* Documenting the history of corruption within the Erie Railroad, Charles attacked the new elite of railway monopolists, epitomized by Cornelius Vanderbilt, as "shrewd, unscrupulous, and very illiterate."[54]

Adams's charges of corruption in the Erie Railroad began to shift influence back to a class of men more like himself and, more particularly, himself. Later that year, he led the effort to form the Massachusetts Board of Railroad Commissioners, the nation's first state railroad regulatory commission. Adams embraced Auguste Comte's positivist conviction that society would inevitably evolve toward centralization and that educated elites needed to manage it. He was content, in theory, with a single corporation owning all the railways in the nation, noting that "everything now tends to consolidation, and consolidation in the hands of able men portends as assured a success as does the massing of troops under brilliant generals in war."[55] It was imperative only that companies be subjected to the supervision of regulatory commissions that guaranteed leadership by the right type of people.[56]

Adams eventually endorsed the single tax on the narrow grounds that it would promote honest tax assessment, though the movement did little to advertise its connection to him. When he died in 1915, the leading single tax publication printed an obituary that praised him for his work on behalf of tariff reduction and proportional representation—eliding his historic work for railway regulation—but ultimately concluded that he could not be "classed altogether as a radical." For Georgists, proponents of expert management who believed in the single tax were still, somehow, something less than real single taxers.[57]

Divisions between single taxers and proponents of regulation were driven by fundamental differences in how they understood monopoly. The economist Henry Carter Adams, in "Relation of the State to Industrial Action" (1887), asserted that some businesses were "natural monopolies" because they accrued increasing returns as they grew in scale.[58] Monopolies were a result of efficiencies from economies of scale; hence, monopoly was a function of size. In contrast, single taxers followed Mill's definition of monopoly as any market where scarcity allowed the seller to set prices out of proportion to the labor expended in production of the good. These monopolies could be, and often were, small—land was the quintessential monopoly because it was finite and each plot was unique. Using this definition, all businesses were monopolistic to the degree that they relied on tariffs, patents, and, most especially, highly sought-after parcels of land. Monopoly power, in this model, was most common in resource extraction and in transportation, which required rights-of-way predicated on extensive and unique networks of contiguous land. While Adams implied that monopolies were part of a natural process of modernization that the state could supervise but not halt, single taxers believed monopoly represented the theft of common property. Once land was socialized, most concentrations of private power would dissipate, and those that survived would do so justly because they reflected healthy and efficient markets.[59]

Conflict between George and Progressive professionals was also driven by debates about the role of expertise in democracy. In 1890 the American Association of Social Sciences invited George to a debate over the single tax. The assault on George was led by E. R. A. Seligman, a professor in the economics department at Columbia University and scion of a wealthy banking family. Seligman was not wholly opposed to land value taxation, but he was fiercely opposed to George personally.[60] It was anathema to him that someone without the credentials of a professional economist should have so much sway over the public's economic views: "In biology, in astronomy, in metaphysics, we bow down before the specialist; but every man whose knowledge of economics or of the science of finance is derived from the daily papers, or one or two books with lopsided ideas, thinks he is a full-fledged scientist."[61] Economics, Seligman believed, should be left to the economists.

George answered that economics should, in fact, be uniquely accessible to nonprofessionals. He alleged that the stakes involved in economics made it subject to bias; "professors of political economy" either "belong to" or "are influenced by" the class that profits from monopoly. George added that economics was too important to democratic government for it to remain beyond the reach of the average voter:

> There is a reason why the great majority of us must, in such matters as astronomy or chemistry, accept what the professors of such sciences tell us. We cannot study such sciences: we have neither the leisure, the knowledge, nor the opportunities. But, if we cannot study political economy,—the science whose phenomena lie about us in our daily lives, and enter into our most important relations, and whose laws lie at the bottom of questions we are called on to settle with our votes,—then democratic republican government is doomed to failure; and the quicker we surrender ourselves to the government of the rich and the learned, the better.[62]

George did not reject scientific expertise but argued that intelligence mattered little in a republic if it was not passed down to the average citizen. In his final book, *The Science of Political Economy* (1898), he alleged that the German-trained historicists had replaced universalism of classical economics with a "lack of definiteness and want of consistency" intended to obfuscate rather than inform.[63] Their efforts to professionalize economics, George believed, was a direct reaction to the fact that the most widely read economist of the age was himself, a man whose "alma mater was the forecastle and the printing-office."[64]

During the debates over the Wilson-Gorman tariff bill and the income tax, Seligman led efforts to form a new school of taxation, rooted in the concept of ability to pay. He resented the role that single taxers played in the debates over the bill, going so far as to challenge Shearman's frequently cited statistics on the maldistribution of wealth, though they were substantiated by a federal statistician.[65] Seligman's ability-to-pay concept in taxation was ostensibly progressive in that it required those with higher incomes to pay more; however, it also shifted the focus away from wealth. Advocates of ability to pay argued that wealth taxes were disruptive because one might own wealth and receive little income, so wealth taxes would force one to sell off assets. This was exactly what single taxers aspired to, since they supported wealth distribution to level the playing field.

Ability-to-pay economists often embraced a corporatist vision in which employers owed the workers comfort in return for obedience. Progressive economists studied under German academics such as Karl Knies and Otto Gierke who used the biblical metaphor of the church as the body of Christ to contend that corporations were rooted in a medieval ideal of individuals merging into a single body. This mystical corporate ideal dictated the supremacy of the community over the individual, but did so in hierarchical terms; the working class would be protected as society's hands but would also be subordinate to its head.[66] Hence, while the economist Richard Ely supported organized labor's right to contest its earnings, he rejected labor's demands for workplace autonomy, because "certain functions must be trusted almost wholly to the executive head."[67] He glowingly profiled the "enlightened absolutism" of the company town of Pelzer, South Carolina, noting that "paternalism" thrived in the South because "at the top" there were "gifted, well-disposed, kindly natures, accustomed to the exercise of authority," whereas "at the bottom" there were "amiable, tractable classes of men and women."[68] Ely extended this paternalistic ideal to the public sphere, praising Prussia's three-class franchise, which gave more representatives to the wealthy, because "not every citizen is qualified to perform all the public functions."[69] For Ely, the single tax dream of equal opportunity was a nightmare that jeopardized the efficiency of large accumulations of wealth under expert management. High taxes that forced farmers to sell off their land would put wealth in the hands of people less adept at cultivating it and would jeopardize the fortunes that bolstered charity. Land was "the basis on which . . . existing foundations and institutions for the relief of suffering and social betterment" rested, and therefore the abolition of landed property would have "an unfortunate influence upon all endowments."[70] The economist John Bates Clark framed this exchange of comfort for obedience in a more liberal way by arguing that mass consumption promised new vistas of freedom and democratic participation, but this was itself a way to reconceptualize democracy as consumerism instead of popular control of politics.[71]

Georgists had more amicable relations with American farmers, though their interests were misaligned. At its founding, the Knights of Labor had attempted to shape the direction of the emerging Populist Party, and the party's "Omaha Platform" borrowed liberally from the results of the St. Louis Industrial Conference, conducted in collaboration with the K. of L. Hamlin Garland and Jerry Simpson had "conspired" at the conference to introduce a Georgist land plank, but farmers were predictably not keen on taxing land. The single tax plank in the preamble of the Knights of Labor Platform, however, was incorporated into the Omaha Platform, albeit in a less precise form. Removing taxation from the plank left a vague but powerful statement in favor of communal rights to land: "The land, including all the natural resources of wealth, is the heritage of all people, and should not be monopolized for speculative purposes."[72]

The People's Party posed a serious dilemma for George because, while the two shared a common spirt, his experience had soured him on third-party politics. George's *Standard* encouraged its readers to avoid the new party, declaring that "the advantage to the single tax movement of prodding the Democratic Party on in the way . . . it has been going . . . is too obvious for discussion."[73] Nevertheless, the *Standard* celebrated when the Populist William Peffer was elected to the US Senate, because "a Kansas Legislature has risen superior to corruption."[74] Despite their differences, single taxers had sympathy for a party that represented the common people.

Single taxers, however, rejected the anti-monopoly legislation passed in reaction to agrarian protest. Congress established the Interstate Commerce Commission in 1887 and empowered it to regulate railways. In 1890 Congress passed the Sherman Anti-Trust Act, which authorized the federal government to prevent every combination in "restraint of trade." Single taxers disliked both because trust-busting was a dangerous extension of federal power and "if the government undertakes to manage railroads while they remain private property . . . it will find itself in a corrupt partnership with the worst elements of railway monopoly."[75] To the credit of single taxers, neither law was used effectively to control concentrated wealth for at least a decade, and the Sherman Anti-Trust Act was quickly mangled by the courts, which reinterpreted it to attack labor unions as conspiracies in restraint of trade.[76] Courts even cited the Sherman Anti-Trust Act in issuing injunctions mandating jail time for those who provided food to striking workers. While single taxers had seen their ties with labor weakened by the rise of the AFL, they still maintained strong support among workers in company towns, extractive industries, and high-rent metropolises. The one time when Gompers lost the presidency of the American Federation of Labor was to the former Knight of Labor John McBride of the United Mine Workers, who unseated Gompers in a campaign that demanded that the union fight for government ownership of utilities and the single tax.[77]

These new anti-union powers accidently created by anti-trust law would be tested in Pullman, Illinois, a model company town that had been constructed by George Pullman to house workers building his luxury Pullman Sleeping Cars. When the Panic of 1893 sent business activity into a spiral, Pullman cut wages by 28 percent while holding rents steady, so that in many instances workers' earnings hardly covered rent. Workers called a strike led by Eugene V. Debs, and railway workers across the nation refused to handle trains carrying Pullman cars, impeding rail traffic. Two federal circuit court judges, citing the Sherman Anti-Trust Act and the Interstate Commerce Act, issued injunctions that barred Debs from encouraging workers to strike or even communicating with other union officials. President Grover Cleveland sent troops to put down the strike in Chicago, provoking a bloody riot. Debs was arrested for ignoring the court injunction and became the first labor leader tried for violating the Sherman Anti-Trust Act. The single tax lawyer Clarence Darrow defended Debs in court and, though Darrow lost the case, he and other Georgist labor lawyers, including Samuel Seabury, would wage a long war against these new abuses of "judge-made law."[78]

The Pullman strike would be socialism's coming-of-age party in the United States, though that result was hardly a forgone conclusion. Debs emerged from prison both a newly minted convert to the doctrines of Karl Marx and a populist leader with broad appeal among common people. Debs interpreted the industrial warfare he had been party to as a natural result of the struggle between labor and capital. However, other observers, such as Jane Addams, believed the peculiar thing about Pullman was that it was a company town in which the Pullman corporation owned and leased all the land, threatening anyone who challenged its authority with eviction.[79] Debs, perhaps recognizing the important role that land played in this dynamic, would flirt with the single tax but ultimately rejected it, arguing that it would "make competition infinitely sharper than it is today."[80] The workers Debs organized felt differently; according to press reports, five hundred unemployed Pullman workers made plans to move to Blakely, Alabama, and form a single tax colony.[81]

A New Democracy

The Pullman strike shattered the comity that existed between George and President Cleveland. George had already soured on Cleveland when he stalled on tariff reform to push the gold standard. Then, the Wilson-Gorman Tariff Act of 1894 failed to reduce tariffs as much as anyone, including Cleveland, had hoped. But the president's decision to send federal troops to crush workers' protests rankled both George's libertarian instincts and his sympathy for the masses. George declared he "would rather see every locomotive in this land ditched, every car and every depot burned and every rail torn up, than to have them preserved by means of a Federal standing army. . . . That is the order in keeping of which every democratic republic before ours has fallen. I love the American Republic better than I love such order."[82] Nevertheless, Louis Post would eventually relish Cleveland's betrayal because "a logical result . . . was William J. Bryan's nomination by the Democratic Party on the free silver platform of 1896."[83]

William Jennings Bryan, who secured the presidential nomination of both the Democrats and the Populists, was ideally suited to reconcile the movement's lingering ambivalence about mainstream parties. George attended the Democratic National Convention in 1896, reporting for William Randolph Hearst's *New York Journal*. He wrote presciently that the Democratic Party that "emerge(d) from the Chicago convention is not the old Democracy."[84] George supported Bryan, though he cared little for Bryan's pet issue, silver currency, preferring instead government-issued paper money. Opposite Bryan was William McKinley, whose support for high tariffs, the gold standard, and eventually imperialism embodied a Republican faith in government support for the nation's industrializing core. Theodore Roosevelt groused that Bryan represented those who "pray for anarchy," and, like the Paris Commune, his insurrection needed to be suppressed "by taking ten or a dozen of their leaders and shooting them dead."[85]

Not all single taxers were ready to rally around a candidate whose platform shared so little in common with their own. George wrote a series of nationally syndicated articles reporting on the depth of Bryan's support among working people. He fell short, however, of explicitly endorsing Bryan. In October a group led by Thomas Shearman issued a public declaration, reprinted by the *New York Times*, condemning George's effort to attach their movement to Bryan.[86]

The day before the election, George returned fire against "those friends of mine, the few single taxers who, deluded, as I think, by the confusion, propose to separate from the majority." To them he wrote: "The banks are not really concerned about the legitimate business under any currency. They are struggling for the power of profiting by the issuance of paper money, a function properly and constitutionally belonging to the nation. . . . They are concerned about their power of running the Government and making and administering laws." In many ways, George's statement was bolder than a direct answer to the silver issue. He claimed the producers and "the forces of aristocratic and special privilege" were locked in battle over control of democratic government. "All great struggles of history have begun on subsidiary issues," claimed George. The single tax would stand not alone but as part of a larger battle against "privilege."[87] His argument that a broad battle against elites would culminate in the single tax pushed the movement into a coalition with variegated currents of dissent, even where they had little direct bearing on the land issue. According to Henry George Jr., "Tom L. Johnson, Louis F. Post, and a great majority of the single taxers" followed into Bryan's camp.[88]

After Bryan lost the election, George made one last effort at the mayoralty of New York. This 1897 campaign demonstrated how far George had propelled his movement into mainstream politics. Twenty years earlier, George had run on the United Labor Party ticket; now his party was the "Democracy of Thomas Jefferson." The name implied that he had ceased to be an independent and was instead reclaiming the mantle of the Democratic Party. Contemporaries understood that George's campaign was about control of the Democratic Party. Carl Schurz observed that the campaign was "started by Democratic organizations outside of Tammany Hall. . . . They found in the failure of Tammany Hall to endorse the free-coinage plank of the Chicago platform a welcome opportunity to set up for themselves a claim to be recognized as the 'regular' Democratic organization in New York."[89]

In his acceptance speech at Cooper Union on October 5, George made clear that he was fighting alongside Bryan for control of the Democratic Party: "A little while ago it looked to me at least that the defeat that the trusts, the rings and money power, grasping the vote of the people, had inflicted on William Jennings Bryan was the defeat of everything for which the fathers had stood, of everything that makes this country so loved by us, so hopeful for the future. . . . You ask me to raise the standard again; to stand for that great cause; to stand as Jefferson stood in the civil revolution in 1800. I accept."[90] At the heart of the most important speech of the campaign, George positioned his race as a continuation of the one that had convulsed the country a year earlier. The party's platform called for municipal ownership of franchises; expanded parks, libraries, and museums; and a ban on the use of court injunctions to end strikes. Most important, it declared for the Chicago Platform that Bryan had campaigned on.[91]

In private, unobscured by flowery rhetoric, George's campaign agents made it clear that their intent was to bully New York's Democratic machine into adopting Bryan's national platform of reform. Willis Abbot, chairman of the campaign committee, wrote to Bryan that he had "started the campaign to keep in agitation the issues of the Chicago platform. I succeeded by forcing the Tammany people, who ignored our platform in their local platforms, to discuss all our national issues on the stump." Another member of the campaign committee wrote Bryan that "you can't hope for anything from Tammany Hall except so much as you are able to extort from them. The leaders do not like you nor the platform. Only the pressure from the ranks made them pretend to support you last fall."[92] George was a bludgeon battering Tammany Hall into allegiance with Bryan.

Tammany's agents appealed to Bryan for an endorsement, only reinforcing the appeals of the George campaign. They professed that they had been entirely "true and loyal" in the 1896 campaign, though that had clearly not been the case.[93] They asked Bryan to "write a letter of encouragement for them. . . . Is it but fair to expect as the regular organization of Greater New York that they should receive your hearty support?" In a statement that betrayed a conception of democratic governance rooted in patronage and loyalty rather than popular will, they asked, "What right has Henry George and his followers to undertake to destroy and to kill, politically, an organization that was as true as true could be?"[94] Tammany's appeal to Bryan was a daft move that only proved George had the power to chastise Bryan's enemies. It was leaked, almost certainly by Bryan, to the press. There it was interpreted as evidence that Tammany was "afraid of George."[95]

During the campaign, Bryan was urged by one of the most respected voices in the Democratic Party to incorporate the insurgents into the party. John Altgeld's governorship of Republican-leaning Illinois made him the party's leading representative of urban reform. A month after George accepted the nomination in New York, he wrote Bryan:

> Where in Nebraska and in perhaps most of the agricultural states, the silver question is the one that principally interests the people, there are in Chicago and in fact in all the great cities . . . large bodies of men whom we cannot interest in silver at all. . . . I have found . . . that the majority of what are called

> the "Henry George" men, a large portion of the progressive element of the
> Republican party, feel very little interest in the silver question, but are
> becoming intense on the question of municipal corruption, government by
> injunction, etc., etc., and they are ready to act with us solely because they
> believe that fundamentally we are right on these questions.

Georgists had generally been aligned with the Republican Party when it was the party of abolition but were increasingly breaking with it over its postwar economic policies. Altgeld predicted that Bryan could expand the Democratic Party's reach into the cities by appealing to them. "We both need and want the assistance of these people," he explained. "As a rule, they are an active class, and are successful in forming sentiment." As his career progressed, Bryan reached out to urban constituencies to expand the Democratic base, and, after George's second mayoral bid, single taxers were one of the groups that he courted most assiduously.[96] A week after Altgeld sent this letter, a rumor broke in the press that Bryan had written associates in New York suggesting they oppose Tammany in the mayoral election. Bryan was now placing his bets on George, even if it meant alienating the king-making Democratic machine in New York.[97]

George clearly thought his 1897 campaign had some deep significance other than his election, because he embarked on it confident that it would bear a heavy cost: his life. In 1891, George had suffered a bout of aphasia, probably a stroke from which he never fully recovered. His doctor had informed him that campaigning would likely kill him, a diagnosis that he appears to have accepted. Before joining the race, he reminded his wife, Annie, that she had once said Michael Davitt should stand by the people of Ireland even when "it should cost him his life." He now asked her permission to make the same sacrifice.[98] Although he understood the consequences, he campaigned as zealously as he had in 1886. On October 28, he delivered five speeches. The next day, with four days remaining before the election, George died.

Attendance at George's funeral was estimated at two hundred thousand. Daniel Beard, who had introduced George at his last public event, remembered: "The funeral of Mr. George was the most impressive one I have ever witnessed, and in a way it was the most solemn one. I witnessed General Grant's funeral and was deeply impressed by the loyalty of the mass to the great general, but on the occasion of Henry George's funeral it was deep affection and reverence that seemed to permeate the crowd. As the cortege moved along, men and women stepped out into the street, fell on their knees and prayed."[99] After the procession, the crowd assembled at Grand Central Palace for an ecumenical service. Catholic followers were represented by Father Mc-Glynn. The influential Protestant minister Lyman Abbott spoke, declaring that "he who lies before us in death was honored by all men."[100] The theme of universal acclaim was continued by the noted German American rabbi Gustav Gottheil, who claimed that "friend and foe stand side by side in reverent awe by his lifeless frame."[101] The final speaker, John Crosby, a relative unknown, delivered a secular encomium that positioned George alongside Thomas Jefferson in the democratic tradition.

George was unable to split open the Democracy in 1897, but he did earn the gesture from Bryan that had probably been the real object of his campaign. Bryan sent a statement praising the deceased leader: "He was one of the foremost thinkers of the world. His death will prove a loss to literature, society, and politics." Bryan betrayed his political instincts with an ambiguous statement that made him sound sympathetic to partisans of both sides of the land issue: "Those who agreed with his theories found in him an ideal leader, while those who opposed him admitted his ability and moral courage." That Bryan praised George with a clear eye to politics only reinforces the movement's new role in the party system. George entered the fray with a declaration of war on the two-party system, but in death he was escorted out by the Democratic Party's peerless leader.[102] The relationship would only grow stronger; Tom Johnson, the man whom George chose to lead his movement, would literally be carried to his grave by Bryan.[103]

In describing George's funeral, the *New York Sun* conveyed how confident New Yorkers were that the tide of history was flowing with George: "The densely packed streets, the silence of the vast multitude of bystanders, the solemn black-clad line of men without the glint of a single uniform, moving along the dim streets behind the lofty catafalque, while a crescent moon, half hidden behind gauzy clods, shed its uncertain light, made up such an event as the New York of today will tell to its children, and they to their children, until it has become history more living and vivid than any historian can write into his pages."[104] George, for his part, died confident that he had inspired "movements whose practical success is only a matter of time."[105]

CHAPTER 6

A Great and Glorious City

The Single Tax and Urban Reform in Ohio

> I cannot play upon any stringed instrument; but I can tell you how of a
> little village to make a great and glorious city.
>> Themistocles, as quoted in George, *Progress and Poverty*

Before his death, Henry George purchased a plot in Brooklyn's Greenwood Cemetery. The burial space had one distinguishing feature: it was adjacent to the family plot of Tom L. Johnson. George's decision to be buried next to the former streetcar magnate reflected not only their close relationship but also the historic mission he attributed to Johnson. George believed Johnson was the man to carry his standard into popular politics. His foresight was accurate in this case. Johnson would continue—and would surpass—George's legacy as a mayoral candidate. He became the dominant political force in one of the nation's largest cities (Cleveland, Ohio), a model for mayors around the country, and one of the more successful municipal statesmen the country had ever known.

Since George had "tutored" Johnson in politics over many years, Johnson's mayoralty was a coda to George's own career, and perhaps his most important work. In Cleveland, the principles that public and private spheres should remain separate, that the people should rule, and that imperfect markets should be socialized were applied to a vast array of civic functions, transforming philosophy into substantive policies that circulated throughout the nation. Cleveland had an independent, modern urban government concerned with the public interest. This model stood in stark contrast to the reigning philosophy of urban governance summarized by the Tammany sachem George Plunkitt: "I seen my opportunities and I took 'em."[1] Johnson finished George's efforts to integrate the movement into the Democratic Party. Johnson's anti-rent policies, high taxes, and expanded public services introduced urban voters who typically favored Republican high-tariff policies to the Democratic doctrine of progressive taxation. Johnson and his imitators would in this way play a pivotal role in expanding the Democratic coalition.

Even while victorious, Johnson's career highlighted the tension between George's radical liberalism and democracy. While single taxers saw themselves as saving democracy, the odds of the democratic public enacting a vision of liberalism as extreme and narrowly defined as the single tax were vanishingly small. Democracies, in fact, have struggled to enact anti-corruption and anti-rent policies because rent imposes a small, sometimes imperceptible burden on a large but disorganized public, while providing powerful advantages to an organized and resourceful interest, eager to fight diligently on its own behalf.[2] Single taxers blamed the shortcomings of democracy on the concentrated political and economic power of the "interests." Because they stressed the importance of the democratic process and popular participation, they embraced propaganda and hardball politics as a corrective for securing their aims within the confines of a system skewed in favor of privilege. Their skillful political machinations often appeared to disrupt the calculus of interest group politics. Setbacks during Johnson's mayoralty raised doubts that charismatic individuals could, through wit and will alone, reshape democracy. For the time being, though, history seemed to be on their side.

The Urban Democracy

In July 1900, the Democrats met in Kansas City to renominate William Jennings Bryan for president. Tom Johnson, who was a delegate to the convention, took the stage to present a bust of the candidate sculpted by Richard George, son of Henry George.[3] The symbolic gesture underscored the alliance between Johnson's movement and the Democratic Party. In 1900 Bryan campaigned against the annexation of the Philippines after the Spanish-American War and won the support of single taxers whose abolitionist histories had tied them to the Republican Party. Even William Lloyd Garrison II joined with the party that had redeemed the South.[4] Voters, however, did not follow him; Bryan lost in a landslide and single taxers followed him to defeat. Only one Georgist, Robert Barker of Brooklyn, survived in Congress.

A beachhead for economic reform also developed during these years within the GOP, but it was a type of Progressivism that Georgists generally were not attracted to. Within months of securing reelection, President McKinley was shot by an anarchist in Buffalo, New York, making Theodore Roosevelt the Republican Party's standard-bearer. In his first speech to Congress, Roosevelt called for anti-anarchist legislation and limitations on immigration.[5] This poor record on civil liberties rankled Georgists like Louis Post.[6] Some single taxers, such as Hamlin Garland, were drawn to Roosevelt's conservationism, but his economic program did not break hard enough from Republican orthodoxy for most. Most problematic, Roosevelt pushed the party further in the direction of imperialism, intervening extensively in Latin America in the wake of the Spanish-American War. This was anathema to Georgism, with roots in anti-colonialism that dated back to *The Irish Land Question*. The *Johnstown (Pennsylvania) Democrat* explained: "Every single taxer understands that imperialism has but one spur—and that is greed. . . . It has gone to grab franchises, to gobble up land, to appropriate valuable natural opportunities, to grasp new privileges and through these to exploit labor."[7]

Georgist anti-colonialism was out of place in the rising current of Progressivism, which often embraced empire as an extension of its unbounded faith in expert rule. In *Democracy and Empire* (1900), the sociologist Franklin H. Giddings dismissed the apparent contradiction between democracy and empire by arguing that consent of the governed was not desirable, because "it means that practically the test of moral government is nothing more than mere approval by human numbers, who may be ignorant or even depraved."[8] Giddings was echoing Theodore Roosevelt, who griped during the debates over the annexation of the Philippines that he had no patience for those who "who cant about 'liberty' and the consent of the 'governed.'"[9] Giddings evinced the elitism that cemented Progressivism and imperialism together, linking the nation's expanding empire with its burgeoning industrial sector, where "there will be a greater deference than exists at present to natural leadership—to the minority who have the capacity to direct and organize."[10] The only significant segments of the working class that Giddings believed had not embraced the doctrine of expert management were "the disciples of Henry George, and the believers in theoretical anarchism."[11]

Denouncing imperialism during a moment of martial jubilation had pushed the Democratic Party to the margins of national government, but this mattered little to the single taxers who identified "local taxation" as the best avenue for George's program.[12] Even during his time in Congress, Johnson had dedicated much of his energy to ensuring that property assessments in Washington, DC, reflected the real value of land.[13] By the time he left Congress, he was confident that "the place to begin is in the city."[14]

Although control of the governor's mansion would give single taxers more influence over taxation than the mayor's office, agrarian opposition made that impossible. In 1898 California Democrats nominated for governor James Maguire, a blacksmith-turned-lawyer who had advised George during the drafting of *Progress and Poverty*. Republicans attacked Maguire for his professed faith in the single tax, which they claimed would greatly injure small farmers. Maguire ran instead on the public ownership of railroads and yet still lost across the state.[15] Similarly, in Colorado, Democratic state senator James Bucklin led a study of land value taxation in Australia and New Zealand and then introduced a referendum enabling cities to exempt improvements. The referendum lost overwhelmingly in rural districts, where it was attacked as a step toward the single tax.

At the same time, it became evident that Ohio's cities would support a radical program. In 1898 Samuel Jones was elected mayor of Toledo. Jones had amassed a fortune in oil and embarked on a career in manufacturing. He was deeply affected, however, by the hardships his workers endured following the Panic of 1893. Jones searched of a new philosophy and found the Christian radicalism of George Herron and Leo Tolstoy. Imitating Tolstoy's decision to forfeit his land, Jones invested the profits from his Acme Sucker Rod Company in benevolent projects, including a school, a park, an auditorium, higher wages, eight-hour days, paid vacations, and a cooperative insurance system. Samuel "Golden Rule" Jones—a moniker that became synonymous with Tolstoy's doctrine of Christian nonresistance—was so committed to personal freedom that he did not ask his employees to clock in.[16]

Jones had a fiercely independent streak but moved closer to the single tax movement with time. He was idiosyncratic—a vegetarian who fasted often and could sometimes be found meditating on his head or sleeping on his porch, irrespective of the season. His attire was that of a Gilded Age bohemian, marked by a "flowing cravat" of the sort that, Brand Whitlock observed, "for some . . . reason artists and reformers wear."[17] He was influenced by the Georgist writings of Herron and Tolstoy and believed that land and utilities were a source of inequality, but, like many Christians who read George, he also embraced a post-millennialist faith in an earthly kingdom of God that would make capitalism obsolete.[18] Jones, therefore, was initially close to the Socialist Party and Eugene Debs.[19] But he supported Bryan for president in 1900 to block the annexation of the Philippines. Endorsing a Democrat was an intolerable violation of Marxist orthodoxy that prompted an onslaught of criticism from the Socialist press. Jones repudiated these attacks as "the spirit of Partyism" and added, "One kind of Partyism is as hopeless to me as another."[20] Before long, Jones would find a new ally in Tom Johnson, whom he called "the freest man that is at all prominent in partisan politics in America."[21]

Winning the People (and the Experts) of Cleveland

Cleveland at the turn of the century was a transit and industrial hub, the seventh-largest US city in population and rapidly growing. The city's streetcar system was a subject of fierce controversy. In the early 1890s the movement for municipal ownership began in the Franklin Club, a debate organization for single taxers, socialists, and Bellamyites. Pressure for change grew when the Cleveland Electric Railway Company (Con-Con) increased the speed of cars and hit several pedestrians. By 1899 the system was paralyzed by striking workers and a series of bombings that invited comparisons to a war zone. Hundreds were arrested in riots that summer. When the strike was crushed, citizens turned to the ballot box. Sam Jones ran for governor on a platform of municipal ownership. His campaign was organized by Peter Witt, a former molder who had been blacklisted for his work with the Knights of Labor. Witt, an agnostic and single taxer, had a reputation for fiery, often profane rhetoric nurtured by years of poverty. Jones lost the state but won in Cleveland's Cuyahoga County with more votes than the Democratic and Republican candidates combined.[22] Witt, who was both the campaign manager for Jones in Cuyahoga County and president of Cleveland's Central Labor Union, helped carry that symbolic victory.[23]

By demonstrating support for public ownership in Cleveland, Witt was paving the way for Tom Johnson to claim the mayoralty on a Georgist platform. This result was possibly intentional. Witt and Johnson had met years prior, in 1894, when Johnson was campaigning for Congress. Witt, an "angry, earnest man, with flashing eyes and black locks hanging down on one side of his forehead," came out to heckle the city's streetcar magnate during one of his speeches.[24] Johnson invited Witt onstage to discuss the issues, transforming Witt into one of Johnson's fiercest supporters.[25] Johnson had lost his congressional seat in a Republican wave in 1895, but, as unrest spread through Cleveland in 1899, he retired from business, and rumor spread that he was planning a return to politics.[26]

Johnson feigned surprise when, in February 1901, petitioners arrived at his door with 16,000 signatures demanding he stand for office. In fact, a month earlier he had begun the campaign with a subtle stunt. On January 25 he attended negotiations over a new streetcar franchise in Columbus. The city was entertaining a twenty-five-year franchise with a five-cent fare, but Johnson intervened with a proposal to operate the franchise at three cents and to reduce fares further if the line earned more than 6 percent return on investment. Reports were that on his trip to Columbus "wily" Tom also met with Democratic Party leaders in the capitol in preparation for an undisclosed campaign. Columbus officials refused Johnson's franchise.[27] This was a foregone conclusion because the deal had been presented so late, but the city's rejection of Johnson's offer reinforced the narrative that franchises were given to political allies, not the best bid. Furthermore, the stunt established that Johnson was willing to wager his own money that he could run an unprecedented three-cent line. As someone who had operated a streetcar system, Johnson leaned on his business experience to contend for the feasibility of publicly owned three-cent streetcar service.[28]

Fare reduction was a winning platform; Johnson was elected with a comfortable plurality of 6,000 votes, carrying a solid majority of working-class, immigrant, and suburban voters. It was less obvious that fare reduction was Georgist, because it fell short of establishing public ownership. However, *The Public*, which Johnson funded, explained that with a three-cent fare, "arrangements for municipal ownership can be made" because reducing profits would ease resistance to municipal ownership. Further, with a cheaper fare "the consequent rise in land values, giving to landlords the money value of these municipal benefits, will popularize Henry George's single tax reform."[29] Georgists believed that land was the "robber that takes all that is left"; sparing the people monopoly traction rates, therefore, would only increase rents proportionally, further illustrating the central role that land played in inequality.

In the very act of taking office, Johnson proved that he would not be bound by political norms. His predecessor, Mayor John Farley, had granted valuable lakefront property to the Pennsylvanian Railroad Company, but Johnson refused to concede public land rights. Foregoing the traditional two-week transitional period, Johnson orchestrated an ad hoc inauguration within two days of the election so that he could invalidate the contract before it went into effect. This maneuver precipitated the first in a series of legal battles for his administration. It would be followed shortly thereafter by his controversial decision to appoint Peter Witt to lead a tax school. The school was consistent with George's ideals of state promotion of an engaged and educated citizenry but was perceived by his critics (and the courts) as using public funds to promote partisan viewpoints.

Although he had the air of a fiery populist, Johnson proved adept at recruiting experts. He saw expertise in government as a necessary step toward public ownership. When Johnson appointed the Republican statistician Edward Bemis to lead the water department, he observed that "there is no better recommendation for municipal ownership of other utilities than to show that the ones now operated are run in the interests of good service, with economical and efficient management."[30] Johnson ran his city like a business because he believed the city should be in business. He made merit, rather than party, the principal criterion in hiring and ended the practice of requiring civil servants to donate to the Democratic Party. These policies bore fruit; Bemis designed an intake tunnel that cut utility prices and reduced the incidence of typhoid by 90 percent.[31] Like George, Johnson was neither a populist nor a fetishist of expertise. *The Public* explained the proper role of "expertism in government": "The people know what they want better than any expert in government can tell them. . . . But with reference to the details of what they want, the experts know best. Given a nation in which the people regulate details, and you soon have chaos; given one in which experts determine policies, and you evolve bureaucracy, and ultimately absolutism."[32] Technical expertise was a tool that could effectuate the public will, but expertise should not supplant the role of the majority in democratic decision making.

This struggle to reconcile democracy and expertise was embodied in Frederic C. Howe, a mugwump Republican who had studied under the economist Richard Ely. Howe had acquired from Ely a faith in experts and the notion that "reform" meant empowering the "Anglo-Saxon" "to carry on civilization."[33] Howe was offended to find that Johnson believed "my class was not as important as I thought it was."[34] However, once Howe was elected to the city council from the Republican Party, Johnson won him over, and Howe became his representative in the city council and state assembly. Retaining some of the faith in expertise he had obtained from his professors at Johns Hopkins University, Howe embraced Germany's model of making "scientific research, an adjunct of the state"; however, unlike his mentor Ely, he now derided the country's "paternalism and autocracy" for fostering the spirit of caste.[35] Howe argued that expert administration should be subordinated to the democratic public. Ultimately, he emphasized that much of Germany's success stemmed from the policies that it shared with Georgists—government ownership of natural monopolies and land—and looked past autocratic Germany to Georgist Denmark as his model "cooperative commonwealth."[36]

Johnson's most gifted recruit was Howe's college acquaintance Newton D. Baker. Baker had been a conservative southern Democrat. After meeting Johnson, Baker's ideas transformed rapidly. When asked about his beliefs, Baker replied simply, "I am a follower of Tom Johnson."[37] Among friends he identified as a "devout single-taxer."[38] Baker remained in many senses a conservative, slow to countenance policies such as public poor relief or a federal ban on child labor, but he would constantly prove himself a radical when confronting injustices that Georgists saw as monopolistic privilege.[39] Regarded by Oliver Wendell Holmes Jr. as one of the great lawyers of the age, Baker was elected city solicitor of Cleveland in 1903 and defended the administration's programs against armies of corporate lawyers.[40] After a laborious workday Baker would read in his study, sometimes devouring "a 300-page book . . . in an evening."[41] As a matter of course, he perfected extemporaneous speech. "He speaks without a line of writing before him," George Creel observed, "yet when he has finished after half an hour or an hour, what he has said could be printed as literature without the change of a word.[42]

Johnson's capacity to convince experts like Baker to sacrifice their own well-being and devote themselves to public service ought to be mystifying. As Johnson himself noted, Baker had "held his public office at constant personal sacrifice." Johnson added, "This low-paid official has seen every day . . . lawyers getting more often five times the fee for bringing a suit that he got for defending it."[43] Baker answered this riddle in a remarkable piece of marginalia scrawled into his copy of *The Life of Henry George* (1902):

> Its greatest lesson lies, I think, in its vindication of the truth that real power and effectiveness in men lies in uncompromising and unswerving fidelity to ideals. After all is done and said neither the peace nor pomp which flows from success in sympathizing with the world's prejudices produces a fraction of the satisfaction which must beautify the life of a man who can say that he has not yielded a jot or tittle of his allegiance to the truth as he saw it; and if happiness be the true end of life who could hesitate a moment to choose between the lot of Henry George and that of any man of his time?[44]

George's utopian vision offered a sense of purpose during a period of doubt. As a consequence, it pulled some of the most capable experts in the country into the service of democracy.

Johnson's War on the Interests

Johnson's first battle was against the state tax assessors, who he claimed undertaxed the property of powerful railroad corporations. He tasked Edward Bemis and Peter Witt with an extensive study of property taxes in Ohio. It purported to show that while homes were assessed at 60 percent of their value, railroads were assessed at only 10 to 20 percent. Establishing taxes on railroads, Johnson believed, would allow him to build bridges with otherwise-hostile farmers.[45]

Johnson traveled to meetings of county and state auditors with a trailing cohort that included his experts and Samuel Jones. Johnson impugned the honesty of the board of auditors by presenting statistical evidence showing that railroad corporations which gave free passes to assessors were taxed at lower rates. Johnson hired detectives to follow assessors, proving that they met with railroad executives the day before they officially convened. Rather than mount a substantive defense, assessors tried to ignore Johnson or simply fled in terror. The *Stark County Democrat* joked, "All you've got to do to produce a scatterment in the throne room at the Stark county auditor's office is to yell 'Tom Johnson.'"[46]

These theatrical displays papered over nuanced differences in economic philosophy. Assessors justified discrepancies between the stock market value of railroads and their own assessments by noting that the tax system touched only property, not the intangible assets that constituted much of the value of railroads. Georgists argued, conversely, that the bulk of the valuation of railroad corporations consisted of their monopoly value and that this was, in fact, tangible because their monopolies were a function of their ownership of exclusive access to rights-of-way. Rights-of-way were land and land was a tangible asset, subject to taxation. The noise and danger that speeding trains brought to communities often suppressed the value of adjacent land, but the land under the tracks was immensely valuable because it was the basis for a monopolistic transportation network and was difficult to cobble together without government support. Johnson's administration argued that because assessors did not understand the social value of land, they did not tax railroad property at its full value. Assessors undervalued the land of railroad corporations by evaluating it as they did adjacent properties, when in fact its value was immensely higher because it was integrated in a contiguous strip and was thereby transformed into a vital artery for commerce.[47]

Because state constitutions acted as a straitjacket on legislative tax reform, these technical debates became indispensable for challenging inequitable tax systems. The core dispute was whether utilities should be valued at their original cost of production or their reproduction cost, defined as the price of rebuilding the utilities at the time of assessment. Progressives generally favored valuing corporations at the original cost of production, even though this method disincentivized efficiency by allowing corporations to claim interest on all expenditures, regardless of whether they were necessary.

Reproduction cost valued utilities at what it should cost to rebuild them, but this value assessment included the present cost of the land, which was likely to have grown since the utility was first built.[48] Much of the debate over the valuation of utilities for price controls, public purchase, and taxation, therefore, would center on whether corporations had a right to capitalize on rising land values.[49] After Edward Bemis joined the advisory board of the Valuation Division of the Interstate Commerce Commission, he explained his objection to reproduction cost valuation: "A few sky-scrapers go up between the Grand Central and the Pennsylvania stations, in New York, enhancing the site values at those depots. In consequence, the freight and passenger rates from New York to San Francisco must be raised."[50]

Johnson failed to persuade county and state assessment boards, but he made a leap forward in municipal taxation by taking extraordinary measures to expedite tax reform. Cleveland's property was assessed by a six-member Board of Equalization. The mayor was empowered to make only two appointments a year to the board. Impatient, Johnson offered two members lucrative government jobs to leave their positions, opening a majority on the board. In July 1901, the reconstituted board increased assessments on a host of major companies; Con-Con's assessment increased from $595,000 to $6 million. The board also established a system of land value assessment designed by W. A. Somers. As an assessor in St. Paul, Minnesota, Somers had developed what became the standard method for calculating land values. He used sales records to extrapolate from a handful of properties (preferably vacant or minimally improved lots) the value of land within a portion of the block. He then referred to a series of maps that charted the average variation of land values within a block according to standard premiums for corner lots, light, ventilation, and other conveniences.[51] This system allowed Somers to quickly extrapolate land values throughout the block with data from one or two underused lots. Johnson applied a similar system to the taxation of riparian rights. When the Otis Steel Company objected that the city might as well tax air, Baker shot back that it wouldn't be worth much because "you have put too much smoke in it." The goal was to tax scarce resources: "All of us have air and light, but just a few of you have Lake Erie."[52] As Johnson increased revenue from taxing natural resources, he ended licensing fees for professionals, shifting taxes from labor to land.[53]

While increasing taxes on property, Johnson reduced the city's revenue from vice enforcement. As the *San Francisco Chronicle* observed, "Whoever believes in . . . getting extra money from those who . . . engage in unsocial occupations involving police expenses . . . can never be 'single-taxers.'"[54] The singleness of the single tax meant the city would not tax vice. But the issue went deeper than that because single taxers believed that regulating private enterprise—including criminal enterprises—inevitably did more to corrupt government than to purify society. In New York, the young Georgist judge Samuel Seabury presided in the case of a police lieutenant who contracted a murder in order to hide his role in an illegal gambling establishment. Afterward, Seabury summarized the Georgist position on vice enforcement: "The sums collected by the police excite the greed of certain politicians who demand their shares, and in turn they protect the criminal branches of the law. The presence of politics brings strength to the system and makes it harder to break up."[55] Concluding as George had that deploying the coercive powers of the state only reinforced privilege, Peter Witt wrote, "I am convinced that the dream of Socialism can be realized with less, instead of more, government."[56]

The sweeping implications of separate public and private sectors were most evident in law enforcement. Johnson eliminated fines for saloons, gambling establishments, and houses of ill repute.[57] In 1907 Johnson's police chief, Fred "Golden Rule" Kohler, announced that Cleveland's police officers would no longer pursue minor offenses like public drunkenness. From 1907 to 1909 the number of arrests in Cleveland declined from 30,418 to 6,000. Yet, from 1907 to 1908, arrests for larceny and burglary increased from 169 to 224 despite a decline in the incidence of these crimes.[58] Similarly, Johnson's police commissioner, Manuel Levine, convicted twenty judges of colluding with debt collectors to wrongfully convict poor defendants. Levine argued that these abuses were a result of the bounty system under which judges were paid by the case. He led the push to create a modern salaried judiciary.[59] Levine continued his campaign to eliminate the power of money over the justice system by introducing the small claims court to Cleveland, making it the first major city in the nation to allow the poor to seek redress for small financial claims without expensive legal counsel.[60]

Johnson's criminal justice policies reflected a faith that people would, under optimal conditions, become good citizens. Director of Charities Harris Cooley purchased two thousand acres outside the city for the rehabilitation of juvenile delinquents. Providing land to criminals was intended, according to Cooley, to reveal "the path up which the crime has come": in the absence of land monopoly, criminals would be productive citizens.[61] Johnson pardoned convicts detained at the workhouse for inability to pay fines.[62] This approach contrasted not only with Spencer's dream of using law enforcement to wean out the genetically unfit but also with the Progressives at the American Economic Association, which published flimsy statistical research linking crime to racial inferiority.[63]

In an age when Progressives railed against liquor and "white slavery," tolerance of vice was rare, but in neighboring Toledo, Tolstoyan, Georgist anarchism reigned.[64] Jones or his assistant, Brand Whitlock, would often assume control of the police court and acquit everyone who came before them.[65] Jones took clubs from the police. He stopped enforcement of vice laws, particularly Sunday closings. Jones believed that "law in America is what the people will back up. If the people back up what the mayor does, then what the mayor does is law; and if they do not back it up, then it is not law."[66] He put this principle to the test when Gilbert J. Raynor, district superintendent of the Anti-Saloon League, wrote a piece for the *Toledo Bee* criticizing Jones's moral laxity. Jones proved his point by enforcing the most antiquated and oppressive blue laws. In the first week of the experiment, the proprietor of the Valentine Theater was arrested for hosting a Marine Band concert on the Sabbath. The demonstration had its intended effect; within a week the city council convened to strike down Toledo's blue laws.[67]

These tolerant vice policies arrayed the churches against Ohio's urban radicals. An assembly of a hundred Cleveland ministers labeled Johnson's vice policy "diabolic" and unanimously agreed to attack the mayor from the pulpit.[68] The *Catholic Bulletin* published a series of articles declaring the single tax "anti-Christian."[69] Single taxers alleged that Christian charity was just paternalism, which, by legitimating economic inequality, promoted vice. "How small the work of philanthropists with their gifts of dollars appears, compared to the work of this man who gave them *hope*," Johnson noted. Echoing a popular Georgist slogan, he called for "*justice* and *not charity*."[70]

Liberating the City

In the face of this radicalism, the Republican governor of Ohio, George Nash, worked to limit the power of urban radicals. Although Ohio's cities were some of the most liberal in the nation, the state's countryside was historically conservative. Ohio's farmers never rallied to the People's Party and instead spent the 1890s demanding lower property taxes.[71] The state assembly barred mayors from sitting on police benches, halting Jones's mass acquittals. The legislature also empowered the governor to veto local tax assessment boards.

The governor then overturned the land value taxes that Johnson had established in Cleveland.[72]

Georgists, however, remained unassailable in their urban strongholds. Governor Nash signed the Chapman bill, which required mayors to secure a two-thirds majority in the city council to make appointments. Absent a supermajority, the governor filled vacancies, effectively putting urban government under state control. However, when Johnson was reelected in 1903, candidates who signed his pledge to support the three-cent fare, "equal taxation," and a municipally owned electric company won twenty-three out of thirty-two seats on the city council, allowing him to retain power despite state intervention.[73] Jones won 70 percent of the vote—nearly as much as the Democratic and Republican candidates combined.

In response to Governor Nash, Johnson argued for liberating urban democracy. William Jennings Bryan invited Johnson to deliver the keynote speech at his Fourth of July celebration in 1903. Johnson drew upon the themes of democratic sovereignty in the Declaration of Independence and demanded they be applied to the city, "for the true unit of all government in modern times is the municipality."[74] Johnson aimed to overturn state constitutions that prevented cities from setting tax policy, directly operating businesses, and owning their own utilities. After securing home rule, Johnson promised, the city would be able to realize principles proposed in *Progress and Poverty*, including tax reform, public ownership of streetcars, and an end to private contracting.[75]

Although it had pragmatic roots, home rule as imagined by the Johnson administration embraced a romantic vision in which socialized ground rent funded a richer, more democratic urban life. In *The City: The Hope of Democracy* (1905), Frederic C. Howe imagined that "home rule would create a city republic, a new sort of sovereignty, a republic like unto those of Athens, Rome, and the medieval Italian cities."[76] He predicted that "here concerts, lectures, and human intercourse will be offered. A sense of the city as a home, as a common authority, a thing to be loved and cared for, will be developed."[77] The city, offering a localized social democracy, would provide health care and monitor working conditions. Howe's statistics purported to show that rising land values were sufficient to fund existing municipal budgets even without the full confiscation of ground rents. Franchises would become a source for revenue because "rights of way upon the streets are but site values. Their value is created, as are those of the corner lot, by the growth of society."[78] In drawing on the history of ancient city-states and declaring the city "the hope of democracy," Howe completed George's revision of a Jeffersonian tradition that had seen the city as antithetical to democracy.

In 1902 *The Public* counted more than a dozen single tax candidates across the country, yet the fight for home rule in Ohio dominated the attention of Georgists. That year single taxers held two gubernatorial tickets: Franklin Lane in California and Lucius Garvin in Rhode Island. The latter, in a historic win, became the first Democrat to carry a northeastern state since 1896. Surprisingly, however, Post chose to focus on Herbert Bigelow's campaign for home rule as a candidate for secretary of state of Ohio.[79] A child runaway, Bigelow had become pastor at the historic Vine Street Church, a traditional abolitionist stronghold whose parishioners had largely concluded there were no more social problems left to solve after emancipation—until Bigelow arrived, preaching the single tax and demanding that Black people be admitted to the church. Bigelow made the church into a sanctuary for radical liberalism, decorated with quotes from Henry George, Thomas Jefferson, William Lloyd Garrison, Wendell Philips, Giuseppe Mazzini, and Leo Tolstoy.[80]

Bigelow's campaign brought home the importance of capturing the Democratic Party machinery. Bigelow won Cleveland but lost the state in a landslide. *The Public* concluded that the conservative Democratic machine in Cincinnati had betrayed Bigelow supporters and recommended running them out of the party.[81] Subsequently, when eight democratic legislators approved a fifty-year streetcar franchise in Cincinnati, Johnson traveled to these legislators' districts and campaigned successfully to defeat them. In the process, Johnson scared the state party into his camp.

After that display of power, Johnson won the gubernatorial nomination in 1903. He lost the race but later claimed that his objective had never been to become governor but rather to capture the party.[82] The *New York Times* reported that when Johnson "ruthlessly unseated delegates, and crushed with an iron heel the frail opposition. . . . His real object was to insure the sending of a delegation from Ohio to the next National Convention of the party that would stand for the radical programme." Johnson, the *Times* insisted, had no interest in the office; he was looking "far ahead."[83] He pushed through a party platform that included home rule, the initiative and referendum, municipal ownership, popular veto power over franchises, a salaried officialdom, and a two-cent-a-mile steam railroad fare. According to Howe, Johnson had come "into control of the Democratic Party."[84]

The Traction War and the Democratic Public

As the battle over home rule took shape, a parallel struggle to achieve Johnson's three-cent fare was under way. On February 10, 1902, Johnson found a bidder to build a track that would compete with the established lines under conditions that included the right of public purchase, a ten-hour workday, union arbitration, and profit sharing with the city after ten years. The courts invalidated several of these provisions, and construction was stalled by a series of seventy-seven injunctions over a period of eight years. During these legal challenges to the new line, the franchise of Con-Con's lines expired, but the courts allowed them to continue operation.

Stuart Chase described what came next as "Tom Johnson and the 'interests' wrestl[ing] naked in the public streets of Cleveland."[85] In December 1905 Cleveland annexed the suburb of South Brooklyn because it had a small electric power plant that provided a backdoor avenue to public competition with private power. Soon rumor spread that, in the two days between the filing of paperwork and the annexation of South Brooklyn, the village council planned to sign a twenty-five-year franchise with Con-Con that would force Cleveland to acknowledge Con-Con's franchises. Johnson was out of town when news reached City Hall. Peter Witt, acting as city clerk, took charge. Three police officers were sent to South Brooklyn and placed outside the town hall with orders to arrest councilmen if they convened for a vote. Others were sent to follow the councilmen and intervene if they tried to meet privately. The affair ended without further incident, but even supporters referred to the episode as the "dictatorship of the city clerk."[86] Such robust use of executive authority was standard in Johnson's Cleveland. When franchises expired the following year, Johnson defied a court injunction and tore up sections of Con-Con's track.[87]

This expansive use of executive power was supposed to be in the service of democracy. The traction debate was never about whether the public should exercise control over the streetcar system; this had always been the case. Streetcar lines generally ran through public streets, owned by the city, so companies negotiated with the city for leases—known as franchises—in which the city could demand fare reductions or lump-sum payments in return for franchise rights. This system often failed because it was more cost-efficient for traction companies to bribe legislators than to bid for a fair franchise. The alternative to Johnson's public ownership and fare reductions was not laissez-faire, but regulatory commissions in which experts determined a fair rate of return. As Cleveland fought a protracted traction war, one such commission had been established in Columbus with hardly any opposition. Railroad corporations often advocated for commissions as preferable to vesting elected officials with the power to set rates.[88] Xenophobia encouraged skepticism about the urban electorate's ability to manage such complex issues; 35 percent of Cleveland's population in 1910 was foreign-born, and another 40 percent had at least one parent born abroad. Johnson, on the other hand, noted that in his time as a streetcar magnate he had easily manipulated regulatory commissions. Only democratic control, through the concerted efforts of elected officials, could manage transit. When legislators in Columbus proposed a bill for statewide regulation, Johnson denounced it as "the worst measure of its kind ever offered for the consideration of any state legislature."[89]

Johnson led a vigorous campaign of political education to prove the urban electorate's ability to govern itself. The New Dealer Raymond Moley remembered Johnson as a "public educator" and claimed that in Cleveland the "average citizen was as ready in his discussion of such abstractions as franchise, over-head values, and cost of operation per mile as the ordinary citizen is with regard to baseball."[90] Declaring that parks were for the people, Johnson removed "Stay off the Grass" signs and allowed all speakers to address the people without permits.[91] To realize his dream of public space for public discourse, Johnson commissioned the "Group Plan," a complex of public buildings constructed in Greco-Roman style around a large green space in downtown Cleveland.[92] After hours, public schools were converted into "community centers" where citizens debated issues. Although Johnson's tax school was ruled unconstitutional, he found other ways to take his message to the public. His supporters transported giant tents around the city, allowing Johnson to travel to the people for large events. In the tent meetings, his terse style proved an asset. He turned to his audience, inviting them to ask questions. Responding to Clevelanders in a simple, direct style, he cultivated a strong relationship with voters, whom he treated more like pupils than constituents.[93]

These popular campaigns also combated a hostile press. Johnson was never short on publicity, but good press was rare. The *New York Times*, the *Washington Post*, the *Chicago Tribune*, and the *Atlanta Constitution* each mentioned Johnson on average more than once a month during his mayoralty. Each described him as a possible presidential candidate. However, they neglected his practical accomplishments in favor of tabloid attacks on his personage. The *New York Times* claimed the "length, breadth, and thickness" of his "economic and political principles" were that of a "rat . . . [who, h]aving grown gray and prosperous," sent out "pious exhortations to renounce gross and carnal pursuits" that he had pursued when young.[94] In one editorial, the *Wall Street Journal* claimed that citizens should doubt his judgment because he was like those politicians from "other climes, where men are volatile and nature is often more kind."[95] To the editorial writer, not only was Johnson a traitor to his class, but he had assimilated the racial features of the fiery, irresponsible immigrants he represented.

But a handful of writers stood on the horizon, ready to challenge the press's narrative. On July 12, 1904, Samuel Jones died. With his death, Johnson gained a new, charismatic literary partner. Newton Baker remembered traveling to Toledo for the funeral and meeting Brand Whitlock, who appeared to be an intellectual aristocrat at home among the people: "He was tall, slender, and strikingly handsome with the easy, unconscious superiority of mind and elevated but uncondescending approach to his audience which marks the only valid distinction permissible in a democracy. His audience consisted of acres of people who packed the lawn in front of the Jones house. . . . The crowd was a family bereft of its father, and Brand was the oldest son and heir, counting up the gains and glorifying the hope for which the family traditions stood."[96] Whitlock preferred literature to politics but was anointed as Sam Jones's heir in Toledo, almost against his will. More so even than Jones, Whitlock looked to Johnson as the national leader "most thoroughly grounded in sound economic principles."[97] Unlike Jones, Whitlock was decisively a single taxer and served as an editor of *The Public*.[98] It was this philosophy alone that kept him in political life; his assistant Albert Jay Nock noted that Whitlock despised "the difficult general discipline of an alien life." Whitlock aspired to a literary lifestyle, but he also "sought philosophical consistency and found it and *established* it in himself."[99]

Whitlock was a realist who believed art should faithfully convey social conditions.[100] He demonstrated the power of realist literature with *The Turn of the Balance* (1907). The book—an indictment of the criminal justice system modeled after Tolstoy's *Resurrection*—coincided with his fight for a statewide ban on capital punishment.[101] It followed the story of German immigrants whose lives had been ruined by a railroad accident that forced them into crime. These poor criminals were destined to a life of moral corruption by a system that guarded privilege. The real heroes of the book were drawn from the producing class: a sturdy, flannel-wearing mechanic who refused to swear an oath to enforce the death penalty; a rising lawyer who repudiated his class to defend the downtrodden; and a woman who abandoned her gendered preoccupation with charity when she realized that the church's paternalism merely disguised the sins of the urban elite. The Anglo-American elite enjoyed aristocratic privileges. Free to bend the law at will, they frequented the Tenderloin and rented their properties to criminals at exorbitant rates. Legal fees, high rents, law enforcement, and grafting prison contracts were tools for privileged interests to skim off the high margins of criminal enterprises. The whole narrative, Whitlock claimed, was based on his actual experiences as a lawyer.[102]

The response to *The Turn of the Balance* was tremendous. Critics called it "dangerous," "pessimistic," even "anarchistic."[103] His most vocal critic was the local preacher Cyrus Townsend Brady.[104] Whitlock believed he had offended "the Reverend Cyrus and those wealthy parishioners of his" because "the streetcar company in which they are interested . . . cannot get the kind of franchise it wants so long as I am mayor. Or it may be that his antagonism may arise naturally out of the fact that he is a romanticist in fiction and I am a realist, the first time in history, I think, that the two schools ever clashed in politics."[105] The book also won accolades from critics around the nation. Ben Lindsey and Thomas Mott Osborne, prominent Georgist criminal justice reformers, sent letters of support. Upton Sinclair and Jack London both praised the book.[106]

Whitlock followed with *On the Enforcement of Law in Cities* (1910), the definitive statement of the left libertarianism that prevailed in Ohio's municipalities. Originally written as an extended letter to the Federation of Churches, it was later republished as a pamphlet. Here Whitlock blamed the incidence of crime on "this social system, with privileges for the few, and proscriptions for the many." He attributed the desperation and poor behavior of "women of ill-repute" to "exorbitant rents." His property tax reforms did more for law and order than the legal system did.[107] At its heart was the argument that criminal law would be invalid until it was brought into accord with the natural law that established social property alongside private property: "In that philosophy, it is as great an offense to steal a railroad as it is to steal a ride, as great a crime to appropriate a coal mine as it to pick up coal along the tracks: in that philosophy public property is as sacred as private property."[108] The Federation of Churches promised a reply, but never delivered. Twenty years later, Albert Jay Nock, Whitlock's personal assistant at the time, would cite *On the Enforcement of Law in Cities* in his attacks on prohibition.[109] He would also popularize the term "libertarian" to describe people like himself, opposed to both moral legislation and economic planning.

No writer, however, was more important to the Johnson administration than Lincoln Steffens. The goateed Greenwich Village bohemian revolutionized American journalism beginning in 1902 with the publication of "Tweed Days in St. Louis," which exposed corruption in Missouri's first city. It was a pivotal moment in muckraking journalism. According to William Allen White, Steffens had found that "the thing we call capital has become a part of this government."[110]

The idea that there was something akin to an "invisible government" was not new; everyone understood that behind the scenes cities were run by unelected machines. But Steffens argued that there was a deeper layer to the corruption—that behind the foreign surnames in smoke-filled rooms stood the "better" people of the city, the very same Anglo-American elite that "good government" reformers would empower. Steffens assailed expert regulatory commissions because "government prohibitions drive vicious businessmen into politics to save their livelihood." Instead he demanded, as announced in the title of one of his books, "the struggle for self-government."[111]

Steffens began to crack Republican dominance in the state of Ohio in 1905 with his article "Ohio: A Tale of Cities." Here he alleged that Mark Hanna and other traction interests had been running the Republican Party through boss George Cox, a portly saloonkeeper. According to Steffens, Ohio politics was settled with bribery and brawls—revolvers were often a necessary accoutrement in the civic life of the Buckeye State.

Then Steffens traveled to Cleveland, where he met Johnson and transformed him into the national standard for urban governance. For the first time in all his travels, Steffens had found a city with no corruption: Cleveland. He wrote the oft-quoted line, "It seems to me that Tom Johnson is the best mayor of the best-governed city in the United States."[112] Johnson became the hero of all of Steffens's stories, part of the lineage of "great leaders" that descended "from Moses through Jesus to Henry George and Johnson."[113]

Steffens's article broke Republican dominance in Ohio; in 1905 it inspired a wave of anti-boss sentiment that elected the state's first Democratic governor in fifteen years.[114] Johnson's crowd then used its foothold in state government to solidify the Democracy's place in Ohio. Howe was serving in the state senate when a colleague informed him that there was reason to suspect the Republican state treasurer of serious improprieties. The colleague had been unable to raise interest in the charges, but Howe had the Johnson crowd's flare for publicity. As an elected official, he had the constitutional authority to inquire as to where the state's money was held. So the intrepid Howe led a group of reporters to question the treasurer, who replied, "It's none of your damn business, either as a senator or as a citizen where I keep the money or how I run my office." The senate instantly began a probe that found the Republican treasurer and auditor had both deposited state money in the private banks of their associates, where it earned little if any interest. When the auditor was asked why he often did not turn over state money promptly, he replied, "Probably I didn't want to."[115] It would be more than a decade until the once-solidly Republican state elected another Republican governor.

Johnson retained control over the Democratic Party platform, eventually achieving most of the reforms of the once-radical 1903 platform.[116] The state established a two-cent-per-mile fare for steam railroads. Steam railroads saw their taxes skyrocket 300 percent, electric companies 500. New laws intended to reinforce municipal home rule required franchises to be approved by referenda and expanded the mayor's power to construct city works without private contractors.

Free from state control, Johnson realized George's policy of ending public-private contracts with spectacular ramifications for public finance. Under direct public operation the cost per vapor lamp declined from \$28.95 per annum to \$22.34, and the price of garbage collection fell from \$3.24 to \$1.69 per ton. This occurred in tandem with substantial gains for employees: wages for garbagemen grew by 10 to 20 percent, while their workday was reduced from twelve to eight hours. With the acquisition of two small power plants, the price for city lights dropped from \$87.60 per year to \$54.96, producing an estimated annual savings of \$90,000.[117]

The improved fiscal state of Cleveland expanded the city's Democratic base. A city that had once been predominately Republican now reliably elected Democrats, and Johnson became the city's longest-serving mayor. The basis of Johnson's power was a record of public improvements established with progressive taxation. While the state overturned some of Johnson's initial tax reforms, many corporations voluntarily increased their assessments to blunt Johnson's movement. The Electric Illuminating Company, widely understood to be Johnson's next target, volunteered to nearly double its assessment.[118] Assessments on real estate increased by nearly 50 percent, while assessments on personal property remained almost static.[119] One of the mayor's pamphlets highlighted that whereas the city had paved 185 miles of road in its entire history up to Johnson, in eight years Johnson paved 210 miles. When Johnson entered office, the sewer system was 311 miles long; he expanded it by 250 miles. He built twenty bridges and three public bathhouses and acquired 282 acres of new parkland. Cleveland had 893 electric streetlights in 1901. In 1909, it had 1,900.[120] One periodical explained Johnson's mayoralty: "Many students of municipal affairs claim that Cleveland is the best governed city in the United States. It is at this time making wonderful progress and millions and millions of dollars' worth of public improvements are under way. The tax rate is excessively high, but the people have something to show for their taxes."[121]

By April 1908 Cleveland was primed to have the closest thing to a publicly owned streetcar system extant in any major US city. Courts had established an injunction against the completion of Johnson's line, but he had the line constructed under cover of night and then forbade Cleveland's police from enforcing the injunction. Johnson's three-cent Forest City Company was operational and was absorbing Con-Con's lines as their franchises expired. Con-Con agreed to sell it assets. Johnson regarded the new company, the Municipal Traction Company, as a "holding company" reined in systematically to act in the public interest until the state constitution was amended to permit public ownership. The franchise established the three-cent fare, allowed for public purchase of the line, and capped earnings at 6 percent interest based on the original cost of construction. *The Public* advertised the corporation's stocks. The system, run by Johnson's allies, would be barred by law from receiving excessive rates of return—what Johnson would consider monopolistic rents.[122]

It quickly became clear, though, that the public was not as committed to this vision of public interest. In a bid to win support, Con-Con had promised its workers a two-cent raise if its franchise was renewed. Johnson was unwilling to redeem this promise. Former Con-Con employees went on strike and used dynamite to blow up cars. Lincoln Steffens, embodying the movement's skepticism toward unions, complained that "organized labor struck as fiercely as organized capital ever did at municipal ownership." Johnson was confident that the administration would weather the storm, because "we counted, as we always have, upon the general public, the disinterested vote, the people at large."[123] But, because of the strike, the Municipal Traction Company lost $55,000 in its first month and $22,289 in its second. Beset with service problems, more vigorous fare enforcement was established, and some riders, including police and firefighters, were asked to pay streetcar fares for the first time.[124] Georgists saw these policies as prioritizing the community's interest in lower fares over the special interests of workers.

Johnson had pushed for a law that would require franchises to be approved via referendum, but now that policy came back to haunt him. Voters stuck down the franchise for his Municipal Traction Company by a razor-thin margin of 605 votes out of 75,893 cast. Whitlock attributed this to the way Johnson had alienated workers and civil servants. But it also represented a failure of Johnson's political acumen. "One day," Whitlock recalled, Witt "went into the office and found the mayor using a long roller, trying to flatten the strips of tickets which had been found to be too thick to go readily into the fare boxes. In this way the situation got away from him, and I do not think he ever fully appreciated the extent of the dissatisfaction and opposition."[125] George had prepared his supporters for the end to history, in which the triumph of his reforms would create a millennium of progress and obviate social conflict. Johnson, lulled into overconfidence, gave up the struggle, settled into his new role as expert administrator, and failed to see that history was moving on without him.

The failure of Johnson's signature policy undermined his mayoralty. He lost his reelection campaign in 1909.[126] Johnson's defeat was especially disillusioning because the movement placed so much faith in democracy. Whitlock confessed to Steffens that his "faith has drifted just a little from the poll." But then Johnson explained, "The people did right in those two referendum elections; every time the people vote they reach a little higher level of intelligence." Johnson reportedly said, "It doesn't matter what becomes of us or whether we win or lose, the cause is won already and the world is ours. All I ask is to be allowed to go on fighting for that cause . . . until someday I stub my toe and fall into the grave."[127] Steffens concluded that "he puts up a very bold front, but I have the feeling that he has been hurt to his very heart."[128]

Johnson had shown the first signs of illness around the time of the failed franchise referendum. He was still a celebrity, able to proudly watch the progress of his cause. In April 1910 Joseph Fels arranged a dinner in his honor in the British Parliament as the battle for the People's Budget brought George's dream closer to realization than ever before. But, plagued by an intractable stomach ailment, Johnson died on April 10, 1911. Two hundred thousand attended his funeral parade in Cleveland.

William Jennings Bryan acted as a pallbearer at Johnson's funeral and declared that "no man during the past generation has done more effective work for the people than Tom Johnson, and certainly no one has been called upon to pay a heavier price for that labor than he."[129] *The Public* released a seventy-page memorial issue of remembrances from newspapers throughout the nation.[130] A majority in the US House of Representatives voted to memorialize Johnson. Newton Baker organized a drive to establish a monument for him on the mall of the Cleveland Group Plan that Johnson had commissioned for public discourse. The memorial includes several stands for public speakers. Johnson is depicted sitting, copy of *Progress and Poverty* in hand, with the inscription: "Beyond his party and beyond his class / This man forsook the few to serve the mass. . . . And ever with his eye set on the goal / The vision of city with a soul."[131]

Finishing the City on a Hill

Johnson's faith that he was winning the war, even when he was losing his battles, proved true. The same election that cost Johnson the mayoralty established land value taxation in Cleveland. Johnson's representatives in the statehouse passed the Quadrennial Assessment Act in 1909, which returned the appraisal process to local officials. With home rule in taxation, a slate of Johnson's followers was elected to the Quadrennial Assessment Board. They invited W. A. Somers to implement his system of land value taxation. In his autobiography, Howe entitled his chapter about his time on the board "Single-Taxing the City." This was an exaggeration; the board could not, for example, exempt personal property. But real estate taxes were shifted from buildings to land. The total valuation of Cleveland property increased from $200 million to $500 million, with some assessments increasing tenfold.[132] As with so many other Cleveland innovations, Somers's land value assessment spread rapidly throughout American cities.

Despite the failure of the referendum, Johnson's streetcar plans eventually triumphed. In 1910 the courts engineered an agreement whereby the lines would be operated by Johnson's "holding company." From 1911 to 1914, the system charged a three-cent fare. Peter Witt, the fiery labor agitator with a fifth-grade education, now ran the system; he even designed his own streetcar.

At Ohio's constitutional convention in 1912 Johnson's followers had an opportunity to establish the direct, local democracy they idealized. Daniel Kiefer, shortly to become the movement's financier, arranged for Tom Johnson, Brand Whitlock, and others in their group to fill Bigelow's pulpit as he spearheaded a campaign to establish direct legislation in the new constitution.[133] Bigelow presided at the convention as it enacted a home rule amendment designed by the Ohio Municipal League, of which Newton Baker was president. Cities were empowered to design their own charters and granted all powers not explicitly forbidden in the constitution, including the right to own and operate utilities. Another amendment barred the Ohio Supreme Court from holding laws to be unconstitutional if more than one judge dissented. Amendments banning the use of injunctions against striking workers, eliminating the word "white" from the state constitution, abolishing capital punishment, and enfranchising women were approved by the convention but failed on referendum.[134]

The amendment establishing direct legislation embodied a significant new direction for the movement. Rural delegates at the convention recognized that overturning the uniformity clause would make it easier to establish the single tax, so they agreed to it only on the condition that the constitution ban the taxation of land. Bigelow accepted this concession because direct legislation was also included in the compromise and the new referendum system permitted the amendment of the constitution with a simple majority of voters. Thus, direct legislation emerged as a leading priority of the movement because it allowed the people to cut through constitutional restrictions and establish the single tax in one fell swoop.[135]

The greatest vindication of Johnson, however, was the landslide election of his lieutenant. In 1911 Newton Baker, Johnson's city solicitor, was elected mayor with 62 percent of the vote, the largest margin the city had ever granted a candidate. Baker dominated the immigrant vote, winning 100 percent of the German, Czech, and Irish electorate. Baker declared, "This overwhelming victory is a vindication of the ideals and ideas . . . Tom L. Johnson taught us, and I shall do my best to carry out those ideas."[136]

Baker continued the campaign for public ownership by waging war on the local electricity provider. He secured a $2 million bond to expand the Municipal Electric Light and Power plant that Johnson had established to supply power to public facilities. When contractors refused to supply him with machinery, Baker, a master of Johnson's forceful politics, threatened to go to Congress and have their tariff protections removed. The utility reformer Morris Cooke glowingly remembered that "he got his machinery."[137] Baker's victory was historic on two counts: precedents for public power in large cities were few, and it reduced the price of electricity in Cleveland to half what state-level regulatory commissions had established nearly simultaneously. Thus, Baker's victory would become the leading example of a powerful new principle in utilities: the public yardstick.

Baker has been depicted as both a radical and a conservative because he followed the Georgist model of socialized monopoly and free markets. He had little interest in social welfare, and during the economic downturn of 1914, refused to increase assistance for the poor. Yet in 1913 he proposed a Garden City–style suburb in which the city would act as landlord, leasing five hundred houses. Although this plan was thwarted by the lobbying of the Cleveland Real Estate Board, Baker did form a municipal fish sale, ice cream stand, dance hall, and orchestra. These each reflected, for various reasons, public interests; the ice cream stand, for example, was in a public park and therefore entailed locational advantages belonging to the city. These public enterprises, like his electrical system, often functioned as a way for the public to establish what prices would be without monopoly. He quickly discontinued such projects when he was confident that private industry was operating competitively.[138]

While cities throughout the country were drifting toward public ownership, Cleveland was the benchmark. In his landmark study of American utilities, Delos Wilcox wrote that the Cleveland and Chicago campaigns "occupy a field by themselves among American street railway grants. They represent the outcome of long-contested local transit situations whose importance and the intelligence with which they were fought out, made them of nation-wide interest. These franchises represent the high-water mark thus far attained in municipal franchise granting in America."[139] With these two struggles as examples, Wilcox became an outstanding opponent of statewide regulation, favoring instead home rule, municipal ownership, and the single tax. As the chairman of the Committee on Franchises of the National Municipal League, he propagated these views among fellow experts.[140] He was employed to advise and conduct valuations for franchise disputes in Grand Rapids, Detroit, San Francisco, New York, Los Angeles, Newark, St. Louis, and Denver.[141]

Without an experienced cadre of reformers like Cleveland's, streetcar struggles often came to naught. Prior to Johnson's tenure in Cleveland, Hazen Pingree—known as "Potato Patch" Pingree for inviting the poor to farm vacant land in the city—had waged the nation's most prominent traction dispute in Detroit. But in Detroit, Johnson, as a businessman, was bidding for his own franchise. Pingree had privately approached Johnson with his suspicion that his offer was not in the public interest. Johnson was willing to admit the deal was bad but unwilling to explain why. Steffens recounted the confusion that followed: "When the hearing was held, Pingree couldn't make his position very clear; he tried to, hesitated, and then he blurted out that he didn't understand the ordinance, but he pointed at Johnson and he said: 'But I can tell you this. Tom Johnson there told me that if he was in our places he'd see Tom Johnson in hell before he'd grant it.' Everybody looked at Johnson, who laughed heartily. 'Yes I did say that,' he admitted, 'but it is a dirty trick to tell on me.'"[142] Pingree's inability to comprehend the situation had consequences other than a few humorous incidents at his expense. The deal Pingree negotiated was poorly constructed and riddled with inconsistencies. Its principal concession—a three-cent fare during commuting hours—exacerbated congestion.[143]

Johnson's legacy had at least as much to do with its writers and propagandists as its administrators, though there was rarely a clear line between the two. Johnson often trampled on norms to obtain his ends. One obituary remembered that he was "sometimes careless of law and yet kept half his fellow citizens sure that he was an exemplar of justice."[144] The publicity campaigns that kept "half of his fellow citizens" in the dark have come only to dominate our perception of him more with the passage of time. A poll of historians conducted in the 1990s ranked Johnson the second-best American mayor of all time, next only to Fiorello La Guardia.[145] Johnson is remembered so fondly because of a solid contingent of literary supporters who highlighted his successes and drowned out the flood of newspaper criticism. In 1907 Johnson wrote Whitlock that "between you, Fred Howe and Steffens you are immortalizing the memory of this great struggle."[146]

It seems ironic that Johnson's radical democracy would become a template for expert-driven urban reform. However, Progressives often admitted that their doctrine of expertise ran against the grain of popular sentiment. Unsurprisingly, voters were more willing to employ experts when Johnson pitched them as instruments of the public will than when Ely advertised them as autocratic usurpers of democratic power. While many professionals were gratified by the argument that they deserved greater say, many others were inspired by the promise that their work could craft a fuller democracy. This subordination of expertise to public will was thus a useful myth that found some substance in Cleveland's informed and animated public, but also encountered many complications. Johnson's battles sometimes cast doubt on whether the voters were devoted to his ideals and whether his lieutenants stretched the powers of their office beyond custom (and sometimes the law). The administration believed it overreached to secure popular will against powerful, privileged interests, but it fought so consistently for its own stridently ideological vision of a free society that it is hard to imagine it was a pure incarnation of democratic sentiment. The faith that moral sentiments gravitated toward the natural law embodied in *Progress and Poverty* underwrote Johnson's belief that fighting for the single tax and fighting for democracy were one and the same. The movement would grow in coming decades, but so would the tension between its liberal ideals and the public will.

CHAPTER 7

Seeing the Cat

Ideology and Movement Culture

> Until there be correct thought, there cannot be right action; and when
> there is correct thought, right action *will* follow.
>
> Henry George, *Protection or Free Trade* (1886)

James Maguire, democratic candidate for governor of California in 1898, coined one of Georgism's most popular idioms: seeing the cat. The term was derived from a landscape drawing that, viewed from the right perspective, revealed the image of a cat. In his account, Maguire struggled to find the cat, but once he had, it was all he could see. This was a metaphor for the "complete and absolute mental transformation" that he attributed to the single tax. George, he said, had anticipated the impact of his ideas in *Progress and Poverty* when he claimed: "There are pictures which, though looked at again and again, present only a confused labyrinth of lines . . . until once the attention is called to the fact that these things make up a face or a figure. This relation once recognized is always afterwards clear. It is so in this case. In the light of this truth all social facts group themselves in an orderly relation, and the most diverse phenomena are seen to spring from one great principle."[1]

George formulated an all-encompassing belief system in which land tenure explained the rise and fall of civilizations. In a letter to John Reed, Amos Pinchot brushed aside his doctor's diagnosis of arthritis: "It is as easy as pie to cure, especially in the case of a radical who believes in single tax and government ownership of railroads. We can cure anything with those."[2] Pinchot was making a joke at his own expense, but there was truth to the cliché that Georgists believed the single tax could fix anything. William Gorgas, Woodrow Wilson's surgeon general, argued that the single tax would cure disease by reducing poverty, funding hospitals, and filling in vacant lots.[3] Although the term was not current during the period, Georgism fits Hannah Arendt's definition of ideology as "a total explanation for everything."[4]

George hoped this ideology would unite his movement around a shared democratic philosophy. He distrusted organization. To the extent that single taxers were organized, it was in local clubs or front groups, designed to build coalitions around single-issue campaigns. Throughout the world, the movement was characterized by streams of financing, ad hoc pressure groups, local activists, and influence peddlers. George argued that a clearly delineated and comprehensive system of thought could mold individual action into a unified movement better than mass organization. Single taxers did, in fact, develop a surprisingly coherent movement without formal organization. Although a rift opened between Progressive Georgists and adherents to the "single tax limited," Georgism rarely suffered from the disruptive schisms that plagued Marxism. Instead, the movement replicated the same policies around the nation without centralized coordination.[5]

There were, however, institutions and subtle hierarchies that helped flesh out the implications of Georgist philosophy and create a movement culture. Single taxers turned to those who had been closest to George, including Henry George Jr., Louis Post, and Tom Johnson, to mediate disputes and define orthodoxy.[6] The policies of Tom Johnson in Cleveland served as a national model propagated through the movement press, particularly *The Public*. A chain of correspondence between Johnson's group and municipal officials reinforced the role of a cohort of George's close associates as the movement's nerve center.

Louis Post and the Single Tax Press

Louis Freeland Post was born and raised near Hackettstown, New Jersey, descended from Puritans who had followed Thomas Hooker in his rebellion against the state of Massachusetts. Rebellion and the pursuit of a perfect social order were ingrained in Louis's sense of identity.[7] He showed talent as a child and was advanced a grade, though he then struggled and left school at fourteen. Post's father had been a county official ("a chosen freeholder") with the Democratic Party, though he lost his office after bolting to the Republican Party at the beginning of the Civil War.[8] Post, devoted to abolitionism, was too young to enlist in the army, but as a budding printer and writer, he demanded the rebels be punished to the full extent of the law. He would always be cognizant that his middle-class origins allowed him opportunities not afforded to those on whose behalf he fought.[9] In the late 1860s he moved to New York City to study stenography and law. In 1870 Post received an appointment to work as a stenographer and law clerk for South Carolina state senator David Corbin and moved to the South to promote equal opportunity.[10]

Post's fight for the underdog began in the Reconstruction-era South. As a stenographer in prosecutions of the Ku Klux Klan, he recorded more than eight hundred pages of testimony about Klan violence. Concluding that "patriotic fever of a certain type knows no law but that of the savage," Post acquired a lifelong antipathy to ethno-nationalism.[11] He published an account of his experience in South Carolina that challenged the narrative of academic historians in which Reconstruction had failed because Black legislators were inept or corrupt. Instead, he argued that white terrorism overthrew a system of forward-looking multiracial democracy.[12] Post argued in movement periodicals that St. Helena, where plantations were "virtually confiscated" by property taxes, evolved into a model Black community because it was one of the few places were Reconstruction-era land redistribution had been implemented.[13]

But the South refused to be reconstructed, so Post instead tackled the cause of the working class. In 1872 he returned to New York, became active in the Republican Party, and secured a patronage position as assistant US attorney. He quickly realized that the Republican Party had drifted from the idealism of Lincoln, and he left politics to practice law privately. Private employment, though, left unsatisfied his desire to perform work of greater social import. In 1879, one of his clients began to publish a penny daily and Post left the law for journalism. *The Truth*, with its cheap price tag and large circulation, became the leading labor periodical of New York City. Post also became legal counsel for the Central Labor Union (CLU).[14]

It was as a labor writer that Post first learned of George. For an abolitionist, the great struggles of the age seemed to be over, and Post complained to William McCabe, foreman of *The Truth*'s composing room, of the "deadly dearth" of editorial content. McCabe, the Irish Maori New Zealander who would lead the first Labor Day parade, had known George from the printing trade in San Francisco and recommended *Progress and Poverty*. He claimed, presciently, that "there are enough editorial subjects in that book to last you a lifetime."[15] Post was skeptical; what he knew of George suggested that he was "a man no patriotic American would care to know."[16] But Post followed McCabe's advice and was immediately struck by *The Irish Land Question*, including its "commonsense statements, its cogent reasoning, and its attractive diction."[17] George reinvigorated Post's fading reform sentiments: "Always temperamentally sympathetic with human suffering, I saw my field of sympathy expanding. . . . Slavery ceased to be a mere racial institution of our Southern states which Lincoln had abolished. It took on an aspect of economic serfdom which still existed."[18]

Post quickly became one of George's most important lieutenants. He serialized *Progress and Poverty* in *The Truth*, introducing the city's workers to land nationalization. In 1883 Post became president of New York's first

Georgist organization, the American Free Soil Society, whose name evoked the old cause of anti-slavery. The organization evolved out of "bohemian" dinner parties, usually held in an Italian restaurant that served spaghetti by the yard to humans and rats alike.[19] More auspiciously, Post was one of the people George consulted when he struggled with his decision whether to accept the CLU's nomination for mayor in 1886. During the campaign, Post managed the party's periodical, *The Leader*, and later the Georgist periodical *The Standard*. Post quickly emerged as George's most trusted writer.

It is hard to overestimate Post's bond with George, who was both a close friend and an object of veneration. Post called George a "prophet" and observed that "Henry George was soon widely felt to be a man into whose spirit God had breathed a vital economic truth in the realm of love one's neighbor."[20] These attitudes were common; Post noted that when he organized a banquet at Delmonico's for George, Felix Adler objected because, as "the author of a great literary and sociological book," George was above anything as ephemeral as a banquet, as if philosophers need not eat.[21] One would think such reverence could not survive prolonged contact with a flesh-and-blood person, but it did. Post certainly observed George's foibles—he was forgetful of engagements, sloppy in dress, oblivious to convention, and careless about most things he was not deeply invested in—but these faults only confirmed that George lived on a higher plane.

The other leading figure in Louis's life was Alice Thacher. Like Post, Thacher was a Swedenborgian, a member of the transcendentalist-inspired "New Church" that promised communion with God through nature. Beginning in 1889, Thacher served as editor for the aptly named *New Earth*, a Georgist Swedenborgian journal. In 1893, she became Alice Thacher Post. After she married Louis, Alice remained politically active and engaged in Louis's publishing ventures. Louis argued in *Ethical Principles of Marriage and Divorce* that natural law dictated that marriage be an equal partnership readily dissolved when the two parties failed to meld into one. During this age, family served as a bulwark of conservatism, modeling supposedly natural inequalities and justifying the males' rapacious pursuit of wealth as a sacrifice for their loved ones. But Louis imagined marriage not as an iron bond to the past, but an equal and free contract that should be dissolved freely if the partnership failed—an idea that had once languished along the most radical edges of abolitionist and feminist thought.[22]

Six months after George died, Tom Johnson funded the new journal, edited by Louis and Alice Post, *The Public: A Journal of Democracy*. The timing suggests that the publication was meant to serve as a nerve center for the movement after its leader's passing. It was hardly the only single tax paper; there were a multitude of local papers. There was also one national magazine, the *Single Tax Review*, that served as the mouthpiece for the movement's anti-statist wing. However, *The Public* was the undisputed leader of the more politically influential Progressive wing. Post rejected a narrow application of George's philosophy, arguing that "the reform advocated by Henry George is not a substitute for all reforms, as superficial reformers have lightly inferred, but that it is, as Henry George himself declared, the only foundation on which other social reforms can be secure and effective."[23] Based in Chicago, the periodical thrived at the meeting point between eastern railroads, western railroads, and Lake Michigan, a geographical confluence that gave the Windy City a monopoly over much of the commerce of the Midwest. By 1925 Chicago's land values had grown to a level greater than that of all the aggregate farmland in twenty-three states, effectively mirroring the hinterland that its transportation and communication networks dominated.[24] As boosters' dreams of general prosperity gave way to the reality of rising rents, Chicago, like many bourgeoning midwestern cities, proved fertile ground for the single tax.[25]

The Public placed single-tax thought within the broader context of democratic movements. Its title hints at a faith that democracy could embody the interests of the whole people—that conflict existed only because the electorate failed to understand its own unity of interest and ideals. Although it was typically affiliated with the Democratic Party, Post insisted that it was not a party paper but a small-*d* democratic paper, in the tradition of Thomas Jefferson, Abraham Lincoln, and Henry George.[26] In fact, it rarely split with the Democratic Party, except on the issue of race, over which it railed against racist southern Democrats.[27] Throughout its twenty-one-year run, *The Public* took up causes as diverse as anti-imperialism; the commission form of government; initiative, referendum, and recall; scouting; progressive education; price controls for urban transit; government ownership of railways; Zionism; and proportional representation. At various points, it published regular columns on women's suffrage, cooperativism, and the "color line." At a time when academic journals generally ignored the scholarship of W. E. B. Du Bois, *The Public* hailed his seminal book *The Souls of Black Folk*.[28] *The Public* implied that these issues were connected to the single tax and praised people who could "see the cat." The journal described A. B. du Pont—descendant of the physiocrat Pierre du Pont—as "one of the ablest exponents of the Singletax doctrine" because, "as he apprehended it, the philosophy ramified in more diverse directions and to more remote conclusions than the average so-called Singletaxer could dream of."[29]

By treating all social problems as a function of land monopoly, *The Public* sometimes veered into reductionism, perhaps nowhere more severely than on the issue of race: "Those who talk about the black menace or the yellow peril are merely thinking of the possibility of the black or yellow man monopolizing a particular part of the earth and preventing the white man from making a living. Some day we shall learn that the earth is big enough, and that if we will but remove the barriers there are plenty of jobs for all men regardless of color." Nevertheless, *The Public* did not succumb to the pitfall of indifferent waiting for the coming dawn. It continued: "Is there anything to be done until this millennial day of industrial and economic freedom? Yes, much. Men who work in powder mills must learn not to scratch matches. Racial animosities can never be extinguished until the cause is removed. But we can prevent these critical outbreaks which mark our national record."[30] Along these lines, *The Public* editorialized against housing discrimination, which it argued was a conspiracy to create artificial scarcity and exploit African Americans with high rents.[31]

Post's racial egalitarianism was atypical for a period when Progressives gravitated toward hereditarian thinking. Francis A. Walker argued that the solution to poverty was for the state to assume control over the evolutionary process: "We must strain out of the blood of the race more of the taint inherited from a bad and vicious past before we can eliminate poverty, much more pauperism, from our social life . . . a wholesome surgery and cautery must be enforced by the whole power of the state."[32] In some cases state action was not even necessary; Walker argued that African Americans would naturally go extinct due to their racial inferiority.[33] Edward Ross coined the term "race suicide" to describe how Anglo-Saxons were being replaced by inferior new immigrants from Eastern and Western Europe. That term entered the public arena when President Theodore Roosevelt appropriated it in 1902. Even traditional liberals, weary after the sacrifices of the Civil War failed to usher in a better world, adopted biological determinism. The Supreme Court justice Oliver Wendell Holmes Jr. survived a Confederate bullet in the neck and another in the chest to become the era's most emblematic and dyspeptic artifact of the liberalism of yesteryear. Yet even he famously embraced eugenics with the line that "three generations of imbeciles are enough." His opinion in *Buck v. Bell* legitimated the forced sterilization laws adopted by most states.[34]

The Public's repudiation of eugenics embodied the movement's faith that humankind could reach moral perfection through free and equal opportunity. George had once told a Black voter that "if you will notice the men into whose minds these ideas have entered, you will find them rising above all prejudices of nationality, or race, or color, because the bottom principles for which we contend—the whole basis of the theory—is that we are all the equal creatures of a common God."[35] Eugenics was anathema both because of its essentialism and because of the authority it bequeathed to experts. Clarence Darrow remembered that George had come from a poor family and concluded that if eugenicists could "have a political convention to determine the fathers and mothers of the human race, then it is pretty sure that few of the great would be born."[36] The single tax never seems to have obtained any sway among the voting (i.e., white) public of the Deep South, but many expatriates from the Southland set aside ancient prejudices when they embraced George's doctrines. The southerner A. B. du Pont led the charge to move the location of the 1911 Single Tax Conference when the LaSalle Hotel in Chicago insisted on segregating Black and white delegates.[37] Similarly, William Lloyd Garrison II testified on behalf of Tom Johnson: "Born in a slaveholding state and in a family actively identified with the Confederate cause, he has emancipated himself from his early influences and stands unflinchingly for universal rights, regardless of race, sex, color or condition."[38]

Many African Americans, in turn, would be drawn to the movement both because of its racial liberalism and because of landed inequality in the South. The Colored Farmers' Alliance, representing mostly sharecroppers, was the first large, national organization to endorse the single tax.[39] T. Thomas Fortune, one of the leading Black journalists in the nation, advocated the single tax as the solution to Black tenancy and economic oppression.[40] The Harlem Renaissance thinker Hubert Harrison engaged in occasional single tax work. Harrison was a Socialist, but he struggled with the Socialist Party's abdication to what he called "Southernism"—a mixture of socialism and white supremacy—that drove him toward friendlier, single tax groups.[41] W. E. B. Du Bois sometimes discussed George's paradox of progress and poverty and in Chicago spoke under the auspices of the Henry George Lecture Association. Du Bois was unsure whether the single tax would have the effects attributed to it, but recommended George to Black readers because "monopoly of land and its products is the most sinister thing that faces modern industrial progress, the rise of the laboring classes, and the emancipation of the Darker World."[42]

For the single tax movement, the axis along which the question of race was most divisive was not the Mason-Dixon Line but the Continental Divide. Although in later life George emphasized that the Chinese were not "essentially inferior," he continued to oppose Chinese immigration on cultural and economic grounds.[43] In California the movement was led by friends of George from his nativist years who never broke from white nationalism. In their darkest fantasies, white civilization would reject the single tax and collapse, allowing more enlightened nonwhite civilizations to eclipse it.[44] In 1893 James Maguire supported the Geary bill, which required Chinese nationals in the United States to carry a resident permit. William Lloyd Garrison II compared the bill to the Fugitive Slave Act and wrote to George that the movement was in theory and practice hostile to this type of racism: "You minimize the probability of dissension in the Single Tax ranks. Already it is cropping out. The men and women who were drawn to your great truth by its universality and its brotherly love for all mankind are beginning to measure such professions with the defense of such a flagrant contradiction as the Geary Act. . . . I have no hesitation in saying that the majority of single taxers, outside of California, will be a unit in this regard."[45] When James Barry began to push Japanese exclusion in 1902, *The Public* repudiated it as "an unwarranted and unworthy race intolerance."[46] While the single tax had developed from a racialized struggle for California's natural wealth, it was built on a dream of equal opportunity that undermined racial caste.[47]

Initially produced largely by Louis and Alice Post, *The Public* grew into a respectable paper with an impressive cadre of backers. In later years, David Starr Jordan, the first president of Stanford University, served as its foreign affairs expert. Other contributors included the feminist Charlotte Perkins Gilman; Sun Yat-sen, the father of Chinese nationalism; and the novelist Herbert Quick. Even Syngman Rhee, the first president of South Korea, contributed an article. *The Public* cultivated an aura of respectability, advertising endorsements by leaders of public opinion such as William Jennings Bryan, Ray Stannard Baker, Horace Kallen, Thorstein Veblen, and Carrie Chapman Catt.[48]

The Public's circulation grew from a modest 3,500 to 16,000, but its supporters emphasized the quality, not the quantity, of its reading public.[49] William Lloyd Garrison II said of Post: "You teach the teachers, and the good goes broadening down surely if slowly."[50] Looking back, the editor George Knapp contended that *The Public* had "helped to form the men who have formed the liberal thought of America. . . . Its circulation was never large; but its influence could not be measured by that yardstick. It went to editors and editorial writers all over the land."[51] Upon receiving *The Ethics of Democracy,* a compilation based on Post's essays in *The Public,* Mark Twain wrote, "I thank you very much for this book, which I prize for its lucidity, its sanity & its moderation, & because I believe its gospel."[52]

Post consummated the integration of the movement into the Democratic Party by bonding with its "peerless leader" and three-time presidential candidate. William Jennings Bryan cultivated relationships with many single taxers, but few so assiduously as this short, stout editor, with his bushy beard, glasses, and disheveled hair. *The Commoner* advertised Post's paper, and the two exchanged material for publication.[53] Eventually, Bryan came to consider Post "amongst the soundest as well as the most discrete of" his "political advisers."[54]

Bryan sometimes helped advance Post's cause, particularly in the case of municipal home rule. It is doubtful that Bryan shared Post's diagnosis of social problems, but, as a man of democratic principle, he was willing to sweep away constitutional restrictions against the single tax and put the issue before the people.[55] In reference to local option (i.e., municipal home rule), Bryan wrote Post that he was "very glad to endorse the experiment. I believe that a new system should be experimented with before it is generally adopted in order that the theory may be tested by practice and it is entirely in harmony with the idea of local self-government."[56] Shortly thereafter, in February 1902, *The Commoner* published an editorial supporting the right of cities to establish their own tax laws, thereby lending its support to a campaign that had been the focus of local single tax politics after the uniformity clause in Maryland's constitution was used to invalidate land value taxation in Hyattsville.[57] When Bryan was invited in 1906 to recommend items for the constitution of the soon-to-be state of Oklahoma, he suggested the legislature should have the "plenary power" to tax as it wished, including a tax on "the improved or unimproved value" of land, "as experience may prove best."[58] Oklahoma's constitution, ratified in 1907, provided for home rule in taxation.

Post embraced Bryan as a devotee of popular sovereignty, yet Georgists sometimes doubted his liberalism. Certainly Bryan, who denounced Theodore Roosevelt for eating dinner with the Black leader Booker T. Washington, was too closely allied with southern segregationists to embrace natural rights.[59] Frederic C. Howe recalled a night Bryan spent at Tom Johnson's house when the former streetcar magnate confronted the peerless leader with all the loopholes in his regulatory policies. Johnson argued that regulation would fail and that it was only necessary to erase the laws—like private ownership of land—that permitted special privilege to take root. Howe reported that Johnson was unable to break through Bryan's "moralistic armor" or win him over to the "philosophy of freedom."[60] In 1908 Daniel Kiefer wrote Lincoln Steffens that several of their Georgist friends thought Bryan more "fitted to be the pastor in the strictest Methodist church" than president. One of the critics he identified was Clarence Darrow, who would famously defend the First Amendment rights of John Scopes in 1925 opposite Bryan, who as prosecutor sought to enforce the state's ban on teaching evolution in public schools.[61] On the stand, Darrow embarrassed Bryan, who days later went to his grave. It was an ironic conclusion for the former allies, but it was not altogether surprising considering long-standing concerns with Bryan's boundless faith in state action on behalf of Protestant piety.

With its clout in the Democratic Party, *The Public* helped spread Johnson's municipal reforms, particularly in its hometown of Chicago. While *The Public* was distributed nationally, circulars advertising support from Chicago civic leaders suggest that it both aspired to be, and to a degree was, ensconced in the city's municipal politics.[62] Post appears to have taken a particular interest in promoting Cook County circuit court judge Edward Dunne, publishing his speeches on a variety of topics aligned with the single tax ideology, including municipal home rule, property tax evasion, and anti-imperialism. One of these speeches, calling for municipal ownership to eliminate the "rent" of utilities, was given under the auspices of the Henry George Lecture Association.[63]

In 1905 Dunne was elected mayor of Chicago on a platform of public ownership. Clarence Darrow, appointed special traction counsel, served as an intermediary between Dunne, Post, and Johnson, helping to bring insight from Cleveland into Chicago's traction dispute. Dunne's policies so consistently resembled Johnson's that the press often complained that Chicago had become a colony of Cleveland. Ultimately, Chicago, like Cleveland, established a traction line with a cap on return on investment to prevent the company from collecting monopoly rents.[64]

Dunne inserted Post directly into politics with an unusually contentious school board appointment. Dunne's path to the mayoralty had been paved by the Chicago Teachers Federation (CTF), a union that represented mostly Irish Catholic, working-class elementary school teachers. The CTF was organized by Margaret Haley, a radical who had been inspired, if not altogether converted, by George while in college.[65] In 1899 she began an investigation into Chicago's tax records that found utility companies had not paid taxes on their franchise values. She then initiated a lawsuit, with Clarence Darrow and

John Altgeld as legal counsel, demanding utilities be taxed at their full value in order to pay the salaries of teachers who had been denied their full earnings due to municipal shortfalls. It was then–circuit court judge Dunne who rendered a verdict in favor of the CFT. The organization rallied to Dunne's policy of public ownership to ensure that the city received its due and teachers could be paid.[66] Haley secured Post a position on the school board, taking a night train from Chicago to Cleveland to beg Johnson to release Post from his editorial obligations with *The Public*. The school system was rife with graft, so Post and other appointees of Dunne fought for better contracts, including higher rents on property the school board leased to the *Chicago Tribune*.

The Dunne school board's biggest struggle, however, was over the control of knowledge, not finances. William Rainey Harper, president of the University of Chicago, objected to raises for teachers because they already earned "as much as my wife's maid." Harper also led efforts to centralize curriculum design in administration.[67] Haley attacked Harper's vision of a system in which the superintendent "was assumed to be an educator . . . and six thousand teachers in the system merely takers of orders."[68] When Post assumed his position on the school board, he objected to "a despotic business man's education policy that makes marionettes of teachers."[69] In protest, Haley and Post devised a "democratic" teacher promotion plan based on regular evaluations, timed promotions, and continuing education, overturning Haley's system that, they alleged, evaluated teachers "on their loyalty to immediate authority rather than on their loyalty to ethical and educational principle."[70] Middle-class Progressives committed to the ideal of professional expertise were so hostile to the Dunne board's plan that, when Fred Busse unseated Dunne as mayor, he fired Post and other members of the board before their terms expired. Even the Progressive stalwart Jane Addams opted not to protest the purge of her peers from the board. While Post, Haley, and Dunne failed to realize their educational reforms in Chicago, they managed to block a bill that would have tracked many students into a vocational curriculum by the seventh grade.[71]

The battle for democratic education in Chicago represents the Georgist commitment to a liberal pedagogical ideal focused on civic discourse. John Dewey, who labeled Harper's vision of an expert-led school reform in Chicago as "autocracy," traveled to the single tax commune of Fairhope, Alabama, to observe the Marietta Johnson School of Organic Education. In *Schools of Tomorrow* (1915) he reported of Johnson's school that "on the whole, it's the best I've ever seen."[72] Johnson's pedagogical ideal was student-directed inquiry, which she believed was rooted in the Georgist philosophy of her community, because "if sincerity and openness of mind could be preserved in every school by eliminating external standards," it would ameliorate the "inability of the man in the street to recognize the fundamental injustice of our monopolistic economic order."[73] Dewey visited Johnson's school for a series of observational studies. The following year, he published his seminal *Democracy and Education* (1916), which popularized student-centered, progressive education emphasizing civic and ethical learning with practical illustrations that bridged the divide between intellectual and manual labor.[74] It is probable that Dewey, who often praised George's social philosophy, saw his educational doctrines as related to George's democratic philosophy. Certainly, his supporters did; Johnson's Organic School and Dewey's laboratory school were supported by the single tax philanthropists Joseph Fels and William Kent, respectively.[75]

George Creel's Committee of Correspondence

Upon first inspection, the backgrounds of Louis Post and George Creel could not have been more different. Creel was born in Missouri in 1876, at the tail end of Reconstruction. Although Missouri was a border state, Creel had no doubt that it was part of the "solid South." He grew up listening to the yarns of southern "Colonels" and imbibed the region's prejudices. His family's plantation had been graced with the presence of Stonewall Jackson, a distant cousin, and some of Creel's relations had fled south of the border rather than submit to Yankee dominion. Yet it was Creel's very familiarity with the aristocratic ethos that made him such an implacable enemy of it. He noted that his father was "reared as a 'gentleman'" and therefore had "neither training nor industry." After slavery was abolished in Missouri, Creel's father "went back to diligent drinking," and his family fell into poverty while his mother carried the burdens of the household.[76] Confronted with the visible disdain of his son, Henry Clay Creel occasionally threatened to take a job as a day laborer. When George, who could not comprehend the enslaver's disdain for work, responded that this sounded like a capital idea, the family descended into maelstroms of recrimination.

By the time he reached adulthood, Creel was pure ambition. He ran away from home at fifteen and traveled around the state, working odd jobs at county fairs.[77] At twenty he hit it big writing for the *Kansas City World*. Creel felt lucky. Although he had a remarkable literary talent cultivated by his mother's readings in the classics, Creel had never started high school. He seized the job with "demoniac energy," but the opportunity fizzled after he was assigned to the society section.[78] When reporting on grand parties, he "hoofed it with the best at every dance" and "sat down at tables with never a thought that I might be unwelcome."[79] He sulked out of town in embarrassment after realizing that high society had not, in fact, welcomed such familiarity from a proletarian reporter. These concerns about respectability stuck. In later years he joined San Francisco's elite Bohemian Club and wore fashionable suits with glittering tie studs. Yet he was deeply self-consciousness about his broad, slightly misshapen nose, his short stature, and his self-conscious predisposition to speak through his teeth.[80]

Creel was driven by the desire to be his own boss. He started over in New York City, where his lack of credentials barred him from serious journalism. Instead, he made a try at the comics section, but struggled there too. A night spent on a park bench outside Madison Square lit a fire under Creel. The next day he sold a few jokes and began a career as a comic writer. But he soon grew impatient because at the ripe old age of twenty-two, he was still the "cheapest sort of hack."[81] In New York's literary circles, he befriended the poet Arthur Grissom, who had recently married—to the great consternation of her parents—the daughter of Kansas City's richest banker. In 1899 Creel moved back to Kansas City to start *The Independent* with Grissom, his father-in-law providing the financing. However, Grissom's marriage quickly dissolved, no other investors were recruited, and Grissom abandoned the venture, leaving Creel the paper's sole proprietor. Without capital, Creel took on the task of writing and publishing *The Independent* almost single-handedly. On the side, the pugnacious publisher slugged it out as an amateur boxer. Creel's journey from poverty to independent proprietorship was reminiscent of Henry George's story and embodied the lives of many of his followers, who prized social mobility and identified Georgism with equal opportunity.

As with Post, Creel's conversion would come in the search for ideas to inform his writing. Upon assuming ownership of *The Independent*, he concluded that he needed to find "the right gospel . . . to be a true guide."[82] He had heard of Marx in New York City and so made an investigation of *Das Kapital* but was appalled by the "hate of achievement, hate of the competitive struggle, hate of demonstrated superiorities."[83] In contrast, he thought the single tax was "heaven" because it would "end the monstrous injustice of having individuals appropriate the wealth created by the community."[84]

Creel did not reference the single tax as much as one would expect from a "guiding philosophy." This was characteristic of the movement. As a minority faith with strong adherents and equally strong opponents, Georgism was often referred to obliquely through coded language about "natural resources" and "special privilege."[85] J. J. Pastoriza, elected mayor of Houston in 1917, complained: "Later on I saw clearly that we Singletaxers acted as though we were really afraid that we might get the Singletax, so we kept on giving it to our auditors in sugar-coated doses, as though we were ashamed of the philosophy which we had espoused."[86] Antonio Bastida, a Cuban American financier active in the New York Single Tax Club since George's first mayoral campaign, criticized single taxers for embracing accommodationism to integrate themselves into mainstream politics. In "Emasculated Single-Tax or Common Property in Land," Bastida asked, "Are Single Taxers known as abolitionists of property in land? Does the Democratic Party reward confessed abolitionists of private property in land with appointments and nominations?"[87] Brand Whitlock once observed that Georgists were "the most opportunistic of reformers."[88]

As a recent convert to Georgism, Creel wrote to the movement's leaders to better catch the image of the cat. Tom Johnson, Newton Baker, Frederic Howe, Sam Jones, Brand Whitlock, Ben Lindsey, Francis Heney, and William U'Ren helped flesh out orthodox policy and thought through epistolary exchange that Creel compared to Jefferson's Committee of Correspondence.[89] In these letters, movement leaders defined less obvious implications of their ideas. Creel, for example, had, in his duties as editor, taken a keen interest in the problem of prostitution, which was rampant in cities. He had no clue how to solve the problem. So he wrote to Brand Whitlock, who supplied a long, detailed response, "dismissing punitive laws and the police as a cure" and instead arguing for gender equality and sex education.[90] This reflected the movement's libertarian bent, as well as its focus on popular edification. When Creel returned to the issue of prostitution, it would be as an advocate for public ownership of collective farms on which former prostitutes could support themselves. At a meeting of the People's Institute at Cooper Union, he explained: "The condition caused by commercialized vice, is not a moral question, but purely an economic one. It is due to housing conditions, tenements, and low wages. And that gets us back to the big fight, the fight against involuntary poverty, and then you get back to the single tax."[91]

Creel, though, misapprehended the scope and character of this "committee of correspondence." Maybe at some point he would be considered part of the inner circle, but odds were good that the Ohio crowd saw him not as a core participant but as only one of many spokes emanating out of Cleveland. Johnson and Whitlock received a constant stream of letters asking for advice on urban questions.[92] Some of these letters came from Georgists closely aligned with the Cleveland crowd, and others from elected officials who merely saw Cleveland and Toledo as models for municipal governance. While the Ohio reformers provided some guidance to Creel, they were intimately involved in traction disputes in Chicago and Springfield, Illinois.[93] Thus, the *Kansas City Star* claimed that "Cleveland shared Tom Johnson with all its sister municipalities. Not another city entered a franchise fight or planned an extension of activity for the general well-being . . . that it did not receive help and inspiration from Cleveland's public servant."[94]

Creel stood out most in this committee of correspondence when he briefly provided institutional structure. Creel was inspired by the itinerant and idiosyncratic Charles Ferguson, a lawyer, minister, and journalist who had worked his way into Johnson's orbit in Cleveland. With a "rich, powerful voice" that "had as many stops as an organ pipe," and given to mystical discursions on Augustine, Ambrose, and Innocent, Ferguson successfully pitched wild schemes to Creel and later to Woodrow Wilson.[95] To Creel, he preached the gospel of the "University Militant," a vaguely etched vision of an educational institution that would turn the academy's objectivity and disinterestedness on its head by welding intellectual inquiry to practical social change. Creel was both enthralled and baffled by Ferguson, whose idea of founding a university in the remote desert West seemed impractical. Instead, with his associate Frank P. Walsh, Creel worked to build a "Municipal University" that published educational material about urban reform.[96] He drew on his "committee of correspondence" for articles that would guide urban reformers around the nation. The backbench stuff they submitted had been rejected elsewhere, suggesting that most contributors were less enthusiastic than Creel. While Ferguson pushed Creel to ignore the "triviality" of the news business and emphasize the advancement of "the sciences and the humanities," the average newspaper reader in Kansas City preferred the simple and sensational style of the magazine of public exposure.[97] With Creel's bank account overdrawn, the Municipal University suspended operation in March 1908 after just four months.

Chastened, Creel left Missouri again, resolving to relocate to Denver to work with the boyish, mustachioed reformer Ben Lindsey. Creel's ticket to Denver was a job working with the *Denver Post*, a frankly mercenary paper. One of its proprietors explained how he got his start as a bartender: "There were no cash registers in those days and I tossed up the dollars as they rolled in. If they stuck to the ceiling, the house got 'em."[98] Lindsey was skeptical of the *Post* bringing in a new, big-name writer, who he assumed would begin a new campaign against him. Lindsey contacted Brand Whitlock, and once again Creel's committee of correspondence came to the rescue. Whitlock testified on behalf of Creel; Lindsey met with Creel and wrote back that Creel was "a magnificent fellow. He certainly 'sees the cat.'"[99]

Ben Lindsey was known around the country as the reformer who had conceived of the juvenile court. Built on the premise that children should be rehabilitated rather than punished, he ran his court like a social worker, seeking to discover why children had been drawn into crime.[100] When the young Franklin Roosevelt received a letter from Lindsey, the future president glowed that it "really means a great deal to me" and that Lindsey "had real influence on younger men" entering politics.[101] Lindsey's faith in rehabilitation stemmed in part from the fact that he believed the real crime—the one that was at the root of all the others—was the private ownership of land. To the evangelist Billy Sunday he wrote: "If you could only point out a little more definitely the fundamental causes of poverty and injustice and therefore one of the chief causes of sin, you would perhaps be doing in this world one of the greatest works since Christ came to earth. I wish you would read *Social Problems* and *Progress and Poverty* by Henry George."[102] This attitude, which had also inspired the criminal justice reforms in Cleveland, was widespread in the movement. In 1913 Clarence Darrow explained to a group of prisoners in Chicago: "The only way in the world to abolish crime and criminals is to abolish the big ones and the little ones together. . . . Abolish the right of private ownership of land, abolish monopoly, make the world partners in production."[103]

Creel would be at the forefront of dispensing justice to these "big" criminals. As an editorial writer at a series of large newspapers, he led campaigns to establish the referendum and initiative in Colorado. With his encouragement, the electorate voted in favor of a publicly owned water utility, but eleven Democratic legislators held up development. Creel accused them of graft and called for their lynching. One of the legislators Creel had threatened sued him for libel. In the trial the intrepid newsman took the stand and gave stump speeches against his accuser. Creel's lawyer, trying to moderate his client's behavior, asked if he had used "rope" metaphorically when referencing the lynching of corrupt legislators. In response, Creel yelled "No! The hemp! The hemp!"[104] Creel was acquitted, and in 1912 a wave of reform sentiment in Colorado carried the "citizens ticket" into office. Creel became police commissioner.

In his controversial six-month stint as police commissioner, Creel instituted a host of reforms. Citing Cleveland and Toledo as precedents, he took batons away from police officers and established public farms for the rehabilitation of petty criminals and prostitutes.[105] The anvil of justice, he argued, should instead fall on those who owned the property on which prostitution occurred.[106] He fired police officers whom he accused of ballot stuffing. Creel broke from the convention of arresting anarchist speakers and ordered police not to harass members of the Industrial Workers of the World. When an officer disobeyed, Creel pressed charges against him and personally bailed the anarchist out of jail.[107]

Although many of Creel's policies as police commissioner were derivative of the Ohio Georgists, he had one major innovation: the nation's first female cop. Josephine Roche, a Columbia-trained sociologist, delighted in the challenge to gender norms her appointment posed, though in practice she was more like a modern social worker, using counseling to reach Denver's prostitutes and wayward youths.[108] Creel's decision to hire Roche reflected his views on gender. Shortly before appointing Roche, Creel married the actress Blanche Bates, who announced to the press her surprise that her husband had no interest in her being an "old-fashioned" wife, instead encouraging her to continue her stage career.[109]

Creel credited his support for women's suffrage to his mother and her herculean efforts to provide for and manage the household. However, his views also fit into the broader contours of a movement with a deep faith in democratic equality.[110] Some Georgists were slow to make the connection but did so easily when prompted. Tom Johnson claimed never to have thought about women's rights until Marie Howe, wife of Frederic, asked, "You who are so democratic in everything else, why are you not democratic about women?" Within a matter of weeks, Johnson became one of the first leaders in Ohio's Democratic Party to support women's suffrage.[111] George Peabody served as the principal financial backer and president of the Men's League, which normalized male support for suffrage during the Progressive era.[112] Elizabeth "Lizzie" Magie became famous in 1906 when she took out a newspaper ad sarcastically selling herself to a hypothetical suitor as a "young woman American slave." This not-so-subtle critique of traditional marriage earned her years of hate mail for her aspiration to be a "self-sustaining" working-woman.[113] Magie because most famous within the movement for inventing *The Landlord's Game*, which demonstrated how the progress of the community under a system of private ownership would slowly concentrate wealth into the hands of a few people. Ultimately, Parker Brothers would appropriate the concept for the boardgame *Monopoly*.

What made Roche's appointment unusual for the movement was that a woman had assumed a prominent outward-facing role. Women such as Alice Thacher Post, Carrie Chapman Catt, Mary Fels, and Anna George were important within the movement, but they were never part of the hero's gallery that fought the great battles.[114] Politics at the time was a space in which women were rarely allowed, and when they were, it was because they leveraged their gendered roles as moral authorities on topics such as charity and the prosecution of vice.[115] These were not topics that resonated with Georgism, and when female Georgists like Magie appropriated themes of producerism, the reading public was scandalized by the proposition that women should be independent. The brief law enforcement careers of Creel and Roche in Denver speak to the limits of female political participation. James Barry complained that women in the movement "not only 'miss all the joy of battle.' But oftimes they bear the brunt of it. Do you think I could have published the *Star* so long without the aid and sympathy of my wife? No, indeed. Yet, *I* receive *all* the credit."[116]

The democratic character of the reforms Creel and Post fought for was not inherent to urban Progressivism. The general trend throughout the nation was in the opposite direction, as traditional elites expressed skepticism about the fitness of the working class to participate in democracy. By 1912 voter turnout dropped by 15 to 20 percent in northern and midwestern states. Reformers overturned laws allowing noncitizens to vote while establishing tighter registration and voting requirements. Often, democracy was dispensed with altogether, as elected officials were replaced with appointed experts. Expertise served as a thinly veiled rationale to empower the traditional Anglo-American elite as it lost the numerical heft to win elections.[117] More democratic Progressives such as Jane Addams believed the immigrant working class could acquire the skills of citizenship under the tutelage of the native-born elite. Far to the left of all these were Georgists, who believed that the average landlord or franchise holder committed greater crimes than the petty larcenists who filled the prisons. By merely providing equal opportunity, the lowliest in society could outstrip the highest in education and prosperity.

Movement Culture

Although Post and Creel had disparate backgrounds, their stories converged at the twilight of the Progressive era. Both served in the administration of

Woodrow Wilson. Both were called before Congress to answer charges of subversion even as they helped organize a war to make the world safe for democracy. Post was ruined by the experience; Creel would have better days ahead but hit many bumps on the front end, including slander charges, boycotts, unemployment, and financial ruin. Georgists often paid a heavy price for their beliefs. When the Oregon reformer William U'Ren began campaigning for the single tax, he lost so many clients that he could not cover office expenses at his law firm. Many former clients bluntly declared that they would not come back while U'Ren was "working for Singletax."[118] It is no accident that two of the most outspoken Georgists—George Peabody and Tom Johnson—were also so wealthy that they never needed to worry about their finances.

Why did men like Creel, who were fueled by ambition and lacked family fortunes to fall back on, devote all their energy to careers that were as likely to ruin as to make them? U'Ren explained that his sacrifices were justified because the single tax gave him "ideas and ideals worth living for, writing and fighting for." He noted that Tom Johnson "got very full dividends for the money and the life he put into the work he loved. . . . From the banker's standpoint he died on the red-ink side of the ledger, but he didn't think so."[119] James Barry diverted thousands of dollars a year from his printing business to fund *The Star*, was imprisoned by the Supreme Court of California for contempt of court, and spent $12,000 fighting legal challenges, bringing his business to the brink of collapse. Still, Barry felt that he had "gotten all back, with dividends regularly paid and interest compounded."[120] Herbert Quick said of his faith, "It changed my whole life. It was a barrier to advancement to the best places in my profession of the law, but it made my life richer in every other respect."[121] *The Public* asked, "What is it that leads men to brave the scorn, the hate, the persecution of mankind?" It answered: "The servants of Truth are paid by the knowledge of the Truth, for them alone is it given to know the good from the bad, the right way from the wrong."[122]

This need for a philosophy was palatable in fin de siècle America. The Civil War had impressed upon Americans the importance of great causes, but social and scientific developments had left Americans bereft of many of their traditional commitments. Darwin threw religious doctrine into question. Industrialization and corporatization undermined the independence of labor. Urbanization precipitated the decline of self-contained communities with their stable value systems. Railroads and telegraphs reduced the cultural isolation and uniformity of small-town America. Middle-class affluence made struggle superfluous for a significant segment of the population.[123] The single tax provided Americans with something to believe in. William James famously argued that Americans needed a "moral equivalent of war" to rectify the lack of purpose that had brought many, including himself, to psychological break-downs.[124] Speaking to the Single Tax Club of Chicago, Clarence Darrow hit on a similar theme: "I have always believed in peace, in a way, but there is something worse than war—peace without purpose is worse than war, for it releases the petty and small and insignificant in man. . . . Men and nations must have an inspiration to live. Henry George had it. . . . We can learn from Henry George . . . that one must have a meaning, one must devote himself to some-thing, or he cannot live."[125] Along similar lines, Herbert Bigelow noted that the single tax had given him "purpose in life" by giving him something "capable of immediate and progressive application" yet rooted in "loftiest patriotism and the purest religion."[126] The single tax subsumed traditional faiths in republi-canism and Christianity and imbued the normal course of political change with a sense of progress toward the millennium.

There is another shared thread in the stories of Post and Creel: they were both writers. In the *Atlantic Monthly*, Alvin Johnson observed of Georgists that "their strength is especially great in that wing of the middle class which is active in molding public opinion, the 'intellectuals.' . . . It is this fact of an exceptionally influential personnel that chiefly lends political importance to the movement."[127] A large percentage of single-taxers were aspiring literati or devoted students of literature. Brand Whitlock was a novelist even while he served as mayor of Toledo. Henry George Jr., Stoughton Cooley, Daniel Car-ter Beard, Frederic C. Howe, and George Creel all wrote fiction.[128] Mark Twain's *A Connecticut Yankee in King Arthur's Court* drew parallels between feudalism and modern industrial capitalism and featured illustrations drawn by the Georgist Daniel Beard that labeled the Knights of the Round Table "absorber[s] of unearned increment."[129] Because of this cultural clout, ele-ments of single tax philosophy, like the critique of landed property implicit in the board game *Monopoly*, were embedded in popular culture.

The way that Georgists wrote says a great deal not only about how they influenced opinion but also how they related to truth. They were uniformly proponents of realist literature, and through Hamlin Garland, James A. Herne, Edwin Markham, George Inness, and William Marion Reedy served as the backbone of the realist movement in America.[130] Realists purported to il-lustrate social truths through fiction and sometimes claimed that all they wrote was based on fact. This was encouraged by George himself, who wrote Herne to praise him for the way his play *Shore Acres* told a "wider truth" by allowing "things not seen to be felt."[131] While the social injustices that realist fiction depicted were generally factual, these were woven together with a connective tissue of narrative that was fabricated to provide the story with structure. These liberties represented a faith that there were normative, emotional, and social truths that could better be conveyed through fiction than through empirical description. Needless to say, academic progressives did not embrace fiction as a truer form of truth and generally kept to a style that ensured they breathed a rarified air, unsullied by the general public. But the idea that facts obtained significance only when they were sharpened into weapons had its own pitfalls. This sentiment is likely why one single taxer—George Creel—would be labeled the "chief evangelist of American propaganda" after World War I.[132]

When *Progress and Poverty* turned twenty-five in 1904, some 250 notables assembled in New York to celebrate. The list of attendees included many predictable names: Louis F. Post, Henry George Jr., William Lloyd Garrison II, Hamlin Garland (who served as toastmaster), and Daniel Beard. Congressman John De Witt Warner was there, as were the poet Edwin Markham, a young Samuel Seabury, Norman Hapgood, Lincoln Steffens, Ida Tarbell, and P. F. Collier. George Bernard Shaw sent a letter. Oswald Garrison Villard, editor of *The Nation*, declined the opportunity to participate but reassured George Jr. that he "hope[d] the time will come when I can publicly record my affection of your father's many public" works.[133] The keynote speaker was William Jennings Bryan.

In his speech, Bryan spoke little of George, eschewing the predictable encomium. Bryan began:

> The greatest day of my life was that day a little over a year ago which I spent with Tolstoy. There were two Americans of whom he spoke to me. The son of the one of them sits here at my right, the son of the other at my left [Henry George Jr. and William Lloyd Garrison II]. He spoke in the highest terms of Henry George and endorsed his economic theories. He showed me something he was reading, a preface to the life of the older Garrison. It is interesting tonight for me to meet here for the first time the poet whose words have touched the consciences of so many. It is a notable thing that there should be at this board the son of Henry George, the son of William Lloyd Garrison, and Edwin Markham.[134]

Rather than single out the author of *Progress and Poverty*, Bryan focused on the people in the room. George's movement, not George, was the object of his praise. It was alive, it was known around the world, and even the voice of the Democratic Party could be awed by it. The title of Bryan's speech was "Equal Opportunity." He did not endorse the single tax, but he made it evident that he shared Georgists' faith in a level playing field. The movement was more than one man, and more than one tax; it was a broad, encompassing philosophy of democratic equality that was a major force in the United States and—as Bryan's conversation with the Russian author Tolstoy suggested—throughout much of the world.

CHAPTER 8

The Good Ship Earth

The Global Single Tax

> It is a well provisioned ship, this on which we sail through space. If the bread and beef below decks seem to grow scarce, we but open the hatch and there is a new supply, of which before we never dreamed. And very great command over the services of others comes to those who as the hatches are opened are permitted to say, "This is mine!"
>
> Henry George, *Progress and Poverty* (1879)

The significance Henry George ascribed to land has often been seen as an idiosyncratically American artifact of the Jeffersonian ideal barely clinging to life as the site of social conflict transitioned inevitably to the factory floor.[1] The single tax movement, however, was global and so consistently populated by nonconformist, urban artisans that it is hard not to conclude that it was a type of class ideology. Where and how it manifested usually reflected substantive concerns about rent and the power of landed property as industrialization concentrated population in dense areas with high rents or drew labor out to remote encampments where the employer exercised social control. In Denmark small farmers supported land value taxation, but in general, landowning farmers were stalwart opponents of Georgism.

Interest in George's ideas was often more pronounced abroad than it was at home. His reimaging of British liberalism resonated in the United Kingdom. Some commentators, in fact, saw George as only a particularly charismatic agitator for John Stuart Mill's philosophy. Liberalism was a transnational ideology, so these arguments had cachet around the world, particularly in developing nations where the single tax was seen as a route toward modern liberal nationalism that bypassed the inequalities industrialization had engendered. George's appeal to Judaism was also remarkably persuasive. In contrast, his anemic following among American tillers of the soil speaks to the ways his Jeffersonian republicanism was strained by repositioning the city as the seat of civic virtue. While *Progress and Poverty* echoed Jeffersonian themes about wealth inequality undermining democracy, his plan to abolish landed property turned Jefferson's hope for universal land ownership on its head. This urban republicanism would be influential within the movement, but among the reading public it tended to confuse George's ideas with agrarianism, without ingratiating him to agrarians.

The single tax movement was transnational. Throughout the world, Georgists were conscious of one another, exchanged ideas, and often worked on intertwined campaigns. This transnationalism reflected a rootedness in cosmopolitan cities, immigrant communities, and itinerant businessmen. In the world of the single tax movement, New York City was closer to Dublin than to Poughkeepsie. These exchanges would sharpen the movement's internationalist and anti-colonial sentiments and shape its response to the coming world war. Although George began his career allied with anti-Chinese nativists, single taxers, embracing the inclusive implications of their natural law philosophy, welcomed China as its most promising prospect.

In this transnational exchange, American Georgists acquired ideas and credibility. In the United States the war between George and the academy persisted, but in much of the world his ideas were more amenable to the intelligentsia. Most theoretical innovations to Georgist philosophy had international roots. Furthermore, demonstrations of land value taxation abroad gave the movement valuable evidence to legitimate its arguments.

The People's Budget and the Global Renaissance of the Single Tax

In 1872 the British Parliament commissioned a study of the ownership of landed property known as the Return of the Owners of Land. The results showed that a mere seven thousand families controlled 80 percent of Great Britain's land.[2] In 1897 the British economist J. A. Hobson noted that England was primed to accept George's message, both because of this unusual concentration of landed wealth and because of "the phenomenally rapid growth of industrial towns, with their close concentration of working population."[3] Hobson dismissed George as an original thinker, noting that the "English science of Political Economy . . . from John Locke to J. S. Mill, may be regarded as continually engaged in undermining the ideas of justice and social utility attaching to private property in land."[4] George was a persuasive agitator who "cooperated with the spirit of the age," though he had "exercised a more directly powerful and formative educative influence over British radicalism of the last fifteen years than any other man."[5]

In turn-of-the-century England, a "New Liberalism" developed that questioned the free market, using George's concept of socially created value as a bridge to tie plans for expansive economic reform to classical liberalism. Hobson observed, "The slow education which the land question has conducted upon the nature of monopoly and socially created values, was bound in time to bear fruit in a growing recognition of similar elements of monopoly and social values inherent … throughout the industrial system where competition is impeded or estopped."[6] British New Liberals and Fabian socialists saw socially created "rents" and "unearned increments" wherever scarcity existed—even in the wages of individuals with exceptional skills.[7] For Fabians, this attack on returns from finite factors was at the heart of a critique of property rights, an assault reconciled with the philosophy of Smith and Mill through George's argument that society, rather than the individual landholder, deserved the rents it created. Therefore, the New Liberalism and Fabianism did not, according to Hobson, involve "any violent breach of continuity with liberal traditions."[8]

Hobson's account reinforces the idea that Georgism was not just a tax but also a philosophy embedded within the worldview of a certain class. He noted that many Englishmen did not share all of George's views but "are disciples of Henry George because they regard unqualified private ownership of land to be the most obviously unjust and burdensome feature in our present social economy."[9] In their class and religious views the average British Georgist was like their American counterpart: they were generally urban, upwardly mobile, skilled laborers. J. A. Hobson wrote that in every city where he lectured, he encountered "a certain little knot of men of the lower-middle or upper-working class, men of grit and character, largely self-educated, keen citizens, mostly nonconformists in religion, to whom Land Nationalization, taxation of unearned increment, or other radical reforms of land tenure, are doctrines resting upon a plain moral sanction. These free-trading Radical dissenters regard common ownership of and equal access to the land as a 'natural right,' essential to individual freedom."[10] Hobson describes a comprehensive Georgist identity, similar to that which prevailed in the United States: self-educated, civically engaged workers, religious nonconformists, liberal free traders, individualists, and adherents of natural law doctrine.

The British land tax movement grew through the first decade of the twentieth century. As in the United States, the single tax movement in Britain had focused on securing the right of municipalities to enact land value taxation. The Glasgow City Council, the London County Council, and 516 other municipal or rating authorities petitioned Parliament for the power to tax land values or, as they were often called in England, "site values" to emphasize the importance of location.[11] The movement was strongest in Scotland. In 1907 and 1908, the House of Commons passed the Land Values Taxation Bill, granting Scotland the right to assess land values.[12] On both occasions the bill was vetoed by the House of Lords, dominated by the landed aristocracy.

In 1909 land value taxation took center stage in one of English history's greatest political struggles. That year the Liberal chancellor of the exchequer, David Lloyd George, used popular support for land value taxation to engineer a battle to undermine the House of Lords. He introduced a budget that included higher taxes on income and luxuries, as well as three types of land taxes: a tax on the "unearned increment" when property was transferred, a tax on existing land values, and a tax on mineral extraction. Henry George Jr. praised the last of these as a reassertion of control over "national resources."[13] David Lloyd George claimed that these taxes were required to support the nation's recently enacted old age pensions and could fund new unemployment and health insurance programs.

This "People's Budget" embodied a web of overlapping questions about finance, political power, and taxation. Land value taxation was at the very heart of this conflict, but not for the obvious reason. David Lloyd George grew up poor in rural Scotland and came to loathe the landowning peerage. He had supported site value taxation throughout his career, though he was never a principled or consistent statesman.[14] He would sometimes brag that he had inserted site value taxation in the budget primarily to entrap the House of Lords.[15] If so, it worked. The House of Lords, largely composed of the landed aristocracy, would never tolerate the taxation of their estates. Defying precedent, they vetoed the budget and precipitated a constitutional crisis. The taxation of land, the welfare state, and the rights of the majority had all fused into a single confrontation.

The progress of the People's Budget was watched with fascination around the world as New Liberalism's high tide. Samuel Gompers, who traveled to England to witness the struggle, convinced the American Federation of Labor to endorse it.[16] The American journalist William Allen White reported during his visit that a quarter of a million "laboring men, merchants, and professional men" marched for the People's Budget in "the greatest political meeting ever held in Hyde Park."[17] Marchers, who included the whole of the British Liberal government, sang the "Land Song," with lines such as "Why should we beg for work and let the landlords take the best? Make them pay their taxes for the land, we'll risk the rest! The land was meant for the people."

The People's Budget did not propose the single tax exactly, but the Liberal Party's understanding of land was closer to George than to Mill. Lloyd George argued that the value of land was created by the community, a view that reflected the distinctly Georgist theory of social value.[18] Winston Churchill was a young liberal lion at the time—he would return to the Conservative Party after World War I—and, serving as one of Lloyd George's closest allies, made a series of rousing speeches on the "People's Land." *The Public* was ecstatic to report that Churchill told a Scottish crowd: "It is quite true that land monopoly is not the only monopoly which exists, but it is by far the greatest of monopolies. It is a perpetual monopoly, and it is the mother of all other forms of monopoly."[19] Smith, Ricardo, and Mill had considered land a monopoly, but Churchill took these ideas much further, adopting the decidedly Georgist principle that the landlord reaped the whole value of all social progress. In one speech, republished in *The People's Rights* (1909), he told the story of a toll along the Thames at which most of the working people in the neighborhood paid six pence a week for their daily commute. Recognizing an injustice, the toll was removed and "within a very short period from that time the rents on the south side of the river were found to have advanced by about 6d. a week, or the amount of the toll which had been remitted."[20]

Everyone understood that the People's Budget was fought on Georgist terms. John Stuart Mill had argued that justice permitted the taxation only of the "unearned increment"—increases in land value—but the People's Budget followed George's principle of taxing the full value of land. Whereas British liberals had thought of land rent mostly in terms of agricultural capacity, the People's Budget targeted the value of urban land and natural resources. Thus, the Tory prime minister Arthur Balfour denounced the People's Budget: "If this is not . . . the precise principles of Henry George, I do not know the meaning of the English language."[21] The Georgist Joseph Fels provided much of the funding for the Liberal Party during the conflict. At the Hyde Park rally, William Allen White was amazed to see the whole of the Liberal cabinet and most of the Parliament marching under slogans he recognized from Kansas single taxers. He concluded that "it is a long jump from Jerry Simpson to Lloyd George, Lord Chancellor of the Exchequer, but progress seems to have made it in 'two jumps.'"[22]

Lloyd George disappointed single taxers in the end, though he accomplished far more than they realized. The People's Budget culminated in the Parliament Act of 1911, which reduced the power of the House of Lords. It also instituted new progressive taxes that financed the emerging welfare state. Some land taxes were included in the law, but before a national assessment could be completed, the United Kingdom was engulfed in World War I and Lloyd George suspended the process indefinitely. For an otherwise pivotal moment in British history, the conclusion of the fight for land taxation seems anticlimactic, but only if our vision is narrowed to this small island in the North Atlantic. The People's Budget lived on past 1911 and caught fire around the globe. Land value taxation obtained a new prominence in global political discourse. It failed in England, only to conquer large swaths of the world.

In Canada, land value taxation had seen steady progress. By the early teens, land value taxation was taking root in western Canada. The development of profitable extractive industries had fostered a Georgist labor movement in which the Knights of Labor played a prominent role. Land value taxation promised to affect idle timberlands so that owners would sell their property and workers could afford to become independent producers.[23] Before the People's Budget, British Columbia, Saskatchewan, and Alberta had enacted laws that required municipalities to tax land at a higher rate than improvements. Under these laws, municipalities retained the discretion to increase the percentage of the tax levied on land. The newly formed town of Edmonton had, without fanfare, shifted the whole value of property taxes from buildings to land.[24]

Then the People's Budget brought international attention to the question of land value taxation, and it took off in a dramatic way. In 1910, as the battle in the United Kingdom was fought, the mayor of Vancouver, Louis D. Taylor, led the effort to remove all taxes on improvements, and Vancouver became North America's first major "single tax city" in that its real property tax assessed only land (other taxes survived). Western Canada was developing rapidly, and urban leaders believed land value taxation would draw settlers from rival municipalities.[25] Promising that the single tax would spur densification, Taylor claimed that "under the Single Tax, as it is operated in Vancouver, a new sky line is being built up for the city."[26] He disseminated statistics purporting to demonstrate that land value taxation had caused Vancouver to grow more rapidly and densely than such neighboring cities as Seattle. British Columbians who attended provincial hearings generally accepted the public's right to unearned increases in land values as a fundamental moral principle. Even many farmers who believed it would injure them personally testified that it was unjust for the benefits of the region's rapid development to accrue to those who did nothing to develop it.[27]

It was no accident that Vancouver became a "single tax city" during the fight over the People's Budget. Mayor Taylor was an urban booster who recognized his moment. He bragged that "the city awoke one morning and found itself famous," capitalizing on international interest in the reform. Municipal officials around the world wrote Taylor asking for information about the experiment. Taylor was especially eager to report in his newspaper, *The World,* when an associate of David Lloyd George promised to visit and report back to the chancellor of the exchequer.[28] One of the British Empire's youngest cities was now a model for the metropole. Taylor's boosterism suggests that this was the point.

The example of Vancouver was felt around the world, but particularly in western Canada. Statistics suggesting that land value taxation had caused Vancouver to boom convinced municipalities that as they vied to be the great metropoles of the future, land value taxation was necessary for competitive advantage. Although George was often discussed in British Columbia, and usually positively, the idea lost its political character in the scramble for growth. Victoria voted by a margin of eight to one in favor of land value taxation.[29] By 1914, approximately two-thirds of cities in British Columbia, all cities in Alberta, and one-fourth in Saskatchewan placed the burden of property taxes exclusively on land values.[30]

Similarly, land value taxation had gradually spread across Australia and New Zealand in the years before the People's Budget.[31] In Australia the movement was first promoted in the 1880s by John Farrell. Before Farrell became a writer for the *Bulletin,* he had been a small farmer, miner, timber cutter, and brewer. He shared with other Australian single taxers a penchant for eccentric dress, often combining elements of elite, bohemian, and working-class attire to protest class norms. Georgism developed a large following among the nation's unorthodox clergy and lay preachers. Australians resented the leasing of crown land to wealthy pastoralists. Most wanted to open more land for peasant proprietors and so, often against the protests of strict Georgists, established land taxes with exemptions on individual homesteads that have persisted into the twenty-first century.[32] In New Zealand a land value tax had first been instituted in 1878, the year before *Progress and Poverty* was published, though it was quickly overturned. George's influence revitalized the movement to tax land, and it gained newfound strength in cities, leading to the establishment of a progressive land tax in 1891.[33]

In 1910, just as Vancouver was becoming a "single tax city" in the wake of the People's Budget, Australia established a national graduated land value tax. Billy Hughes, former president of the Balmain Single Tax League and future prime minister of Australia, campaigned that year on land value taxation. Hughes pointed to Lloyd George as evidence of a global war on land monopoly.

Australians established a tax that closely followed precedents in New Zealand, where the land value taxation had been hailed for splitting up large estates and allowing small proprietors to take advantage of the booming wool market. Opposition to the land tax would also be transnational; British financers campaigned against it, arguing that capital would flee the country, but Prime Minister Andrew Fisher pointed to Australia's prosperity in the wake of the new land tax to rebut these claims. Fisher's Labor Party government went still further in 1911 when it commissioned a new capital city, Canberra, where all land was owned and leased by the government. A Georgist architect from Chicago, Walter Burley Griffin, was awarded the commission to design the city.[34]

Interest in land value taxation after the People's Budget would not be confined to the English-speaking world. In 1910 Germany passed a national increment tax on the rising value of land.[35] That year the Bund für Bodenreform (Organization for Land Reform) claimed 640,000 members behind its Georgist platform, though most members belonged only to affiliated industrial and municipal organizations that endorsed the Bund's program. As was common with Georgism, it was a coalition of variegated interests instead of a disciplined mass organization.

Although the Bund für Bodenreform won its largest national victory on the heels of the People's Budget, the group had deep roots in Germany. It won its first victory in Germany's Chinese colony, Jiaozhou There, the commanding admiral and Chinese commissary, von Diedrichs and Dr. Shrameir, respectively, instituted a tax of 33.33 percent on the unearned increment of land. Georgists credited land value taxation with the progress of Jiaozhou from the thirty-seventh- to the seventh-busiest port in China. The example proved persuasive and, by 1908, 113 German cities and communes had enacted laws that shifted taxes onto land.[36] The Bund also exploited ancient laws against the privatization of land to establish public ownership of urban property.[37]

Special circumstances made farmers in Denmark unusually receptive to land value taxation. Beginning in the 1660s, the government's revenue system had relied upon a tax on potential agricultural yield, a sort of primitive land value taxation. These taxes were revoked in 1903, sparking a backlash among farmers whose intensive methods were suited to the traditional tax. Whereas US farmers were notorious for acquiring more land than they could manage in hopes of a speculative rise, Danish farmers worked small plots of land intensively. A tax that would free up land for purchase spoke more powerfully to them than fears of paying taxes on their small plots.[38] Between 1902 and 1909 the Georgist lawyer Sophus Berthelsen secured endorsements for land value taxation from the country's three major agricultural associations, arguing that land value taxation would modernize the traditional tax on agricultural yield.[39]

Denmark took its first steps toward land value taxation in the wake of the People's Budget. In 1911 the government appropriated funds for a national assessment of land values.[40] Georgists left the Radical Party in 1919 to form their own party, the Retsforbundet (Justice Party). A year later, the government began to establish land value taxation. Beginning with a tax rate of one and a half per thousand of the capital value of land in 1922, the tax was increased again in 1926, 1933, and 1937. According to the chief of the Danish Land Valuation Department, the tables used to ascertain values were "very similar to that used in several American cities," apparently a reference to the Somers system for assessing land values that Tom Johnson had popularized.[41] While the Georgist Justice Party was always a minor party, it secured power as part of a coalition with the liberals and socialists. As late as 1952, the Liberal prime minister Erick Eriksen spoke at a Georgist conference, sharing the stage with Agnes George De Mille, granddaughter of Henry. A segment of the conference, even then, was devoted to remembering the People's Budget.[42]

The first charismatic leader from the Global South to embrace George was José Martí, who helped inspire the fight for Cuban independence from Spain. Martí compared *Progress and Poverty* to the Bible and wrote: "George's book was a revelation not only to the working man, but to the thinker. Only Darwin in the natural sciences has left on our world a mark comparable to that of George in the social sciences."[43] Marti, who lived in New York during George's 1886 mayoral campaign, had been close enough to catch the flavor of the movement and to observe the power that it exerted on its members. "Such fervor," he wrote, "has never been seen outside of religious movements. Even in physical attributes these men seemed to be endowed with superhuman strength. They never became hoarse from talking. They needed no sleep. They forged ahead as if they had discovered in themselves a new being."[44]

Martí exemplified anti-colonial leaders drawn to George; he aspired to bring the liberal values of personal freedom, democracy, and social mobility to his country but hoped to bypass the inequality that had followed industrialization. When Martí moved to the United States in 1880, he marveled that "at last I am in a country where everyone looks like his own master."[45] Yet, while watching George's 1886 campaign, Martí concluded, "With liberties, as with privileges, it follows that they prosper together or are endangered." George led "the downtrodden for purposes of helping them and mitigating the physical and spiritual servitude in which they live."[46] George's dream of extending liberal freedom from the political to the economic sphere was especially attractive to someone like Martí, for whom the absence of freedom was a lived reality.

In colonized nations, the single tax was often associated with liberal modernizers. The great Chinese leader Sun Yat-sen had cut off his braid, moved to the cosmopolitan city of Hong Kong, converted to Christianity, adopted Western attire, and traveled throughout Europe and North America. During his travels, Sun read about the European nationalist revolutions of the nineteenth century, important precedents in his struggle against the archaic Chinese monarchy. Sun also, however, believed that these liberal revolutions had ushered in an economic system disadvantageous to the common people. Sun became a Georgist and befriended Henry George Jr. on his travels through the United States.[47]

Land value taxation was particularly appealing to Sun because it united modern liberal sentiments with Chinese tradition. China had historically taxed land. Sun wanted to modernize this tradition.[48] The ancient tax used three rates reflecting agricultural fertility. Sun argued for a system that, in accordance with George's ideas, captured the value of urban land: "Taxes ought to be levied according the value, not the area of land. For land varies much more than in the ratio of these three degrees. I don't know by how much the land in Nanking differs in value from land on the Bund in Shanghai, but if you rate it according to this old method of three degrees you cannot assess it justly."[49]

The exiled leader was vindicated in 1911 when his supporters succeeded in overthrowing the monarchy. On January 1, 1912, Sun returned to China and announced the birth of the Chinese Republic. He pronounced three pillars for China: democracy, national independence, and *"minsheng,"* translated as the "People's livelihood." He explained in an interview that day: "I intend to devote my future to the promotion of the welfare of the Chinese people as a people. The teachings of your single-taxer, Henry George, will be the basis of our program of reform. . . . We will embrace all the teachings of Henry George and will include the ownership by the national government of all natural monopolies."[50]

For a glimmering moment in 1912, it appeared as if one of the great nations of the world was on the verge of establishing George's utopia. In fact, Sun Yat-sen's control was fleeting, but it nevertheless roused the movement's transnationalist impulses. The Scottish Land League sent a letter congratulating Sun, who returned a kind letter of support to the Scots. The American Zionist Joseph Fels then forwarded the exchange to the Vancouver mayor, Louis D. Taylor. Taylor then published the exchange in *The World* to demonstrate the global support for his reforms. By then the exchange had traveled across the world, encompassing citizens of four nations, most of whom were on intimate terms with one another.[51] Although these hopes would be dashed when Sun lost control of China, they would not go unrealized. When nationalist forces fled to Taiwan in 1949, they established land value taxation as a constitutional principle to prove that they, rather than the mainland Communists, were Sun's true heirs.

In Latin America, Sun's story was paralleled by that of José Batlle y Ordóñez of Uruguay. Urbanization and liberalization were again crucial to Georgism in that country, where nearly a third of the population lived in the capital city of Montevideo. Uruguay had also been home to a fifty-year civil war dating back to the height of liberal nationalism in Europe. The Italian hero Giuseppe Garibaldi had even fought alongside the nation's liberals in the 1840s. In 1904, Batlle finally led Uruguay's liberal Colorado Party to victory. He was elected president in 1911 and stood on a platform that included both expansive social welfare programs and land value taxation.[52] *The Public* attributed the movement's salience to the urban character of the nation, noting that "nowhere in the world is the cost of living so high as in Montevideo."[53]

Georgists celebrated the progress of their idea in Latin America. By the 1910s, *The Public* was publishing a stream of optimistic news about the region. Writers pointed to municipal land taxes in Brazil. The mayor of Nictheroy, Brazil, purportedly demanded that his municipality implement "the doctrine of the singletax of Henry George." In Argentina, *The Public* observed, members of the Liberal and Radical parties in the country's parliament fought successfully for a national investigation of land value taxation. In Costa Rica the president had announced that the single tax "excites our sincere enthusiasm."[54] The *Joseph Fels Fund Bulletin* noted that Paraguay had established a graduated land value tax with heavy penalties on unused land.[55]

The single tax even won support in a diasporic nation. In *Moses/The Crime of Poverty*, Henry George had argued that the biblical Jubilee, in which land was redistributed every fifty years, illustrated that private property in land was contrary to Mosaic Law. This argument held wide sway among Jews on both sides of the Atlantic. The German academic Franz Oppenheimer, one of the principal architects of the kibbutzim, swayed many European Zionists with George's argument, including Theodor Herzl. On the other side of the

Atlantic, the leading American Reform rabbi Stephen Wise counted his boyhood trip to listen to George one of his "very precious memories."[56] By 1918 Wise had become active in New York City movements to establish land value taxation. He naturally carried these ideas over to his Zionist commitments. Speaking as the president of the American Zionist Organization in 1918, he urged his coreligionists: "What a great thing it would be . . . if the ideal which goes back to the Mosaic commonwealth, which was revived by a man of prophetic genius, Henry George, and again by that man and real Jew, Joseph Fels, should at last find fulfillment in the Jewish Land."[57]

The American Zionist Organization followed Wise's advice and issued a statement supporting the common ownership of land at its annual conference in Pittsburgh. Louis Post was commissioned to write a pamphlet about the application of Henry George's ideas to the Holy Land.[58] With this endorsement, Bernard A. Rosenblatt, president of the American Zion Commonwealth, went to the London Inter-allied Zionist Conference a year later, in 1919, and convinced it to endorse land value taxation.[59] When Israel was established in 1948, common ownership of the land became the second of the Basic Laws.

Land nationalization in Israel reflected both belief and economic necessity. Scholars have argued that nationalization was closely intertwined with colonization; if the land remained in the possession of Palestinians, the immigration of Jews would only make the landholding Palestinian population wealthier and more powerful.[60] This is confirmed by Rosenblatt's account of the 1919 London conference, where one leading figure told him that he disagreed with the single tax but voted for it because it was "an economic expedient for the restoration of Palestine as the Jewish Homeland."[61] Ironically, *The Public* and the most devoted single tax Zionists—Joseph and Mary Fels—were far less keen to use the single tax to undermine Palestinian land claims, arguing that Palestinians should keep their land and decide for themselves whether to embrace land value taxation in an emerging multiethnic state.[62] Georgists would sometimes bend their principles to establish the single tax, but in this case their commitment to national independence remained strong.

Global Ideology, Global Consciousness

Bertrand Russell demonstrates the intellectual heft George carried outside the United States. Russell was a founder of modern analytic philosophy and a Georgist until World War I. Russell's key insight was that philosophical discourse had run around in circles because terms were never clearly defined.

Russell used mathematical symbology to avoid words that had multiple or indefinite meanings. He appreciated George, with his clear and rigorous diction, likely because he avoided the slippery language that Russell's symbology was meant to eliminate. Conversely, he criticized Marx, who had inherited German idealism's penchant for making profound points with terms whose explanatory power was predicated on their imprecision. Russell protested, for instance, that Marx had never defined or consistently used the term "rent." Marx had "refuse[d] to regard rent as an independent category," separate from capital, because doing so might undermine the argument that capital was the source of inequality.[63] In fact, Marx fully understood the dilemma rent posed to his ideas; in his early works he had tried to write it out of existence, predicting land would lose value with time because it was static, whereas industrial capital was growing rapidly. That argument, however, held only if rarer things fetched a lower value than abundant things.[64]

Another British intellectual, the economist J. A. Hobson, helped Georgists define the relationship between land and imperialism. In most respects, Hobson's economic theory was nearer to Mill's than to George's. But Hobson's most memorable contribution closely resembled George's theory of industrial depressions; according to Hobson, economic downturns were the result of rent redistributing wealth away from productive enterprise.[65] Hobson was arguably the most prominent advocate for an "underconsumption" theory of economic downturns until the 1930s. In his *Imperialism* (1902), Hobson applied this theory to foreign affairs, arguing that elites looked to conquered territories as an outlet for surplus goods. The solution to imperialism was "a sound system of taxation." A tax on "unearned increments of land values" would "strike at the very root of the malady" that caused imperialism.[66] Within a year of *Imperialism*'s publication, Tulane professor James Dillard introduced readers of *The Public* to Hobson's theory.[67] It would have grand, historic consequences outside the movement; mirroring Hobson, Vladimir Lenin developed his own underconsumption thesis for imperialism. By replacing "rent" with "surplus value," Marxist anti-colonialism was born.[68]

Working at the intersection of land, imperialism, and the state, Franz Oppenheimer had a particularly long and improbable impact on American thought. Chair of sociology at Goethe University, Oppenheimer was a German intellectual remembered as the inspiration for Israeli kibbutzim. For Americans, his principal contribution was *Der Staat* (1908), a book heavily advertised in *The Public*, which published the English translation. The book offered a Georgist answer to the Marxist theory of the state. Like Friedrich Engels, Oppenheimer defined the "state" in opposition to "government" as an oppressive institution designed to exert the will of a ruling class. Engels argued that the state emerged with the development of capital and that, prior to private property, decisions had been reached through consensus, as among the tribal Iroquois. This consensual model was "government."[69] Where Oppenheimer differed from Engels was in pointing out that nomadic herders had exhibited great disparities in wealth, but these were constantly changing and never reinforced through political power. Thus, the birth of capital did not inaugurate the state. Instead, Oppenheimer argued that the state emerged when imperial powers conquered their neighbors and established land claims that required the organized application of violence to protect their economic power. Oppenheimer then traced how the state had developed throughout history to protect landed property acquired through conquest, with the implication that after the abolition of landed property a community of interest centered on freedom would emerge that would usher in the abolition of the "state" and the rebirth of "government." This theory was foundational to Albert Jay Nock's *Our Enemy, the State* (1935), a seminal tract for American libertarianism.[70]

Surveying the progress of Georgism around the world, single taxers adopted a global perspective. In 1913 Herbert Quick, a novelist famous for his stories about Iowa farmers, wrote *The Good Ship Earth* (1913), a Georgist interpretation of world affairs. Quick presented evidence that global warming and the exhaustion of natural resources would force the migration of peoples. The result would be either an ever-expanding series of international conflicts or a concerted decision by the people of the world to treat the earth as common property. Quick called for a "United States of the World" to manage resources and negotiate accord. Though burdened with some racial stereotypes, Quick's book repudiated the imperialist's notion that it was the "white man's burden" to civilize other peoples because "good government, to be worth anything, must be won through the evolution of popular government."[71] Quick's vision of liberal international order evoked the coming of Wilsonian internationalism; Wilson, in fact, appointed Quick to the Federal Farm Loan Bureau after the book's publication.

Whereas Progressive economists stressed citizens' obligations to the nation, Georgists deemphasized nationality because they perceived individuals as subject not to collective, particularistic norms but to universalist natural law.[72]

When *The Public* opined against splitting Eastern Europe into ethno-national states, it explained: "We believe, not so much in concentration and segregation, but in the efficacy of the liberal melting pot. We believe, not so much in the liberation of groups as in the liberation of individuals."[73] The single tax movement was, reflecting its urban character, filled with immigrants from the Irish and Jewish diasporas as well as international businessmen like Joseph Fels and Max Hirsch.[74] Single taxers found their sense of community less in the nation than in the city, which they believed had a collective right to the values it created. Thus, it was natural that Tom Johnson's lieutenant Newton Baker would both lead the movement for the internationalist League of Nations and coin the term "civitism" to promote identification with one's city.[75]

Violent anti-colonialism, however, would encounter crosswinds within the movement because of the influence of the Russian novelist Leo Tolstoy. Tolstoy, himself an aristocrat, understood the power inherent in landed property. Since he espoused a mechanistic theory of history, as evidenced in his masterpiece *War and Peace*, he was doubtless drawn to the way George explained historical development as a function of landed proprietorship. Tolstoy contributed to Georgist thought an extreme philosophy of nonresistance that bordered on anarchism. In *Resurrection* he told the story of an aristocrat who became concerned with the fate of a poor prostitute, converted to Georgism, and distributed his land to the peasants.[76] Tolstoy argued that the criminal justice system was an oppressive relic of inequality and that the single tax would lay the foundation for a society in which nonviolence reigned.[77] This idea influenced Georgist legal reformers such as Clarence Darrow and Brand Whitlock, who called this repudiation of state violence the "golden rule." It would also feed into a broader philosophy of nonviolence; Mohandas K. Gandhi, who corresponded with Tolstoy, was inspired by the Russian author.[78]

These transnational currents intersected in surprisingly dense ways before World War I. George Creel watched these trends of nonviolence and anti-colonialism square off in his hometown of Denver. There Lincoln Steffens had passed through, preaching the Tolstoyan doctrine of nonviolence and gathering converts among Creel's associates. But Creel pointed them to the example of Sun Yat-sen, who had been in Denver about a month prior. Creel had asked Sun how he managed to convince his people to abandon nonviolence; the Chinese leader responded, "because they came to see the truth that evil had to be fought."[79] While the United States was struggling with whether to enter World War I, *The Public* published a speech by Sun Yat-sen's son, Sun Fo, to California single taxers. Sun Fo demanded that they embrace "struggle between democracy and autocracy."[80] By then, *The Public* was closely tied to Woodrow Wilson. After the United States entered the war, more Georgists, including Creel, joined his administration to lead the war on colonialism and German "autocracy."

CHAPTER 9

Justice, Not Charity

The Fels Fund and the Implementation
of Land Value Taxation

> I do not believe in charities. They are agents of pauperization. Neither am
> I a philanthropist. . . . Carnegie, Rockefeller, Morgan and other captains of
> industry are robbers and their millions are ill-gotten gains. . . . I admit that
> I, too, have robbed the public and I am still doing it, but I propose to spend
> the accursed money in wiping out the system by which I made it.
>
> Joseph Fels (1910)

Daniel Kiefer was a businessman in Cincinnati's textile industry in the 1890s with little interest in politics. In 1896 he joined the Republican Party to stop the election of William Jennings Bryan. However, his conservatism began to crack when President William McKinley ordered the US occupation of the Philippines, precipitating a brutal war to assert American imperial power. Then, he found the single tax. A portly man with short-cropped hair and a goatee, he became a vegetarian, in line with a movement that, on questions like vivisection, periodically extended its creed of natural rights to the animal kingdom.[1] Kiefer quickly emerged as the movement's most energetic organizer and fund raiser. In Cincinnati he found Herbert Bigelow's single tax Vine Street Church in poor financial condition and organized the Bigelow Press Bureau, which placed the church on a sound financial footing by syndicating Bigelow's sermons in more than two hundred periodicals. In 1907 he ran a fund-raising drive that saved *The Public* from bankruptcy. Kiefer's stridency made him effective in seeking donations. He once wrote Whitlock about reactionary Cincinnati businessmen, "I am looking for a good sized French Revolution to hoist some of this same number off the earth," adding that he would personally pick up "torch and guillotine" to see the job through.[2] With this zeal, Kiefer would test the single tax commitment to democracy and lay bare the tension between its strict strand of liberalism and the messy democratic process.[3]

Kiefer made his most important pitch near the end of 1908 when he traveled to the single tax colony of Fairhope, Alabama, to meet Joseph Fels. Fels had been born in Virginia and then made a fortune in Philadelphia after he met the inventor of a new laundry soap in 1893 and signed onto a partnership, managing the finance and marketing of Fels-Naphtha Soap. The soap made Fels a fortune, which he used to sponsor single tax projects like the Fairhope community and farming on vacant lots in Philadelphia and London, the two cities in which Fels split his time. A devout Jew, he was active in the Zionist cause as well and believed that George had proven in *Moses/The Crime of Poverty* that land nationalization was a tenet of the faith. When Fels and Kiefer met in Fairhope, Johnson had recently lost the traction referendum in Cleveland and the movement needed direction. Following Kiefer's urging, in 1909 Fels offered $25,000 a year to support local tax reform in the United States. He also offered £5,000 a year to the faithful in England, Canada, Wales, New Zealand, Switzerland, and Denmark. He promised to match all other contributions. Fels assumed a passive role in the organization, which Kiefer ran.[4]

In many ways the Fels Fund Commission was a profoundly democratic organization. It provided the public with an enormous quantity of educational literature on taxation and served as the primary impetus for the adoption of direct legislation in many states. In providing funds directly to a handful of capable individuals to spearhead state campaigns, it institutionalized the Georgist preoccupation with charismatic leaders who could carry the people behind them. That approach failed, however. Land value taxation did spread across US cities during the 1910s, but that proliferation was, ironically, due to the following it obtained among administrative experts. The implementation of land value taxation was usually quiet, if not secret. By the end of the decade, Kiefer acknowledged that educating the public had been less effective than chicanery. Democracy had failed to sustain the liberal ideal.

The Resurgence of Land Value Taxation

The events of the People's Budget and its aftermath piqued Americans' interest in land value taxation. In 1909 *The Public*'s circulation nearly doubled. The *San Francisco Chronicle* had always been hostile to the single tax, but it now reported positively on the German Increment Tax.[5] The professoriate would never be doctrinairely Georgist, but a growing circle of economists, including Irving Fisher, H. J. Davenport, T. N. Carver, John Commons, Frank Graham, and Arthur Hadley, acknowledged that land was a uniquely efficient and just source of public revenue.[6]

The People's Budget sometimes fed directly into new municipal battles for land value taxation. The Boston press followed it closely, probably because it intersected with the question of Irish home rule, important to the city's large diasporic community.[7] In 1911 John F. Fitzgerald, Boston's first Irish-Catholic mayor (also grandfather of the nation's first Irish Catholic president, John F. Kennedy) asked the city finance commission to investigate a tax on the "unearned increment."[8] The commission refused, arguing that filling the city's coffers would advance "state socialism." Even so, Henry George Jr. took a victory lap, giving a speech at Oxford Hall in which he applauded Fitzgerald's effort.[9] In his inaugural address in 1912, Fitzgerald again called on the legislature to investigate the "single tax," citing land value taxation in England and Germany as well as the progress of the Somers system in US municipalities.[10] Subsequently, Fitzgerald was invited to speak at the annual Fels Fund convention, where he "made concrete applications of single tax principles . . . pointedly and forcibly."[11]

There were glaring structural problems with the general property tax—and particularly the tax on personal property—that opened an opportunity for local tax reform. The International Tax Association concluded: "That the general property tax has broken down in administration may be regarded as an established fact."[12] From 1910 to 1911 Albert Jay Nock published a series on the general property tax in the muckraking periodical *American Magazine*. The tax, according to Nock, had become absurd: "Indiana begins by asking the citizen how much money he has on hand and ends by asking how many female dogs he owns or harbors." The idea that citizens would accurately report their personal property was ludicrous: "This plan might work admirably in a community of just men made perfect, but in the United States it does not work at all."[13] Nock told the story of retired farmers saddled with taxes higher than their actual earnings. He contrasted their plight with that of the wealthy magnate August Belmont, who was able to evade $40,000 in taxes by deeding his property (in name only) to the Rothschild family.[14] The rich had a litany of legal devices to avoid taxes; what they did pay, Nock argued, was a voluntary contribution to preserve the illusion of good citizenship. Nock's critique of the property tax was persuasive because he was now able to point to a practical alternative. He concluded his series with articles discussing the success of land value taxation in Canada, particularly highlighting the boom in urban construction in Vancouver.[15]

In the United States, the Somers system emerged as an important mechanism for spreading land value taxation. The Somers system became more sophisticated with practice, but the crux of its design was a series of mathematical models that predicted the average variation in land values within a block according to its proximity to roads and other improvements. This allowed assessors to take data from the sale of underimproved lots and rapidly extrapolate the land values of adjacent properties.[16] Somers joined the Manufacturers' Appraisal Company, with which municipalities contracted for land value assessments. Although business was initially slow, when Johnson's ally Dunne came to power in Chicago, the Windy City contracted him. Then, in 1909, the system was established in Cleveland. Frederic Howe and Newton Baker lent their reputations to it. Baker claimed that with more equitable assessments the base rate of property taxation in Cleveland was cut in half.[17]

After its adoption in Cleveland, the Somers system spread rapidly. In the following two years Somers was contracted by Columbus, Denver, three Illinois towns, and Philadelphia, though the courts blocked implementation in the City of Brotherly Love.[18] All told, between 1910 and 1926, seventy cities contracted with the Manufacturers' Appraisal Company for assessments, including Milwaukee, Buffalo, Savannah, Baltimore, Phoenix, and Newark. Some of these implemented land value taxation in part or in whole, while others used it to improve existing assessments.

The Somers system made land value taxation a reality in municipal governance, but its success had little to do with popular enthusiasm for the single tax. While some Georgists invited Somers to town, officials seem not to have understood the connection in most instances. Somers was hired in Baltimore because he offered a realistic method for updating outdated assessments without costly in-person visits to every property. Newspaper reporters were rarely able to describe the system other than to say that it was a "scientific" method of assessment designed by an "expert."[19] As land value taxation became a question of value-neutral expertise, real estate interests requested presentations on the system.[20] Cities were eager to obtain professional assistance with their broken tax systems, but the Somers system's spread was often halted once locals understood its radical origins. After J. J. Pastoriza led a fight for the single tax in Houston under the mantle of the Somers system, municipalities throughout the Southwest began to look askance at it.[21]

Single tax assessors throughout the country increased assessments on land without amending the law. When in 1900 the Chicago Single Tax Club had proposed endorsing assessors who would implement the single tax unilaterally, many members, including Louis Post, resigned in protest of this undemocratic abuse of power. However, this faith in democratic tax reform was at odds with the reality of US taxation. Assessors were subject to little, if any, supervision, and even courts refused to exercise their powers of judicial review over assessments unless it could be proven that they had intentionally violated the law. Where single tax legislation was passed, assessors could, and did, simply decide to ignore it.[22] Eventually, even Louis Post accepted the fact that local tax reform was a question of administrative rather than legislative policy and embraced assessors who campaigned on implementing the single tax.[23]

The nation's leading Georgist assessor was Lawson Purdy of New York City. Purdy had been treasurer of the New York Bank Note Company before he converted to the single tax. He then gave up his top-tier finance job to become a soapbox orator around Madison Square. When Thomas Shearman began his fight for municipal home rule in taxation, Purdy joined as secretary of the New York Tax Reform Association. The picture of a genteel expert, he was, in the estimation of *American Magazine*, "distinguished by every charm of culture and urbanity," and "his advice is so much in demand that he is really a national figure."[24] Purdy served as president of both the National Municipal League and National Tax Association, helping to mold assessment methods around the nation. Robert Murray Haig, no fan of the single tax, conceded that Purdy was "the acknowledged authority" in property taxation.[25]

Before becoming New York City's assessor, Purdy had used his position with the New York Tax Reform Association to lobby for legislation that would increase tax revenue. In 1889 he drafted a law that served as the test case for taxing franchise values.[26] Then Purdy rallied support from the Chamber of Commerce for a local option bill. In 1903 he secured passage of a bill requiring the assessment of land and improvements separately. In the following year, tax revenue in New York City increased by 42 percent to $1.5 billion. The assessments on properties across from Central Park increased by nearly 100 percent, whereas in Brooklyn assessments increased by only 27 percent. Encouraging assessors to consider site value had shifted the burden toward fashionable neighborhoods.[27]

In 1906 Purdy was appointed president of New York City's Department of Taxes and Assessment and, in that position, further increased taxes on land. For more than a decade he served as the chief architect of the city's property tax regime. Arguing that assessments on land values had not been fully equalized with those on improvements, he increased the tax rolls by $900 million in 1911. Critics claimed that he was overvaluing land, but he had substantial support, including, ironically, from real estate interests. Many realtors supported his heavy assessments because they funded new transit options that increased the value of their properties. Thus, even those who bore the brunt of Purdy's taxes embraced them as a perpetual growth engine in which higher taxes, land values, and improvements would feed off one another.[28]

Throughout the country, single-tax assessors placed heavier burdens on land. Purdy's separate assessments were instituted in at least thirteen states.[29] Tax assessors from Los Angeles wrote to *The Public* that they had increased the tax on land by 40 percent while decreasing the tax on improvements by 10 percent. In Vermillion, South Dakota, assessor August Peterson doubled the rate on land while decreasing the rate on improvements and personal property. It is unclear whether these assessments were actually "equalizing" valuations or if they were illegally shifting the tax burden onto land. The *New York Times* publicized accusations that a Georgist assessor in Bayonne, New Jersey, instituted the single tax when he raised assessments by as much as 10 percent on International Tin Company. In Piedmont, California, Mayor Hugh Craig, a single tax assessor, more than tripled local taxes on land to $7.2 million during his first year in office. He held the tax on improvements steady at $1.2 million.[30]

Growing support for land value taxation among assessors seems to have been common enough to register nationally. Robert Murray Haig believed the undervaluation of improvements was a ubiquitous, though largely invisible, phenomenon: "It is impossible to enumerate the municipalities which undervalue buildings as compared with land without the sanction of law. Such undervaluation is very common both in Canada and the United States. Usually it is accomplished merely by the informal action of the assessor and the fact not extensively advertised because of its illegality."[31] In 1902 real estate and personal property were assessed at nearly the same rate relative to their actual value: 38 and 31 percent, respectively. By 1922, assessors valued real property on average at nearly twice the rate of personal property: 46 and 24 percent, respectively.[32]

The final instrument Georgists used to increase the tax burden on land was the special assessment, a staple of municipal finance. In special assessments, construction was funded with taxes on property that was directly benefited by the improvement.[33] From 1902 to 1932 the percentage of bonded indebtedness of districts with special assessments relative to total municipal debt increased from 0.3 percent to 9 percent.[34] Much of this increase was practical; debt limits made it difficult to fund major public projects without special assessments. But many urban experts also advocated special assessments to capture the unearned increment that accrued to property because of public works.[35] In his first five years as mayor, Tom Johnson increased revenue from special assessments by an average of 46 percent compared to the preceding five years.[36] Fred Kern, the Georgist mayor of the small, predominately German town of Belleville, Illinois, followed a similar policy. Using special assessments, in 1903 he added twenty miles of paved road and thirty miles of sewer. Before, the city had only about a mile of each.[37]

The flip side of revenue was spending, and Georgists won votes with the urban social services and improvements they financed. Particularly significant was the case of George L. Record. Record was a charismatic, though slightly eccentric, public figure.[38] His hand was mangled during a childhood industrial accident. Yet he worked his way through college to become a successful lawyer. His life in politics began in 1901 when he approached Jersey City mayor Mark Fagan with the case for the single tax. Fagan appointed Record Jersey City's corporation counsel. The city conducted a study of the local tax regime that discovered more than a million dollars of untaxed corporate property. Lincoln Steffens observed that with this new tax revenue Fagan was able to "buy a site for a new high school; begin one school, finish another, put up eleven temporary schools"; he also "built a free bath; established free dispensaries, extended one park, bought another, improved two more, and [gave] free concerts in them."[39] Fagan was backed by a coalition of small property owners, who saw their taxes decline, and working-class constituents, who appreciated new social services. Everyone understood that behind Fagan stood Record, and Record used these accomplishments to become the boss of a Progressive contingent of "New Idea" Republicans.[40] When Woodrow Wilson became governor of New Jersey in 1911, he allied with Record to pass reforms that transformed him into a presidential prospect. Thus, Wilson would begin his career building bridges with Georgists to reach urban constituents.

The Fels Fund and the Failure of Popular Agitation

The Fels Fund began with the goal of implementing the single tax in at least one state, a departure from the administrative reforms that had emerged in municipalities as the natural course for the single tax movement. It held national conferences, but these only justified the organization's decisions to donors. Real power was vested in an executive committee that included Lincoln Steffens, Frederic Howe, Jackson Ralston, and George Briggs. Tom Johnson served as treasurer and Daniel Kiefer as chair. After Johnson's death, A. B. du Pont took his position, and the suffragist Carrie Chapman Call joined the board. As a rule, the Fels Fund Commission financed only individual local activists. In this way, the commission deepened the movement's reliance on heroic personalities. Efforts were made at annual conferences to incorporate those excluded from electoral politics; Alice Thacher Post, for instance, led discussions. The conference relocated in 1914 when the hotel refused to cater to an integrated audience that included Francis H. Warren, a Detroit activist who tried to organize a Black single-tax colony in Liberia.[41]

Embracing an incremental approach, the Fels Fund Commission devoted its first year to campaigns for the initiative and referendum. Direct legislation had deep roots in the movement; James Sullivan, an editor of George's *Standard*, had traveled to Switzerland in 1888 and published a series of articles describing direct democracy there. His 1892 book, *Direct Legislation by the Citizen through the Initiative and Referendum*, introduced Americans to the concept of direct legislation. Afterward, Sullivan became coeditor of the *American Federationist* and found a ready audience for direct legislation in the American Federation of Labor, whose leadership understood that with it they could put labor issues directly on the ballot without evoking the party loyalties that divided workers. A variety of state organizations were formed, with a single organizer—usually a single taxer—lobbying for direct legislation in alliance with local labor groups. Direct legislation fit with the movement's democratic sensibilities, but it was also a means to an end. At the first national Fels Fund convention, in 1910, donors were told that "the chances for putting the land value system into effect are unquestionably best in States where the people have the constitutional initiative."[42] The purpose of the referendum was to bypass state legislatures and, more particularly, uniformity clauses in state constitutions, so that land value taxation could be established without a constitutional amendment.[43]

The Fels Fund Commission chose William U'Ren to be its national figurehead for direct legislation. The son of a blacksmith who emigrated from Wales, U'Ren had studied law at night while working as a miner in Colorado. In 1889 he despaired that his life lacked purpose and traveled to Hawaii to end it. Then, he encountered *Progress and Poverty* and rediscovered his will to live.[44] Elected to the Oregon house of representatives as a Populist in 1896, U'Ren engaged in horse trading with state Republicans to pass a direct legislation amendment in 1902.[45] The sponsorship of the Fels Fund allowed U'Ren to become a full-time reformer, promoting Oregon as a national model for democratic Georgism.

U'Ren was an unknown quantity to many at the first Fels Fund conference in 1910. In the remote Pacific Northwest, he had no vital connections to the movement's main currents. He was a puzzling, even baffling figure; he refused a chair and spent the conference squatting against a wall, the image of western implacability. U'Ren appealed to donors at the conference by explaining that his struggle for the referendum was just a shortcut to the single tax:

> I read "Progress and Poverty" in 1882 and I went just as crazy over the Single Tax idea as anyone else ever did. . . . I thought I could get it by agitation and was often disgusted with a world that refused to be agitated for what I wanted. In 1882 I learned what the Initiative and Referendum is, and then I saw the way to the Single Tax. So, I quit talking Single Tax, not because I was any less in favor of it but because I saw that the first job was to get the Initiative and Referendum, so that the people, independently of the Legislature, may get what they want.[46]

U'Ren would later claim that "all the work we have done for Direct Legislation has been done with the Single Tax in view."[47]

With Fels's support, U'Ren took a leading role in the national campaign for direct legislation. The commission disseminated a pamphlet highlighting the victories of direct legislation. The timing was propitious.[48] The governor of New Jersey, Woodrow Wilson, though initially opposed to direct legislation, was reconsidering. George L. Record arranged a meeting between Wilson and U'Ren, and the commission paid for U'Ren to make the trip, which he claimed he never could have afforded without Fels's backing.[49] U'Ren won Wilson over, producing, according to the historian Norman Hapgood, "the biggest change in [Wilson's] thought made by anybody."[50]

The Oregon campaign secured the first statewide victory for the commission. In 1910 U'Ren campaigned for a referendum to eliminate the poll tax and institute municipal home rule in taxation. He built a coalition with the Oregon State Federation of Labor, which endorsed land value taxation to force timberland onto the market.[51] The Fels Fund Commission sent every registered voter in the state a 128-page pamphlet with a detailed breakdown of how land value taxation would affect different classes of property owners.[52] The referendum passed with a plurality of 2,044. Multnomah County, home of Portland, contributed 2,000 votes in favor.[53]

U'Ren and the Fels Fund Commission, now overconfident, saw the election of 1912 as the moment to consolidate their gains. They pushed a ballot measure to exempt all personal property and improvements in Oregon while imposing a graduated tax on land values, rights of way, franchises, natural resources, and waterpower. But, instead of reaching the promised land, U'Ren and the Fels Fund Commission ran the Oregon movement into the ground.

The bill was poorly constructed, allowing owners with property spread out across multiple taxing jurisdictions to fall into a lower tax bracket. Local papers railed against Fels, an out-of-state Jew, for influencing Oregon politics with his fortune. The proposal lost with only 27.8 percent of the vote. In contrast, a referendum for the single tax in 1908 had secured 34.5 percent.[54] The backlash was so strong that the home rule amendment was overturned. However, assessors in Portland began quietly shifting the tax burden onto land, so bureaucratic activism triumphed where popular campaigning had failed.[55]

In 1912 the Fels Fund Commission made an even bigger miscalculation in choosing Missouri, with its numerous property-owning farmers, as the location for a campaign to gradually implement the single tax via referendum. The single tax movement was strong in St. Louis, where rents were almost as high as in New York City.[56] But the rural reaction to the referendum was visceral. Appeals to the movement's transnational accomplishments struck an unwelcome chord in rural Missouri. Locals resented "foreigners," even those from other states in the Union. One agitator from Colorado reported that local governments refused to protect him when citizens threatened his life. The British member of Parliament Francis Neilson, an actor, playwright, and director who had fought for the People's Budget, traveled to Missouri to campaign for the single tax. But there, a representative of the British government advocating the confiscation of land values did not resonate well. Neilson narrowly escaped a lynching. The referendum secured 42 percent of the vote in St. Louis. Outside the state's four largest cities, however, it obtained only 5 percent of the vote.[57]

In deciding to win over an entire state, the commission had committed itself to reaching past its urban base to the countryside, but the reaction to Nielson and Fels hints that this objective was difficult not just for economic but also for cultural reasons. Single taxers argued that rural land was so cheap that it would benefit from the single tax. According to them, the 1910 census demonstrated that the combined farmland of California, Oregon, Washington, Idaho, Nevada, Arizona, New Mexico, Utah, Nevada, Wyoming, and Colorado had less assessed value than the land of New York City alone.[58] But these assurances meant little when spoken with a foreign accent. In a speech on the floor of the US Senate in 1917, Illinois Republican Lawrence Sherman articulated the rural critique of the single tax, claiming that it was "a principle born of the miasma of a great city." Its adherents were those who "never see daylight except, filtered, bleached-out rays in the great canyons of the office buildings." These were people who "do not know what a corn pone tastes like . . . have so little leg and lung power they could not run half a mile" and ultimately "obtain a lopsided, unhealthy view of life."[59] A year later, Sherman delivered a similar tirade in which he emphasized not only the urban but the cosmopolitan character of the movement. Single taxers were "gentlemen who have no idea where a potato comes from—whether it grows on a tree or whether it is concocted by a French cook in the kitchen of some high-class hotel."[60]

When the commission shifted its focus to Colorado, it became increasingly clear that its style of popular education was less effective than either interest group appeals or administrative reform. With the establishment of home rule in Colorado, land value taxation went up for a vote in Pueblo, Colorado Springs, and Denver. In 1913, the Pueblo election was won by a single activist, George Knapp, who ran a shoestring campaign. He estimated the assessment of every parcel under land value taxation and mailed a circular advertising the rates to every voter in town. Knapp attributed his victory to a combination of labor support and opportunistic voters eager to reduce their tax bills.[61] In 1915, Denver single taxers waged a vigorous, ideological campaign, with full-page newspaper adds, large banners, and public debates, but lost with only 22 percent of the vote. Refusing to take the less strident approach that had triumphed in Pueblo, the activist Louis Wallis emphasized doubling down on "propaganda," and local activists planned in 1917 to unleash an army of canvassers and send every voter in the city a copy of George's "The Crisis of Poverty" and "The Single Tax."[62] But in neither case did the election matter. In Pueblo the assessor refused to enforce the law, and it was overturned in 1915. Conversely, in Denver, the Somers system was instituted with little notice or controversy. In the end, all that mattered was who held the assessor's office.[63]

In Houston, J. J. Pastoriza sought to blend the commission's faith in civic education with administrative activism, but these proved irreconcilable. Pastoriza was the son of Spanish immigrants and was orphaned at age two. Pastoriza became an iron molder's apprentice, then a printer, finally making a small fortune speculating on real estate. In 1911 Pastoriza was elected tax commissioner by a large majority, garnering ten times as many votes as the Socialist candidate. During the campaign, he argued that the sitting mayor had already quietly begun shifting the tax burden onto land to great success.[64] Once elected, however, Pastoriza added $12 million in land value to the tax rolls, claiming that the land had been undervalued.[65] He went further than other assessors by admitting that he had broken the law to establish land value taxation and, in 1912, promised to exempt all personal property from taxation.[66]

A group of real estate speculators with large holdings of vacant lands sued to overturn their high assessments, and in 1915 the courts found Pastoriza's valuations unconstitutional since he acknowledged violating the state's uniformity clause.[67]

Pastoriza sacrificed land value taxation in Houston for publicity, but it was good publicity. Pastoriza claimed that, in the two-year period from 1912 to 1913, building permits in Houston increased by 55 percent, bank deposits grew by $7 million, rents dropped 20 percent, and the population increased by 25 percent. Opponents argued that these "magical" results were the product of natural growth, but the voters of Houston believed Pastoriza's narrative.[68] Between 1911 and 1915 his vote increased from 3,587 to 5,659. Although the courts overturned Pastoriza's work in Houston, his policies were imitated in Galveston, San Antonio, Beaumont, and Waco.[69] Pastoriza was invited to speak to the state legislature, and the Texas house of representatives voted 63 to 55 to establish land value taxation, though a two-thirds majority was required. This high level of support for land value taxation outside the city likely reflected the state's concentrated land ownership and rising rates of tenancy; in 1880, 37.6 percent of Texan farmers were tenants, and by 1910 the proportion had risen to 53 percent.[70] Pastoriza's example extended even outside the Southwest; as far away as Allentown, Pennsylvania, the city council announced its intention to follow the "Houston Plan."[71] Capitalizing on his publicity, Pastoriza in 1917 campaigned for mayor of Houston. Despite the city's conservative reputation, Pastoriza embraced his radicalism, noting that "the Singletax was my religion, and that I would not go back on my religion for any office in the United States."[72] In a four-man race, Pastoriza won the Democratic primary with 43.9 percent of the vote. The victory, however proved hollow. Pastoriza died from heart failure eighty-three days after his election.[73]

The focus of the Fels Fund Commission's work was California. In 1914 single taxers in that state received $16,978, nearly half the commission's annual budget.[74] This was due partly to California's size and partly to the strength of the local movement. Its leading figures were friends of Henry George from his early days in San Francisco. These included onetime gubernatorial candidate James Maguire and the editor of the *San Francisco Star*, James Barry. The movement made great strides in 1911 with the establishment of direct legislation, a unanimous vote in favor of home rule by the California Municipal League, and the election of a mayor in Berkeley, J. Stitt Wilson, who identified as a single taxer and a Christian socialist. The Fels Fund Commission sent a copy of Tom Johnson's autobiography to every mayor in California to solidify its vision of municipal reform in the Golden State.[75]

Once again, the commission pushed the movement too far and sabotaged it. Single taxers in the California League for Home Rule in Taxation began a series of referendums to establish home rule. In 1912, they secured 40.9 percent of the vote; two years later they secured 41.6 percent. On both occasions they garnered large majorities in Los Angeles and San Francisco.[76] But the Fels Fund Commission grew impatient and shifted its funding to activists in Southern California who proposed the immediate statewide confiscation of all land values. Because this referendum would ban all other sources of revenue, it was the most direct single tax proposal put to a vote in the United States. The movement behind this referendum, known as the "Great Adventure Movement," precipitated a schism between Progressive Georgists and their more libertarian peers. The Great Adventurers, such as Luke North, were largely Southern Californians with no personal connections to George. They resented the gradualism of mainstream Georgism. George's old associates, in turn, felt that reading their papers was "cruel and unusual punishment."[77] State single taxers organized a conference in 1917 to reunite the movement, but the Great Adventurers walked out because they felt underrepresented.[78]

The Great Adventure made a splash but set the movement back. Upton Sinclair paid to have ads supporting the referendum printed in the *Los Angeles Times*, *The Record*, and the *Pasadena News Star*.[79] But Progressives feared it would exempt franchises from taxation, and conservationists thought that, without provisions for natural resources, the encouragement to use land intensively would hasten deforestation.[80] In 1916 the referendum obtained only 32 percent of the vote. Whereas home rule picked up votes with each election, the Great Adventure lost them. Because the proposition continued to win in San Francisco, James Barry thought home rule would have secured an important sentimental victory if the Great Adventure had not hijacked the movement.[81] He wrote Anna George De Mille that if the movement had stayed its moderate course "in this very City where your father 'The Prophet' wrote 'Progress and Poverty' of which I 'set type'—we would very soon, I think, have had Single Tax."[82]

The last of the great popular battles for land value taxation was in New York, where high rents gave the movement broad appeal. In 1908 a group of social workers asked Benjamin C. Marsh to organize an exhibit on the congestion of population. More than seventy thousand people visited the exhibit when it was displayed at the American Museum of Natural History and the Brooklyn Institute of Arts and Sciences. It depicted conditions in New York and compared them unfavorably to European cities with land value taxation. The exhibit estimated that the average factory worker spent a third of his income on rent. The centerpiece of the show consisted of two cubes, one barely more than half an inch across, the other four and a half feet. One was a scaled representation of the value of land in Manhattan in 1624, the other the value in 1907; the display asked the audience "Who created it? Who gets it?"[83] A bell rang every five minutes, indicating that the city's land values had increased by another thousand dollars.[84]

Marsh's work caused such a stir that Mayor William Jay Gaynor was directed by aldermen to appoint a committee to investigate rent. Henry George and Gaynor had been on amicable terms; in 1897, George had promised to step out of the mayoral race if Tammany nominated Gaynor. After Gaynor finally won City Hall in 1909, he earned a reputation as a philosophical mayor with libertarian attitudes toward law enforcement.[85] His appointment of the City Commission on Congestion of Population launched a campaign to reduce rents through land value taxation. Marsh was appointed its secretary. Frederic Howe testified. The commission released a report calling for the rate of taxation on improvements to be halved over a period of five years. In 1911 this proposal was introduced in the state legislature by T. D. Sullivan and Assemblyman William Shortt. The Sullivan-Shortt bill was endorsed by the city's three largest labor unions: the Central Federated Union, the Central Labor Union of Brooklyn, and the United Hebrew Trades. The Municipal League of Savings and Loan Associations and the Tenants Union also endorsed it, with the latter pointing to the example of Vancouver to argue that land value taxation would reduce rents.[86] The People's Forum hosted speakers in favor of the reform, including Walter Laidlaw, executive secretary of the Federation of Churches; John Flynn, of the Central Labor Union of Brooklyn; and J. Aspinwall Hodge, representing the People's Forum itself.[87] One "mass meeting for lower rents" featured John J. Murphy, tenement house commissioner; several Yiddish-language speakers; and Progressive rabbi Stephen Wise.[88] Speakers emphasized that the construction boom caused by land value taxation would reduce rents.

Most important was the endorsement of Mayor Gaynor. At a speech for the Lower Rents Exhibit at Union Square, Gaynor admitted that "the chapter in Mr. George's book that proposed to do it right off the reel . . . did not commend itself to me." However, he continued, "the taking of ground rent by taxation may be the perfect system of taxation, as philosophers and economists admit the world over." Gaynor endorsed the Sullivan-Shortt bill because it would implement George's plan "so gradually and slyly that we neither feel it nor know it." He concluded that "any system of taxation . . . which multiples the number of buildings, automatically and necessarily lowers rents."[89] Although George had never taken City Hall, his ideas had.

Despite popular clamor for it, the Sullivan-Shortt bill made little progress. Governor William Sulzer supported it, but it was blocked in the state legislature by resistance from upstate legislators.[90] The Long Island Real Estate Exchange claimed credit for its defeat.[91] In 1914 the incoming mayor, John Purroy Mitchel, appointed the Committee on Taxation, which proved less favorable than Gaynor's commission. The committee's report, released in 1916, included a long study of land value taxation in western Canada conducted by Columbia University professor Robert M. Haig. Haig suggested that land value taxation in Vancouver probably had encouraged construction and lowered rents, though claims about its efficacy were inflated because the region was already developing rapidly. He warned that many large owners of real estate would be unable to bear land value taxation, forcing them to dispose of their property.[92] The effects on property owners that Haig reported served as justification for a majority of the committee to issue a report opposed to land value taxation.

The Committee on Taxation's report illustrated the difficult politics of rent reduction: it benefited a great number of people in a small way but injured a small number of people in a severe way. The majority report concluded firmly against the idea that public interest superseded special interests. "Losses and gains," they observed, "must be weighed against each other. It would . . . be neither fair nor wise to cause the owners of real estate . . . to suffer diminution in the amount of their invested capital because of vague and uncertain benefits to other classes that might ultimately be expected."[93] In his dissent, committee member Franklin Tomlin concluded bitterly that "practically all the argument against an increased tax on land is based on the claim that it will injure the business of land speculation."[94] This was in a way true, though it oversimplified deep philosophical differences over which took precedence: the public interest or property rights.

The Ambivalent Legacy of the Fels Fund Commission

By the time Joseph Fels died in 1914, the commission's campaigns had failed. However, there was some evidence that the publicity was paying dividends. Shortly before Fels's death, in May of 1913, single-taxers secured an unanticipated win for the Sullivan-Shortt principle of gradually exempting buildings. It was won not in New York, but in two Pennsylvania cities: Pittsburgh and Scranton. Although the Fels Fund Commission was largely inactive in the state, the idea came to the attention of Pittsburgh residents when Benjamin Marsh, then working for the commission in New York, presented his work at the Carnegie Institute in Pittsburgh.

Concerns about the high price of living in Pittsburgh prompted the city to commission a study that determined the average value of an acre of land in the First and Second Wards of Pittsburgh was $285,500 whereas it was only $205,500 in Manhattan. Single-taxers attributed Pittsburgh's aberrantly high rents to a tax system that was opposite of land value taxation: improved properties were taxed at as much as twice the rate of unimproved properties, disincentivizing construction. The obvious solution was to reverse course. A bill shifting the property tax from buildings to land in Pittsburgh and Scranton sailed through Pennsylvania's legislature without Scranton city officials even registering an opinion on it.[95]

Similarly, as World War I brought workers to urban areas, rents rose rapidly and the agitation for the untaxing of improvements in New York was finally victorious. In 1920 the state allowed cities to exempt from taxation new units built within two years. Increases in land value were still taxed, thus shifting a larger percentage of the tax burden onto land.[96] Once passed, untaxing new buildings rapidly lost support because of concerns that it was insufficiently Progressive. Fiorello La Guardia, president of the Board of Aldermen, and Mayor John F. Hylan criticized the procedure for exempting luxury apartments as much as it did working-class accommodations.[97] This was not actually true. But the complaint indicates that policy leaders were increasingly focused on whether taxpayers were being assessed according to their ability to pay.[98]

The Fels Fund Commission had dedicated tremendous resources to establishing the single tax on the state level with campaigns that preached the gospel of Henry George. But land value taxation obtained electoral victories mainly by stripping it of its radical philosophy and marketing it as a tax cut. The commission's long-sought-after dream of state-level single tax legislation was realized in 1919, when the Nonpartisan League of North Dakota pushed through the legislature an exemption for "farm improvements." In reality, the bill shifted the burden of taxation onto land, railroads, commercial-use property, and stocks, which were the only types of property not subject to exemption.[99] Exempt "farm improvements"—a deceptive term that misled farmers into thinking they received special treatment—included all structures on agricultural land, urban residences up to $1,000 in value, personal property up to $300, workingmen's tools up to $300, and farm implements up to $1,000. The *New York Times* observed, "They are going to bring Henry George to North Dakota."[100]

North Dakota poked an enormous hole through the Georgist faith that the public would embrace the public interest if properly informed. The commission had blanketed cities and states with pamphlets and books on the single tax. At the last Fels Fund Conference, held in 1914, there were calls to pull out of politics altogether and focus completely on "propaganda" to educate voters on the merits of the single tax.[101] And yet, when the dream of the Fels Fund was finally realized, it was by tricking farmers into believing they were getting a tax exemption that served their special interest. The National Single Tax League, which Kiefer chaired, observed sardonically that though the movement had been accused of injuring farmers, now "we see that the Singletax is designed to give the farmer an unfair advantage."[102]

The 1910s tested whether the single tax movement was as committed to a bottom-up vision of democracy as it was to a tax on land. The results were mixed. It is a testament to single taxers' dedication to popular democracy that, as their cause was embraced by urban administrators across the nation, the movement spent its resources on statewide educational campaigns to convince farmers that they were better off without landed property. That, however, did not work. As the tension between democracy and natural law liberalism became clearer, single taxers embraced quiet administrative reforms, expertise, and political subterfuge. Even their advocacy for direct legislation had ambivalent implications for their faith in democracy; the point of the referendum was less to empower the people than to facilitate constitutional change. Incidentally, in many places where land value taxation or nationalization took root—including Taiwan, Mexico, and Israel—it did so as constitutional law, too foundational to be left to the democratic public. This growing sense that the single tax needed to be forced onto the public would prime Georgists to adopt Wilson's vision of a war to spread democracy.[103]

Although the single tax was not always popular, single taxers were. Whether or not the average voter understood or cared about professional land value assessments, they supported people who implemented the changes, such as George Record and Tom Johnson, because of the promise of new social services and lower tax burdens. Urban working-class constituents, who typically voted for Republicans because they believed high tariffs protected their jobs, increasingly turned to Democratic Georgists who promised progressive taxes and active government. As single taxers entered national politics, they did so on platforms that built directly on these municipal accomplishments.

That these urban tax reforms were bubbling up to the national level became apparent in the wake of the 1912 presidential election. That year Theodore Roosevelt and the Progressive Party rejected urban home rule, instead emphasizing the primacy of the national government.[104] Roosevelt's campaign staff had been confident that he would win with a lock on large, traditionally Republican cities.[105] But Wilson, who reached out to Georgist mayors, significantly expanded the democratic coalition in urban areas. After the election, Roosevelt endorsed not only home rule but land value taxation as well: "We believe that municipalities should have complete self-government as regards all the affairs that are exclusively their own, including the important matter of taxation, and that the burden of municipal taxation should be shifted as to put the weight of land taxation upon the unearned rise in the value of the land itself rather than the improvements, the effort being to reduce the undue rise in rent."[106] That Roosevelt would come to Jesus in the wake of losing the presidency was unlikely; the same plan for home rule in taxation that Roosevelt now endorsed had won 57 percent of the vote in San Francisco in 1912. In 1916, California would pick the president with a margin of fewer than four thousand votes. Single taxers had begun to flip partisan affiliation in big cities, and both Roosevelt and Wilson understood that national party power hung in the balance.

CHAPTER 10

Conservation for the People

Land Nationalization and Conservation

> What have the buffaloes done to us that we should sacrifice the heritage
> of our children to see them extirpated before we die?
>
> Henry George, *Our Land and Land Policy* (1871)

As Georgism reshaped urban tax regimes, it also left a durable mark on the public domain. That impact was invisible to scholars who imagined George as a tax reformer looking to re-create a republic of yeoman farmers, but that was never who he was. He branded his program "land nationalization" and argued for a tax that would be analogous to government leasing of land. When his ideals were realized across a vast swath of the nation, it was through a leasehold system that offered environmental administrators crucial land management tools.[1] This result was possible due to a coalition with conservationists that highlights how the concept of land rent attracted new constituencies to environmental policy.

Laying the Foundations for Leasing

American Indian policy was one of the first issues in which Georgists engaged with the question of federal land leasing. As George campaigned to be mayor of New York City, Chief D. W. Bushyhead told the Cherokee Nation that "labor should not be taxed" but land that "belongs to all alike . . . should be paid for in the form of a just tax for the excess used."[2] Thus, when Senator Henry Dawes visited Indian Country in 1885, he was not exactly wrong when he observed with disdain that tribal land tenure was the "Henry George system." Dawes introduced a bill abolishing tribal ownership and allotting indigenous land privately. Many indigenous people resisted, sometimes citing Henry George as evidence that private ownership had failed.[3] Tribes that managed to retain subsoil rights, such as the Osage, sometimes prospered with hearty checks for collectively owned natural resources, leading the press to marvel at what could be achieved when the "unearned increment" was saved for the "needy."[4] Privatized land, conversely, often ended up in the hands of encroaching whites. Beginning with a campaign to nominate a sympathetic Indian commissioner in 1893, Georgists lobbied to revert indigenous land to tribal leasehold.

In 1904 Robert Baker, a Georgist congressman from Brooklyn, met President Theodore Roosevelt. Baker asked Roosevelt to consider legislation that would revert tribal land to a leasehold system. Roosevelt was surprisingly receptive to the idea. Up to that point, Roosevelt's policy had been, with the passage of the Desert Reclamation Act of 1902, to find ways to privatize the public domain even when it seemed impractical. Now, however, he told Baker that from an "'academic' standpoint he was more largely in agreement with us than we might imagine." Roosevelt objected not to the principle of leasing but to the double standard of applying it exclusively to Americans Indians. He promised, however, to find another opportunity to take up the question of leasing "in the near future."[5]

Two years later Senator Robert La Follette proposed a bill to lease mineral deposits on the public domain. Then, the passage of the Antiquities Act in June 1906 empowered Roosevelt to protect areas of the public domain from development, and by July he had begun withdrawing 66 million acres of public land presumed to contain coal. Later, in September, he used the act to withdraw land for national parks, starting with Devil's Tower in Wyoming. In February 1907, Roosevelt proposed a new plan for mineral deposits on the public domain, arguing that "the nation should retain its title to its fuel resources and its right to supervise their interest."[6] In preparation for leasing, the US Geological Survey was tasked with classifying lands according to their most valuable usage.

Roosevelt's acceptance of leasing represented a radical turn in conservationism. Conservation has been labeled a "gospel of efficiency," a technocratic faith that everyone would benefit from sustainability and the rational use of resources.[7] Leasing represented a more radical current of conservationism, however, that emphasized the distribution of national wealth. By the 1910s it was common for conservationists to propose conserving resources "for the people." This phrase referred to conserving resources under collective ownership, so that the windfalls, like those of the Osage, would fall to the whole people, not just monopolistic firms. This line of discourse usually echoed Georgist ideas, in part to draw Georgists into the conservationist movement.

An alliance between conservationism and Georgism was less comfortable than it might seem. George rejected the Malthusian theory that population grew too quickly to be supported by natural resources. In 1981, the economist Julian Simon cited George's arguments about mankind's ability to innovate around resource constraints in order to contend that there were no inherent "limits to growth."[8] This formulation oversimplified George, who believed rational management and conservation where among those powers of innovation that could prevent humans from running up against natural constraints on progress; he bemoaned, for instance, the wasteful extermination of bison. In *Progress and Poverty*, George cited government leasing of Alaska fisheries as an example of how public ownership had facilitated the conservation of resources. Even so, one of the promises of the single tax was that it would open resources for extraction.[9] Georgists adapted their position as it became apparent that leasing was likely a more sustainable policy than taxation. Most did not see leasing as a significant departure from the single tax. In 1889 Louis Post had considered whether leasing would be preferable to taxation and concluded: "No principle will be involved in the question. It will simply be one of expediency."[10]

A Coalition to Conserve the People's Resources

As Roosevelt's chief forester, Gifford Pinchot had been instrumental in developing the conservationist agenda. However, he remembered obtaining a sense of the economic importance of land only after President William Howard Taft took office. Then, it was revealed that a group led by Clarence Cunningham had flouted homesteading laws by filing thirty-three claims for coal land in Alaska and selling them to a syndicate associated with J. P. Morgan. Pinchot alleged that the secretary of the interior, Richard A. Ballinger, was complicit in the fraud. Pinchot's campaign against Ballinger ruined the conservationist credentials of his boss, President Taft. According to Pinchot, the "Pinchot-Ballinger controversy" had an equally important impact on his thinking. He realized that "the saving of natural resources for the benefit of the people through the conservationist movement involved the whole monopoly question. At first the idea seemed to me fantastic," but then he concluded "that the concentration of natural wealth in the hands of monopolists is one of the great problems of conservation."[11]

After the Pinchot-Ballinger controversy, Pinchot's speeches called with increasing stridency for conserving resources "for the people." Pinchot now observed: "The American people have evidently made up their minds that our natural resources must be conserved. That is good. But it settles only half the question. For whose benefit shall they be conserved—for the benefit of the many, or for the use and profit of the few?" Pinchot argued that resources should never be alienated from the commonwealth. They should remain the property of the nation and leased for public revenue. The alternative was "excessive profits from the control of natural resources, monopolized by a few . . . not worth to this nation the tremendous price they cost us."[12]

Pinchot echoed many of the principal tenets of Georgism when he argued that land was the source of monopoly, that "speculation" garnered "unearned" profits, and that land belonged to the people in common. In fact, Pinchot was probably never a Georgist or, at least, not a devout one. Beginning with the Ballinger controversy, however, Gifford's younger brother, the single taxer Amos, became an important ally, cowriting much of Gifford's material and often pushing it in a decidedly Georgist direction.[13] Moreover, Pinchot's National Conservation Association reached out with increasing frequency to Georgists for research, publicity, and political support. The organization's secretary, Harry Slattery, appealed to the editors of *The Public* and Pastoriza for data on "land monopoly."[14] Slattery also reached out to influential Georgists for help in publicizing the organization's campaigns.[15]

Many single taxers saw land in a narrow economic sense, with little regard for its aesthetic value. There were always some, though, who perceived land as more than a dangerous monopoly, and many of these figures had gravitated toward Roosevelt. Hamlin Garland lamented that land speculation had hindered the development of civilized frontier communities, yet also celebrated the West's natural beauty. In 1910 Garland wrote *Cavanagh*, dramatizing the work of a forest ranger in the growing national park system. Daniel Beard, who introduced George in his last public appearance, had been drawn to him by the idea that private ownership cut youth off from healthy play in nature. Beard had helped form the Boy Scouts to fight that trend. In 1913 he lobbied for a new line in the Boy Scout oath: "I promise to serve my country by guarding its natural resources."[16]

But no one more effectively bridged the divide between Roosevelt's conservationism and Georgism that William Kent. Kent was raised in Marin County, California, and grew up in the shadow of Mount Tamalpais. His father was a successful businessman, and Kent learned about the value of land in a practical way, inheriting both expensive Chicago real estate and expansive ranches throughout the Mountain West. As an adult, Kent moved to Chicago to administer the family fortune, but he was drawn into local politics. Elected as an alderman, he befriended Louis Post and led campaigns against traction monopoly. His sharp wit and aggressive writing style helped tear down the local machine and put his friend Edward Dunne in the mayor's office. Kent became a hero to younger reformers like Harold Ickes.[17]

Kent naturally bridged the politics of conservation and urban reform. Even in his busy Chicago days, he routinely escaped to the wilderness for long camping trips. Eventually, he returned to Northern California, where he used his fortune to help conserve the region's natural resources. Eager to save remaining redwood groves, he purchased three hundred acres in 1908 and then donated them to the government as a national park. What became Muir Woods National Monument, however, was only one of his many gifts to the public. He also gave Marin County an ownership stake in its water provider, along with its interests in the Mount Tamalpais watershed. He helped preserve parts of Lake Tahoe.[18] Kent imagined a future in which "no great center of population in the world could obtain anything like such an outdoor playground as may be secured by San Francisco and the other bay cities."[19]

Kent's interest in conservation overlapped, though not exactly comfortably, with his faith in land nationalization. Single taxers identified him as one of their own and supported him in all his election campaigns, even though he ran as a Republican or an independent. Yet Kent often expressed some independence from the movement. In 1909 he wrote to *The Public* to say that it was "so right most of the time" but that he was furious with its negative coverage of Roosevelt.[20] Arguing that California's natural resources were overburdened, Kent campaigned for alien land laws to dispossess the state's growing population of Japanese American farmers. This position aligned with the movement's early roots in white settler colonialism but was at odds with the increasingly cosmopolitan disposition of the movement outside California; Stoughton Cooley, the new editor of *The Public*, opined that unless California similarly confiscated the holdings of large oil companies, it would be clear that the Alien Land Law was a mere "display of bigoted prejudice."[21] Kent was, conversely, more concerned than the average single taxer with the way the full taxation of rent would disrupt continuity of tenure among small, white owners who were often barely staying afloat even without the government asking them to pay rent. Instead, he endorsed government leasing, traditionally seen as more moderate, because it entailed compensating landowners by purchasing their property. Though not always perfectly aligned with the movement, Kent was certain as to where he had obtained his faith that the land of Northern California belonged to its people: "We owe to Henry George the impulse toward the destruction of landowning privilege."[22]

The tension between Kent and the single tax movement was emblematic of the divide between Georgists and conservationists. Taxing land was intended to foster intensive use, but this incentive would encourage owners to extract resources as quickly as possible and dispose of their exhausted property to avoid paying taxes on it. Despite these differences, conservationists and single taxers shared an interest in community rights to land and could find shared ground in plans for leasing. The National Conservation Congress issued a statement in 1914 condemning the single tax and arguing that it would speed deforestation by encouraging owners to raze their resources. Yet, the organization declared that "it is wholly unlikely that the public would seriously consider exempting all speculatively owned forests from taxation."[23]

Concerned about a fight with conservationists, the Fels Fund Commission organized a committee including Amos Pinchot to clarify the Georgist position on extractive industries. The Fels Fund Commission adopted the committee's recommendations, which declared that the government should own and lease extractive resources. The government would assess a rental value equivalent to the value of the land without resources. Resources would be assessed at the time they were extracted. Because proprietors would pay royalties on resources after they were extracted, the full value of resource land would be captured without incentivizing the destruction of resources to reduce taxes.[24] In pitching leasing to its readers, *The Public* highlighted a conversation between Henry George and the legal reformer David Dudley Field in which George observed that "public policy forbids anything that would hasten the cutting of timber."[25]

The National Conservation Association, under Gifford Pinchot's leadership, was eager to accept an alliance with Georgists on the question of leasing. At the time, it was consciously reaching out to them. Its internal "plan for publicity" proposed planting stories in newspapers by reaching out to affiliate groups. The memo, for example, suggested "an article, on say the Nationalization of our Water Powers—a first factor in Industrial Reconstruction. Such an article, if only made into a pamphlet, could be sent to the periodical list, economic leaders, perhaps to some of the near radical businessmen."[26] Conservationists believed that social ownership of natural resources expanded the movement's appeal to a variety of economic interest groups: consumers concerned about high prices, taxpayers eager for alternative sources of public revenue, workers in extractive industries discontented with their bosses, and small producers fearful that large businesses would monopolizing natural resources.[27]

Georgists provided conservationists with publicity to reach new constituencies and expand their influence in a potentially hostile political climate. Pinchot had won his early victories with a Republican president, but in 1912 Republicans lost control of Congress and the White House. In their place stood a Democratic president who was friendly to Georgists and a

Democratic Congress that included many members sympathetic to George. Key administrative powers seemed to be in the hands of Georgists. Wilson initially offered the position of secretary of the interior to Newton Baker, Tom Johnson's lieutenant.[28] Baker refused to cut short his term as mayor of Cleveland, so the position passed instead to the Californian reformer Franklin K. Lane, a former friend of George who counted the prophet of San Francisco one of the "three greatest forces in the last thirty years."[29]

Lane, popularly considered presidential timber if not for the fact that he was born in Canada, was regarded as the type of policy expert who "renders government by the people effective."[30] In 1889 Lane was assigned to New York as a correspondent for the *San Francisco Chronicle*. He arrived in New York a Godkin liberal, but then met and befriended George.[31] When he returned to California, Lane began a law practice, wrote San Francisco's city charter, and was elected as the city and county attorney of San Francisco. In 1902 he lost a race for governor of California, though he ran well ahead of the Democratic ticket, with strong support from the San Francisco Bay Area. By the end of the Wilson administration, Louis Post would raise doubts about Lane's orthodoxy, but during the campaign he readily identified Lane as a single taxer.[32] In 1906 Lane was appointed to the Interstate Commerce Commission (ICC), where he led efforts to put the Hepburn Act into practice.[33] When the ICC was first established, Louis Post compared it to a vice cop; captured by industry bribery, the commission would do more harm than good.[34] Yet, when Lane was appointed to the commission, Post praised him as "incorruptible" and approvingly reported on his work to remake the commission into a rate-setting body.[35] In practice, the narrow Georgist vision of state building proved difficult to insulate from expert regulation.

In Alaska Secretary of the Interior Lane developed a model for nationalization with broad political appeal. Lane proposed leases of Alaskan coal land of a maximum of 2,600 acres—the average size of an individual coal mine operation—with 13,000 acres reserved for the navy, a fixed annual rent, and additional royalties for each ton of coal extracted. Royalties contributed to the Alaskan Development Fund. Land was also reserved for construction of a government-owned railroad to bring resources to market. Retaining public ownership of coal land appealed to conservationists, as did assessing royalties in proportion to the quantity of coal extracted. Limitations on the amount of land that could be leased assured voters that small producers, not large monopolists, would profit from the leases. Opening Alaska for development was popular on the West Coast, where Lane's plans were expected to reduce energy costs. Navy coal lands could be put into operation during a crisis to combat scarcity and price hikes. Lane's proposal for nationalizing Alaskan resources sailed through Congress. Resistance to similar plans would be stiffer in the contiguous United States, where a greater number of developers were eager to claim the resources for themselves, but Alaska provided a popular blueprint that Lane and his allies used to promote leasing the public domain.[36]

Throughout his tenure as interior secretary, Lane fought to spread the Alaska model, campaigning for federal leasing of coal, potash, phosphate, and oil lands on the public domain. Pointing to the success of leasing in Alaska, Lane argued that the system would put an end to speculative grabs at the public domain: "We have realized … that no man should have land he does not use, and that it is mainly because a few men are allowed to have and hold lands they do not use that others have difficulty in securing land they need for use." A broad application of the policy would line the public's purse. Lane estimated that if the federal government had retained coal lands in Pennsylvania, it would, under his plan, have secured $2 million annually in royalties.[37]

Kent, elected to Congress in 1913 as a Republican-leaning independent who supported Wilson, would be important as an intermediary between conservationists and single taxers in the fight for leasing the public domain. In the campaign for public waterpower, Harry Slattery solicited a list of Georgists in Congress from Charles Ingersoll. Ingersoll told Slattery that there were approximately thirty devout congressmen and that the reading clerk of the House maintained a list of members belonging to what amounted to a Georgist caucus.[38] A few months later, Slattery mailed out a circular to select US representatives asking for support in a campaign to lease waterpower sites. The letter, designed for a Georgist audience, was signed by William Kent and claimed that the bill "guarantee[ed] the future against having to pay rates based on community created land values."[39]

Throughout Wilson's presidency the House of Representatives fought to pass a waterpower bill based on the proposition that the value of these finite resources grew with and belonged to the community. Gifford Pinchot opposed one of the early iterations of this plan, the Shields bill, because it would allow hydroelectric companies to keep "the unearned increment."[40] Slattery, as secretary of the National Conservation Association, wrote of hydroelectric power: "We should not forget that land value or monopoly profit is the heart of the waterpower question. All human experience teaches that this value will increase enormously as population grows. Any legislation which prevents the public from retaining, so far as practicable, this unearned increment is wrong in principle."[41] George's theory of social value provided the intellectual justification for this departure from the tradition of fee simple ownership. While plenty of constituents embraced leasing for practical reasons unrelated to the single tax, the single tax stood philosophically near the center of the coalition for nationalization.

Kent led the charge for public waterpower with the backing of the National Conservation Association. When Newton Baker was appointed secretary of war, Kent wrote Wilson to advocate that Baker be tasked with writing waterpower legislation. This was hardly a natural task for a secretary of war, but, Kent observed, Baker was a "Tom Johnson Democrat."[42] Kent then wrote Baker to encourage him to draft a bill that would prevent power producers from retaining the "unearned increment."[43] Wilson assented to Kent's plan and gave Baker the job of crafting the administration's waterpower plan. Ultimately, Baker helped draft a waterpower bill with Franklin Lane and Josephus Daniels. This bill allowed the federal government to confiscate "excess profits" from hydroelectric projects and purchase dams for the price of land and capital at their initial value, not including rising land values.[44] The bill faced a tough fight in the Senate because of resistance from western states, which resented federal ownership of land within their borders and considered leasing "contrary to the spirt of our free institutions."[45]

Under the supervision of the National Conservation Association, Kent, himself a cattleman, also led the fight for a bill that would lease the open plain for grazing. The Kent bill of 1916 secured the support of the National Livestock Association, whose members understood that what remained of the public domain was not fertile enough to warrant purchase. Regulated leasing would protect the public domain and allow ranchers to extend their operations without investing in marginal land. Kent argued that this strategy would in turn increase the supply of meat, benefiting consumers. The most vehement opponents in the West were wool growers who feared discrimination after many long years of frontier wars with powerful cattlemen. However, most of the opposition came from conservatives in the East who saw the idea of government as landlord as contrary to the nation's free-market principles.[46] The Northwest Ordinance, authored by Thomas Jefferson, had provided for the leasing of the nation's scarce lead supplies, but this experiment was short-lived. The ruling precedent had been to distribute the public domain to individuals. Securing a permanent federal stake in natural resources was a radical, mostly new principle.

To those unfamiliar with Georgism, Kent's support for leasing might be surprising given that he generally sounded less like a radical socialist than a

Barry Goldwater–style, anti-government, western cattleman. Kent prided himself on being the most committed free-trade Republican in Congress. In his first speech to Congress he exclaimed, "If we can tax ourselves rich, we can prove poker to be a productive industry." Kent argued that soldiers' pensions were counterproductive boondoggles because any tax on capital would negatively impact wages. Yet, in his arguments for free trade, he suggested that tariff reductions be paid for with "heavy taxation of community-created land values."[47] Only George's argument that land was uniquely social could square his antipathy for taxes with his support for land nationalization. His faith in these ideas even enticed Kent to work against his own interests as a businessman, lobbying for the socialization of his extensive landholdings and lifting trade protections on industries he invested in.

Ultimately, leasing prevailed because conservation "for the people" was more popular than simply preserving resources. While many congressmen saw leasing as antithetical to American ideals, it promised to open new resources for exploitation.[48] After more than a decade of struggle and a dawning realization that conservationist sentiment was too powerful to overcome, opponents acquiesced. In 1920 Congress passed the General Leasing Act, which began the leasing of oil shale, oil, gas, coal, sodium, and phosphate deposits on the terms Lane proposed. Congress also passed a bill for leasing of water-power sites based on Baker's draft. Congress did not approve Kent's grazing bill, but it was resurrected during the New Deal, and in 1934 the policy was established with the Taylor Grazing Act of 1934. By the end of the 1930s, the United States had fully adopted a leasehold system for the public domain.

In this way, a country purportedly founded on the institution of private property adopted a system in which more than half of the land of certain states would remain federal property in perpetuity. America's stark divide between free markets and socialized land mirrors the ideology of Henry George, and while George might not be its sole author, he was instrumental in its formation. The major figures in the fight for the public letting of land overwhelmingly embraced the principle that land was uniquely communal because its value was created by society. Those who never opened *Progress and Poverty* still turned to people like Pinchot who echoed its lessons. George did not invent the American fascination with land, but he did turn it on its head. No other person was as important for transforming it from a fetishization of yeoman farmers into a philosophy of rational, public management.

It is also evident that during Woodrow Wilson's administration, George's ideas developed a new salience in national politics. Although Wilson's "New

Freedom" promised a more liberal method of leveling the playing field, as a popular refrain has it, in practice it only expanded on existing policies that regulated industrial monopolies. But Wilson's role in establishing public water-power and a leasehold system on the public domain demonstrates that his administration was thinking about monopoly in ways so different from trust-busting that historians have failed to comprehend them as anti-monopoly policies at all.[49] In fact, Wilson would strike major blows at all three of the Georgist pillars of monopoly—land, the tariff, and railroads—along lines that were often more consistent with Georgist ideology than with the interests of the Democratic Party's predominately agrarian constituents. Wilson would take the country further in the direction of George's radical, new liberalism than could ever have been expected.

CHAPTER 11

The Point of Least Resistance

Woodrow Wilson and the Single Tax Movement

> That Cleveland group which sat at Tom L. Johnson's feet, which learned
> from him, worked with him, saw his vision, knew his aspirations for
> Cleveland, and his reasons and motives and methods,—upon them at any
> rate a mantle has fallen, his mantle, which they must not but worthily
> wear. No truer memorial of him could they offer the people of the city, of
> all cities, of the whole country, than to take up his program of public
> service where Death command he laid it down.
>
> Louis Post, 1911

In 1909 Herbert Croly published *The Promise of American Life* as a manifesto
for "nationalism." Croly endorsed few specific policies and made little effort to
convince his readers that the status quo was rotten—he assumed that, by this
point, "average well-intentioned Americans ... are likely to be reformers of
one kind or another."[1] Croly's book was an exercise in national mythmaking, in
which he identified two warring American traditions: the Jeffersonian tradition of individual liberty and the Hamiltonian tradition of strong national
power. Croly excoriated democratic reformers who identified as "liberals,"
such as the single taxer Lincoln Steffens, for exciting hostility to businessmen
who had "contributed enormously to American economic efficiency."[2] Like
the abolitionists, liberals divided the nation rather than bringing it into harmony.[3] A strong central government was required to balance the class interests of the nation, which, as his father's positivist philosophy had predicted,
would inevitably become more stratified. A strong central government, Croly
argued, would be more "democratic" by embodying the national will. Croly
defined democracy at best loosely. He denied that "popular majorities" were
the "sovereign will" of the people and doubted that Blacks and immigrants
were fit for the franchise.[4] Real democracy was control by a nationally minded
elite: "The essential wholeness of the community depends absolutely on the
ceaseless creation of a political, economic and social aristocracy."[5]

Croly's object was neither freedom nor equality but rather national unity
and imperial power. Croly pointed to modern France, with its large class of
peasant proprietors, as headed down the path toward "national corruption and
dissolution" because its prosperity discouraged it from following Friedrich

Nietzsche's advice to "live dangerously."[6] Croly much preferred the "legitimacy of German aggression."[7] He took for granted that colonial expansion was a "manifest deduction" from nationalism.[8] These ideals would be realized by a strong, messianic leader; he compared Theodore Roosevelt to "Thor wielding . . . a sledge-hammer" but predicted the rise of an even greater leader, "armed with a flaming sword."[9] After publishing *The Promise of American Life*, Croly came under the sway of John Dewey's liberalism and acknowledged the value of some civil liberties, though under his leadership the *New Republic* would still excuse Benito Mussolini's authoritarianism as a necessary expedient to a higher goal.[10] When Croly praised Mussolini for substituting "visions of great future for collective pettiness," he illustrated the dark implications underlying his dream of organic national will.[11]

Needless to say, *The Public* rejected Croly's nationalism: the solution to inequality was more, not less, freedom.[12] Single taxers were no friendlier to Croly's *New Republic*. Amos Pinchot observed that it ignored the fundamental issues and instead "concentrates attention on symptoms," adopting an air of "impregnable virtue, already cast in the mold of respectable middle age." Albert Nock coined the phrase "Crolier than thou" to mock the publication's hauteur. *The Promise of American Life* sold only 7,500 copies in Croly's lifetime, but it won the support of middle-class intellectuals, for whom it distilled a growing consensus about elite control. Croly's most important fan was Theodore Roosevelt, who praised the book.[13]

Theodore Roosevelt, therefore, did not endear himself to Georgists when he campaigned for president in 1912 on the platform of a "New Nationalism" that seemed to echo Croly's ideas. After President William Howard Taft brought anti-trust charges against U.S. Steel, George W. Perkins organized Roosevelt's presidential campaign, soliciting donations from major corporations that aspired to establish anti-trust exemptions for benevolent monopolies. Roosevelt wholeheartedly supported Perkins's philosophy that government and monopolies should work together to end the insecurity of the competitive market. He classified Perkins as a good monopolist because U.S. Steel established profit sharing with its workers and insurance programs for old age, disability, and death. Roosevelt was not bothered that Perkins's workers labored seventy-two hours a week and were barred from organizing unions, hardly making them equal partners with U.S. Steel, whose budget was larger than that of most national governments. But that was not the point. Roosevelt was preoccupied with building a strong, imperialistic state. Corporate welfare staved off economic discontent that would divide the nation and ensured that workers could afford to have children to become cannon fodder. Roosevelt's affinity for strong-man politics led Louis Post to label his philosophy "Napoleonic Democracy" and predict that, if he were elected to a third term, US democracy would abandon consent of the governed for the benevolent paternalism of a powerful leader.[14]

In contrast, single taxers were drawn to Woodrow Wilson's "New Freedom." Wilson argued that democracy and monopoly were incompatible, and, rather than regulating or splitting up bad monopolies, the playing field should be leveled. In practice, Wilson—to the consternation of Georgists—would also regulate monopoly, but *The Public* distinguished between "Roosevelt's paternalism and Wilson's democracy" on issues such as the tariff, where it imagined Wilson's free trade policies would promote real competition.[15] Henry George Jr., a congressman by the time of Wilson's 1912 campaign, read *Protection or Free Trade* into the *Congressional Record*. Using congressional franking privileges, the Fels Fund distributed at least 100,000 copies of the book to support Wilson's planned tariff cuts, repeating Johnson's stunt from two decades earlier.[16]

Political pragmatism would also drive Wilson and Georgists together. Georgists had slowly transitioned from the abolitionist Republican Party to the free trade, anti-imperialist, and anti-monopoly Democratic Party. As leaders in the nation's big cities, they had brought many of those cities with them, convincing constituents that progressive taxation, rather than high tariffs, would best serve working people. Woodrow Wilson quickly recognized the role Georgists could play in expanding the Democratic coalition.

A Pragmatic Alliance

Wilson had begun his career working with Georgists. Elected governor of New Jersey in 1910, he was the first Democrat to hold that office since Bryan seized control of the party in 1896. Wilson's victory was possible not only because the Republican Party had lost popularity under President Taft but also because "New Idea" Republicans, hostile to party leadership, had split the party. The single taxer George L. Record had used his accomplishments in Jersey City to become the boss of this group. Once elected, Wilson worked closely with Record to win Republican support for his legislative agenda, with Record drafting the governor's election and corrupt-practices bills. Wilson appointed Record to the state board of assessors. Later, as president, Wilson tried unsuccessfully to appoint Record to the Federal Trade Commission, cementing a lifelong alliance.[17]

It did not take long for Georgists to recognize Wilson as a probable ally. Record worked to coax Wilson toward Georgist politics, arranging for William U'Ren to meet Wilson and convince him to endorse direct legislation. U'Ren wrote Joseph Fels and Daniel Kiefer (the Fels Fund had sponsored the trip) that he was confident he had convinced Wilson of not only the value of the referendum but also "a good deal more than that."[18] Not long afterward, *The Public* began promoting Wilson's still-hypothetical presidential candidacy.[19] At the Democratic National Convention in Baltimore in 1912, Newton Baker successfully fought to alter convention rules so that Ohio delegates could vote for Wilson and thereby help to secure his nomination.[20] Meanwhile, the Georgist Thomas Mott Osborne, son-in-law of William Lloyd Garrison II, worked with Franklin Roosevelt to cajole delegates to back Wilson at the convention.[21]

Urban Georgist machines constituted a small percentage of Wilson's base, but they held together the coalition's most precarious elements. No Democrat had secured a majority in a presidential election in two decades; even Wilson won only because Theodore Roosevelt split the Republican vote. Eager to reach out to urban constituents, Wilson befriended socialists such as Max Eastman and even made a successful pitch to civil rights activists like W. E. B. Du Bois, who would be severely disappointed with his presidency.[22] But Georgists were more natural and powerful allies, able to reach traditionally Republican voters. In 1912 Warren Worth Bailey, longtime editor of the Georgist *Johnstown (Pennsylvania) Democrat*, was elected to Congress from the district centered in Johnstown, which had never elected a Democrat. Henry George Jr. became the third Democrat since the Civil War elected from his Brooklyn district. The Cleveland district that had booted Tom Johnson in 1896 had become solidly Republican, until Johnson's ally Robert Crosser won it back. These victories were part of a Democratic wave in 1912, but unlike many new congressmen, Georgists held onto their districts in the next cycle. The *Joseph Fels Fund Bulletin* bragged in 1914 that "every Single Tax member who was nominated was re-elected."[23]

In Congress, Georgist representatives built on the success of their local reforms, fighting for policies that were straight out of Tom Johnson's playbook, including traction reform in Washington, D.C., and nationalization of the telegraph system.[24] George Jr. led an investigation into the equalization of property taxation in the District of Columbia that attracted such celebrities as Terence Powderly and Gifford Pinchot. Samuel Gompers testified, demonstrating how Georgism's international reach and urban victories had built bridges with labor. After George's 1886 campaign, Gompers had rejected the single tax as irrelevant to labor's concerns.[25] But in 1912 he testified before Henry George Jr.'s committee that he had witnessed the effects of land value taxation in Vancouver and found that it made "as much general satisfaction among the people as we shall have for a long time to come."[26] Land value taxation, he claimed, had lightened the tax bill of small homeowners and spurred construction that bolstered the building trades.

Georgists were lukewarm about Wilson's first two years in office. Whereas Wilson had promised to destroy rather than regulate monopolies, his Clayton Anti-Trust Act and Federal Trade Commission continued Roosevelt's regulatory approach. Even Croly and the luminaries at the *New Republic* slowly gravitated to Wilson, earning a harsh rebuke from their former hero Roosevelt, who now denounced them as "three anemic gentiles and three international Jews."[27] *The Public* branded Wilson's Clayton Anti-Trust Act "nonsensical" until language was introduced protecting labor unions from court injunctions.[28] The paper's response to the Wilson tariff reductions and his new Federal Reserve system were generally positive but muted. Reviewing the whole of Wilson's legislative agenda up to 1914, *The Public* concluded that all that Wilson's New Freedom consisted of was "palliatives," nothing "fundamental."[29]

Georgists remained content, though, because Wilson offered them more administrative influence than they could have hoped for. Contributors to *The Public* debated the merits of Wilson's Farm Loan Board, only to conclude that it would likely drive up the value of land by pumping federal money into the real estate market. However, the appointment of Herbert Quick ensured that the board "should have at least one member who realizes that the difficulty exists and knows what must be done to overcome it."[30] Quick, in his position, would have no authority to establish a land value tax to deflate farmland, but the fact that he was there was sufficient comfort. Louis Post was appointed to be the first assistant secretary of labor after lobbying by Warren Worth Bailey, William Jennings Bryan, and William B. Wilson.[31] *The Public* opined that "a remedy exists, and it is seen and appreciated by high government officials now occupying strategic positions from which they could procure its application."[32] In private, Georgists were more direct. Warren Bailey beamed about the administration: "These chaps are all land value taxers."[33] Henry George had preached the doctrine of political expediency, arguing that "the political art . . . consists in massing the greatest force against the point of least resistance." The Wilson administration would be that point.[34]

This pursuit of position during the Wilson administration could at times seem craven, but power was a means to an end. Senator Lawrence Sherman of Illinois, a frequent critic of single taxers, cynically reported that "a coterie of single-tax pegs have been crowded into Democratic holes. It is a painful fit, but even a single-taxer can stifle his lifetime conviction of yesterday to get on the Government pay roll."[35] Georgists, though, did use even the smallest fiefdoms of executive power to realize their convictions. In 1914 Wilson appointed Frederic C. Howe commissioner of immigration at Ellis Island to build support for Democrats among reformers in New York City. The position gave Howe time to speak and write but also provided an opportunity to introduce some of Johnson's democratic policies to the main artery of European immigration. As in Cleveland, Howe opened the lawn of the immigration complex for communal use and turned it into a space for free concerts and movies. Howe continued Johnson's war on government contractors, fighting for direct government provision of food services on the island. When New York's Republican congressman William Bennet quietly removed a proposal to end subcontracting on the island, Howe campaigned against him and got a Democratic representative elected in his place.[36] Howe had imported something of Johnson's schoolhouse of democracy to the main artery of European immigration and, as Wilson had hoped, expanded the urban base of the Democratic Party.

The Single Tax Goes to Mexico

If Georgists aspired to bypass congressional reactionaries, there was no better place than in foreign policy, where the executive branch encountered little oversight. Their timing was opportune. As Wilson entered the White House, Mexico was in the middle of a revolution. The Fels Fund Commission adopted a sophisticated and multipronged lobbying campaign. In 1914 Daniel Kiefer wrote a Californian single taxer asking him to travel to Mexico to lobby the revolutionary leader Pancho Villa. The recipient, who was probably William G. Eggleston, replied that his health was too poor for the trip and that Villa was not the person to lobby. Instead, he recommended targeting representatives of the Constitutionalist revolutionaries who were spearheading propaganda missions in the United States. In addition, he proposed lobbying Wilson to support the Constitutionalists and push them toward the single tax. According to this plan, Georgist congressmen Keating, Bailey, and Kent would talk to the president directly. Kent would also lobby Secretary of the Interior Franklin K. Lane, and Post would lobby Secretary of Labor William B. Wilson, to push their case on Wilson. The goal was to win over the president, who would be "the big lever" in a campaign to turn Mexican land reform toward the single tax.[37] This lobbying campaign speaks to a startling level of cohesion, coordination, and influence. Although the Fels Fund Commission initiated the campaign, it relied on a network of ideological allies in high positions. Steffens, for example, reached out to Secretary of War Newton Baker on revolutionary leader Venustiano Carranza's behalf because Baker "could understand it all, being a Tom Johnson man."[38]

The campaign to establish ties with Mexican revolutionaries was surprisingly auspicious. Carranza dispatched emissaries to the United States to solicit support from US radicals and win Wilson's favor, framing the Mexican fight for land reform in an idiom Americans would understand.[39] In 1916 Modesto C. Rolland, an associate of Carranza, wrote to *The Forum* to explain the objectives of the Mexican Revolution. He claimed that "the policy of the Revolutionary leaders is the first step toward the doctrine of the single tax."[40] The Mexican Bureau of Information, founded by Rolland in New York, pointed to land reforms in the Yucatan, wherein it was claimed that "the Henry George theory is being applied with remarkable effect."[41]

The Fels Fund Commission pursued, with some success, its ambitious plan of directly lobbying Mexican revolutionary leaders. Lincoln Steffens, a commission director, traveled to Mexico. His first trip was a bust, but on his second, Wilson secured him a place as an official envoy. Steffens had no title, but this suggested to Mexican officials that he had a special relationship with the president. Steffens became intimate with soon-to-be-president Carranza and vigorously argued the Georgist position. Steffens introduced Carranza to J. W. Slaughter, who wrote in *The Public* that revolutionary leaders were coming around to the idea of a graduated land tax.[42] Steffens believed that Carranza "and his successors accepted and enacted as much as they understood of the [single tax] theory."[43]

Wilson turned to Georgists for advice about Mexico and agreed with their diagnosis. In May 1914 Wilson told the *Saturday Evening Post* that the revolution "was a fight for the land—just that and nothing more." Land barons had built their empire on theft, so "doing away with the land monopoly and dispersing it among the proletariat" would be a just "restoration."[44] The president counted Steffens the "second best informed man in the U.S. on Mexico" next to himself.[45] He recommended the appointment of Frederic C. Howe to the Joint High Commission on Mexico because Howe was one of the "the closest and most comprehending students of such questions as those which undoubtedly lie at the bottom of the whole Mexican domestic settlement."[46] Howe had no expertise in Mexican politics, only in the land question. Secretary of Interior Lane, whom the Fels Fund had recruited to lobby Wilson on behalf of the constitutionalist revolutionaries, led the commission.

Georgists celebrated victory in Mexico. On the sidelines, Roosevelt argued law and order should be restored by backing the reactionary dictator Victoriano Huerta or establishing an American protectorate in Mexico.[47] Steffens, however, encouraged Wilson to back Carranza among the crowded field of Mexican revolutionaries. When Carranza's government wrote Mexico's new constitution, Article 27 vested all rights to land and natural resources in the government. Steffens believed he had influenced the crafting of Article 27, and although some have credited him with drafting it, the extent of his involvement is unclear.[48] Whether he played a major role, clearly many Georgists had wanted him to. Mexico served as the proving ground for Wilson's liberal internationalism, and Georgists were in the vanguard, exploiting their power to influence foreign governments.

The Single Tax and Industrial Democracy

During the Wilson years, conflict at home solidified the relationship between Georgists and labor. On April 20, 1914, the Colorado National Guard fired on a colony of striking coal workers at Ludlow, killing dozens, including women and children. Because the strike occurred on state land, the tragedy bolstered arguments for removing natural resources from corporate control. In response to the "Ludlow Massacre," George Creel rushed back from New York to support the workers. Within three weeks, Creel pulled together a protest of about ten thousand people at the state capitol in Denver. On the platform, he argued for "a constitutional amendment . . . that will permit the state to develop its own natural resources, dig its own coal, harness its own streams, water its own deserts, to the end that workers may be protected and parasites destroyed."[49]

The Ludlow Massacre provided fodder for Georgists to make the United States Commission on Industrial Relations (USCIR) into a radical spectacle. Authorized during the Taft administration to investigate industrial conditions in the United States, the commission was chaired by Frank P. Walsh. Walsh, a labor lawyer and Irish nationalist, had been Creel's ally in Missouri. When the Missouri single tax referendum was provoking lynch mobs, Walsh returned and told the state Democratic Party that "the single tax is the only thing that has in it the final solution of these industrial problems."[50] Later that year, Wilson appointed Walsh to chair a national study of industrial relations.

Walsh's handling of the USCIR reflected the movement's faith that popular education took precedence over neutral fact-finding and objective science. As chair of the USCIR, Walsh refused to submit to "experts and the like." He feared that if he acquiesced to the techniques of the academics on the board, "fundamentals" would "remain practically untouched." Walsh worked assiduously to scare off the professors, including economist John Commons, who, he complained to William Reedy, was too temperate in that he "asserts that he is a single taxer, and he has the fundamental knowledge of the land question, but I am afraid he would put the soft pedal on that."[51] Creel, who advised the commission, poked holes in the statements of the Colorado Fuel and Iron Company, embarrassing its representative, the purported founder of public relations, Ivy Lee.[52] Then Walsh subpoenaed John D. Rockefeller Jr., who owned the mines in Ludlow. Never had an industrial giant been so viciously handled by federal officials, and the press was fixated on the spectacle.[53] The final report compared Rockefeller to Louis XVI and his charities to the paternalistic noblesse oblige of the aristocracy.[54]

The USCIR's final report articulated a Georgist philosophy. It endorsed land value taxation as a remedy for an array of social and economic wrongs including farm tenancy, housing shortages, and unemployment.[55] It called for the nationalization of "natural monopolies," including telegraphs and telephones. It criticized company towns as "feudalistic." Clarence Darrow testified to the commission that private police in company towns barred labor leaders from speaking, and concluded, "I don't think we live in a free country or enjoy civil liberties."[56] Public ownership and leasing of natural resources, the commission argued, would expand freedom in a nation where monopoly now had the power to deprive citizens of their rights.

The USCIR popularized a new brand of labor unionism: industrial democracy. Rather than emphasizing conflict between labor and capital, industrial democracy resembled the labor republicanism that had once wed Georgism to the Knights of Labor.[57] It suggested that labor focus on shoring up democracy in- and outside the workplace. Instead of autocratic, top-down, Taylorist management, workers ought to have a say in the process of production. *The Public* declared that under this banner labor would be "the great democratic movement of our times."[58] Thus the 1910s witnessed a reconciliation between labor and Georgists. In 1916 the Missouri Federation of Labor endorsed land value taxation, followed by the United Mine Workers of America in 1917.[59] In 1913, even Samuel Gompers reminisced, while speaking to the San Francisco League for Home Rule, that he "count[ed] it a great privilege to have been a friend of Henry George, to have taken the stump for Henry George for mayor in New York. . . . You speak about the Single Tax and I believe in it with you."[60]

As in Mexico, Georgists exceeded their democratic mandate with the USCIR. Congress refused to renew the controversial commission after the release of its report in 1915. But the commission reconstituted itself as a private entity, occupying its former offices and title in order to preserve a disingenuously official veneer. Conservative members were replaced with sympathetic voices such as Frederic C. Howe and Amos Pinchot. For funding, the USCIR turned to Daniel Kiefer, who solicited donations from Georgists by observing that the USCIR and the Fels Fund now had an interlocking directorate.[61] Using a fake institute to spread its propaganda—a strategy popularized by PR guru Edward Bernays a decade later—the USCIR then distributed en masse the sections of the USCIR final report that favored land value taxation.[62] Initially, the organizers planned on using coded language to produce "not necessarily a blunt single tax piece but an article dealing with special privilege, freeing of natural resources, etc., through a just system of taxation." But the millennium appeared to be nigh, and Walsh argued for a "blunt single tax piece" under the banner of what had been a federal commission.[63] Walsh would cite the USCIR to support the Crosser bill, the closest thing to single tax legislation that could be mustered.[64]

The Crosser bill, proposed by Cleveland Democrat Robert Crosser in 1916, reimagined the old free soil ideal along Georgist lines, with the government retaining title to the land and leasing it out at its full site value. Leasing was the most direct way for the federal government to collect land value, since a federal land value tax was generally considered a violation of the constitutional ban on unapportioned direct taxes. Post recruited the young Benton MacKaye to write a report for the Labor Department showing that the Crosser bill would increase the wages of urban workers by providing opportunities for self-employment. MacKaye then argued in *The Public* that the movement shift its focus to direct ownership. Of Secretary Lane's reforms in Alaska he wrote, "With two of these resources—the timber and the coal—the principle of 'Singletax' is actually on the job. Only there is no taxation about it. The public doesn't 'take' the ground rent; it just keeps it."[65] MacKaye would later become famous as the father of the Appalachian Trail, an idea he attributed to a conversation with Alice Thacher Post during this period.[66]

The Crosser bill attracted some attention as a labor proposal, though not nearly so much as the George report on municipal taxation. The latter built on the success of the urban movement, but the principles of the Crosser bill were abstract and untried. Congressman David Lewis, a Democrat from Maryland, organized hearings at which prominent Georgists such as Louis Post, Frederic C. Howe, and Benjamin Marsh spoke about the bill. Former United Mine Workers treasurer William B. Wilson and Arthur Holder of the International Association of Machinists testified on the bill's behalf, but to little effect. The Crosser bill died without much notice, though it would be resurrected after the war created new opportunities for political experimentation.

Preparedness and the Election of 1916

In June 1914, Archduke Franz Ferdinand of Austria-Hungary was assassinated, precipitating World War I. With international trade halted, tariff revenues declined to one-third of their prewar norm, which was particularly troublesome in the midst of calls for military preparedness. In 1913, Congress had established a small federal income tax with the congressional leader Cordell Hull arguing for taxation according to ability to pay. Economist E. R. A. Seligman, however, noted that most of the support for an income tax came from agrarians hoping to shift the burden of federal revenue from tariffs, and even Hull cited free trader Benton McMillin as his inspiration for the income tax.[67] Wilson was reluctant to expand the income tax because of Republican opposition and initially pushed through the Emergency Revenue Act, which hiked excise taxes and the sugar tariff. These new levies were both unpopular and ineffective. Enforcement was so expensive as to offset most new revenue. By 1916 Wilson was committed to expanding the income tax, but, as a salve to conservatives, intended to expand the number of people who paid into the system, rather than raising the rates for high earners.

Georgists led efforts to instead establish a tax regime that soaked the rich. Charles O'Connor Hennessey, Charles Leubuscher, George L. Record, John Dewey, Amos Pinchot, and Charles Ingersoll founded the Association for an Equitable Federal Income Tax to lobby for a steeply progressive income tax. Land value taxation, its pamphlets argued, was preferable, but it was "not feasible for many years because of provisions in State constitutions, and in the Federal Constitution, which it would require years to amend."[68] Given the exigencies of war, an income tax that exclusively targeted the very wealthy was the next best thing because "every great fortune in the country was secured through some privilege: tariff, freight rebates, patent rights, control of credit— or the fundamental privilege—monopoly of land, and natural resources."[69] The organization's executive director, Benjamin Marsh, spoke to large crowds in major cities, presented his case to Congress, and went to the White House to speak with Wilson.[70]

The income tax seemed to violate the Georgist tenet that monopolistic rent should be the only object of taxation, but there were pragmatic reasons for Georgists to coalesce around it. Benjamin Marsh sent out a letter soliciting support for the income tax on letterhead of a New York City single tax organization beginning with the salutation "Dear Single-Taxer" and the injunction "NOT TO BE GIVEN TO THE PRESS." It pointed to a movement to introduce the income tax on the state level and thereby reduce reliance on the property tax, which had been used to implement land value taxation. A federal income tax would limit pressure to use income taxation as the chief source of state and local revenue. Furthermore, Marsh argued that an income tax would be easier to replace than the tariff, which was supported by wealthy interests. This was an argument that Tom Johnson had made in Congress in the 1890s.[71] What might look like ideological flexibility was, in fact, a movement so well organized and cohesive that it could secretly be coordinated to bend its own principles for a long-term goal. Competent observers understood that Georgists never did anything without a view toward the single tax. The National Tax Association correctly diagnosed the Association for an Equitable Federal Income Tax as a "Machiavellian" single tax ploy.[72]

Georgists would play an important role in shaping the wartime revenue regime. Warren Worth Bailey corralled a group of twenty-one representatives and convinced them to write letters to the president, vowing to block any tax legislation that was not steeply progressive. Wilson was forced to abandon his broad-based income tax: without this group he lacked the votes for a tax bill. Wilson benefited from the resistance; the new, progressive taxes were popular enough that one historian credited them with his reelection. It also inaugurated a new, progressive tax regime that, for nearly a century, constituted one of the few ways—along with anti-monopoly legislation—that the United States was more egalitarian than most Western European nations.[73]

The Revenue Act of 1916 included one provision that was particularly appealing to Georgists: the excess profits tax. Many countries had implemented excess profits taxes to collect sharp increases in income from war profiteering, but the American version was different. Taxing all profits over 8 percent interest, it targeted neither large businesses nor firms that had seen a steep increase in profit during the war, but ones that earned rates of return that Georgists associated with monopolistic rents.[74] Ability-to-pay economists attacked the excess profits tax because it could fall heavily on small businesses, but it effectively implemented Tom Johnson's plan to limit interest rates on monopolistic businesses throughout the national economy.[75] It raised more revenue in its first year of operation than the corporate and individual income taxes combined.[76]

As Wilson campaigned for reelection in the shadow of the European war, Georgists threw crucial support behind him.[77] His opponent, Charles Evans Hughes, had a sterling Progressive reputation but, afraid of alienating mainstream Republicans, spent the campaign hiding from the issues and snubbing reformers.[78] Wilson hired George Creel to manage publicity for his campaign. Creel helped popularize the slogan "He kept us out of war" and wrote the best-selling campaign book *Wilson and the Issues*.[79] William Kent, who had been elected to Congress as a Republican, served as chair of the Woodrow Wilson Independent League, a national organization designed to promote Wilson as the bipartisan Progressive candidate.[80] Kent's status as the leading independent in California was crucial, since that state decided the election by a mere 4,000 votes.

The departure of the remaining Republican Georgist to Wilson's camp had been set in motion two years earlier as it became clear that even Progressive Republicans subscribed to a philosophy antithetical to the single tax. In 1914 Amos Pinchot, one of the founders of the Progressive Party, circulated a letter to all its leading figures calling for the removal of its chairman, the monopolist George Perkins. Although Pinchot claimed to "believe in large units of production," he did oppose businesses that have "crushed competition not through efficiency but by monopolizing railroads, pipe lines, and natural resources, etc."[81] When Pinchot reached out to party regulars, a parade of hate mail followed from which Pinchot discerned that members of the Progressive Party believed "that competition is played out, and that we must have trusts and government regulation."[82] Lyman Abbott accused Pinchot of subscribing to Wilsonianism.[83]

The controversy around Pinchot's letter served as a rallying point for disaffected Republican Georgists. The few positive responses Pinchot received were almost invariably from other Georgists. In 1912 George L. Record had been director of the Progressive Party's Popular Government Branch.[84] But in the wake of the Pinchot controversy, it became clear that Wilson better represented his ideas:

> All that we radicals can do is sit quiet and let Roosevelt make an effort to carry
> through the program that is already laid down in four or five states, and if our

view is right his attempt will result in dismal failure, and then perhaps they will be ready to talk with us about a radical program. In the meantime, an article in this week's *Saturday Post* indicates that Wilson is beginning to understand the land question, as he insists that the distribution of land among the rank and file of the people in Mexico is to be the foundation of his policy in that country.[85]

Ben Lindsey, one of the few Georgists who had supported Roosevelt in 1912, expressed his assent to Pinchot's letter and observed that audiences he spoke to seemed enthusiastic about socializing natural resources.[86] Samuel Seabury, whose support for Wilson had cost him Roosevelt's backing in his own gubernatorial campaign, responded that the Progressive Party had "thrown all liberalism and democracy overboard."[87]

The electoral influence of Georgists was clearest in Ohio. Wilson had appointed Newton Baker, Johnson's disciple and successor to the mayoralty of Cleveland, as secretary of war because "it would greatly strengthen my hand."[88] A diminutive lawyer with no military experience, Baker had been appointed to shore up support among pacificists and in the key swing state of Ohio.[89] Baker offered his resignation—though Wilson refused to accept it—less than two weeks after the president's reelection, with a letter that assured him "you now have the sanction of a majority of our people," adding that "the fine vote in Ohio was your vote and not mine, and the people of the state will not misunderstand."[90] In a note to Whitlock, however, Baker offered a different interpretation, observing that "the pivot in the last election was Ohio, and there Tom's work, and that of Jones and yours showed wonderfully."[91] Of the three counties in Ohio with the most new Democratic voters, two were in Cleveland and one was in Toledo, the state's Georgist strongholds. Whereas the Democratic Party picked up an additional 5 percent of the electorate in the rest of the state, these three counties saw a Democratic surge of 16 to 19 percent. Had the nearly 60,000 new Democratic voters in these three counties stayed with the Republican Party, Charles Evans Hughes would have been the twenty-ninth president of the United States.[92]

Whether or not it was true, the press promoted the narrative that Johnson's machine had, through long and patient work, flipped Ohio. The *St. Louis Republic* asked and answered, "Who put Ohio into the Democratic column? The influence of a man, who being dead, yet speaketh—Tom Johnson."[93] The *Springfield Republican* observed that "in 1904 Col. Roosevelt carried the city of Cleveland by 20,000; this year Mr. Wilson carried Cleveland by 18,000. During the intervening years the late 'Tom' Johnson and the younger leaders like Newton D. Baker had re-educated the Ohio democracy to a new vision of public service."[94] Republican congressman Simeon Fess more bluntly claimed Wilson had been elected because of his state's misplaced faith in the single tax and socialism.[95] By redistributing wealth at the municipal level, Johnson and his acolytes had built the Democratic brand in Ohio. Now credited with the president's reelection, Georgists entered his second term with unprecedented influence.

The Public Goes to War

When Germany threatened to resume bombing US commercial vessels, Wilson declared war, and Georgists took prominent positions next to him. Of the four major figures in the defense council, two were unequivocally Georgists: Newton Baker and George Creel. *The Public* became a champion of Wilsonian internationalism. The "Henry George Book Store," operated by *The Public*, distributed Wilson's speeches on internationalism. The administration, in turn, maintained a close association with *The Public*. Newton Baker's private secretary, Ralph A. Hayes, contributed articles about the War Department's economic program, emphasizing policies to limit the monopoly profits of military contractors.[96] In the same issue, Secretary of War Baker endorsed a Christmas edition of "The Law of Human Progress" from *Progress and Poverty*, as "a gift to the mind of each recipient."[97] *The Public* raised funds so that the War Department could distribute copies of the publication to every military camp and then, after this had been accomplished, began sending books by Brand Whitlock, John Altgeld, Frederic C. Howe, and Henry George to the front line.[98] When future South Korean president Syngman Rhee contributed an article advocating his country's independence to *The Public*, he doubtless did so because he believed the administration was reading.

Georgists generally set aside Tolstoyan pacificism because they knew that their people were leading the charge. Albert Jay Nock was an outspoken critic of the war after the fact. But, during the war, he was able to "see the force of the idea that it might be better for a few chaps like you [Whitlock] and Baker and Howe to be helping run this thing than for it to be altogether in the hands of the professional-criminal class."[99] Nock, a friend of the nation's propaganda czar, argued that the war against autocracy must also attack feudalism's economic foundations—land, tariffs, and franchises.[100] Similarly, Clarence Darrow, who had spent his career criticizing incarceration, pled with audiences to accept wartime detentions because "I have known [Baker] for fifteen years, and know

[him] to be an intelligent, high-minded, humane man, one of the best I ever knew."[101] Frank Walsh had indicted the preparedness campaign as conspiracy by a "class of special interests." Once war began, he concluded that he should "do as we have always done" and use the opportunity "either to agitate or to put over some of our basic 'constructive proposals.'"[102] Walsh, appointed co-chair of the National War Labor Board, used his position to punish employers who did not permit workers councils that gave employees representation in the workplace, a sort of industrial democracy that would be co-opted by new, employer-sponsored worker organizations in the postwar years.[103]

As secretary of war, Newton Baker believed his principal duty was to put the economy on a wartime basis. He envisioned this task broadly as constructing "such an organization of the industrial, commercial, financial, and social resources of the nation as will enable them to be mobilized, both to support the military arm and to continue the life of the nation during struggle."[104] When George Peabody suggested that Baker take over the Treasury Department because of his "trained economic mind," Baker responded that his current job of "saving . . . money is complementary to the Treasury's obligation to raise money."[105] Toward that end, Baker worked to eliminate monopolistic rents in private war contracts. Georgists like Kent and Howe argued for nationalizing the munitions industry, much as Johnson had ended private subcontracting in Cleveland.[106] Following these lines, Baker and Josephus Daniels drafted the National Defense Act of 1916, which empowered Baker to research government production of munitions.[107] Because the United States' stint in the war was brief, some of these experiments, including a plant in Toledo, were never finished.[108] However, after a series of unsatisfactory negotiations with the DuPont Chemical Company, Baker began the federal production of gunpowder, cutting the cost for the public approximately in half.[109]

Nationalization, however, was an uphill battle, and the emergency of war called for Baker to follow the precedent Johnson had established with his Municipal Traction Company: capping the rate of return. On May 28, Baker wrote Wilson with his plan for the War Industries Board (WIB): it would serve as the central purchasing agency of the federal government and set prices under the "unwholesome and unsafe high level" prescribed by current conditions. Threatening nationalization if companies did not comply, Baker intended to use the WIB to limit contractors' profits to the fair returns they could expect in a competitive market.[110] However, Secretary of the Treasury William McAdoo and his appointee Bernard Baruch used the WIB's power much differently, overpaying on contracts to develop a clientelist political relationship with contractors and win enough clout to influence prices, wages, hours, and the production process. McAdoo, who would go on to become one of the New Deal's most notorious wielders of patronage, represented a new style of politics that Baker disdained.[111]

Baker fought for another cause that he had inherited from Johnson: public power. In addition to drafting the Water Power Act, he composed the National Defense Act, which empowered the War Department to produce nitrates used for explosives and fertilizer.[112] Under these provisions, Baker found a site in the Muscle Shoals region of Alabama where hydroelectric dams could be constructed. Property owners agreed to allow access to the land for a proprietary stake in the project, imagining that Baker would put expediency first. They miscalculated his priorities: Baker refused to develop the land under anything other than public ownership.[113] He won in negotiations, and the first plant was completed on January 11, 1919; the second, which he named Wilson Dam, would not be completed until 1924. These two federally owned hydroelectric plants sparked a decade-long controversy that would culminate in the creation of the Tennessee Valley Authority.

Georgists entertained a national land value tax that drew much attention but little action within the administration. *The Public* reported that "a Washington Group" comprising "many of the strongest men and women in the movement" debated the issue and concluded that a constitutional version of the tax would be unworkable, but proposed an investigation into whether recent court decisions had expanded federal tax power.[114] President Wilson, at the urging of George L. Record, encouraged Secretary of the Treasury McAdoo to investigate the feasibility of a national land tax.[115] Attorney General Thomas Gregory, however, concluded that the tax would be unconstitutional, unless it was apportioned by state.[116] Even then, the question continued to be pursued within the administration, though most admitted that it was infeasible.[117]

Instead, Post resurrected plans for land nationalization, now packaged as a patriotic war measure. Veterans of every war from the Revolution to the Civil War had been rewarded with free land. Post suggested a departure from the traditional fee simple arrangement, arguing that history had proven that such land would be gobbled up by speculators. Land should be held in public hands and leased at its unimproved value. While the plan loosely evoked the free soil tradition, it was also echoed by Georgists on the other side of the battle lines. In 1915 the *Joseph Fels Fund Bulletin* reported that the German Bund für Bodenreform had proposed a program of leasing land to returning soldiers at its full rental value.[118] Post presented the plan to Secretary of Labor

William B. Wilson. Secretary Wilson took the idea to the president, who, according to Post, responded "favorably." Because the plan would involve the coordination of the Departments of Labor, the Interior, and Agriculture, Wilson requested that all three department heads assent to it. According to Post, opposition by Interior Secretary Franklin K. Lane blocked the plan.[119]

Lane, however, took the lead in developing a more moderate soldier resettlement program. He designed his proposal so as to create tight-knit farming communities. He emphasized regulations that would foster something like a cooperative farm organization.[120] More problematically, Lane proposed that soldiers be allowed to earn the title to their land over time. *The Public* accused Lane of needing "glory" and, when his proposal failed, observed that "liberals need shed no tears."[121]

Lane's motives remain opaque, but practical politics likely played a role in his decision to embrace private ownership. He had already introduced several bills for leasing that had stalled. Giving land to soldiers proved a popular way to reward veterans. The *New York Times* editorialized in favor of it, the National Catholic Welfare Conference released a pamphlet supporting it, Roosevelt promoted it in his last published article, the American Legion endorsed it, more than a hundred thousand veterans signed petitions for it, and twenty-seven states appointed commissions to cooperate with the secretary of the interior on the plan.[122]

Despite the consternation of Georgists, the Lane bill bore the imprint of their movement. Lane pitched the measure to Congress as a remedy for land monopoly, contending that "the acreage should be limited to that which will be sufficient to reasonably support a family." To prevent concentrated land ownership, which Lane argued would undermine democracy, he proposed a spate of regulations that would prevent "speculative ventures in the unearned increment."[123] Although Georgists protested, they came around to the Lane bill. Frederic Howe wrote *The Land and the Soldier* (1919) to support the bill. Howe argued against granting soldiers land in fee simple.[124] But if it were the only option available, he supported the bill because, by limiting how much soldiers could own and making ownership contingent upon use, it made "the community" into the "landlord."[125] *The Public* published a report adopted by the Harvard Liberal Club that conceded the plan was a "necessary makeshift" in lieu of the "proper remedy."[126]

The war also provided an opportunity to secure nationalization of railroads. In December 1917 the federal government nationalized the railroad system in order to coordinate the shipping of war matériel. Although it was a temporary expedient, Georgists hoped to make it permanent. In April 1919, Glenn Plumb, attorney for the railroad brotherhoods, published his proposal for government ownership in *The Public*. The Plumb Plan appealed to diverse constituents by deftly weaving together industrial democracy, public ownership, and the single tax. It called for the government to take ownership of the railroads and lease them to private businesses, which would have a third of the seats on the board of directors. Another third would be reserved for presidential appointees, and the final third for representatives of railroad workers. All new railroad construction would be funded by special assessments on adjacent land.[127] The Plumb Plan League was organized by former congressman Edward Keating and promoted in the periodical *Labor*, which obtained a circulation of 500,000.[128] The railroad brotherhoods promised to campaign against congressmen who opposed it.[129] The Fels Fund Commission financed a separate lobbying effort, the "Conference on Democratic Railroad Control," and Frederic Howe resigned from his post at Ellis Island to lead it.[130]

Both the Lane bill and the Plumb Plan would become victims of organized farmers, as they transitioned from visionary populists to a narrow interest group. Farmers protested the Lane bill because it would bring more land under cultivation, thereby reducing crop prices.[131] Farmers soured on nationalization when the Railway Wage Commission, led by Lane, approved a $300 million wage increase for rail workers, who were so severely underpaid due to years of rate regulation that there were urgent concerns discontented workers would either tear up the rails or simply abandon their jobs.[132] To cover these higher labor costs, the US Railroad Administration increased freight rates by an average of 25 percent. Party leaders informed Wilson that anger among shippers, particularly farmers, would almost certainly result in Democrats losing control of the House of Representatives in the 1918 election.[133] The New York Georgist Benjamin Marsh formed the Farmers' National Council to lobby farmers for passage of the Plumb Plan, but the organization was quickly exposed as lacking farm support. The nation's largest farm organizations, the Farmers' Union and the National Grange, argued for a return to private ownership.[134]

Ultimately, Wilson bucked his agrarian constituents and produced a settlement of the railroad issue whereby excess profits would be confiscated. Efficiency experts protested that the old system of state and local railroad regulations had starved the transportation sector while making operation across state lines inefficient.[135] Shippers protested changes to a regime that had prioritized low freight rates over every other concern. Wilson nevertheless vetoed the Federal Control Act, which would have resurrected the status quo ante.[136] A compromise was reached with the Transportation Act of 1920, which reestablished the Progressive era regulatory regime while encouraging the consolidation of rail lines into a unified national system with all profits in excess of a 5.5 percent rate of interest recaptured. Taxing railroads encapsulated a shift from the Progressive regime that had focused on reducing rates for farmers and other shippers. This approach was broadly seen as Georgist, building off the model that Tom Johnson had established in Cleveland.[137]

Georgists even managed to advance racial liberalism in an otherwise hostile administration. In 1913 Wilson permitted department heads to segregate federal agencies. The Department of Labor, where Louis Post, a founding member of the NAACP, was assistant secretary, remained integrated. Post aspired to do more and, on May 1, 1918, formed the Division of Negro Economics under the leadership of the Fisk University sociologist George Haynes. Post and Haynes told officials in Mobile, Alabama, that they would need to improve working conditions for Black workers or have their federal war contracts revoked. The pair issued the same threat to northern employers who took advantage of housing scarcity among Black workers to operate exploitive boardinghouses. At the end of the war, the department negotiated a deal with Carnegie Steel to retain a third of its Black employees, setting a precedent for retaining Black wartime migrants in the north and giving them a beachhead in a region where they would wield vital political and cultural clout. In effect, the Division of Negro Economics was the first national fair employment program, an almost inconceivable—and certainly unsustainable—accomplishment for an administration that had ridden to power on the backs of southern Democrats. Congress refused to renew the Division of Negro Economics, which it claimed was illegal, and one senator anonymously proffered the prediction that if the program did not end soon, "it will topple the cornerstone of the Democratic South."[138]

Ultimately, Georgists shaped Wilsonian liberalism in their image despite, or perhaps because of, divisions within the president's coalition. Although Georgists and agrarian anti-monopolists both distrusted centralization, they differed irreconcilably on questions such as race, civil liberties, and labor rights. Wilson managed these divisions by allowing bureau heads remarkable autonomy. This, in fact, did little to placate the various wings of the coalition as the war heightened fundamental differences. Yet it gave Georgists the leeway to realize their visions. Georgists held disproportionate power because they were perceived as expanding the Democratic coalition. They managed to secure major, though usually temporary, settlements on their terms. The tax system was redesigned to target exorbitant rents, railroads were to be taxed in accordance with rent theory, and much of the nation's land was placed under a leasehold system. When the Republican senator from Illinois Lawrence Sherman argued that the Wilson administration was trying to "conquer Germany with the single tax," he was not far from the mark.[139] While a national land value tax never materialized, the Georgist critique of monopoly rent inspired wartime economic planning geared toward capping excess profits.

Thinking Locally, Acting Globally

Although Georgists smoothed some of the illiberal edges off Wilson's presidency, they were unable to tame the beast they rode to power. Randolph Bourne, a former acolyte of John Dewey, anticipated their dilemma when he asked, "If the war is too strong for you to prevent, how is it going to be weak enough for you to control and mould to your liberal purposes?"[140] While Georgists took center stage in the process of defining Wilsonian internationalism, that vision never had a monopoly over the public's perception of the war. Theodore Roosevelt, who had been one of the first to argue vigorously for war, led Republicans in their attacks on Wilson's "Peace Without Victory." Demanding national unity to assert "race supremacy," Roosevelt attacked American pacifists and "hyphenated Americans" with a rhetorical vehemence that aped, if it did not create, a wave of violence against the marginalized. The conclusion Roosevelt drew from Germany's invasion of Belgium was that international law was ineffectual and that national military strength was the path forward.[141] Roosevelt's pleas combined with new concerns about radicalism in the wake of the Bolshevik Revolution and a more ethno-national view of "Americanism" to provoke a wave of jingoism that undermined Georgists at the height of their power.[142]

It was evident from the beginning that Georgists would become the target of this new nationalism. In October 1917, the Georgist minister Herbert Bigelow was taken into the woods outside Newport, Kentucky, and horsewhipped because of his history of pacificism. In fact, Bigelow had come to support the war after Wilson made the United States' stated objective the development of a liberal international order.[143] Baker expressed a "certain suspicion that the fellows who took him into the country and whipped him cared very little about his opinions on the German question and very much more about his opinion on certain other economic questions in which he was constantly agitating on the Democratic side."[144] Baker encouraged Attorney General Gregory to investigate the incident and issued a statement: "The cause of the United States," he wrote, "is not aided, but is hurt, by this kind of thing. No nightriders are needed, and when the country is at war for liberty and justice they make a humiliating contrast to our national ideals and aims."[145]

Georgists worked to head off calls for censorship but threw themselves into the fray. When Frederic Howe was ordered as immigration commissioner to summarily deport foreign-born socialists, he insisted that he would not authorize deportations without trials.[146] These deportation cases came under the authority of the Labor Department. Louis Post presided. Asserting that membership in a communist organization was not sufficient proof of disloyalty, he reviewed 1,600 cases and canceled 1,140 deportations, provoking howls of disloyalty and subversion.[147] Before the war was over, Post, Howe, and Creel were each called by Congress to answer charges of radicalism. Republican congressman Edward Hoch passed a motion to impeach Post. In a testament to how divided Wilson's coalition was, the administration turned on itself; Attorney General A. Mitchell Palmer claimed he was not surprised that "when the opportunity . . . presented itself [to Post] in an official way to render a service to those who advocate force and violence," he "should employ it to the limit. He has always been sympathetic to that sort of thing."[148]

Georgists embraced Wilson's calls for self-determination not as nationalists but as liberals who believed in localized democracy. In October 1917 Frederic Howe presided over the first Congress of the League of Small and Subject Nationalities, which drew delegates from across the world, including Ireland, India, Scotland, Korea, and Assyria. *The Public* warned against using ethnicity as an organizing principle and pointed to the Balkans, where efforts to draw borders based on that standard would create a situation "comparable to a bag full of cats." It argued for a "Balkan Melting Pot" because "nationality is an exceedingly fluid and relative affair."[149] Independence was a question of economic exploitation: "Oppression," the article continued, "is a land problem soluble by a sufficient degree of local autonomy to break the tyranny of the feudal estates."[150] Georgists had fought for the economic autonomy of the city from the state and now fought to free small nations from empires. In both cases, the principle was the same: direct, local democracy was more likely to realize sound economic principles.[151] Georgists once again struggled, however, with whether democracy took precedence over the single tax. In one article *The Public* embraced the idea of mandates—former colonies placed under the control of the League of Nations—so long as "the fiscal policy of these colonies should be based on the principle that natural resources belong to the people in common, and that land values—which are created by society—should be taken in the form of a tax to defray the cost of government."[152]

Fearing censorship and eager to promote a liberal war message, Georgists turned to civic education or, less generously, propaganda. Newton Baker and George Creel wrote the president proposing a program of "voluntary censorship."[153] On April 14, 1917, Wilson unilaterally created the Committee on Public Information (CPI) with Creel as its chair.[154] Faced with efforts by the German government to circulate divisive propaganda, Creel explained that "you cannot cure such an evil by cutting it out. A better way is to crowd it out."[155] Albert Jay Nock appreciated Creel's vision but doubted that the passions of war could be managed: "You are sincere and loyal to the core. . . . If you do not succeed,—and you won't—it is because it isn't in the job."[156]

George Creel struggled to ground the war effort in liberal ideas of democracy, rather than nationalism. He minimized stories of German war atrocities and framed the war as a struggle between democracy and "autocracy."[157] This was not self-congratulatory patriotism, however; it elevated an ideal that America still needed to strive toward. CPI pamphlets advertised a future of industrial democracy, fair wages, and eight-hour workdays.[158] Suffragists called on their old ally Creel as the person most likely to sway Wilson, and Creel wrote Wilson to convince the president that if the United States was fighting a war for democracy, it was a "war necessity" to prove that commitment by bringing democracy to women. Ultimately, Wilson embraced women's suffrage in his State of the Union address, supporting the narrow passage of the Nineteenth Amendment.[159]

On the other hand, Creel attacked those whose growing calls for "Americanism" were rooted in a sense of ethnic identity. To the Chicago Association of Commerce, Creel denounced "chauvinists, with their gospel of hate and disunity," and he campaigned against laws that would ban foreign languages.[160] He criticized the way "Americanism" was being used to excite violence against African Americans, organizing a conference of Black editors that demanded antilynching legislation. Together with Newton Baker and Emmet Scott, Creel pressed Wilson to make a statement against lynching, which spurred the white press to editorialize against the growing wave of racial violence.[161]

The CPI's work fit the dicta of Georgist propaganda, according to which citizens needed to be educated but that philosophy and ethics took precedence over empirical fact. The CPI did not typically barter in outright lies or fabrications. It did, however, simplify the war, which it depicted as a struggle between democracy and a "medieval military oligarchy."[162] Creel enlisted academic historians to lend credibility to this narrative, but most understood— or came to understand—that these characterizations were overstated.[163]

Furthermore, this narrative had a political slant. Creel employed radical speakers such as Charles Edward Russell, who in Iowa attacked local conservative representatives.[164] Crawford Vaughan, an Australian Georgist, embarked on speaking tour among labor groups under CPI auspices.[165] Edward Riis, son of the muckraker Jacob Riis, served as commissioner of the CPI in Denmark, where he spread the message that America was engaged in "a holy war . . . between the old feudalism, autocratic rule, and the people's right to self-determination."[166] On occasion, Creel used his authority to put his finger down on the scales of US politics, as when he testified to the patriotism of the Nonpartisan League, which had initially been opposed to the war. When its opponent, the Republican governor of Minnesota, Joseph Burnquist, called Creel dishonest and politically motivated, Creel retorted that Burnquist and his "lynch-law patriots" were the ones misrepresenting America.[167]

Creel encouraged Wilson to identify his war aims in short, easily disseminated points, and then, after Wilson delivered his Fourteen Points, used postcards, movies, and posters to spread the message from South Africa to Japan. Creel told Wilson that "for the first time in history the speeches of a national executive were given universal circulation, and I am proud to tell you, sir, that your declarations had the force of arms."[168] The effect of Creel's propaganda was to stoke hopes for freedom around the globe. In Beijing sixty thousand marched in solidarity with the Allies' victory in Europe, some shouting "Long Live President Wilson."[169] Reports circulated of Italians branding Wilson the Messiah.[170] Ho Chi Minh journeyed to the peace conference in Versailles with a petition for Vietnamese independence.

Creel failed to reach the hearts and minds as effectively as the ethnonationalists did. The nation was overtaken with a wave of anti-German sentiment and racial violence on a scale not seen since Reconstruction.[171] Hollywood promulgated hate with overwrought depictions of German brutality. So too did parts of Wilson's administration, particularly the Treasury Department, which advertised war bonds with images of dark-skinned, blood-soaked "Huns."[172] Attorney General Palmer stoked fears of an imminent communist revolution. Republican senator Lawrence Sherman alleged that the administration was "a collection of radicals imbued with the vagaries of Karl Marx and of Lenine and Trotzky [*sic*]."[173] When Senate Democratic Whip James Lewis proposed nationalization of railroads, telegraphs, and telephones, it was labeled a "programme of state socialism." The conservative Republican Indiana senator James Watson continued that "all of the radicals that are not in jail are in office under the Administration."[174]

Simultaneously, Wilson's allies were disillusioned as liberal internationalism was outmaneuvered in the peace talks at Versailles and blocked in Congress. Creel himself acknowledged that he had stoked expectations for a postwar Eden so high that disappointment was inevitable.[175] *The Public* would be washed out with the tide of Wilsonian internationalism, ceasing publication without explanation in December 1919. The feature of the final issue was written by Sun Yat-sen. Here, the father of Chinese nationalism drew upon Wilsonianism to advocate for the development of his nation.[176] Not long after the Versailles talks concluded with the Japanese in control of northern China, Sun flirted with Marxism. In the new Soviet Union, Lenin appealed to Wilson's discontents with talk of national independence. While Sun ultimately repudiated Marxism, Mao Zedong built on anti-Versailles protests to form a budding Communist movement in China. Liberal anti-colonialism had failed, and Marxism emerged as the most credible challenger to imperialism.

Georgists had played a role in this Wilsonian moment by fighting for Wilson's reelection and propagating his ideas on an unprecedented scale. This work grew out of faiths ingrained in movement culture: anti-colonialism, decentralization, democracy, and popular "education." Georgists brought to a global conflagration a set of practices that had been fleshed out in the crucible of urban reform and adapted them only slightly, approaching the management of international opinion with all the tact and delicacy of a municipal muckraking crusade. In the aftermath, Georgists emerged as leading exponents of a world order predicated on global democracy and national independence. To a crowd in Los Angeles in 1935, Creel reported that he had visited Wilson often after his stroke, and with "a terrible desolation in his eyes" the former president would cry out, "I failed." But Creel promised vindication for the fallen leader: "He was deceived by his agony and despair. We, the living, know that he did not fail. The fire that he kindled in the souls of mankind still burns, and its flame will someday show a hate-sick world the path to the heights."[177]

The High Tide of the Single Tax Movement

During the waning years of the Wilson administration, Creel developed an interest in Mexico's experiment with socialized natural resources. Although Article 27 of the constitution established land and natural resources as public property, this was a mere statement of principle without any design for implementation. One of the most important questions was how to deal with American oil companies, which the US State Department and the Yankee press insisted should retain their property rights. Creel, still an official agent of the government, worked to ease fears of retaliation if Mexico seized national resources from American companies. On October 2, 1919, he sent a telegram through Manuel Carpio to the Mexican Senate. Carpio, who was part of President Carranza's outreach campaign to the United States, had been a contributor to *The Public*.[178] In his telegram, Creel urged that the government "not gratify oil interests by legislating at their pleasure."[179] Creel's letter was purportedly "commented upon generally in Mexico City." The Mexican consul general in New York, R. P. de Negri, wrote to Mexican senator Flavio Borquez, "You are probably familiar with the statements made by George Creel . . . on President Wilson's views with regard to the nationalization of petroleum in Mexico." He concluded that the "working classes, radical socialists, and honest intellectuals" in the United States were open to "nationalizing natural resources."[180]

By 1920 the CPI had been terminated unceremoniously, with Congress refusing even to provide for the collection or storage of its records. But in October of that year the president turned to Creel one last time, now as an unofficial envoy to Mexico, circumventing the State Department in negotiations to give official recognition to the new Mexican government. Creel met with Wilson twice and then, under an assumed name, snuck across the border and began to negotiate terms for recognition with interim Mexican president Adolfo de la Huerta. According to Creel, he undertook this mission unofficially and at his own expense with Wilson's blessing.[181] As head of the CPI, Creel had already earned the wrath of the State Department for encroaching on its territory, making this effort a serious affront.[182]

While Creel's diplomatic mission to Mexico was intended to be secret, he was followed across the border by an informant of Republican senator Albert Fall, an ally of the oil industry. News of the trip was leaked to the press. The State Department under Secretary Bainbridge Colby denied that Creel's mission was diplomatic and gave every indication that it was opposed to hastening the pace of recognition. While in Mexico, Creel publicly dissented from the State Department, arguing that the oil question should not be a factor in whether the United States recognized Mexico. His comment provoked an unnamed "high official of the State Department" to respond that the department was inflexible on the oil issue. Two days after Creel returned to Washington, he conferred with Wilson and Secretary of State Colby. Colby announced that he would expedite the process of granting recognition. To save face, Colby claimed that Creel had no impact on the State Department's decision. Despite the president's directive, Colby again stalled negotiations to recognize Mexico, which were then halted altogether when the conservative Harding administration took office.[183]

With the question of recognition still hanging in the air, the new president of Mexico, Álvaro Obregón, issued a letter appealing to the American people to accept Mexico's rights to its resources. The letter claimed that "the natural resources of the country made enormous fortunes for the few; wholesale campaigns of dispossession gathered the land into great estates owned by absent landlords; industry was dragged back and fifteen million people led lives of misery." Mexicans hoped to "finance the national progress through the medium of our natural resources." Nationalization of natural resources would provide Mexico the wealth to build a stable democracy, and "honest taxation" would "put an end to this policy of land monopoly and non-productivity."[184]

Astute observers in the American press noticed a fair share of "Creelisms" in Obregón's statement and noted that Creel was in Mexico as part of the "Obregon retinue."[185] Creel denied that he had written the president's letter, but the multiple drafts in his personal files suggest otherwise. Four months earlier, Creel had written an article positing a course for postwar Progressivism. He concluded with the plea, "But why not hit at the source? Why not prevent the accumulation of that sort of wealth that is not the product of courage and energy and effort? Why not fight for the adoption of Henry George's theory, or as it is better known, the single tax?"[186] The *Single Tax Review* published, without comment, Creel's article side by side with the statement attributed to Obregon.[187]

Fifty years after publication of *The Irish Land Question* brought the single tax into public discussion, it was endorsed by the former spokesman for the United States both under his own name and that of the president of Mexico. It was the high-water mark of the movement's struggle for position. Creel's statement was not just a declaration of personal faith but also the culmination of a national mobilization. Long, dispiriting fights over franchises, taxes, and urban social services had gradually built urban constituencies potent enough to make Georgists crucial to the Democratic coalition. To a remarkable degree this was a fulfillment of George's plan. This brand of partisan power was what he envisioned when he dictated that those who supported his cause follow him into the Democratic Party under Bryan's banner. It was the course Johnson pursued when he fought for hegemony over Ohio's Democratic machine. In the end, even the highest posts in a globally transformative administration proved insufficient to inaugurate the single tax. To realize their ideal, they had regularly overstepped the mandate voters had given them. However, Georgists had secured a platform for a liberalism that advanced equal opportunity—locally, nationally, and globally—at a time when even many Progressives accepted the inevitability of growing social inequality.

CHAPTER 12

The Will to Believe

The Decline of the Single Tax and the Rise of Regional Planning

> The Uplift as a crusading spirit, as a dedication, as a religion, is coma-
> tose . . . strangled both by the war and its own ineptitude. It was inept
> because its moral judgments took the place of sound analysis. It dealt in
> blacks and whites; it deified a muzzy and mystical conception of democ-
> racy and found horns underneath every plug hat; it was too logical and not
> sufficiently psychological. . . . But it was a gallant spiritual adventure, and
> before its chieftains and martyrs we stand at salute.
> Stuart Chase, "Where Are the Pre-war Radicals?," 1926

After World War I, the single tax movement crumbled. Many of its former exponents lost faith, though they retained the outlines of George's philosophy. A
movement that had been rooted in a loose network now lacked cohesion. This
precipitous decline can be credited to several causes: the rise of communism,
ethnic and racial tribalism, the growing popularity of the ability-to-pay principle of taxation, and disillusionment with Wilsonian internationalism. Most
important, though, was the dissipation of the conditions that had sparked the
growth of the single tax: the growing accessibility of the automobile made it
easier to commute to places of employment, escaping high urban rents and the
oppression of company towns. An exodus from urban areas undermined the
movement's glorification of the city-republic. A love affair with sprawl
made the single tax, which would penalize holding idle land in order to encourage intensive use and densification, obsolete. What impact Georgism retained was due to the legendary status of the movement's chieftains, and the
precedents they set. These traditions influenced younger reformers in vague,
often contradictory ways.

Georgists lost faith not so much in the single tax as in the democratic public
it was intended to foster. Georgists had believed that, under the right social
circumstances, the public would be rational and disinterested, inherently
drawn to a natural law philosophy that would unleash social progress. Instead,
the events of the 1920s suggested that the electorate was animated by self-
interest, irrational, and tribalistic. Some, like John Dewey, turned to Georgism
to create a truly democratic society. Others, like Albert Jay Nock, rejected de-

mocracy as incompatible with natural rights. The tension between liberal philosophy and democracy had come to a head. The precedents Georgists had set helped pave the way for a rights revolution. Yet it became clear that the battles they had fought on behalf of democracy were contingent upon a faith in the redemptive power of the single tax, and this appeared increasingly remote. They had played a significant role in creating a more democratic society of which they were increasingly skeptical.

Losing the Public

By the 1920s, hopes that the public would embrace the single tax evaporated. In 1899 Thorstein Veblen, in *The Theory of the Leisure Class*, had depicted farmers as the archetype of the honest producer. Experience, however, had proven that untrue, and when Veblen published *The Vested Interests and the Common Man* in 1919, he concluded that farmers' interest in land values had made them the chief defenders of the privilege to hold unearned income: "The reason . . . American farmers have been led . . . to side with the vested interests . . . comes of the fact that the farmers are not only farmers but also owners of speculative real estate."[1] In 1925, Rexford Tugwell asserted of George that "none of the reformers with his system of reform has been able to sufficiently capture the imagination of the people to persuade them to its adoption," though, he added, "it is not often denied that the premises upon which their arguments were based are true enough."[2]

The Fels Fund Commission and its referendum campaigns proved only that the democratic public offered no clear path toward the single tax. The novelist Upton Sinclair, though a socialist, had donated time and money to the 1918 single tax referendum in California. After this "great adventure" failed, Sinclair concluded that the single tax was politically unobtainable. In his *Book of Life* (1922), he wrote, "Theoretically the movement has a considerable percentage of right on its side." However, he claimed, "to understand it requires a knowledge of the complexities of our economic system which the voters simply have not got." Sinclair did not abandon the land problem, but he turned to answers that were more straightforward, including "cooperative agricultural colonies for our returned soldiers."[3]

George's vision of a "great and glorious city" in which land value taxation would spark densification seemed at odds with the public's trend to relocate outside cities. By the 1920s, the higher rates of home ownership and lower rents of an automobile society had taken hold. Now, as many as 57 percent of workers in Muncie, Indiana, commuted more than a mile from home to their place of employment. During the same period, the construction of new rental properties in Muncie all but ended.[4] The migration away from sites of employment was mimicked in larger cities such as New York, with Manhattan losing 18.2 percent of its population during the twenties.[5]

As the automobile expanded housing opportunities, the leverage that landholders held over tenants declined. While home ownership fell slowly from 1900 to 1920, during the twenties it increased by 5 percent, more than compensating for the slump of the preceding decades. At the same time, the explosive growth in real estate prices slowed. From 1912 to 1922 the aggregate value of real estate grew at an average rate of 8.85 percent every year; from 1922 to 1928 this slowed to 5.33 percent, even though the decade witnessed record home construction and rising construction costs.[6] The autocratic company town largely disappeared by midcentury, as workers choose to commute rather than live under the dominion of a boss who could tell them whom to vote for or where to worship.[7] The famed Georgist assessor Lawson Purdy now reevaluated his belief that because land was finite it would grow progressively in value, concluding that it was "accessibility, rather than the aggregate amount of land, that determines price."[8]

Georgists had supported the income tax, believing that, because of business's hostility, it would be easier to replace with the single tax than the tariff, which was supported by an array of entrenched special interests. They soon found, however, that the real power behind the throne was agriculture.[9] After the war, Georgists formed the Manufacturers and Merchants Federal Taxation League and secured endorsements from businesses for a bill that would shift government revenue to a national tax of 1 percent on the value of land.[10] Congressman John Nolan, a former iron molder representing San Francisco, introduced this Ralston-Nolan bill. Congressmen were bombarded with literature supporting the bill, but to no effect. Rural legislators were hostile, with one representative from Iowa arguing that under it the farmer "will be required to produce everything the world uses, wears, and eats, and in addition pay all the taxes." This congressman dismissively observed that Ralston had served as legal counsel for Louis Post and others accused of subversion during the war.[11]

Instead of providing an avenue for the single tax, the income tax popularized the rival doctrine of ability to pay. Georgists believed that land should be taxed to force the abandonment of underutilized land, but ability-to-pay economists countered that taxpayers relinquishing wealth was evidence that they were "unable to pay" and thus the tax was unjust. Robert Murray Haig made several studies of land value taxation in Canada in which he attacked it despite noting that it had seemingly reduced rents and spurred construction. In Vancouver, he observed that it violated ability to pay because "many of the large owners of such property have few resources other than their investments in land" and land speculators would thus be unable to pay their taxes.[12] Haig was called to Saskatchewan in 1917 to produce a report on municipal revenue after a group of property owners complained that land value taxation had produced "a reduction of real-estate prices."[13] Haig concluded that under land value taxation, "land values will be unfavorably affected," in part because "speculators" had concluded that their land was a "bad bet" and released it onto the market.[14] Georgists contended that such easy access to land was an avenue to economic opportunity, but Haig believed it to be a violation of ability to pay. He argued for shifting taxes onto improvements, because tenants would bear the cost in rising rents and it would thus operate "as a type of income tax on the lower ranges of income." Haig even recommended a poll tax to guarantee that all citizens, even the poor, paid what they could.[15] To ensure that property relations were not radically disrupted, Haig argued, taxes should rest on income, rather than wealth, though that might mean the burden of taxation would often fall harder on the working poor than the idle rich.

Haig's judgment that taxes should not redistribute wealth discouraged him from entertaining the complex implications of land value taxation in British Columbia. Declining land values in the 1920s did make land value taxation less sustainable, and British Columbians were literally unable to pay them. From 1924 to 1933, between $7,872,790 and $9,311,721 worth of real estate reverted every year to municipalities in British Columbia when owners fell into arrears. The mayor of Victoria, however, welcomed these tax sales because the properties were primarily in remote areas and "if in private ownership" would have demanded infrastructure such as streets and sewers at "considerable cost to the city."[16] When the city of Vancouver commissioned an expert to study tax forfeitures, he found that "only 4% were on improved properties, many of which, it is understood, were in poor condition" and the rest were on vacant properties that "were in outlying districts acquired more or less as a speculation."[17] During the depression of the 1930s Vancouver leased out these relinquished properties to elderly citizens, relief families, and squatters, before selling them at a considerable profit.[18] The Vancouver City Council, which was unfriendly to land value taxation by the 1930s, reported that the tax had led to "all city property" being "covered by buildings without tenants," which only reinforced the claim that the single tax spurred urban development and low rents.[19] Thus, both supporters and opponents of land value taxation believed that it had—as intended—redistributed wealth, made land a municipal resource, released cheap urban space, curtailed sprawl, and created a dense, well-built renters' market. The question was whether those changes were worthwhile. Haig's myopic focus on ability to pay allowed him to sweep through a thorny thicket of moral questions and provide a scholarly imprimatur to the normative belief that people should keep what they own.

This ability-to-pay doctrine found an audience during the 1920s and '30s as taxpayers staged a revolt against the property tax. The National Association of Real Estate Boards alleged that by 1928 four-fifths of state and local revenue was derived from real estate, imposing an undue burden on a single class of property.[20] In 1923 Rhode Island ratified a constitutional amendment limiting increases in the property tax. Within a decade, six more states had passed similar measures, and by 1936 thirty-five had passed, or were considering parts of, the legislative program of the National Association of Real Estate Boards. Among these was Ohio, which approved a constitutional amendment limiting the property tax.[21] Similarly, in British Columbia, property owners argued that they could not pay high land value taxes and that the burden needed to be shifted to Chinese immigrants or residents of trailer parks.[22]

This tax revolt did reflect legitimate concerns about the ability of owners of real estate—particularly farmland—to pay after World War I. The disruption of European agriculture during the war had produced a large captive market for American foodstuffs and sparked a period of rising prices and speculation. Farm real estate values grew 65 percent during the war as farmers gobbled up land to expand production for hungry markets. After the war, however, prices returned to normal levels and farmers were saddled with mortgage debt for real estate that was declining in value, leading to an agricultural depression and a wave of farm foreclosures that leveled rural banks.[23] John Dewey argued that these economic difficulties could have been avoided if land value taxation had been in place to deflate the value of real estate during the war.[24] Even if this were true, however, adding to the burdens of the agricultural sector after it collapsed in the 1920s would only have further destabilized the economy. Thus, Franklin Roosevelt, who helped popularize ability to pay, argued consistently for shifting the burden of taxation from overburdened and declining real estate values.[25] Georgists had hoped to reduce prices to foster equality, social mobility, and economic efficiency. However, underwater properties in the 1930s tied New Deal liberalism irrevocably to the opposite doctrine of asset price appreciation, fostering a wealthier middle class while progressively increasing barriers to entry.[26]

Losing Faith in the People

In 1918 Lincoln Steffens traveled to Russia and met Vladimir Lenin. "The Russian Revolution hit me very hard," Steffens wrote to Brand Whitlock. "There I saw close up those forces which we used to feel in cities rise up and carry men away like a ship in a storm." While in Russia, Steffens concluded that class war was natural and irreconcilable with his philosophy. He wrote Whitlock that the "liberal notions" they had shared were proven to have "been cultivated human wishes and purposes, having no parallels in nature and no foundation in science."[27] Steffens wanted to believe that George was right but was confident Lenin had proved otherwise. He wrote Daniel Kiefer wishing someone "would write a revision of George's philosophy in the light of the war and revolutions. That is what Lenin thinks some Socialist should do for Marx."[28] Steffens always struggled with the harsher world he now inhabited. In 1934 he wrote Frederic C. Howe that he was "hoping I will be proved wrong the way I used to seek evidence that I was right."[29]

While Georgists generally remained hostile to landed property, they lost faith that voters would ever be disinterested enough to adopt their strict interpretation of liberal natural law. In his 1932 autobiography, Clarence Darrow wrote that he was no longer a "pronounced disciple of Henry George." He noted that "I never believed that land should be reduced to private ownership, and I never felt that any important social readjustment could come while any one could claim the unconditional right to any part of the earth and 'the fullness thereof.'" Yet he rejected the movement's "cocksureness, its simplicity and the small value that it placed upon the selfish motives of men. I grew weary of its everlasting talk of 'natural rights.'"[30] Brand Whitlock, Albert Jay Nock, and Newton Baker turned on their former constituents, expressing concerns that immigrants, particularly Jews, did not sufficiently appreciate liberal ideals.[31] Clarence Darrow, once a fierce critic of eugenics, embraced genetic explanations for crime as his faith that the single tax would abolish inequality evaporated.[32] Whitlock, the novelist mayor of Toledo, now expressed "serious doubts as to whether there is, or ever will be, any such thing as democratic art."[33] Nock argued that George had soiled his philosophy by mixing it with democratic politics.[34]

The tribalism of the 1920s hit Georgists hard. In 1924 Ben Lindsey, the world-famous children's judge who had founded the first juvenile court in

Denver, faced a Democratic challenger supported by the Ku Klux Klan. Lindsey campaigned alongside the Catholic clergy in denouncing Klan nativism and anti-Catholicism. With the ticket split, he won reelection with a mere 130 votes. Lindsey ran afoul of the clergy, however, because of his support for contraceptives and easy divorce. The priest of Denver's Cathedral of the Immaculate Conception demanded his recall; Lindsey proclaimed that "the Cross and the Burning Cross both made war on me."[35] The clergy supported KKK efforts to vacate the election, claiming that the results from a Jewish district that had favored Lindsey should be discarded due to fraud. Lindsey was removed from office and forced to repay his salary to the widow of the Klan candidate; the official himself had taken his life after evidence of his past improprieties came to light.[36] Lindsey was disbarred, forced to rent out his home, and eventually run out of Denver altogether. Nevertheless, George Creel, Lindsey's old ally, preserved his faith in the people, arguing that "by 1928, the Ku Klux Klan will have disappeared just as the A. P. A. and the Know-Nothings."[37] Creel's confidence that the public would learn from its mistakes was in some sense prescient—the second iteration of the KKK collapsed as he predicted—but it also reflected his failure to grasp that the sentiments driving the Klan were an enduring feature of American society. The reenergized nativism of the twenties was inspired, in part, by the congressional Dillingham Commission of 1911, which used Progressive social scientific methods to paint southern and eastern European immigrants as racially inferior.[38]

This narrow "Americanism" would also manifest in a growing fear of socialism. Elizabeth Dilling's *The Red Network*, the first compendium of the secret communist conspiracy imagined to have captured the government, named a litany of Georgists, including Frederic Howe, Newton Baker, Frank Walsh, Lincoln Steffens, Benjamin Marsh, and Ben Lindsey as secret enemies of America.[39] Even though Howe had served in the Wilson administration, his wife, Marie, was arrested by the Secret Service on suspicion of subversion.[40] After the war, Howe retired to Nantucket, where, beginning in 1922, he gave educational lectures. But even here he was hounded by "big patriotic meetings" protesting a "hot-bed of revolutionary propaganda." It was rumored that the Justice Department infiltrated the meetings.[41]

Louis Post had put himself near the center of red scare hysteria during the deportation fiasco by advocating for freedom of speech. He remained in Washington, D.C., during the 1920s, living in Columbia Heights, where he met regularly with the city's liberal notables, including Louis Brandeis, Senator George Norris, Senator Robert La Follette, and Judson King.[42] But after accusations of sedition stemming from his leniency in the deportation hearings, he was unable to secure employment. When he did give public presentations, some of the attendees were agents of the Bureau of Investigation, which, at J. Edgar Hoover's prompting, continued its quest for evidence that Post was aligned with international communism.[43] Post observed that "his services were no longer in compensatory demand" because the single tax was "out of fashion" and because of his "identification with the 'reds.'"[44] He could not find a publisher for his biography of George.[45] His unemployment and the collapse of his life's work sparked disabling bouts of depression that Post described as "trips to hell."[46]

The founder of *The Public* lost faith in the public. He wrote that the country was drifting toward "a plutocratic autocracy" because of the mob sentiment of "pagan patriots" who "support any cause, however menacing to American ideals it may be, if its promoters decorate it richly enough with the American flag."[47] Post turned increasingly to the Swedenborgian Church for solace. Instead of reporting confidently on the progress of the single tax, he speculated that a just God would ultimately lead his people to the promised land. Despite his professed faith, a hint of pessimism seeped into his unpublished autobiography, "Living a Long Life Over Again," the title of which spoke to some doubts about the path he had committed himself to.

On January 10, 1928, Post died. On the day of his funeral the *New Church Messenger* published Post's last piece, "What Could Check Communism." Its conclusion was that we "must expand the concept of 'mine and thine' to 'mine, thine, and ours,'" thus ending the "injustices that arouse and promote communist unrest."[48] Supreme Court justice Louis Brandeis delivered the eulogy at Post's funeral. Brandeis, who was leading efforts to convince the US Supreme Court to adopt a more expansive interpretation of the First Amendment, praised Post in language that evoked the sacrifices the apostle of George had made for dissidents: "Post lived fearlessly, generously, nobly. He struggled without ceasing to preserve our liberties and to enlarge them. He resisted the clamor of stupid intolerance. He exposed shameful, ruthless lawlessness."[49]

Snatching Liberty from the Jaws of Defeat

A year after Brandeis delivered the eulogy at Post's funeral, he bid farewell to the Georgist solution to rail monopoly established in the Transportation Act of 1920. In *St. Louis & O'Fallon Ry. Co. v. United States*, a majority of justices ruled to invalidate the recapture of excess profits established during Wilson's presidency because the ICC's valuations did not take reproduction cost into consideration.[50] In his dissenting opinion, Brandeis justified the exclusion of reproduction cost because it "guarantees a return . . . upon unearned increment."[51] The Transportation Act, which should have been a great coup for the movement, was never effectively implemented because of judicial wrangling over valuation.

Although Post's economic philosophy seemed moribund, his brave effort to protect immigrants accused of radicalism from deportation was validated. The American Civil Liberties Union (ACLU) was formed in 1920 to defend the free speech rights of radicals accused of subversion. At the time, judges gave civil authorities wide latitude to censor material deemed to have a "bad tendency," and the only right vigorously protected by the judiciary was the "right to contract."[52] This jurisprudence met with little protest from Progressives, who generally had little affinity for individual rights, because they believed the will of the community could best be realized by an unencumbered state. Then, in the furor unleashed by World War I, Iowa banned the use of the German language in most public places, and the federal government imprisoned Eugene Debs for delivering a speech condemning conscription. The ACLU, formed in reaction to these abuses, represented a new awareness that as the state grew, it was increasingly necessary to protect individual rights. The protection of radicals served as a beachhead for a wider "rights revolution" in which the ACLU led efforts to incorporate the Bill of Rights into the Fourteenth Amendment, thereby stringently protecting those liberties from government abuse.

While the ACLU employed the legalistic language of constitutional rights, it shared an affinity with the natural rights philosophy of Henry George and its aspiration to preserve a private sphere free from the authority of expanding state power. When the ACLU was formed, it began its fight against the red scare by republishing an account of the deportation cases that Post had presided over. The pamphlet, originally published by the National Popular Government League, was written by Georgists Judson King and Jackson Ralston, with Frank Walsh adding his signature.[53] The Harvard-educated economist John S. Codman, who in 1935 cofounded the Boston branch of the Henry George School of Social Science, led the Civil Liberties Union of Massachusetts.[54] Frederic Howe, whose account of the war in *Confessions of a Reformer* served as the decade's most famous exposition against the Progressive faith in unlimited state power, took a seat on the ACLU's national board.

A wide swath of progressives disillusioned by the wartime state embraced individual rights, though Georgists had generally been there first. During the

Progressive era, even moderate liberals like William Allen White and Oliver Wendell Holmes Jr. believed the First Amendment did not protect speech that promoted violence or illegality.[55] When the anarchist Emma Goldman surveyed Progressive-era liberalism in search of supporters for free speech, she invariably found Georgists. She remembered that "Cleveland had for years been a free-speech stronghold, owing to the libertarian conditions established there by the single-tax mayor, Tom Johnson."[56] The two consistent defenders she identified in the press were the Georgist periodicals, *The Public* and the *St. Louis Mirror*.[57] Amos Pinchot and his wife were among the most prominent supporters of Margaret Sanger's fight to publicly advocate birth control; the New York Georgist Bolton Hall invited arrest at one of her events to serve as a First Amendment test case.[58] The Georgist lawyer Clarence Darrow's defense of labor activists and radicals prior to World War I made him perhaps the nation's preeminent civil libertarian. After the war, he worked with the ACLU to defend the communist Benjamin Gitlow in a case that ended with the US Supreme Court limiting the power of state governments to regulate speech. Under the leadership of Frank Walsh, the Commission on Industrial Relations exposed stunning employer violations of civil liberties and proposed a constitutional amendment that would ban both public and private sector impingements on free speech. Walsh's report became the rallying point for the movement to protect First Amendment rights; even the revolutionary Industrial Workers of the World regarded it as their "Bible."[59]

As the most mainstream faction of the radical coalition emerging around civil liberties, Georgists often played a vital function in legitimating the movement for free speech. The infamously libertine editor William Marion Reedy, in whose *St. Louis Mirror* realist literature from Carl Sandburg and Edgar Lee Masters shared the page with his Georgist orthodoxy, would play a vital role in legitimating revolutionary speech. In 1908 Reedy published "The Daughter of the Dream," in which he labeled Emma Goldman "eight thousand years ahead of her time." Goldman, who praised Reedy as a man of "rich humor," "broad culture," and "courageous spirt," noted that "no finer appreciation of my ideas . . . had ever been written by a non-anarchist."[60] Key to Reedy's appreciation was a utopian liberalism that allowed him to conceptualize anarchism as a distant horizon of his, and the nation's, philosophy: "Without such vision the people must perish. What is democracy but a step forward to this ideal? If that is the best government which governs least, is not no government at all the *summum bonum*? What use for Church and State if man, with every burden cast off, every bond broken, rises to his full

stature and development, with a spirit purified into selflessness by very surrender to the instinct of self!"[61]

An accident of fate made Reedy's defense of Goldman especially significant. Taking Goldman under his wing, he steered her "through the shoals of society luncheons and would-be bohemian dinners." Goldman noted, "His suave manner could smuggle the most dangerous contraband into the enemy's camp."[62] Reedy introduced Goldman to the young Roger Baldwin, whom Reedy described as a "very mild uplifter," until the meeting with Goldman. After meeting her, Baldwin became a "radical of the most pronounced sort." Reedy took great pride (and credit) when, after World War I began, Baldwin formed the Civil Liberties Bureau to defend radicals from wartime hysteria.[63] In 1920, that organization became the American Civil Liberties Union, and Baldwin served as its executive director until 1950. Taking cases that turned the Bill of Rights into a living document, the ACLU precipitated the rights revolution, which ensured the United States adhered to the traditions of rights-based liberalism, even as the administrative state grew steadily. This development embodied, in a sense, George's dream of coupling an ever-expanding social welfare state with a sacrosanct private sphere. By validating the most extreme types of speech, Georgists planted the seeds for the rights revolution.[64]

The Public and Its Problems

Georgists were hardly the only reformers who expressed growing doubts about the capacity of the people to govern wisely. The 1920s witnessed a series of Republican presidents whose candidacies were promoted by glossy photographs and films that showed the imprint of a new class of professional ad men such as Edward Bernays and Bruce Barton. Publicity was hardly new to Progressives, whose muckraking journalists and bully pulpit presidents modernized the art of political persuasion. However, Progressives had leveraged these techniques to expose corruption. In contrast, professionalized public relations experts seemed to be manipulating public emotions. In 1922 America's leading journalist, Walter Lippmann, wrote *Public Opinion*, in which he despaired at the impossibility of real democracy. Lippmann argued that the average citizen was incapable of understanding the issues, was too driven by emotion, and was too susceptible to propaganda.[65] Lippmann proposed the formation of government "Intelligence Bureaus" through which experts would disseminate facts to influence public opinion and shape the legislative process.[66]

Five years later, John Dewey published *The Public and Its Problems*. Dewey shared many of Lippmann's concerns with democracy. He drew a sharp division between "democracy as a social idea and political democracy as a system of government."[67] He had no faith in democracy as a mere set of procedures, arguing that "there is no sanctity in universal suffrage, frequent elections, majority rule, congressional and cabinet government."[68] Instead, democracy was an ideal that had to be realized in social conditions before political institutions could have substantive value. Dewey was one of the few prominent individuals during the decade to move sharply toward the philosophy of Henry George.

Dewey rejected, as Georgists had unerringly done, the doctrine of expert management. Dewey had a profound faith in science to reshape society, but only insofar as its knowledge became ensconced in, and subservient to, the democratic public. Like Tom Johnson, he considered expertise to be utilitarian, something that could find a means to an end but that was not itself capable of identifying the public's needs in a disinterested way. Once experts "become a specialized class, they are shut off from the needs which they are supposed to serve."[69] Only by abiding by the dictates of the democratic process could experts ascertain the ends to which their skills should be applied. Dewey observed that "the man who wears the shoe knows best that it pinches and where it pinches, even if the expert shoemaker is the best judge of how the trouble is to be remedied."[70]

Unlike Lippmann, with his expert-led Intelligence Bureaus, Dewey had little faith in any outside agency to uplift the public. Instead, he ended *The Public and Its Problems* with a plea for the importance of local community in fostering a sense of common purpose. Like George, who associated democratic knowledge with the local-level "collision of mind with mind," Dewey identified democracy's social roots with the Greco-Roman city-state, New England townhalls, and, ultimately, the industrial city.[71] While the written word was important for conveying knowledge, it was "soliloquy"—inherently aristocratic because it imposed the author's ideas without dialogue. Reliance on outside sources for information was dangerous because the public had shown itself incapable of distinguishing fact from propaganda.[72] Dewey argued that "the problem of securing diffused and seminal knowledge can be solved only in the degree in which local community becomes a reality," creating a "fraternally shared experience."[73]

Dewey failed in *The Public and Its Problems* to identify how these local communities could be fostered, but in his subsequent works he clarified that idle land speculation needed to be taxed out of existence. In an essay four years later, he argued that to "remove the barriers that now prevent the circulation of knowledge and ideas," it was necessary to eliminate slums, which built cultural barriers to the development of community.[74] Two years later, in *Art and Experience*, Dewey explained the origins of slums: "Their character is determined by an economic system in which land is used—and kept out of use—for the sake of gain."[75] By that point, he was constantly arguing as president of the People's Lobby that land value taxation was the only way to fix the nation's economic and social ills. He increasingly emphasized George's ideas of social intelligence created by unconscious cooperation.[76] Dewey believed the crux of George's contribution was to show that cultural development was rooted in place and therefore became imbedded in rising land values that barred the less fortunate from access to those resources: "Henry George puts . . . stress upon the fact that community life increases land value because it opens 'a wider, fuller, and more varied life' so that the desire to share in the higher values which the community brings with it is a decisive factor in raising the rental value of land."[77]

It is a truism that, while Dewey was the nation's best-regarded philosopher, Americans rarely followed the lead of this radical, often-idiosyncratic intellectual, who embodied what they aspired to be but rarely were.[78] Whereas Dewey pointed to the development of cities and intensive use of land as the path toward democratic community, most reformers hoped to break them apart. They would pull Americans out of the city and relocate them in new communities where open land would separate them from their neighbors and even larger empty greenbelts would protect them from central cities.

Regional Planning

With little support for taxing land or spurring density, some took elements of George's ideas in a new direction. The regional planning movement traced its roots back to the Garden City Movement in England. The inventor of this new type of community, Ebenezer Howard, had written in *Garden Cities of Tomorrow* that by placing the whole burden of taxation on landowners, George was "little likely to commend . . . [his] views to society." Much of the book was devoted to proving that land rents would be a sufficient and theoretically sound source of revenue, but Howard believed that for the plan to obtain traction, the state would need to compensate landowners, purchasing land for model planned communities. Instead of dense cities, these would be a regional network of small communities with private homes and large lots of communal green space.[79] Howard's idea was profoundly successful. Letchworth, Howard's first garden city, was flourishing by the 1910, attracting imitators from as far away as Russia and inspiring England's popular government-owned "New Towns."[80]

In the United States, the Garden City idea was taken up by the Regional Planning Association of America (RPAA). This organization formed in the late teens when Charles Whitaker, a Georgist, collected a small coterie of like-minded individuals around him in his role as editor of the *Journal of the American Institute of Architects*.[81] The group included Benton MacKaye, who advocated in *The Public* for land nationalization as a more direct route to Georgism.[82] MacKaye, however, was exceptional among the younger generation of radicals for the close relationship he had with men such as Post. Organized around George's family and close associates, Georgist leadership was inflexibly rooted in people of or near his generation. A poll of the New York Single Tax Club at the time found that only 20 percent of its members had joined in the previous decade. This intelligence inspired the upcoming 1911 Fels Fund conference to hold a survey that produced better results, though they suggest that the movement was recruiting fewer new members where better established organizations had entrenched membership in the past.[83] One younger radical reported that he "became an interested member of the single tax group in New York City, but" left after he "found . . . that the group in New York City that was interested in the single tax seemed to be all contemporaries of Henry George."[84]

Regional planning, therefore, constituted a generational shift from the single tax. The regional planner Stuart Chase had been pursuing a degree in business at Harvard when he spotted *Progress and Poverty* on the shelf in the library. In the ensuing "nine hours a sword had flashed and cut [Chase] off from the cumulative ideology of twenty-three years." Chase abandoned business and joined the local single tax club but left within a year, noting that it "was composed largely of elderly men."[85] He bounced around a series of socialist organizations, retaining a faith in the social nature of land, but was in no sense a doctrinaire single taxer. A founding member of the RPAA, Chase used his position as associate editor of *Survey* to coordinate a series of special issues that gave regional planning its first real public hearing.[86]

This generational change mirrored the broader shift of the 1920s toward aesthetic and psychological ideals. Government ownership offered experts the opportunity to plan beautiful communities, not just efficient ones like the dense urban cores Georgists had embraced. Lewis Mumford noted that his was "a generation . . . no longer interested in trying to make the machinery of society more perfect, but that sought to provide that their own lives . . . should be lively and enjoyable."[87] Increasingly the regional planners critiqued land values not for promoting inequality but for producing ugly, dense cities. Frederick Ackerman argued that the real sin of "appreciation of value" in land was that it fostered overbuilt urban centers, because "no speculator in urban lands and buildings will interest himself in an enterprise unless the prospects surrounding it show the promise afforded by growth and concentration."[88] With the nation's rush to the suburbs, even older Georgists accepted that they had been too rational in their focus on urban economics. Newton Baker noted that the movement had emphasized the "economic rather than the spiritual side of man's relation to land" and failed to appeal to "deeper values."[89]

By the end of the 1920s, regional planners had built momentum for policies that would redistribute population away from urban centers. Franklin Roosevelt was an early convert, announcing himself "a great believer in . . . regional planning" interested in a "far-reaching policy of land utilization and of population distribution."[90] Roosevelt's uncle Frederic Delano argued for reversing the logic of the single tax by reducing the taxes on land and increasing them on buildings to slow the growth of cities.[91] Rexford Tugwell took it for granted that "the day of the larger cities has definitively passed." As the leading urban planner of the New Deal, he noted that in embracing the suburb the Roosevelt administration had merely "accepted a trend instead of trying to reverse it."[92]

The regional planning movement sometimes saw itself as rooted in George's critique of private land ownership but was also radically unlike it. In trying to merge the single tax with city planning, regional planners adopted an ethos of expert control which was antithetical to George's philosophy that the unconscious cooperation of the market functioned better than planning.[93] The aspiration for perfectly planned communities failed to acknowledge that cities served multiple, often contradictory purposes and that individual preferences varied widely. At the regional planning conference in 1932, experts reached no consensus on how communities ought to be planned, only that they should be.[94] When the self-taught Jane Jacobs wrote *The Death and Life of Great American Cities* in 1961, she persuasively argued that the discipline of urban planning had been founded on an irrational hostility to urban life, not scientific evidence. Planners' efforts to impose sprawling empty space on the city had hollowed out the natural ecosystem of market exchange that made cities vibrant.[95] Planning, she argued, amounted to little more than a poorly conceived war on the cities as resources flowed to federally subsidized suburbs. Plans to re-create bucolic rural life within the metropolis would likely have received a similarly unfavorable response from George, who believed the absence of cultural exchange in rural communities had turned Americans into "half-savage cowboys."[96]

Chieftains and Martyrs

Stuart Chase might have regarded the "chieftains and martyrs" of the previous generation as too rational for a democracy, but he still idealized their journey as a grand adventure. By the 1920s Georgists were old-fashioned, but many of them were still legends. Although the movement's leading lights were often attacked from both the left and the right for their role in World War I, they retained significant followings.

It was in the early 1930s that Samuel Seabury finished one of George's earliest battles. Seabury had read *Progress and Poverty* in 1894 and, shortly after joining the Manhattan Single Tax Club, met George in his study overlooking the Lower New York Bay. George deemed Seabury one of the "babies of the movement."[97] He had since become a fierce political operator, hatching plots to single-handedly sway two nominating conventions. In 1916 Seabury was nominated for governor but lost, believing he had been knifed in the back by Tammany Hall and Theodore Roosevelt. Seabury returned to private practice, becoming one of New York's most successful lawyers in the barrister tradition (counsel contracted out by other lawyers to handle complex appeals cases). Seabury's contributions to New York were large: he saved Sidney Hillman's Amalgamated Clothing Workers of America from a likely fatal injunction, fought discrimination within the bar, and developed the legal argument for workers' compensation.[98]

Seabury's career reached its pinnacle in 1930, when he was appointed to investigate the magistrates' courts of New York City for graft. No longer a baby, he was now an imposing gray-haired man with a broad forehead, British affectations, and a reserved demeanor that gave way to ferocious independence when he barged into the public sphere. He assembled a coterie of devoted young lawyers to join the "Seabury Investigation" and prepared them to be try a case in the court of public opinion.[99] He got off to a spectacular start when he secured testimony from a thirty-one-year-old Chilean immigrant whom the New York Police Department had employed to frame innocent women and landlords as prostitutes. This scam maintained the appearance of vice enforcement as police left real brothels and prostitutes to operate freely in return for kickbacks. Judges, in turn, helped railroad these innocent women in return for a cut. These judges, often woefully unqualified, earned their sinecures by paying off the Tammany Hall machine, creating a web of illicit activity that stretched from the bottom to the top of city government.

These scandalous charges led then-governor Franklin Roosevelt to authorize a series of probes that unearthed an expanding circle of corruption engineered by Tammany Hall. This investigation culminated in 1932, when Seabury interrogated Mayor Jimmy Walker about large gifts he had received from shady transit franchises. Seabury invited Henry George's daughter and granddaughter to watch the interrogation that ended with Walker's resignation. Seabury had struck a blow against Tammany Hall that it would never fully recover from, bringing a conclusion to the struggle against Tammany that Seabury had fought alongside George in his 1897 mayoral campaign.

After Walker's removal, Seabury became the city's moral center. Although he declined the opportunity to be mayor, he exercised his authority to veto the efforts of the Fusion Party ticket to nominate Robert Moses.[100] Seabury, implacable, forced the reluctant Fusion ticket to instead nominate Fiorello La Guardia, who, on December 31, 1933, was sworn in as mayor at Seabury's home. Adolf Berle Jr. observed that throughout his twelve years as mayor, La Guardia spoke to Seabury as if he were a father.[101] La Guardia appointed Seabury to the Board of Estimate to negotiate the purchase and consolidation of interurban lines into a unified public transit system. Although Seabury encountered setbacks, La Guardia ultimately placed most of the city's transit system under public ownership, realizing Seabury and George's long-standing dream.

Seabury's legend was impressive, but Newton Baker remained the most prominent member of the single tax movement during the interwar period. Baker had been Tom Johnson's choice to succeed him as mayor of Cleveland and then served as Wilson's secretary of war. After the Wilson administration, he had served on the Permanent Court of Arbitration at The Hague and was expected to be a contender for the post of secretary-general of the League of Nations. Baker was widely honored for readying a demobilized nation for total war. His twenty years of public service had left him with few opportunities to accumulate wealth; he was, in fact, eight thousand dollars in debt by the time he left Washington. He returned after a long absence to a highly lucrative private law practice but remained active in so many civic groups that he once observed that the list of those organizations extended for more than two typewritten pages when divided into multiple columns. He was a trustee of six institutions of higher education and president of the Association for Adult Education. Baker's biographer explained his interest in adult education: "One of

Johnson's great services, in Baker's judgment, was that he kept the whole of the population fully informed on his purposes and his plans, with the result that Cleveland had the best-informed body of citizens to be found anywhere in America."[102] Most significant, as a member of the Carnegie Foundation, Baker proposed a project on race relations that became Gunnar Myrdal's groundbreaking attack on Jim Crow, *An American Dilemma* (1944).[103]

After World War I, Baker served as the leading voice for Wilsonian internationalism. A fanciful rumor circulated that Baker had made a deathbed promise to Wilson "never to make a public address without endorsing the league."[104] At the 1924 Democratic National Convention, he wrote the minority report calling for the United States to enter the League of Nations. His speech was aired nationally via radio. Evoking the memory of the recently departed president, he reminded his audience that "I served Woodrow Wilson for five years. He is standing at the throne of God whose approval he won and received. As he looks down from there I say to him, 'I did my best. I am doing it now. You are still the captain of my soul.'" It was an unusually melodramatic speech for the typically analytical speaker, who later adjudged the speech as having fallen short because of several consecutive late nights spent working at the convention. Few others felt that way. He brought several in the audience to tears; William Allen White proclaimed him "a prophet." It did nothing, however, to abate the league's unpopularity. Delegates voted Baker's plank down by a margin of more than two to one.[105]

By 1932 Baker was widely seen as the man most qualified to be president. When the stock market crash of 1929 sent the economy into a downward spiral, the complacency of the twenties gave way to a revival of reform. Educated opinion was largely behind Baker, with one poll in *Outlook* finding that newspaper editors in thirty-four states favored him. Baker even dominated Franklin Roosevelt on his home turf; when polled by *Radio and Amusement Guide*, radio listeners scored Roosevelt's on-air personality an 84, second only to Baker, who was ranked a 92.5.[106] Baker was endorsed by Democrats who depicted him as the heir to the legacies of Woodrow Wilson and Tom Johnson or as the "the Jeffersonian apostle of the North."[107] Walter Lippmann pronounced Baker the "inevitable candidate."[108]

Baker was bitterly opposed by isolationists, particularly the publisher William Randolph Hearst, but his most outspoken opponent was himself; he refused to campaign, disavowed any aspirations for the presidency, and discouraged those working on his behalf. To the press, Baker reported that he did not care for the lifestyle that a residence at 1600 Pennsylvania Avenue would demand, but privately he confessed his lack of confidence. Two years after Roosevelt was elected, he confided to Mary Fels that much of the platform of the leading Democratic contender was "at variance with what I have always regarded as . . . sound theory." But, he added, "I would not know what to do in the crisis with any certainty that my thought is better than his and second, he is at least doing something."[109]

Baker had always feared the unknown implications of untried ideas but had found in Johnson's theories sound cause for action. As his faith in that theory came into question, he was paralyzed by fear: "The older I get the more convinced I am that the only fears I have in the world are fears of ignorance. I am afraid of my own actions when I am acting ignorantly."[110] In his later years he responded to most requests for comment with the observation that he did not know enough about the subject. He wrote that his comprehension of urban policy was as "rusty as my knowledge of the middle voice of Greek verbs."[111]

Baker's faith was shaken but not quite broken. He contributed to a project called "The Henry George I Knew." This was Will Atkinson's desperate attempt to preserve the disappearing history of Georgism. The quest was driven by the realization that historians "did not get from Charles Frederic Adams, before he died, the vivid picture he would have drawn from McCabe, the Maori . . . from Sun Yat-sen, his acknowledgment of the debt New China owes to the Prophet of San Francisco."[112] Baker gave Atkinson a nuanced endorsement: "The world has never suddenly accepted and applied any change in its political or social philosophy so radical as that embodied in the single tax. Great truths have to be accepted piecemeal. Many of the implications of the single tax which were startling in Henry George's day have become commonplace parts of our later thinking and have modified economic doctrines which seemed final before they came into contact with the philosophy which Henry George preached."[113] Baker embraced George's philosophy but no longer affiliated himself with the movement, confirming to Mary Fels that he "believed in the Single Tax" but "is not a Single-Taxer."[114] However, when presented an opportunity, he still engaged. Baker twice visited Mexico to support Antenor Sala, leader of a movement demanding a "sole tax" on land.[115]

Despite Baker's ambivalence, many Georgists fought for his presidency. Mary Fels lobbied him with an enthusiasm that suggested utopian aspirations: "I have always felt the call would come to you when world need became very urgent."[116] George Creel wrote a laudatory article in which he brushed aside Baker's objections as a facet of the "old-fashioned belief that the office should seek the man."[117] Samuel Seabury had wanted the nomination but then swung his support to Baker with the hope of becoming number two on the ticket. Seabury forwarded his charges against Jimmy Walker to Franklin Roosevelt a week before the Democratic National Convention to force him to make a decision that would, Seabury hoped, jeopardize his candidacy by alienating either Tammany Hall or advocates of good government.[118] When Roosevelt squirmed his way out of this dilemma by delaying his decision, Walter Lippmann assailed Roosevelt as "no crusader" or "enemy of entrenched privilege" and, in fact, "no dangerous enemy of anything."[119]

The tradition to which Baker belonged, the force of his supporters, and his record of reform brought the Clevelander surprisingly close to the presidency, despite the candidate's resolve not to stand for election. A small campaign fund, intended to sponsor telegraphs to the convention endorsing Baker, was supported by George Peabody and Wendell Willkie, who had been inspired by Baker's 1924 Democratic National Convention speech to devote his life to internationalism, eventually becoming perhaps the most nationally prominent advocate for decolonization, racial liberalism, and the United Nations.[120] Franklin Roosevelt entered the convention with a solid majority, but party rules required a two-thirds supermajority of delegates to nominate a candidate. Recalcitrant delegates from the South and West refused to concede to Roosevelt's candidacy, and it appeared the convention would, as it had eight years earlier, compromise on a dark-horse candidate who had not been on the ballot. Baker's allies sent telegraphs supporting his candidacy while the young lawyers of the Seabury investigation sent a man to Buffalo to smuggle in Canadian whiskey, which they offered to roving delegates while pitching a Baker-Seabury ticket.[121] After falling short on three successive ballots, Roosevelt was so certain of his defeat that he called Baker to concede. "It now looks," he purportedly told Baker, "as though the Chicago Convention is in a jam and that they will turn to you. I will do anything I can to bring that about if you want it."[122]

Roosevelt's phone call was premature. At that moment, Joseph Kennedy appealed to the publishing giant William Randolph Hearst, an isolationist who disdained Baker and his Wilsonianism. Hearst made a frenzied late-night campaign to sway the Texas and California delegations. William McAdoo, who had clashed with Baker during the war, acted as "his agent." Texas and California swung to Roosevelt, giving him the votes to win the nomination.[123] Half a century after George had encouraged Johnson to pursue power in the Democratic Party, Johnson's protégé nearly fell into the White House. By then, however, Baker knew he had so little of relevance to offer that he made no effort to secure the job.

For a few years, Georgists rallied behind the new president. George Creel and George Peabody acknowledged that they had initially supported Baker but pledged to work for Roosevelt and became close associates.[124] Baker seemed frankly relieved and was happy that the president "knows how to choose counselors": the architect of his "Brain Trust" was Raymond Moley, a former student of his and a longtime admirer of Tom Johnson and Henry George.[125]

Georgists were not wrong to have confidence in Roosevelt; he had obtained political maturity as an independent Democrat in New York when that inevitably meant working with Georgists. He had joined the Wilson administration and there established many close relationships with single taxers, bonding over an interest in land, natural resources, and utilities. Like many people in his administration, he had grown to political maturity looking up to Georgist leaders. Some of the leading minds of his administration considered themselves intellectually indebted to George and his followers, though only loosely. Yet Roosevelt would eventually personify single taxers' disenchantment with democracy.

CHAPTER 13

Back to the Land

The New Deal, Land Policy, and the Single Tax Movement

> As the thoughtlessness and aimlessness of the 'twenties became more and more apparent, I'd grown more convinced that someone must be found who could do on a national scale what Tom Johnson had done in Cleveland. There was no Tom Johnson. But out of the field, by January 1932, it seemed to me that the buoyant likable man in Albany [Franklin Roosevelt] was the only hope.
>
> Raymond Moley

Georgists could have found a lot to appreciate about the New Deal. The security that its welfare programs provided reinvigorated faith in liberal democracy when much of the world veered toward authoritarian nationalism. Roosevelt's Supreme Court nominees expanded the scope and enforcement of constitutional rights. The New Deal was a grab bag of the ideas that had animated reform movements for the past five decades, including some, like economic planning, that Georgists had long detested. But by the end of the New Deal, planning had fallen by the wayside, while programs that emphasized the social character of natural resources, utilities, and housing thrived, sometimes building off precedents set by Georgists. Yet, almost to a man, Georgists left the Democratic Party, as well as their positions of power and influence, because they saw the liberalism of the New Deal as opposed to that of Henry George. They resented the New Deal for expanding the size of government and business, the emphasis it placed on security rather than equal opportunity, and a transactional approach to politics that appeared to transform liberalism into pandering to special interests. After the dispiriting 1920s, many reembraced Henry George with a new vigor, even if just to thumb their nose at the times.

That Georgists failed to acclimate themselves to the New Deal reinforces its significance as a transitional phase in liberalism. Georgists had established many precedents for the New Deal, but they had done so out of an inflexible faith in a narrow reinterpretation of classical liberalism. Former abolitionist evangelists of free labor who reluctantly accepted an argument for socialism even Herbert Spencer acknowledged, would not otherwise have been inclined to embrace the welfare state. Without George, men like Tom Johnson would have remained standpat businessmen. Much of American liberalism had migrated into the twentieth century over a narrow bridge of George's design. It is hard to say how liberalism would have fared if it had endeavored to ford the rapids.

Common Ground

Franklin Roosevelt's opinions followed the polls, but whenever, as an independent Democrat from New York during his formative years, he put his ear to the ground, the single tax was one of the louder rumblings he heard. The Georgist prison reformer Thomas Mott Osborn was a close associate through the 1910s, funding the Empire State Democracy, which Roosevelt used to promote Woodrow Wilson's candidacy in New York.[1] In the Wilson administration, Roosevelt met Louis Post, Newton Baker, and George Creel. He became particularly close to Franklin Lane, for whose widow he endowed a trust fund.[2] In 1916 Roosevelt boasted that he secured the nomination of the single taxer Samuel Seabury for governor of New York.[3] As a young politician, Roosevelt often looked up to older Georgists, including Ben Lindsey and Daniel Beard, whose Campfire Club supported his conservationist efforts as a state senator.[4] Roosevelt admired Beard for drawing the illustrations (many with Georgist undertones) in Mark Twain's *Connecticut Yankee*, the book from which Roosevelt claimed to have taken the slogan "New Deal." Beard, who introduced George at his last public event, mailed Roosevelt his novel *Moonblight*, in which workers appropriate a mine and use the land rent to fund improvements. The president replied, "It is delightful to associate both you and my old friend Louis Post with it. . . . It is of the vintage of 1939—and so are you."[5]

Roosevelt rarely offered his own philosophical views, but he did articulate an interpretation of George that, while it should be taken with a grain of salt, was measured and consistent with his policies. After Roosevelt left the Wilson administration and became governor of New York, the Robert Schalkenbach Foundation, founded in 1925 to promote George's ideas, sent him a copy of *Progress and Poverty*. The governor wrote back that while he did not "go all the way" with George, he was "one of the really great thinkers produced by our country" and that his writings "contain much that would be helpful today."[6] Roosevelt was consistently critical of property taxes for violating the principle of ability to pay.[7] However, most of those around Roosevelt believed the issue to which he was most closely wed was social control of land and natural resources. Raymond Moley claimed that hydroelectric power was the "subject to which Roosevelt had given more painstaking study than he had to any other single one." But this was really, "in a sense, part of a larger policy which had included the conservation of both land and water."[8]

Many around Roosevelt were indebted to the legacy of Georgism. In the lead-up to his election as president in 1932, Roosevelt formed the "Brain Trust," which served as a model for incorporating academic expertise into a presidential administration. Ironically, considering George's conflicts with academia, Georgist thought would have a surprisingly large beachhead in this group. Raymond Moley, born in 1886, was raised in Olmstead Falls, Ohio. At fifteen he bought a copy of *Progress and Poverty* and took to reciting it in the woods and pretending that he was a radical orator.[9] As a newspaper boy in the Cleveland suburbs, he kept a close watch on Tom Johnson and developed a lifelong affection for him. He went to the tent meetings to see Johnson speak, sat at the feet of Frederic C. Howe, wrote a master's thesis on judicial reform in the Johnson administration, and studied property law under Newton Baker.[10] Baker introduced him to Franklin Roosevelt. Moley endeared himself to the governor and in 1932 was tasked with recruiting the Brain Trust. Moley never believed he had traveled far philosophically; he branded Johnson's mayoralty a "more localized New Deal."[11]

One of Moley's recruits was Rexford Tugwell, the chief architect of Roosevelt's land policy. Tugwell had read George in his college days, followed Steffens closely, and depicted Johnson's Cleveland policy as a model for reform. He had studied economics under Scott Nearing, a resident of the Georgist Arden community. From Nearing, Tugwell learned about the Landlord's Game and, at Columbia University, popularized the board game designed as a practical illustration of George's ideas.[12] In a chapter highlighting the influence of Georgist mayors on the New Deal, Tugwell concluded that "of all the possible choices between private and public activity—not excepting the utilities—the ownership and management of land and the manipulation of its values had perhaps the most disastrous consequences."[13] Tugwell argued for building on Johnson's platform of "public ownership of utilities" so that it "might extend to national programs."[14]

According to Tugwell and Moley, the New Deal inherited a great deal from the current of municipal reform in which Georgists had predominated. For Tugwell, agrarian reform, because it had worked through the sluggish medium of the federal government, had produced few results. Most experienced administrators recruited into the New Deal naturally followed, instead, in the footsteps of "city reformers" on whom Henry George's "influence was, indeed, immense."[15] John Collier, for instance, wrote admiringly in 1911 of Milwaukee socialists to the extent that they followed "single-tax tendency common to most American cities" by converting private land to public ownership. Now, as commissioner of Indian affairs, Collier would follow a similar policy by returning privately held indigenous land to tribal ownership.[16] Tugwell concluded that "Tom Johnson, Brand Whitlock, John Purroy Mitchel, and Rudolph Blankenburg had not been permanently defeated, and the patient advocates of better administration had started an evolution essential to the burdens of the welfare state."[17] Speaking to an Atlanta crowd in 1934, Moley argued that Tom Johnson was one of "the Men behind the New Deal."[18] George's argument that urban land accrued social value had reshaped liberalism to incorporate social property: "The tremendous fact which George so diligently promoted," he observed, "was that of social value. To point out that a piece of land in itself is valueless unless there are people who find it useful is to shake the very foundation of all ancient concepts of property."[19]

With this background, the New Deal initially looked little like the quasi-social democracy it would become. Roosevelt's 1932 campaign book, *Looking Forward*, mentioned organized labor once, incidentally, as a source on the unemployment rate.[20] A chapter of the book was devoted to social welfare but argued that it should be reserved to the states.[21] In many respects, the First New Deal would sound instead like another New Freedom, replicating Wilson's Georgist-tinged policies. *Looking Forward* devoted chapters to topics such as the tariff, "state planning for land utilization," "the power issue,: and railroads. Roosevelt's Public Works Administration (PWA) funded publicly owned utilities, and by 1937 the organization's lawyers had drafted more than five hundred state bills to remove obstacles to public ownership.[22] The nation's public lands were expanded as the federal government purchased 22 million acres—approximately 1 percent of the total land mass of the United States—to remove "submarginal" land from cultivation. As the Resettlement Administration moved some farmers off private land, it moved others onto public land, leased by the government. With unemployment hovering at around 20 percent, no factories were requisitioned and forced into operation. But the federal government was tasked with building and operating approximately a hundred communities, thereby extending the leasehold system begun under Wilson.

In 1932 what remained of the Georgist movement rallied around Roosevelt. Frank Walsh, Basil Manly, and Frederic Howe organized the National Progressive League, led by George Norris, to use the public power issue to cleave progressives from the Republican Party.[23] Walsh worked with Judson King to mobilize members of the Progressive-era Popular Government League for Roosevelt. The result was the Roosevelt Campaign Committee of the Popular Government League on Power, Natural Resources, and Forestry. Single taxers including Alice Thacher Post, Edwin Markham, Jackson Ralston, and William U'Ren predominated in the group's leadership.[24] Many Georgists rallied to Roosevelt's trade policies. Will Atkinson formed the All American Reciprocity Union. Roosevelt pledged his support to trade reciprocity and promised to meet with George Peabody, an old friend who was affiliated with the organization.[25] Atkinson also convinced the progressive Republican senator Burton K. Wheeler of Montana to read into the *Congressional Record* an abridged version of George's *Protection or Free Trade.*

Public Waterpower

A decade before the New Deal, Georgists had laid the first bricks of Roosevelt's Tennessee Valley Authority. During the Wilson administration, Newton Baker had presided over the construction of two wartime dams in the Muscle Shoals region of Tennessee. In the waning days of the administration, Baker submitted to Congress the Wadsworth-Kahn bill, under which a federally owned corporation would direct the continued development of the projects. Baker testified to Congress on the bill's behalf. The war, however, was over, and Congress's tolerance for spending had evaporated. Republicans claimed the Wadsworth-Kahn bill was pork barrel legislation for southern Democrats. With no alternative, the fate of the tremendous infrastructure project, funded by taxpayers with an estimated potential yield of $2.9 million annually, needed to be settled. Baker had set up a situation where a fight for public ownership was all but inevitable.[26]

The fight for public hydroelectricity came to a head in 1924 when Henry Ford offered to purchase the dams and produce inexpensive fertilizer for farmers. The prospect of recruiting Ford to work on behalf of farmers proved so attractive that even George Norris, the Senate's foremost proponent of government ownership, initially vacillated when confronted with the offer.[27] Benjamin C. Marsh, who had begun his career fighting for two-rate taxation in New York City, planted the first seeds of doubt about agricultural support for the Ford offer. In Senate testimony he claimed that the Farmers' National Council, of which he was the general secretary, represented eight hundred thousand farmers. The members of his organization, he said, opposed a hundred-year lease of public waterpower to Ford.[28] Newton Baker joined in the effort to blunt agricultural support for the proposal by lobbying W. I. Drummond, of the International Farm Congress, to reach out to Norris. Drummond was persuaded to throw his support behind public ownership by Baker's argument that "the water powers of America are our one great inexhaustible asset and any gift of them to private individuals on practically any terms for long periods of years menaces the future."[29]

Baker was crucial to the fight for preserving public waterpower in Muscle Shoals because he was the leading authority on the project. He had both supervised construction of the dams and written the Water Power Act, which Ford's purchase would have violated. Baker joined with officials from the Wilson administration to form the National Committee for the Defense of the Water Power Act.[30] In March 1924, Representative John Hull of Iowa read a letter from Baker to Congress, describing him as "having more to do with Muscle Shoals than anyone else."[31] He quoted Baker's assertion that the development was "a gold mine . . . everlasting and increasing in value each year."[32]

The Popular Government League had been formed in 1913 with the backing of Georgists to lobby President Wilson, but it now emerged as a leading force in the fight for public hydroelectricity in Muscle Shoals.[33] It was led by Judson King, who had attended the 1914 Fels Fund Convention and served as a pallbearer at Post's funeral.[34] King now argued for "the conservation of water power . . . because it is, next to the land question, the most important economic problem of our day."[35] In classically Georgist language King objected to reproduction cost valuation for utilities, because it allowed utilities to claim "the increase of land values—due almost wholly to social growth and the labor of an entire community."[36]

Judson King and the Popular Government League partnered with Senator George Norris in drafting much of his legislation, including his bills on the Muscle Shoals question.[37] The connection dated back to 1918, when Norris ran for reelection while facing charges of disloyalty because of his opposition to World War I. William Kent took an interest in Senator Norris due to his position on "all the great policies of conservation and democratization of our national resources and national industries."[38] Kent funded a tremendous publicity campaign, including a broadside produced in conjunction with Judson King that was sent to every registered voter in the state. King's Popular Government League continued to rally Georgist donors to Norris after Kent died. During Norris's 1930 reelection campaign, King solicited funds by reminding them that they could not rest on their laurels: "We must beware the similar fate of Mayor Tom Johnson in Cleveland. . . . The generous, white souled Kent has gone the way of all humans. But we are here—Norris is here—and the Old Cause is here."[39] Frank Walsh donated a third of the funds to the Popular Government League's campaign for Norris.

In George Norris single taxers found a champion who would focus reform on the liberal ideal of targeted state action against economic power. In 1930, Norris led the charge against President Herbert Hoover's Supreme Court nominee, John Parker. Parker had a history of establishing injunctions against labor unions and enforcing "yellow dog" contracts, in which workers signed away their right to unionize. Norris, building on the arguments of Georgist labor lawyers like Clarence Darrow, condemned these contracts as a form of involuntary servitude. Rejecting the "freedom" to contract one's rights away, Norris expounded a different vision of freedom. On the floor of the Senate, he picked up an unidentified book and read:

> We speak of liberty as one thing, and of virtue, wealth, knowledge, invention, national strength, and national independence as other things, but of all these, liberty is the source, the mother, the necessary condition. . . . In our time, as in times before, creep on the insidious forces that, producing inequality, destroy liberty. . . . It is not enough that men should vote; it is not enough that they should be theoretically equal before the law. They must have liberty to avail themselves of the opportunities and means of life; they must stand on equal terms with reference to the bounty of nature.

The text, which Norris described as "one of the most beautiful things I have ever read on the preciousness of human liberty," was *Progress and Poverty*. Norris served as the author for a major strand of New Deal thought, and he signaled George's role in popularizing a vision of liberty as hostile to concentrated economic power as it was to overweening government.[40]

During the struggle for Muscle Shoals, Norris asked Baker about the history of the public power service that he and Johnson had established in Cleveland.[41] In congressional debates on Muscle Shoals Norris cited at length Baker's discussion of the plant.[42] Because power had been a municipal question, it was natural for Congress to look to cities for examples. But Cleveland was cited especially often as the principal example of a "public yard stick."[43] Part of the reason was that it was one of only a handful of major cities with municipal power. While municipally owned electricity was not uncommon—Cleveland first obtained its plants by annexing two suburban developments—most public power projects were in small towns that private companies refused to invest in.[44]

Special circumstances had made Cleveland a unique example of the superiority of public ownership to regulation. Senator Norris particularly wanted Baker to confirm that the public plant had come into operation as Cleveland Illuminating Company was subjected to regulatory control. Whereas the private plant in Cleveland had distributed electricity at 12.1 cents per kilowatt-hour (kWh), the public plants sold electricity at a rate of 3 cents per kWh. Norris emphasized to the Senate that the Cleveland Illuminating Company had persuaded the Public Utilities Commission of Ohio that it could not distribute power for less than 10 cents per kWh only six months before public competition forced it to halve that rate. The change was estimated to have saved Cleveland's citizens $13,849,000 from 1915 to 1923. Norris believed the example "goes quite a distance toward demonstrating" that utility regulation was insufficient for establishing fair rates.[45]

As Congress fought a pitched battle over Muscle Shoals in the 1920s, state power disputes demonstrated the political wisdom of public ownership. In Pennsylvania, Governor Gifford Pinchot pitched "giant power," an interconnected state power system that would electrify Pennsylvania under the leadership of the engineer Morris Llewellyn Cooke. Georgists Herbert Quick and George L. Record lobbied to ensure that the governor's report called for public ownership of power plants, but they failed. When it became clear that private corporations had no interest in the expensive task of expanding power networks in rural areas, farm support for "giant power" collapsed.[46] While technocratic supervision of private industry failed in Pennsylvania, Georgist rhetoric was helping make a president in New York. There Governor Franklin Roosevelt nominated Frank Walsh to serve on a committee investigating the state's utility commission. Walsh immediately wrote Judson King to ask for an extended report on the operation of the Cleveland power plant.[47] The Cleveland example served as the foundation for Walsh's argument that regulation was ineffective and that only a public yardstick could set fair rates. Walsh failed to sway the majority of the commission, but Roosevelt endorsed his minority report, making a public yardstick one of his defining positions in the leadup to the presidential election of 1932.[48]

As president, Roosevelt recruited advisors who embraced public waterpower to spur mass consumption and eliminate resource rents. In meetings of the Brain Trust, Rexford Tugwell advanced the arguments of J. A.

Hobson that underconsumption was the result of monopoly rents redistributing wealth away from the consumer.[49] Tugwell quoted at length Hobson's proposal to capture "mineral rights, industrial power, future site, and other land value" and to secure not merely regulation but "ownership i.e. the conservation to the people of specific property rights."[50] President Roosevelt completed the St. Lawrence waterway project that he had campaigned for while governor. He resolved the Muscle Shoals controversy by putting the two existing dams under public ownership and expanding them into a network of hydroelectric sites under the authority of a comprehensive planning board, the Tennessee Valley Authority (TVA).

Public waterpower and rural electrification became the New Deal's most iconic programs, expanding access to consumer goods by introducing affordable electricity to rural communities. The project developed such symbolic significance that the federal government would export the TVA model around the world to demonstrate the strength of the American way. Supreme Court justice William O. Douglas expressed the messianic hopes many liberals attached to public power when he predicted that "the TVA can . . . be utilized as one of the major influences to turn back the tide of communism."[51] During the Vietnam War, Lyndon Johnson, remembering the transformative impact rural electrification had on West Texas, proposed a massive hydroelectric project along the Mekong River: "In the countryside where I was born, and where I live, I have seen the night illuminated, and the kitchens warmed, and the homes heated, where once the cheerless night and the ceaseless cold held sway. And all this happened because electricity came to our area along the humming wires of the REA."[52]

Roosevelt's public waterpower policies were rooted in arguments about the failure of utility regulation that Georgists critical of Progressive expertise had crafted. As special consultant to the Rural Electrification Administration, Judson King would point to the experience of public ownership in Cleveland as one of the origins of New Deal power policy, labeling Theodore Roosevelt's regulatory policies a failure.[53] These policies were also a victory for Georgists in that they treated land, utilities, and natural resources as uniquely suited to social ownership. Eugene Staley, who helped internationalize the TVA model, contrasted the TVA with socialism by observing that "we can have a TVA . . . without nationalizing all the enterprises along Main Street."[54] Stanley had begun his academic career with a book on the history of the Illinois State Federation of Labor that highlighted the influence of that "great book *Progress and Poverty*" on the development of the labor movement.[55]

New Deal Land Policy

While Franklin Roosevelt embraced vigorous government intervention in land, natural resources, and housing policy, these policies differed significantly from the single tax in both their reliance on expert planning and their anti-urban bias. Here Roosevelt followed the trends of the time. Even old Georgists followed a similar trajectory as crashing real estate values and suburban exodus undermined the case for land value taxation. But the ideal of expert guidance proved to be impractical, giving way to a privatized reconstruction of the nation's social geography.

Roosevelt endorsed the doctrine of regional planning, nominating several members of the Regional Planning Association of America to posts in his administration. Many, however, floundered with vague aesthetic principles that were too idiosyncratic to provide a foundation for collective action. Robert Kohn was appointed head of the Housing Division of the PWA. Falling into "a state of paralysis," he was removed after one year's work, during which he had failed to approve a single project.[56] Benton MacKaye was assigned a promising role as the director of the Regional Planning Section of the TVA. MacKaye worked to reconcile the plans of experts in forestry, housing, and water management into a coherent whole. He found these visions, however, to be fundamentally incongruous, with some of parties concerned only with efficiency, others only with aesthetics. By 1934 MacKaye had produced his own plan for distributing population across the entire Tennessee Valley region, but few people paid much mind to what was essentially an expression of individual taste. MacKaye was fired and his plans were scrapped.[57]

Regional planning was most influential in its attacks on urban geography. In some cases, planners would draw on a Georgist critique of speculative land values, but instead of capturing those values, they would aim to eliminate urban rents by dispersing population. In a series of articles in the *New Republic*, Henry Wright argued for a public housing program that would mean "an end to dealing with the fundamental environment of human living as a means of speculative profit—hence the end of the slum and values based on congestion." Wright's prescription was "publicly owning and controlling all the land used in community building" because "planning of the order suggested cannot take place if speculation and private profit continue to be attached to land ownership."[58] Wright worked with the quasi-Georgist regional planner Frederick Ackerman to tear down urban neighborhoods and replace them with public housing. The two led efforts to build the Williamsburg Houses project in Brooklyn, destroying dense urban streets for a settlement that was 70 percent green space and that segregated residential space from the commercial establishments that traditionally gave urban neighborhoods a dense community life. The Williamsburg Houses served as a model for planners who increasingly saw the urban form as a blight that needed to be planned out of existence.[59]

The New Deal's public interventions in land and housing were predicated on both unprecedented environmental problems and an ingrained belief that natural resources had an inherently social character. Gigantic dust clouds sweeping from the plains to the Atlantic dramatically illustrated the exhaustion of the soil. The government began discouraging farming, in part through a policy of purchasing "submarginal land," which was then added to the public domain.[60] Conservation was not the only reason, however, for extending government ownership of resources. In 1934 TVA geologists discovered mineral deposits in Muscle Shoals. Harold Ickes, Harry Hopkins, and Arthur Morgan decided to categorize the land as "submarginal," though it was far from economically barren. Officials noted that, to the contrary, it "will yield an enormous profit," and thus the public should claim it while it had an opportunity to do so.[61]

Rexford Tugwell was responsible for the most radical New Deal housing experiments, which emphasized both public control of land and the dispersion of population from the urban core. Although Tugwell had acquired Georgists' antipathy for landed property, he had little interest in their pet remedy. As his friend Raymond Moley once said, "In the perspective of time" it was George's "diagnosis," more than his remedy, "that was important."[62] As director of the Resettlement Administration, Tugwell was responsible for building or managing more than a hundred government-owned towns, some of them rural settlements populated by farmers who had been resettled from "submarginal" land. Rexford Tugwell's most famous developments were the three large Greenbelt towns, built on the edges of large cities to draw urbanities out to suburban developments with open green spaces. Greenbelt towns embodied both a shift from cities and an assault on the private collection of rent. Tugwell explained that they were to "enable low-income workers to retain more of their earnings for self-advancement because of lower rents."[63] In the process, the New Deal was overturning "the ancient customs of the landlord system."[64]

Many old Georgists were still confident that land was the central axis for economic inequality, but now accepted the inevitability of either government ownership or small proprietorship. Newton Baker forwarded Moley a plan to provide the unemployed with land for homesteads.[65] Frederic Howe sent Roosevelt a letter calling for the government to provide veterans with "low-cost suburban homes or small farmsteads." He claimed this grew out of "ten years of very close association with Mayor Tom L. Johnson of Cleveland."[66] The Great Depression had seen land values across the nation tank. Even New York City struggled to pay its bills, and its once booming real estate market was unable to bear the burden of taxation. Raymond Ingersoll, the Georgist borough president of Brooklyn, had long argued for funding infrastructure improvements with special assessments on the real estate that benefited from the project, but by the end of the 1930s he bragged about shifting those taxes to the city at large.[67]

As Georgists looked for new ways to socialize land, they increasingly saw themselves on opposite sides of the same issue. George Peabody lobbied the administration to pass the Bankhead-Jones Farm Tenant Act, which provided funding for sharecroppers to purchase their own land.[68] The proposal reflected not only Peabody's interest in land issues but his long-standing concern for the condition of African Americans in the South. However, some Georgists refused to accept the shift to small proprietorship, believing it would only exacerbate the problem of land values. Benjamin Marsh, acting as secretary of John Dewey's People's League, argued for modifications of the Bankhead-Jones bill to ensure that loans were not used to purchase land above its value, spurring speculation. He enlisted in his efforts Jackson Gardner of the Agricultural Adjustment Administration (AAA), who argued to Congress that without such provisions it would "impose an indefinite burden on the general public for the owners of land . . . [and] perpetuate rather than end the enormous land speculation."[69]

Efforts to develop a comprehensive policy of national resource management and population distribution reached their zenith in 1937. That year Congress debated bills that would divide the nation into seven regional planning boards, or "Little T.V.A.'s," each with extensive control over land and water policy. Congressman John Rankin, Democrat of Mississippi, testified on behalf of the bill with an exposition on savings from municipal power plants that concentrated on Cleveland, which he called the "pacemaker in low electric rates." Rankin gave an extended history of the project all the way back to Tom Johnson and "his crusade for a 3-cent rate light plant." The president contributed to the debate by submitting a report written by Frank Walsh. Walsh estimated that government ownership of hydroelectric power cut the price of electricity in half. He again impugned the efficacy of regulation, suggesting instead that the "retention of natural power resources for the people" would create sufficient savings to enable a leap in consumer purchasing power that "will mean a great market for electric appliances." Stuart Chase contended that projects should be funded according to "the general theory in municipal practice . . . to assess the abutting property for benefit," an argument that brought the young radical who had found George in Harvard's library back to the principle of land value taxation. This ambitious legislation, however, ultimately fell victim to opposition from an unlikely alliance of southern Democrats, fearful that regional boards would undermine state authority; utility interests, jealous of proprietary rights; and Secretary of the Interior Harold Ickes, who believed that it would usurp the authority of his own department.[70]

The eclecticism of New Deal land policy made it difficult to coalesce around precise policies, even dividing former Georgists. In the 1934 California Democratic gubernatorial primary, Upton Sinclair challenged George Creel on a platform of radical economic reform that he called EPIC: End Poverty in California. The plan's centerpiece was state purchase of land and industrial facilities for workers' cooperatives.[71] George Creel repudiated Sinclair's plan, declaring that "instead of the Socialistic proposal that the state take possession of farms upon failure to pay taxes, turning it over to the unemployed, many of whom never saw a farm, I hold that the state should accept a first lien for delinquent taxes."[72]

Creel hoped to secure small proprietorship, but he still believed in socializing land. In one of his columns for *Colliers*, George Creel surveyed the long list of New Deal land programs and concluded, "More and more the truth is being driven home that no man has the right to say, 'I am absolute owner of my ground, and will do with it as I please.'"[73] Creel added that "the people of the United States never made a greater blunder than in permitting their natural resources to pass into private ownership."[74] Having been part of the California delegation that lobbied for federal funding for the Central Valley Project, he made public hydroelectricity a centerpiece of his campaign.[75]

Despite an acrimonious campaign, Creel and Sinclair briefly reconciled after Sinclair won the Democratic primary. Creel was elected chairman of the state Democratic convention, and the two negotiated a platform that suggested they could still find unity on something like their old platform of the single tax. Small properties worth less than $100 would be exempted from the property tax, but there would be hikes on "large landholdings held out of productive use." The platform further claimed that "our natural resources, which have hereto escaped their just proportion of taxation, must be recognized as natural sources of state revenue."[76] The two leaders split again after the convention when Sinclair returned to advocating state-owned farms. Sinclair lost in the general election amid opposition from fellow Democrats, including Creel.

Ironically, this major fracture in the Democratic Party was spearheaded by two activists who shared a faith that state ownership of land was among the nation's most urgent needs. Once upon a time, the single tax had united people like Creel, who envisioned it as fostering small proprietors, with people like Sinclair, who saw it as a pathway toward expansive state action. As George's proposal fell into the background, the myriad dreams it had encompassed came to be embodied in a diverse and contradictory set of proposals that served as a shaky foundation for collective action.

With the failure of regional planning to establish social control of land outside isolated communities, Roosevelt turned to programs that spurred a private exodus from the city. New Deal infrastructure programs disproportionally funded suburban development; more than half of all Works Progress Administration (WPA) funds spent on roads and playgrounds in New York City went to Queens. Meanwhile, the Federal Housing Administration (FHA) supported loans to prospective homebuyers so long as they purchased in racially homogenous communities with no urban mixed-use design or narrow row houses. Whereas Georgists like Dewey had imagined a democracy rooted in local communities that fostered pluralistic exchange between different races and classes, the FHA funded development that alienated individuals from their neighbors. When the FHA denied funding to the Eight Mile neighborhood in Detroit, developers convinced the agency to reconsider by building a wall to segregate the white neighborhood from adjacent black communities.[77]

Americans would sometimes conceptualize suburbanization as a return to the nation's proprietarian roots, though the differences were stark. By the 1950s, the U.S. Information Agency would advertise America's "people's capitalism" with an exhibit that juxtaposed Lincoln's log cabin with the suburban home, projecting a sense of continuity. As that exhibit noted, however, whereas the settler produced many of his own goods, the modern proprietor purchased consumer goods to reduce household labor.[78] Although mid-twentieth-century Americans would see this access to consumer goods as evidence of progress, it meant that their "crabgrass frontiers" had little relationship to the agricultural frontier that Thomas Jefferson hoped would provide a subsistence living and liberate citizens from dependence on the "caprice of customers."[79] The homestead as a productive farm was a form of capital that partially insulated the owner from the market and often made its owners jealous of concentrated economic power that threatened their independence. In contrast, the suburban home was a consumer good that encouraged residents' reliance on large employers and banks to pay long-term mortgages. Thus, whereas homesteaders were often revolutionary—as when they served as the political base for a war on slavery—the defining qualities of the suburbanite were quiescence, atomistic individualism, and consumerism.[80]

George would have been ambivalent about, though mostly hostile to, this new world ushered in by the New Deal. He accepted the small proprietorships and the territorial expansion of the homesteading tradition as foundational to American democracy, claiming, "All that we are proud of in the American character . . . we may trace to the fact that land has been cheap in the United States, because new soil has been open to the emigrant."[81] He believed that small proprietorship was destined to run up against natural limitations in the supply of land, however, and that sprawl wasted the energy of civilization because economic and social life were better realized in the concentrated life of urban centers.[82] The agrarian quest to destroy cities and their high land values was a vain effort to move backward in time, in that "the attaching of value to land in special—that is to say in particular localities with respect to population—is not merely a most striking feature in the progress of modern civilization, but it is . . . a consequence of civilization, lying entirely within the natural order, and furnishing perhaps the most conclusive proof that the intent of that order is the equality of men."[83] The New Deal effort to engineer small proprietorship fostered a brief period of relative equality for white suburbanites, but it did so at great expense to social and economic life, without providing a sustainable, long-term solution to the inequities of the housing market.

National Recovery Administration

What most alienated Georgists from the New Deal was its embrace of economic planning. While Tugwell acknowledged his indebtedness to Georgists on the land question, he broke with their faith in free competition, arguing that experts needed to manage the increasingly concentrated economy.[84] Tugwell, along with fellow Brain Truster Adolph Berle Jr., were acolytes of University of Wisconsin president Charles Van Hise, who had argued, in his influential *Concentration and Control* (1912), that the concentration of economic power into monopolistic corporations was a natural and progressive innovation. Hise contended that the model of progressive utility regulatory commissions should be applied to all businesses, to ensure that these efficient, concentrated industries served the public interest.[85] Building on this idea, the Brain Trust conceived of a national program of economic planning effected in 1933 with the creation of the National Recovery Administration (NRA). The program embodied a transnational trend in the 1930s toward corporatist alliances between big government and business; its director, Hugh Johnson, hung a portrait of Mussolini in his office and encouraged his staff to read the fascist theorist Raffaello Viglione.[86] The NRA limited work hours, set wages, managed commodity prices, and restricted industrial output. In exchange for control over business, it halted anti-monopoly prosecutions and promised corporations a seat at the table in the design of industrial policy.[87]

Most Georgists were sufficiently interested in the New Deal's land program and attached to the Democratic Party to retain a lingering, ambivalent allegiance toward the New Deal. However, they had inherited ideas about expert planning and competition that were incompatible with the NRA. In fact, one of the most comprehensive Georgist critiques of the New Deal was written before it began. George L. Record died in 1933, leaving him little opportunity to articulate his opinion of the New Deal. But in 1936 Amos Pinchot organized Record's writings into a coherent statement of opinion entitled *How to Abolish Poverty*. Record's extended criticism of regulation allowed Pinchot to frame his corpus to mean that "when the government intervenes, it should be only to assure the free use of capital. . . . No plan, such as that of the New Deal, that fosters monopoly, reduces production and diminishes consumption of goods, should be tolerable to intelligent men."[88] The body of Record's text included only fleeting references to Roosevelt's programs, but in the introduction, Pinchot brought to bear his own personal knowledge of Record's views: "Record admired Franklin D. Roosevelt, and believed in his good intentions, but had little faith in his economic views. He altogether disbelieved in his program of regimentation that is now summed up in the words 'managed economy.'"[89] That Pinchot was able to compose this rebuttal by cobbling together writings that predated the New Deal by decades testifies to how the split between Georgism and the New Deal represented the tail end of a long struggle between Georgists and Progressive advocates of government by experts.

Newton Baker opposed the New Deal for many of the same reasons that he had once fought for public ownership rather than regulation. As a constitutional lawyer he was troubled by the NRA's extensive but poorly defined administrative power. He feared that NRA administrators punished at will much as Hitler did.[90] But Baker was no strict constructionist. In Cleveland and Washington, D.C., he had often worked to circumvent or rewrite constitutional obstacles to reform. His new conservatism was provoked by fears of powerful regulatory regimes. To the progressive businessman Edward Filene, he admitted that he was "instinctively cold" to the programs of the New Deal. Searching for reasons for his hostility, he concluded that "having devoted the major part of my life to the advocacy of liberty and to the defense of every freedom which I found to be assailed, I find it impossible to turn speedily to believing in a system which either invites or demands the surrender of liberty in a wholesale way. Every time I think of business and industry getting together and giving me orders, I want to rebel."[91]

If any Georgist were to reconcile himself to the New Deal, it would have been fellow Clevelander Frederic C. Howe, who was friendlier to government than his compatriots. Howe entered the Roosevelt administration as the consumers' consul for the Agricultural Adjustment Administration. The position was created to ensure that the AAA, designed to increase the price of agricultural products, did not inflate costs at the expense of the consumer. It was a job that required identifying and communicating the public interest, a task that many young New Dealers saw as perfect for Howe. Tugwell expressed the initial enthusiasm with which the announcement was made: "It happened that Frederic C. Howe, who was venerated by all younger liberals as a warrior in many old battles, was drawn to Washington. . . . He seemed an ideal person to represent consumer interests. Above all, as [Agriculture Secretary Henry] Wallace saw it, his presence among us would guarantee that farmers' gains were not to be at consumers' expense."[92] Howe's appointment was purportedly set in motion by his old admirer Raymond Moley and was advanced by a coterie of nostalgic young liberals in the AAA. Louis Bean recommended him to Wallace with the observation that "here's a fine old liberal of the Tom Johnson School." Jerome Frank claimed to have proposed Howe's name for the post because "Fred had been one of the respected men of my college days. He'd written *The City: The Hope of Democracy*, was a great liberal, a friend of Tom Johnson and so on."[93]

It quickly became clear, however, that Howe's views could not be made to fit with the administration's philosophy of planning, and he was immediately excluded from its policy discussions. The department's administrator, George Peek, envisioned the division's role as lifting the price of foodstuffs in the interests of farmers. However, Howe saw his role as adversarial, ensuring that the public interest in lower commodity prices was protected. He spoke weekly on radio and published a *Consumer's Guide* to inform shoppers of price increases.[94] Howe objected to the very principle of planning around which the department was organized: "The main underlying purpose of trade agreements," he contended, "is to legalize monopoly in industry in return for prospective gains to the farm producer and consumer." His position on this had not evolved: "I know fully the difficulties, personally I should say impossibilities, of regulation of monopolies."[95]

Howe never publicly broke with the New Deal, but it would break with him. At the zenith of the New Deal in 1935, Baker confided to a friend about Howe's discontent, noting that he "is often beguiled by beautiful notions, for which the world should be ready but is not, and he is often rather downcast because his fellowmen just will not do wise and beautiful things!"[96] To Steffens, Howe expressed the hope that there was something deeper behind Roosevelt: "He must have a philosophy and it goes pretty far. But wise man that he is, he only exposes a bit of it at a time."[97] Howe was fired in 1935, along with a slate of progressives in the AAA. At the press conference, Secretary of Agriculture Wallace denied that politics played a role, but inquisitive reporters were inclined to believe that Howe had been sacked because of his agitation for lower milk prices.[98]

The financier George Peabody was closer to Roosevelt than any other Georgist, but even he tolerated the New Deal for what he hoped it could be while disdaining what it was. Peabody had introduced Roosevelt to the Warm Springs, Georgia, estate that Roosevelt converted into a treatment center for polio. After the two became close friends, Peabody sent the president a steady stream of Georgist propaganda.[99] Yet privately he complained about New Deal programs, especially the NRA.[100] While he tolerated the NRA under Roosevelt's leadership, he argued that if it survived FDR's presidency, it would point "the way for them [financial powers] to have a Democratic Fascism. If they shall continue to hold the control of the billions invested in railroad and the utilities, they can patiently wait for 1940 when they can utilize a modification of the N. R. A., if still buttressed by control of monopolies, to give them a cinch on government that is way beyond anything in our past history."[101] On his eighty-fifth birthday, perhaps cognizant that his time was running out, Peabody encouraged FDR to "re-read" *Progress and Poverty* and to "build deep and strong foundations." Otherwise, FDR's administration would become like that of Theodore Roosevelt, which "left no record for history."[102]

George Creel best embodied this ambivalence toward the New Deal, as he worked to undermine the NRA even as he ran it. Appointed to the chairmanship of the District Recovery Board, he helped establish the NRA on the West Coast. Following precedents set by the Committee on Public Information, Creel dispatched speakers and organized parades publicizing the NRA. Creel's localism, anti-monopolism, and distrust of regulation, however, made him increasingly hostile to the program he ran. He was disgruntled to find that the national administration refused to accept exemptions he had written for small shopkeepers.[103] He wrote Secretary of Commerce Daniel Roper to complain that the NRA did nothing to "guard against monopolistic practices." He complained of "over-centralization."[104] On September 23, 1933, he sent Roosevelt his resignation as state chairman of the NRA and told the president that California was too far from D.C. to be subject to federal administration.[105] A host of California business and labor groups wired the president asking that Creel be granted the autonomy necessary to keep him in the position.[106] Under pressure, the administration refused to accept Creel's resignation and promised him control over the administration of the West Coast.[107]

This revolt provided Creel the authority to restrain national planning policies. He cultivated an air of independence, challenging the decisions of the AAA.[108] The San Francisco journalist Arthur Caylor referred to the West Coast as the "little NRA" and observed, "It won't do you any good to go over Mr. Creel's bushy head to Washington. . . . matters which come up in this district will be settled right here."[109] To an audience at the International House in Berkeley, Creel defended the thrust of the NRA's work but admitted that "it stands proved already that industry has gone code crazy. Of the six hundred codes either adopted or in the process of adoption, at least three hundred have no excuse whatsoever."[110] Ostensibly, Creel remained a stalwart supporter of the New Deal, but he hid growing discontent. At a closed meeting in 1936, Creel "turn[ed] state's evidence" and confided that he believed the president, as the heir to a family fortune, did not understand poverty.[111]

While Georgists were far less powerful than in the past, their identification with liberalism made them influential critics of planning, thus striking at the base of the New Deal. One of the hardest blows incurred by the NRA came from Clarence Darrow. To manage mounting criticism against his flagship program, Roosevelt organized an independent investigative commission, the National Recovery Review Board. On March 7, 1934, Darrow, presumed to be friendly, was appointed to chair the board. Instead, Darrow produced a report that was "of very great importance" in rallying opposition to the NRA.[112] The report was so scathing that Roosevelt refused to release it, but the rebellious lawyer leaked it to the press, sparking a public controversy. Darrow concluded that the NRA's regulations were designed by major industrial interests to perpetuate monopoly. "There is no hope," Darrow concluded, "for the small businessman or for complete recovery in America in enforced restriction upon production for the purpose of maintaining higher prices." Instead, Darrow suggested, "the hope for the American people, including the small businessman, . . . lies in the planned use of America's resources following socialization."[113] These conclusions, together with Roosevelt's apparent efforts to suppress the report, constituted a casus belli for congressional opponents. Darrow was called before Congress to testify. The People's Lobby, including its president, John Dewey, and a council of old-timer Georgists such as Jackson Ralston and William U'Ren, used the report to attack the NRA. The organization's secretary, Benjamin Marsh, was among the loudest and most provocative opponents of the NRA in congressional hearings.[114]

In 1935, the Supreme Court ruled the NRA unconstitutional in *Schechter Poultry Corp. v. United States*, but in doing so it only saved Roosevelt the embarrassment of addressing the flagging program. Evidence suggested that the NRA had slowed recovery, and backlash against its programs showed that experts could not reconcile the conflicting interests of workers and employers or businesses of different sizes and regions.[115] The dream of disinterested experts managing prices, production quotas, and macroeconomic investment was largely discredited with the NRA, though the failures of similar agencies during World War II were necessary in order to fully disillusion planning's most avid supporters.[116] Georgists played a role in normalizing limits on public power by seeing to its conclusion a long war with the Progressive doctrine of planning. The failure of the NRA, however, was overdetermined. If there was more of Georgism than "expertism" in modern liberalism, it was not because single taxers retained a substantial following but because their policies performed better in the New Deal's crucible of democratic experimentation.[117]

Albert Jay Nock and the Conservative Single Tax

In the 1920s, Albert Jay Nock emerged as the leading intellectual of the single tax movement. Raised in Brooklyn, he had begun a career in journalism in the 1910s, worked alongside Brand Whitlock during his mayoralty in Toledo, and developed close relationships with the Ohio Georgists. Nock shared little about his personal life; his autobiography, *Memoirs of a Superfluous Man* (1943), was a literary triumph without a protagonist, the story less about himself than about the passing of an age. Nock was invariably pictured reclined in his seat, sporting an air of casual intellectual superiority that might appear startingly familiar to anyone who ever watched his protégé William F. Buckley Jr. host *Firing Line*. Unlike many self-educated Georgists, Nock had received a classical education at what is today Bard College, but he shared with his friend George

Creel—who received only a middle school education—a disdain for the new class of university-educated professionals. Whereas Creel saw them as detached, Nock saw them as products of a watered-down German elective system that drilled narrow technical skills without the deep insights into the human condition that a classical education had provided him.[118]

In 1920 Nock founded *The Freeman* with the support of the former British MP Francis Neilson. Louis Post, Lincoln Steffens, and regional planners such as Lewis Mumford contributed to the new journal. In a world that had split between left and right, George's vision of combining individualism with collectivism now sounded dissonant, but Nock exploited that collision to grab his readers' attention. He praised the Russian Revolution because it "liberated the idea that democracy is an affair of economics not of politics."[119] Although *The Freeman* opposed the nationalization of industry, its writers argued that "if the resources of nature were free," there would be a "gradual extension" of "co-operative methods to one plant after another."[120] Yet Nock also struck a starkly libertarian tone, attacking the modern state that Progressives had built. Citing Franz Oppenheimer's Georgist history of the state, he argued that the "state is fundamentally anti-social," and he was "all for improving it off the face of the earth."[121]

The civil libertarianism of *The Freeman* grew from Nock's work with the single tax movement. Just as Nock's mentor Brand Whitlock had opened the saloons in Toledo, *The Freeman* now chided prohibition as a continuation of municipal blue laws. The paper sarcastically observed that illegal brewing ought to adopt an "exceptionally high standard of integrity" without government regulation.[122] Skeptical of the state after the excesses of World War I, it defended Louis Post's efforts to protect immigrants from deportation during the Red Scare.[123]

With Roosevelt's election, Albert Jay Nock emerged as the most outspoken single tax opponent of the New Deal. Believing Roosevelt had misappropriated the term "liberal," Nock with H. L. Mencken popularized the term "libertarian."[124] In this he followed his former mentor Whitlock, who, now living a life of artistic detachment in Cannes, France, wrote fierce missives denouncing Roosevelt as "a robber."[125] Nock during these years abandoned his faith in human perfectibility and concluded that mankind's intellectual facilities were innately limited. The New Deal stood as evidence of democracy's failure: the masses were unfit to rule.

Nock now argued that democracy had corrupted the liberalism of the single tax, which could never be appreciated by the masses. In *Henry George:*

An Essay, Nock posited that George's biggest mistake was to campaign for political office, requiring him to simplify his message to reach a popular audience. As a consequence, his followers had compromised their ideals by becoming "double-taxers" or even "triple-taxers" and losing sight of natural law's divisions between public and private.[126] In laying out a precise model for a free society, the single tax would "continue to locate and identify the ideal which is needful for right guidance, however far in advance of practicability." Nock urged his readers to reject the authority of any government not predicated on George's vision of natural law.[127] If the liberalism of Henry George could not be secured through democracy, that failure was an indictment of democracy, not of George.

In his seminal attack on the New Deal, *Our Enemy, the State* (1935), Nock used the theories of the Georgist sociologist Franz Oppenheimer (father of the Israeli kibbutzim) to validate his idea that the democratic state should be resisted if it fell short of George's ideals. Like Oppenheimer, Nock defined two types of public power. "The state" was inherently antisocial in that it was class government, designed to redistribute wealth by "political means." As an alternative, Nock cited American Indian tribal systems—which rejected property in land—as "government." Because they did not use violence to establish inequality, tribal governments were based on consensus: "the common understanding and common agreement of society."[128] Whereas Oppenheimer had traced the origins of the oppressive state in ancient history, *Our Enemy, the State* was dedicated to telling the story of the state's rise in the United States. In this story, the US Constitution was designed as a power grab by landowners. Nock argued that under a system of "actual free competition," including the abolition of private property in land, society would be resilient enough to resist the state and "a serious or continuous misuse of social power would be virtually impractical."[129] Nock concluded that governments that acknowledged private property in land could never truly be democratic, because their primary purpose was to enforce class rule. Yet Nock no longer believed that democracy could establish the single tax. The only course of action left to a democrat was, therefore, to resist democracy.[130]

In his resistance to the democratic state and the New Deal, Nock made common cause with the rising conservative movement, but still drew on precedents for libertarianism in the single tax movement. At the beginning of *Our Enemy, the State,* he cited William Jay Gaynor's arguments against expanding the police force.[131] In *Harper's* he turned to Whitlock's *On the En-*

forcement of Law in the Cities to argue that there was a distinction between "laws" and "statutes," the latter of which did not have the force of natural law behind them. There was no moral imperative to abide by statutes because natural law was the true source of authority. Whitlock, in positing the distinction, was arguing against moral legislation like prohibition. But both Nock and Whitlock shared a faith that the single tax was the crux of a social order built on natural law. Whitlock's distinction between laws and statues, brought to its logical conclusion, meant that no government had any authority unless it adopted the philosophy of Henry George.[132]

Nock's trenchant anti-statism made him a seminal figure in the history of conservativism. After Nock died in 1945, *The Freeman* was revived by a group of Nock's former associates, including the Georgist Frank Chodorov and Suzanne La Follette. By the mid-1950s, the editorial staff was divided by political infighting, and a wealthy young Catholic, whose father had been a friend of Nock, recruited most of *The Freeman*'s staff to form a new, more broadly conservative magazine. This magazine, William F. Buckley Jr.'s *National Review*, was, in the assessment of historian George Nash, "strikingly similar to the pre-1953 *Freeman*."[133] *National Review* united anti-communists, traditionalists, and libertarians into a coherent movement, serving as the cradle of conservativism.

The conservative movement's relationship to Nock would speak to the ways in which it did—and, more distinctly, did not—inherit the mantle of classical liberalism. When interviewed by C-Span in 2000, William Buckley confirmed that he was intellectually indebted to Nock and had always believed in taxing land because no one could claim the earth as the produce of their own labor. Buckley was not alone; libertarians such as Frank Chodorov and, more recently, writers for the Cato Institute have cited George as an intellectual precursor of modern libertarianism.[134] Yet, as Buckley acknowledged his interest in the single tax, he conceded that he had never pushed the issue, because most of his conservative colleagues were hostile to it.[135] A new group, formed around the Austrian school, was emerging as the leading source of conservative economics. The founder of this school, Karl Menger, rejected the whole of the classical model, especially the Ricardian rent theory that served as the basis for George's analysis.[136] The Austrians were, ironically, an offshoot of the same German historicists who inspired Progressive academics in their attacks on classical liberalism's universal theoretical models, though they split with the Germans on the political implications of their critique of theory. The Austrians argued that inadequate information available to economic actors meant that the perfect competition underlying classic models was unrealizable. The concepts of monopoly price and rent were obsolete, according to the Austrians, because a true, competitive price was an impossible abstraction. Austrians instead argued that all prices were determined by the subjective valuations of consumers and therefore were ipso facto fair.[137] Murray Rothbard, who associated the single tax with what he considered to be the discredited ideas of Smith and Ricardo, objected to it on the grounds that it would make land freely available. Rothbard argued that by controlling resources, landlords and speculators served a vital function as private sector economic planners, allocating locations to their most efficient uses.[138] He rejected free soil because it undermined economic planning by businessmen. Conservatism, then, would embrace forms of economic power to which Anglo-American liberalism had generally been hostile.

Returning to the Faith

While planning fell to the wayside, the New Deal adopted a new philosophy of security that sidelined the question of monopoly. With the rise of mass consumerism in the twentieth century, Americans became less concerned about whether they earned their living as independent producers than whether they were able to afford new consumer goods like washing machines and automobiles.[139] With the collapse during the Depression of traditional safety nets, citizens demanded the federal government provide them a consistent standard of living. Franklin Roosevelt had campaigned against the idea of widespread public welfare and by all appearances was reticent to reverse that pledge. But, by 1935, polling showed that he faced a serious threat from authoritarian third-party challengers, particularly Huey Long. Roosevelt altered course, embracing a new vision of moral capitalism that would guarantee whites (people of color were largely excluded) a standard of living.[140]

Unlike planning, there was nothing in this doctrine of security that was innately anathema to Georgists. They had often advocated for old age pensions. Nevertheless, they were generally troubled by it. This second New Deal bypassed questions of economic power and competition that had been so important to them. Georgists had aspired to purify the market and foster equal opportunity, but security seemed only to promise paternalistic protection. Whereas Georgists believed that concentrated political and economic power was a threat to democracy, the New Deal embraced big business to form a corporatist "iron triangle" of support for the Democratic Party. Many now gravitated closer to orthodox Georgism to identify their complaints with a philosophy that in its broad outlines was not necessarily radically dissimilar from their own.

Raymond Moley, who had organized Roosevelt's Brain Trust, made one of the sharpest turns of the decade. George had been Moley's boyhood idol, but Moley paid the single tax little mind for many years, acknowledging that his "much used copy of *Progress and Poverty*" was rife with evidence that he had "read it with considerable care but not much understanding except to note the main thrust of [George's] extraordinary argument."[141] But at the 1936 Democratic National Convention, Roosevelt harangued the wealthy as "economic royalists." Moley saw it as the beginning of class politics, and so he, according to historian Frank Friedel, "like most of his generation of Ohio reformers intellectually rooted in the doctrines of Tom Johnson and Henry George, moved permanently into emphatic opposition."[142]

In breaking with his onetime ally, Moley joined the conservative movement but also displayed an affinity for the Georgism of his youth. He contributed to *The Freeman* and *National Review*.[143] As late as the 1950s, though, the linchpin of his conservatism was the old faith that "it is the task of statesmanship . . . to eradicate special privileges." Moley now saw in the welfare state a new set of privileged interests that "would threaten the integrity and safety of the state" by demanding that politicians enact an escalating program of redistribution. Streetcar monopolists had been supplanted by "pensioners with a statutory or constitutional first claim on specific tax receipts, labor leaders with legal exemptions not accorded to management, political bosses operating under election laws of their own fashioning."[144] Moley wrote speeches for Dwight Eisenhower. He advised Richard Nixon and Barry Goldwater. He took a special interest in coaxing Nixon back into politics after his loss in 1962.[145]

As a conservative, Moley for the first time seemed to become an orthodox Georgist. In the 1960s he spoke frequently to the Henry George School and served as director of the Lincoln Institute of Land Policy, which was founded by a disciple of George and sponsored academic research on land value taxation. At a presentation to the Henry George School in the 1950s, he explained that he had broken with Roosevelt after his 1936 convention speech because it was about "class against class, and not unity—*not* the forgotten man. . . . Henry George rises above all of this recent disunity."[146] The "forgotten man," a term coined by the social Darwinist William Graham Sumner and used by Moley in Roosevelt's breakthrough campaign speech, referred to hardworking individuals who wanted only to keep what they made. The term embodied a hostility to special interests that liberalism seemed to have shed during the second New Deal. In *How to Keep Our Liberty*, Moley laid out a conservative rubric for public revenue: tax burdens should be determined by voluntary consumption rather than ability to pay; they should be direct rather than covert; and they should be universally felt rather than targeted. Moley singled out property taxes as giving "the citizen a more or less reliable gauge of what he was paying for government."[147]

After Roosevelt passed, George Creel's war with New Deal liberalism seemed to build directly on his youthful battles; the new president, Harry Truman, was a product of the Kansas City Pendergast political machine, which Creel had fought when he began his career as a muckraker.[148] This solidified Creel's suspicion that New Deal liberalism had devolved into a national version of the old urban machines that gifted voters with Thanksgiving turkeys in return for votes. "What started out as a determination to take some of the terrors out of life by the provision of social security," wrote Creel, "has degenerated into *vote buying* on an ever-ascending scale."[149] Creel tried to organize a national organization of conservative Democrats and was aghast when the Republican Party nominated the moderate Dwight Eisenhower. Creel, however, became close to Eisenhower's conservative vice president, Richard Nixon.[150] Still, he believed it was the Democratic Party that had changed, not him. He fondly remembered that "the *clarity* and force of Henry George was heaven" and complained in 1947 that "if anybody . . . had told me that the day would come when the single-tax movement could be housed in a telephone booth, I would have hooted."[151]

The fear that the New Deal was a national machine, expanding its political power by selectively distributing money, was not entirely unwarranted. Roosevelt perfected the process of distributing patronage in tandem with public opinion polls that identified districts that could be swung with federal funds.[152] At the beginning of his career, in a speech to the People's Institute in 1912, Roosevelt had attacked the premise that politicians should be committed to the public interest, which was not "possible to us anywhere outside of a heaven of community of interest . . . where everybody wants the same thing."[153] By the mid-thirties, public opinion polls made it clear that Roosevelt could not keep the masses and their masters happy at the same time, but up until that point, he had worked to balance the interests of elite and popular constituents, granting perks to each. Roosevelt's landmark Banking Act of 1933 included minor provisions whose sole purpose was to allow Bank of America founder

A. P. Giannini to consolidate his financial empire.[154] By the time Creel had abandoned Democrats in the 1940s, the radicalism of the thirties had evaporated, and the party was establishing tax exemptions to favored industries, entrenching political support with special interest politics.[155]

Many of these criticisms hinted at the coming New Left critique of the Democratic Party's broker state. William U'Ren, the father of direct legislation, feared that large labor unions and the "growing influence of the military" were creating a system in which democracy was compromised by the government's dependence on powerful interest groups.[156] By the 1950s, a similar argument would be popularized by C. Wright Mills, who contended that the United States was governed by a "Power Elite" of bureaucrats and interest groups that provided financial and electoral support in exchange for government largesse. Mills's vision of a direct "participatory democracy" was inspired by John Dewey's philosophy of localized democracy.[157] None of the old single taxers would live to see the rise of the New Left, though there is reason to suspect they would have found some common ground. Bertrand Russell had ceased to be a single taxer after World War I, but he carried with him an old-timey radicalism that endeared him to the British New Left.[158] Although Creel joined the conservative war on the New Deal, he held out hopes for a new radicalism. In 1941, he chided the youth of San Francisco for their "stodgy preoccupation with their own personal concerns" and their refusal to pursue "revolts and crusades." The soon-to-be ally of Nixon moralized: "The best proof of the younger generation's utter lack of courage and initiative is found in the fact that the older generation views San Francisco youngsters with tolerance and even approval. What could be more damning?"[159]

The longest-surviving single taxer of prominence to have known George personally was Samuel Seabury, the onetime "baby" of the movement who had prosecuted Tammany Hall. Although Seabury had tried to torpedo Roosevelt's nomination, he came around to the then governor after Roosevelt forced the Tammany mayor Jimmy Walker from office. In 1934 Seabury secured the Republican nomination for governor of New York and stubbornly refused to appease either friend or foe of the New Deal. He praised Roosevelt's Bank Holiday and his emergency relief programs but opposed programs that would run small businessmen out of operation or raise consumer prices, presumably a reference to planning agencies.[160]

As Seabury moved away from the New Deal, he reemphasized his connection to George, who had otherwise played a small role in Seabury's public profile after his 1916 campaign for governor of New York. In 1950 Seabury published *The New Federalism: An Inquiry into the Means by Which Social Power May Be Distributed between State and People to Insure Prosperity and Progress*. The lengthy subtitle spoke to the delicate balance of social power that George had hoped to create by restricting the powers of government to purely benevolent functions while splitting up large conglomerations of wealth in civil society. Seabury began the book with a quote from *Progress and Poverty*. He expressed fears about both the expanding functions of government and its increased dependence on large special interests. New Deal corporatism, with its powerful lobbies, ensured that the people no longer had a say in the government of the United States. To balance the scales, Seabury hoped to reduce the power of government, expand voluntary cooperatives, and, of course, tax land and natural resources: "The masses are not asking for favors but insisting upon equality of opportunity and a full measure of freedom which permits them to receive or suffer the consequences of their own actions."[161]

In 1939 Seabury attended a celebration of Henry George's one hundredth birthday. He spoke there, reaffirming his faith. While he lamented that George's utopia remained unfinished, he knew it had served a purpose: "Although men have not as yet adopted specific remedies which he proposed, they have, nevertheless, absorbed much of his philosophy, and that fact has, of itself, enriched the thought of those throughout the world who believe in democracy."[162] The day before the speech, Adolf Hitler's regime had invaded Poland, marking the climax of a rising tide of authoritarian nationalism that winnowed the number of liberal democracies throughout the world from about thirty-five in 1920 to twelve in 1944.[163] The United States had not been immune to the forces of centralization, class and racial conflict, nationalism, or imperial ambition that had installed authoritarian governments in continental Europe. As George had written *Progress and Poverty*, the South was completing a coup against liberal democracy that much of the country looked upon admiringly. Yet, when many middle-class Americans believed the problem was too much democracy, Georgists had acted as the key instigators for reforms like the secret ballot, direct legislation, urban home rule, and women's suffrage. The movement proved the city could govern itself, vindicated the downtrodden, discredited presumptive authorities, and drew urban constituents away from a "new nationalism" to the "new freedom." Georgists' repudiation of the New Deal established that these efforts were never rooted in an unshakeable faith in popular sovereignty, but rather in a belief that democracy was the best vehicle for securing their vision of freedom and opportunity. Even if the single tax had only been a totem—a magical panacea that tricked the middle class into believing democracy should be salvaged—few Americans of the era could claim to have done as much for liberalism as Henry George.

Conclusion

Henry George and the Promise of Liberalism

In 1932 Raymond Moley wrote Franklin Roosevelt's "Forgotten Man" speech, the most important of the campaign. It spoke to the common people who had been neglected by President Herbert Hoover. The "forgotten man" was a powerful device with a long history, but it had incongruous roots. The phrase had been coined in 1883 by William Graham Sumner. A classical liberal, Sumner had used the term to describe a producing class that was robbed of the fruits of its labor by philanthropists and social reformers. New Deal programs were precisely the sort of thing the forgotten man trope was intended to critique.[1]

The history of the phrase, however, has a logical midpoint in Newton Baker. Baker's reading of George had taught him that for the producing class to reap the fruits of it labor, the state would need to eliminate the private appropriation of rent. In 1926 Baker used the trope in an influential article on the decline of Progressivism. "A liberal," he wrote, "uses his fellow men for their benefit and not for his own. He judges political purposes by their effect on the common good and he has in his mind's eye, as the ultimate object of his concern, the 'forgotten man,' remote, obscure and inaudible in high places. Liberalism of this quality is imperishable and it has many brave servants for the American people."[2] Baker referenced Sumner's "forgotten man" to establish continuity in the liberal tradition, even as he recrafted it into a doctrine of reform. Moley would build on this idea, but he would do so in ways incompatible with Baker's philosophy. The single tax movement was a midway point in the development of American liberalism. By undermining the association between liberalism and private property, George had paved the way for it to become a critique of the market.

Franklin Roosevelt is often thought to have saved American liberalism by converting it into a flexible belief system that emphasized adherence to popular will over strict doctrine.[3] The story of the single tax movement suggests that although this approach was important to salvaging liberalism, it was not necessarily sufficient. Single taxers, as dogmatic liberals, had little sense of how to address the chaos of the Great Depression, and their vision of imposing strict economic principles on the public was unrealistic and eventually raised doubts about whether their ideals were compatible with democracy. Yet the single tax movement was a "great adventure" that paved a heroic path through the Progressive era, expanding and liberalizing the Democratic Party that Roosevelt inherited. At a time when neither the authoritarianism of Herbert Croly nor the majoritarianism of William Jennings Bryan accepted many inherent restrictions on state action, Georgism defined natural boundaries between public and private power that would help shape the parameters of American liberalism.[4]

It is easy to dismiss Georgists after the 1930s as marginal cranks thumbing their noses at popular opinion, but with hindsight we should now be equally skeptical of Roosevelt's tendency to follow the people. This is particularly true regarding the land use issue on which Roosevelt most clearly departed from George: intensive versus extensive development. By subsidizing sprawl, Roosevelt spurred an existential ecological threat.[5] By ensuring that the new suburbs would be homogeneously white, he helped tie the individualism of the suburban home to a sense of ascriptive racial identity, sparking a conservative movement that would slay the very New Deal Liberalism that had sponsored it.[6] The anti-urban policies of the New Deal look especially problematic now as cities across the world serve as the bulwark of liberal democracy against authoritarian headwinds. George's and Dewey's faith that the local community was the only basis for an informed public is justified by our modern epistemological crisis.[7] Scientific expertise has perilously little influence in a democracy that has been constructed to insulate its electorate from society. Roosevelt's political flexibility, then, was no teleological finale for liberalism but only one side to the great, insoluble dilemma of the democratic tradition: that popular will often clashes with social conditions that promote democracy.

Roosevelt's social welfare state has also not entirely withstood the test of time. When John Kenneth Galbraith sought to account for the success of the New Deal's economic redistribution, he concluded, in *American Capitalism* (1952), that oligopoly was so widespread that the competitive market had effectively ceased to exist. Since all major corporations accrued monopolistic rents, unions, consumer groups, and government could function as "countervailing powers" to redistribute rent in a closed, monopolistic system. But by 1993, Galbraith, the leading economist of Keynesian liberalism, understood that that system was crumbling. Competition with Japan had crippled industrial behemoths like General Motors and, "to put matters bluntly, strong labor unions require strong employers. . . . Countervailing power . . . requires that there be a power to countervail."[8] Galbraith attributed the decline of monopoly power in the United States to free trade policies, though, in highlighting the example of Japan, he raised an unsettling possibility. Japan, like most global competitors, had been bombed into rubble when the New Deal state reached its zenith at the end of World War II. Thus, the insulated industrial system that had given the New Deal state the latitude to establish its moral capitalism might have been a historical aberration, resting on the ruins of World War II.

Conversely, Henry George's system was designed to operate under free trade and open competition. George described land as "the robber that takes all that is left," because as monopolies were eliminated—and protectionism was the second-largest monopoly in his account—economic progress would spur increased demand for land and resources, shifting monopoly rents onto land.[9] There seems to have been at least some truth to this prediction. Thomas Piketty calculates that rents from natural resources like petroleum constituted less than 1 percent of global GDP in the early 1970s but approached 5 percent of global GDP by the mid-2000s as rising global consumption increased demand on a finite resource base.[10] As urban areas have regeared to produce for international markets, "global cities" have emerged where specialization in technology, industry, and finance foster economies of agglomeration: networks of expertise and business infrastructure that provide substantial advantages in select cities.[11] These advantages adhere in the value of the land on which those cities rest, so the price of access to the productive capacities of global cities becomes so great that they can hardly support the diverse cultural life that has traditionally been the hallmark of the urban form. The economist Matthew Rognlie has argued that, when depreciation is considered, virtually all the increase in wealth disparity in the United States has been in the housing sector.[12] In England, where a third of the land is still owned by the peerage, land rose from a fifth of national wealth in 1995 to over half of all national wealth in 2018.[13] Nor have rising land values been confined to cities. From 1970 to 2016, the value of Iowa farmland increased by 1,600 percent, more than twice as much as the Dow Jones Industrial Average.[14]

While land value taxation and Henry George remain virtually unknown to the public, they have emerged as popular topics for economists and policy experts, many of whom believe that the survival of the welfare state in competitive international markets depends on the targeted collection of monopoly rents. Chrystia Freeland, the Canadian minster of foreign affairs, argues that we should look to George as a model because "he addressed the obvious inequality of 19th century American capitalism without disavowing capitalism itself."[15] In 2015, Peter Orszag, former director of the Office of Management and Budget under President Barak Obama, came out in favor of a land value tax to fight economic inequality.[16] The Nobel Prize–winning economist Joseph Stiglitz has discussed land value taxation and Henry George as part of a broader critique of "rent-seeking."[17]

The single tax has always risen and fallen with the city, growing with the backlash against urban rents. Thus, it has been discussed as a solution to San Francisco's modern rent problems by the *New York Times* and the journalist Matthew Yglesias. In New York, Mayor Bill de Blasio called for a tax on unused land.[18] The *Vancouver Sun* has suggested the city reinstate land value taxation to control housing prices.[19] *The Economist* recommended land value taxation, estimating that "lifting the barriers to urban growth in America could raise the country's GDP by between 6.5% and 13.5%."[20] Even the *National Review*, following in Buckley's footsteps, has argued for the implementation of a land value tax to fight San Francisco's soaring rents.[21] In response to the affordability crisis in England, former prime minister Tony Blair came out of retirement to endorse land value taxation, which he called "radical but practical; progressive but in a way which aligns with the modern world and is not in defiance of it." In tones that echoed Henry George, Blair suggested that eradicating inequality in landed property would "resolve part of the underlying causes of political alienation and dissatisfaction with democracy."[22]

For experts, land value taxation is often associated with model economies. Most of the "Asian tigers" that famously excel in the competitive global marketplace have established policies to control and collect land rents. Taiwan has a constitutionally mandated system of land value taxation, Hong Kong has nationalized land, Singapore has almost universal public housing, and South Korea has had land value taxation since 1990.[23] Land value taxes in Pennsylvania's cities, established by Georgists in the early twentieth century, have been praised for reportedly sparing Pittsburgh and Scranton the fate of other Rust Belt cities and has spread rapidly to municipalities throughout the region in recent decades.[24] Estonia, which established land value taxation after the fall of the USSR, has the highest GDP per capita among the former Soviet satellite states.[25] Denmark, which implemented land value taxation a century ago, is commonly regarded as an exemplary social democracy. While these governments might not collect substantial revenue from land rents, deflating land values seems to prevent speculative bubbles, increase living standards, and extend state capacity. The Australia Institute estimates that the remnants of the land-lease system in the capital city of Canberra saves the approximately one thousand participating households more than A$9 million in housing expenses per year.[26]

George's economics have likely stood the test of time better than his politics. In Denmark, sudden increases in land value taxation have caused proportional drops in real estate prices, suggesting the tax does, in fact, socialize land rents without burdening citizens, who save in housing costs what they pay in taxes.[27] In Hong Kong nationalization allowed the government to fund rail development through the leasing of adjacent properties, which boom in value after construction. Hong Kong transit has been financially self-sustaining with low fares and a 99.9 percent on-time rate, which nearly substantiates George's promise that under land nationalization free public transit would pay for itself with higher land values.[28] This book begins with George's central fallacy; by imagining New York City as the future, he conflated differences in land value across space and time, projecting a progressive growth in land values. This prediction failed to consider how innovations in transportation and construction could alleviate rents. Land values have not risen consistently enough to make a *single* tax likely. However, land nationalization has functioned well in several nations, and the nationalization of oil has been sufficient in such places as the United Arab Emirates to provide for citizens to a degree that would have made George blush. What has not been sustained in the century and a half since George's writing is his faith that a prosperous republic would necessarily be an enlightened one, free from special interests, judicious in its use of resources, and progressing irresistibly toward a higher, better order. George's utopia was never the single tax; it was liberal democracy.

It is ironic that land value taxation is largely a technocratic fantasy today, since George has often been seen as a wild-eyed populist who substituted Christian faith for sound economic reasoning. This interpretation, however, failed to appreciate the complexity of George's normative philosophy and penalizes him for being a philosopher both in and of democracy. His most influential religious appeal was not to Christianity but to Judaism. His normative arguments were not mere expressions of personal faith but political appeals, undergirded by the belief that popular ideals represented diverse iterations of a natural moral sensibility. Rather than making a priori arguments, George imaginatively reinterpreted the implications of liberal property theory, Christianity, Mosaic law, and republican thought in ways that often turned these doctrines on their heads. Evidence suggests that political persuasion happens when one reinterprets the implications of the inherited values of one's audience, and the power of this approach is evident in the way George built a broad coalition of intellectuals who were often offended by his ideas initially.[29] George's faith that cultural traditions share core commonalities that can bridge differences probably has value in a pluralistic democracy even—perhaps especially—if it is not true.

Marx famously observed that "philosophers have only interpreted the world, in various ways; the point is to change it."[30] If that is the case, George deserves a place in the canon. Other philosophers have had more impact, but he is among a select few whose reputation can survive association with his readers. While his hopes for liberal democracy were probably overly sanguine, they left it better than it had been. His observations about how movements grow and affect change demonstrated an acute awareness of the way his writings would be received by a democratic public. These insights were substantiated when his supporters carried them into the field, bringing the single tax further than could ever have been expected. That most people would regard the impact of this movement favorably is a testament to how he leveraged philosophy to communicate sound ideas. George's greatest accomplishment was not as the author of any book, but as the author of a movement. As he observed: "Until there be correct thought, there cannot be right action; and where there is correct thought, right action *will* follow."[31]

ACKNOWLEDGMENTS

This project benefited from the assistance of many readers. I am indebted to Michael Kazin, who encouraged me to pursue my hunch that there was more to the story of Henry George than had been told. He also served as a meticulous editor. Joseph McCartin deserves credit for shepherding this work through its earliest phases and pointing me in the direction of Louis Post, whose papers were key to developing the outlines of this narrative. Jennifer Burns has had the perseverance to mentor me since my days as an undergraduate and helped me think about how to position George within his historical context. Richard John has proven a generous mentor and a valuable editor whose advice was essential for conceptualizing what it meant to turn a scholarly dissertation into a readable book. Other readers who deserve mention for their contributions to the manuscript include Richard White, Steven Baker, Eric Hubler, Charles McCann, Elizabeth Sanders, Charles Postel, Patrick Dixon, and Stephen Meardon.

My own background left me well prepared to appreciate and capture the aspirational spirit of the movement. Therefore Sylvia England, Marietta Cooper, Jimmy England, Frank Cooper, and Brian Dewey each deserve acknowledgment for this project. I also appreciate everything that my early mentors—particularly Lisa Rubens, Nigel Hatton, and Barry Pateman—did to get me to the place where I could write this book.

I have received generous financial support from many sources: the Robert Schalkenbach Foundation, the Lincoln Institute of Land Policy, the Roosevelt Institute, the Institute for Humane Studies, Mary Cleveland, the History of Economics Society, the Georgetown Scholarship Program, and the History Department at Georgetown University. The hospitality of friends has also helped me stretch my research funding. Thus, thanks go to Yvonne Islas, James Young, David Morar, Pete Pin, and Marc Halusic.

Especial thanks go to my wife, Tameka Porter, for supporting me through this process. This book is dedicated to our son, Theodore England.

This book benefited from two instances of serendipity. The first was at the beginning of my research when Joseph McCartin directed me to Louis Post. Post, as I argue in this book, was a nexus of Progressive-era Georgism, and thus his papers gave me a sense of what that ideology meant in practice and who the key actors in the movement were. This also brought me into contact with *The Public*, which is an inexplicably underutilized source. Often published under the subheading "A Weekly Narrative of History in the Making," *The Public* was a running chronology of the movement that recorded its responses to the events of the time. Beginning this project a skeptic, I was dubious of a narrative that often differed starkly from the historiographical consensus. However, the more I have learned, the more substantial I have found *The Public* to be.

I was also fortunate to be based out of Washington, D.C., when I began this project. This allowed me extensive access to the Library of Congress, a great source for political history, but especially for this project, since most of the manuscript collections associated with the Wilson administration are located there. Many of those collections had been extensively studied but not by researchers with a deep understanding of Georgism. Historians' narrow interpretation of the "single tax" led them to disregard explicit declarations of faith in Georgist principle when an activist exhibited interest in any issue aside from land value taxation. With a thorough grounding in the writings of George and Post, I was able to see these manuscripts in a different light and build a robust narrative that saw beyond the movement's rhetoric to its often-arcane inner workings.

Abbreviations

APP-LC	Amos Pinchot Papers, Library of Congress, Washington, D.C.
BLP-LC	Ben Lindsey Papers Library of Congress, Washington, D.C.
BWP-LC	Brand Whitlock Papers, Library of Congress, Washington, D.C.
DBP-LC	Daniel Beard Papers, Library of Congress, Washington, D.C.
FWP-NYPL	Frank Walsh Papers, New York Public Library, New York, N.Y.
GCP-LC	George Creel Papers, Library of Congress, Washington, D.C.
G. Peabody P-LC	George Peabody Papers, Library of Congress, Washington, D.C.
G. Pinchot P-LC	Gifford Pinchot Papers, Library of Congress, Washington, D.C.
HGP-NYPL	Henry George Papers, New York Public Library, New York, N.Y.
JBP-BL	James Barry Papers, Bancroft Library, University of California, Berkeley
LPP-LC	Louis Post Papers, Library of Congress, Washington, D.C.
LSP-CU	Lincoln Steffens Papers, Columbia University, New York City, N.Y.
LTP-VCA	L. D. Taylor Papers, City of Vancouver Archives, Vancouver, British Columbia
NBP-LC	Newton Baker Papers, Library of Congress, Washington, D.C.
PG-FRPL	Papers as Governor, Franklin D. Roosevelt Presidential Library, Hyde Park, N.Y.
PNSS-FRPL	Papers as New York State Senator, Franklin D. Roosevelt Presidential Library, Hyde Park, N.Y.
POF-FRPL	President's Official File, Franklin D. Roosevelt Presidential Library, Hyde Park, N.Y.
PPF-FRPL	President's Personal Files, Franklin D. Roosevelt Presidential Library, Hyde Park, N.Y.
RMP-FRPL	Raymond Moley Papers, Franklin D. Roosevelt Presidential Library, Hyde Park, N.Y.
RMP-HL	Raymond Moley Papers, Hoover Library, Stanford, Calif.
RTP-FRPL	Rexford Tugwell Papers, Franklin D. Roosevelt Presidential Library, Hyde Park, N.Y.
TPP-CUA	Terence Powderly Papers, Catholic University of America, Washington, D.C.

| WJBP-LC | William Jennings Bryan Papers, Library of Congress, Washington, D.C. |
| WMP-LC | William McAdoo Papers, Library of Congress, Washington, D.C. |

Introduction

1. Richard R. John, *Network Nation: Reinventing American Telecommunications* (Cambridge, Mass.: Belknap Press of Harvard University Press, 2010), 146–147.

2. Henry George Jr., *The Life of Henry George* (New York: Doubleday and McClure Company, 1900), 191.

3. George Wilson Pierson, *Tocqueville in America* (Baltimore: Johns Hopkins University Press, 1996), 645.

4. Frank E. Manuel, *The Prophets of Paris: Turgot, Condorcet, Saint-Simon, Fourier, and Comte* (Cambridge, Mass.: Harvard University Press, 1962), 197; E. P. Thompson, *Making of the English Working Class* (London: V. Gollancz, 1963); Friedrich Engels, *The Condition of the Working-Class in England* (1845; reprinted, Oxford: Oxford University Press, 1999).

5. Arthur P. Dudden and Theodore H. Van Laue, "The RSDL and Joseph Fels: A Study in Intercultural Contact," *American Historical Review* 61, no. 1 (October 1955): 43–44.

6. Eric Foner, *The Story of American Freedom* (New York: W. W. Norton, 1998), 167.

7. Frederic C. Howe, *Confessions of a Reformer* (New York: Charles Scribner's Sons, 1925), 138–139.

8. Guenther Roth, *The Social Democrats in Imperial Germany: A Study in Working Class Isolation and National Integration* (Totowa, N.J.: Bedminster Press, 1963).

9. Robert Johnston, *The Radical Middle Class: Populist Democracy and the Question of Capitalism in Progressive Era Portland, Oregon* (Princeton, N.J.: Princeton University Press, 2003).

10. Robert Blake Yardley, *Land Value Taxation and Rating: A Critical Survey of the Aims and Proposals with a History of the Movement* (London: W. H. & L. Collingridge, Ltd., 1930), 135–143; *The Standard* (New York), July 27, 1889.

11. "A Man of the Century," *Daily Telegraph*, March 6, 1890, in *Henry George: Collected Journalistic Writings*, ed. Kenneth C. Wenzer (Armonk: M. E. Sharpe, 2003), 4:21.

12. Brand Whitlock, "Daniel Kiefer," *American Magazine*, September 1912, 549–553.

13. Jonathan Levy, *Ages of American Capitalism: A History of the United States* (New York: Random House, 2021), 3–387.

14. Agricultural slavery and the premodern merchant marine, for example, anticipated the scale and organization of industrial capitalism. See Edward E. Baptist, *The Half Has Never Been Told: Slavery and the Making of American Capitalism* (New York: Basic Books, 2014); Peter Linebaugh and Marcus Rediker, *The Many-Headed Hydra: Slaves, Sailors, Commoners, and the Hidden History of the Radical Atlantic* (Boston: Beacon Press, 2000).

15. Andrew Herrod, *Labor Geographies: Workers and Landscapes of Capitalism* (New York: Guilford Press, 2001).

16. Josiah Strong, *Our Country: It's Possible Future and Its Present Crisis* (New York: American Home Missionary Society, 1885), 128–143; Washington Gladden, *Social Salvation* (Boston: Houghton Mifflin, 1902), 226.

17. William Lloyd Garrison Jr., "The New Abolition," *The Standard*, September 12, 1891, 7.

18. Caroline Winterer, *American Enlightenments: Pursuing Happiness in the Age of Reason* (New Haven, Conn.: Yale University Press, 2016), 223–251; John Locke, *Two Treatises on Government* (1689; reprinted, London: R. Butler, Bruton-Street, 1821), 82, 300, 359; Quentin Skinner, *Liberty before Liberalism* (Cambridge: Cambridge University Press, 1998), 98; Annelien de Dijn, "Was Montesquieu a Liberal Republican?" *Review of Politics* 76, no. 1 (January 2014): 21–41.

19. Foner, *The Story of American Freedom*, 3–28.

20. Theodore Roosevelt, *The Life of Gouverneur Morris: The Story of His Life and Work* (1888; reprinted, Philadelphia: Gebbie and Co., 1903), 270; Mark Hulliung, *The Social Contract in America: From the Revolution to the Present Age* (Lawrence: University Press of Kansas, 2007), 53–63, 147–158; Eric Foner, *Tom Paine and Revolutionary America* (New York: Oxford University Press, 1976); David Armitage, *The Declaration of Independence: A Global History* (Cambridge, Mass.: Harvard University Press, 2007).

21. Michael McGerr, *A Fierce Discontent: The Rise and Fall of the Progressive Movement in America, 1870–1920* (New York: Free Press, 2003), 183; Thomas Leonard, *Illiberal Reformers: Race, Eugenics, and American Economics in the Progressive Era* (Princeton, N.J.: Princeton University Press, 2016).

22. Christopher Lasch, *The True and Only Heaven: Progress and Its Critics* (New York: W. W. Norton, 1997), 63–66; Robert H. Wiebe, *The Search for Order, 1877–1920* (New York: Hill and Wang, 1967); John Thomas, *Alternative America: Henry George, Edward Bellamy, Henry Demarest Lloyd, and the Adversary Tradition* (Cambridge, Mass.: Belknap Press of Harvard University Press, 1983), 114; Alan Trachtenberg, *The Incorporation of America: Culture and Society in the Gilded Age* (New York: Hill and Wang, 1982).

23. Daniel T. Rodgers, *Atlantic Crossings: Social Politics in a Progressive Age* (Cambridge, Mass.: Belknap Press of Harvard University Press, 1998), 33–112; Pero Gaglo Dagbovie, "Reflections on Conventional Portrayals of African-American Experience during the Progressive Era or 'the Nadir,'" *Journal of the Gilded Age and the Progressive Era* 13, no. 1 (January 2014): 4–27; Steven Hoffman, "Progressive Public Health Administration in the Jim Crow South: A Case Study of Richmond, Virginia, 1907–1920," *Journal of Social History* 35, no. 1 (2001): 177–194; Hulliung, *Social Contract in America*, 192; Emma Stone Mackinnon, "Declaration as Disavowal: The Politics of Race and Empire in the Universal Declaration of Human Rights," *Political Theory* 47, no. 1 (2019): 57–81; Tyler Stovall, *White Freedom: The Racial History of an Idea* (Princeton, N.J.: Princeton University Press, 2021); Steven Hahn, *A Nation without Borders: The United States and the World in an Age of Civil Wars, 1830–1910* (New York: Penguin Random House, 2016), 472–473.

24. Eldon Eisenach, *The Lost Promise of Progressivism* (Lawrence: University of Kansas Press, 1994), 5.

25. Hulliung, *Social Contract in America*, 107, 185–186.

26. Laura Weinrib, *The Taming of Free Speech: America's Civil Liberties Compromise* (Cambridge, Mass.: Harvard University Press, 2016).

Chapter 1 • Progress and Poverty

1. T. W. Moody, *Davitt and Irish Revolution, 1846–1882* (Oxford: Clarendon Press, 1981), 534–558.

2. Eldon Eisenach, *The Lost Promise of Progressivism* (Lawrence: University of Kansas Press, 1994).

3. Moody, *Davitt and Irish Revolution*, 9.

4. Mark Hulliung, *The Autocritique of Enlightenment: Rousseau and the Philosophes* (Cambridge, Mass.: Harvard University Press, 1994), 38, 123; Robert Jacques Turgot, "A Philosophical Review of the Successive Advances of the Human Mind," in *The Turgot Collection: Writings, Speeches, and Letters of Anne Robert Jacques Turgot Baron de Laune*, ed. David Gordon (Auburn, Ala.: Ludwig von Mises Institute, 2011), 343.

5. Peter Groenewegen, *Eighteenth Century Economists: Turgot, Beccaria, Smith, and Their Contemporaries* (London: Routledge, 2002), 222–246; Charles Gide and Charles Rist, *A History of Economic Doctrines from the Time of the Physiocrats to the Present Day* (London: George G. Harrap, 1913), 1–45.

6. Elizabeth Hauser, "A. B. DuPont—An Appreciation," *The Public*, June 28, 1919, 684–686.

7. Victor de Riquetti, Marquis de Mirabeau, *Théorie de l'impôt* (Paris, 1761), 7–8. David Hume also argued that land taxation was a tool to undermine the political and economic power of the aristocracy. David Hume, *Essays Moral, Political, Literary* (1758; reprinted, Indianapolis: Liberty Fund, 1987), 346–348.

8. John Locke, *The Works of John Locke in Nine Volumes* (London: Rivington, 1824), 4:55–57;

9. Adam Smith, *An Inquiry into the Nature and Causes of the Wealth of Nations* (1776; reprinted, London: T. Nelson, 1852), 367, 371, 356.

10. Locke, *Two Treatises on Government*, 209.

11. Smith, *Wealth of Nations*, 27.

12. J. G. A. Pocock, *The Machiavellian Moment: Florentine Political Thought and the Republican Tradition* (Princeton, N.J.: Princeton University Press, 1975); James L. Huston, *The British Gentry, the Southern Planter, and the Northern Family Farmer* (Baton Rouge: Louisiana State University Press, 2015), 11.

13. Smith, *Wealth of Nations*, 61.

14. Thompson, *Making of the English Working Class*; George, *Life of Henry George*, 368–369; Malcom Chase, "The Real Rights of Man: Thomas Spence, Paine, and Chartism," *Bulletin of the Society for the Study of Labour History* 52, no. 3 (1987), 32–40; Linebaugh and Rediker, *The Many-Headed Hydra*, 292–294; Gareth Stedman Jones, *Languages of Class: Studies in English Working Class History, 1832–1982* (Cambridge: Cambridge University Press, 1984).

15. Barbara Fried, *The Progressive Assault on Laissez Faire: Robert Hale and the First Law and Economics Movement* (Cambridge, Mass.: Harvard University Press, 1998), 120–121; Mark Blaug, *Economic Theory in Retrospect* (Cambridge: Cambridge University Press, 1997), 65–84; Maurice Dobb, *Theories of Value and Distribution since Adam Smith: Ideology and Economic Theory* (Cambridge: Cambridge University Press, 1973), 65–95.

16. Robert Dorfman, "Thomas Robert Malthus and David Ricardo," *Journal of Economic Perspectives* 3, no. 3 (Summer 1989): 153–164; Mohamed Salah Harzallah,

"Food Supply and Economic Ideology: Indian Corn Relief during the Second Year of the Great Irish Famine (1847)," *Historian* 68, no. 2 (Summer 2006): 305–322; Thomas Malthus, *An Essay on the Principle of Population* (Washington City, D.C.: Roger Chew Weightman, 1809); Thomas Malthus, *Principles of Political Economy: Considered with a View Toward Their Practical Application* (London: W. Pickering, 1836), 309–413.

17. David Ricardo, *The Principles of Political Economy and Taxation* (1817; reprinted, London: J. M. Dent and Sons, Ltd., 1911), 224–225.

18. Dorfman, "Thomas Robert Malthus and David Ricardo," 153–164.

19. Michael Freeden, *The New Liberalism: An Ideology of Social Reform* (Oxford: Oxford University Press, 1978), 43; David Martin, *John Stuart Mill and the Land Question* (Hull, U.K.: University of Hull Publications, 1981); John Stuart Mill, *Principles of Political Economy* (1848; reprinted, New York: D. Appleton and Company, 1887), 532, 656.

20. Mill, *Principles of Political Economy*, 372.

21. John Stuart Mill, *Programme of the Land Tenure Reform Association: With an Explanatory Statement by John Stuart Mill* (London, Longmans, Green, Reader, and Dyer, 1871), 10.

22. Moody, *Davitt and Irish Revolution*, 238, 291, 318.

23. Drew McCoy, *Elusive Republic: Political Economy in Jeffersonian America* (New York: W. W. Norton, 1982).

24. George Raymond Geiger, *The Philosophy of Henry George* (New York: Macmillan Company, 1933), 187; Benjamin Horace Hibbard, *A History of the Public Land Policies* (Madison: University of Wisconsin Press, 1965), 143.

25. Eric Foner, *Tom Paine and Revolutionary America* (New York: Oxford University Press, 2005), 249–251.

26. Benjamin Franklin, *The Complete Works of Benjamin Franklin* (New York: G. P. Putnam's Sons, 1887), ix, 414.

27. Thomas Jefferson to James Madison, October 28, 1785, in *The Papers of Thomas Jefferson*, ed. Julian P. Boyd et al. (Princeton, N.J.: Princeton University Press, 1950), 8:681–683.

28. Mark Lause, *Young America: Land, Labor, and the Republican Community* (Urbana: University of Illinois Press, 2005), 10.

29. Adam Tuchinsky, *Horace Greeley's* New-York Tribune: *Civil War–Era Socialism and the Crisis of Free Labor* (Ithaca, N.Y.: Cornell University Press, 2009).

30. Henry C. Carey, *Principles of Political Economy* (Philadelphia: Lea and Blanchard, 1840), 3:52; Mill, *Principles of Political Economy*, 241; Jack P. Greene, *The Intellectual Construction of America: Exceptionalism and Identity from 1492 to 1800* (Chapel Hill: University of North Carolina Press, 1997).

31. Jeremy Atack and Fred Bateman, *To Their Own Soil: Agriculture in the Antebellum North* (Ames: Iowa State University Press, 1987).

32. Huston, *The British Gentry, the Southern Planter, and the Northern Family Farmer*, 204.

33. Bruce Laurie, *Artisans into Workers: Labor in Nineteenth-Century America* (Champaign: University of Illinois Press, 1989); Johnston, *The Radical Middle Class*; Eric Foner, *Free Soil, Free Labor, Free Men: The Ideology of the Republican Party before the Civil War* (New York: Oxford University Press, 1970).

34. John R. Commons, *Horace Greeley and the Working-Class Origins of the Republican Party* (Boston: Ginn and Company, 1909); Huston, *The British Gentry, the Southern Planter, and the Northern Family Farmer*, 217, 222; Edward Baptist, "Toxic Debt, Liar Loans, Collateralized and Securitized Human Beings, and the Panic of 1837," *Capitalism Takes Command: The Social Transformation of Nineteenth-Century America*, eds. Michael Zakim and Gary J. Kornblith (Chicago: University of Chicago Press, 2012), 69–92.

35. Eric Foner, *Reconstruction: America's Unfinished Revolution, 1863–1877* (New York: Harper and Row, 1988), 68.

36. Charles Albro Barker, *Henry George* (Oxford: Oxford University Press, 1955), 312, 621.

37. Foner, *Reconstruction*, 376.

38. Foner, 328.

39. "The State of the South" and "Wealth, Debt, and Taxation in the Several United States," *The Nation*, May 28, 1872, 197–200.

40. "'Intimidation' at the South," *The Nation*, September 7, 1876, 145–146.

41. Nancy Cohen, *The Reconstruction of American Liberalism* (Chapel Hill: The University of North Carolina Press, 2002), 211; Richard White, *The Republic for Which It Stands: The United States during Reconstruction and the Gilded Age, 1865–1896* (Oxford: Oxford University Press, 2017), 444.

42. Richard White, *"It's Your Misfortune and None of My Own": A New History of the American West* (Norman: University of Oklahoma Press, 1991), 143, 147; White, *The Republic for Which It Stands*, 120, 142.

43. Delos Wilcox, *The American City: A Problem in Democracy* (New York: MacMillan Company, 1904), 381.

44. Department of Commerce and Labor and Bureau of the Census, *Wealth, Debt, and Taxation* (Washington, D.C.: Government Printing Office, 1907), 21; Richard White, *The Republic for Which it Stands*, 408, 477–516.

45. White, *The Republic for Which It Stands*, 511–517

46. Alexander Keyssar, *The Right to Vote: The Contest History of Democracy in the United States* (New York: Basic Books, 2000), 160.

47. Upton Sinclair, *King Coal* (New York: Macmillan Company, 1917); Jane Addams, "A Modern Lear," *Survey* 29 (November 2, 1912), 131–137; Hardy Green, *The Company Town: The Industrial Edens and Satanic Mills That Shaped the American Economy* (New York: Basic Books, 2010), 3, 5, 30, 59; Oliver J. Dinius and Angela Vergara, eds., *Company Towns in the Americas: Landscape, Power, and Working-Class Communities* (Athens: University of Georgia Press, 2011), 1–20, 115.

48. Herbert Spencer, *Social Statics: or, The Conditions Essential to Human Happiness Specified, and the First of Them Developed* (London: John Chapman, 1851), 324.

49. Michael Ruse, "Social Darwinism: The Two Sources," *Albion: A Quarterly Journal Concerned with British Studies* 12, no. 1 (1980): 23–36.

50. Spencer, *Social Statics*, 132.

51. Mark Francis, "Herbert Spencer and the Myth of Laissez-Faire," *Journal of the History of Ideas* 39, no. 2 (1978): 317–28.

52. Herbert Spencer, *The Study of Sociology* (New York: D. Appleton and Company, 1874), 335.

53. Spencer, *Study of Sociology*, 334.

54. Spencer, *Study of Sociology*, 353.

55. Spencer, *Social Statics*, 13.

56. Levy, *Ages of American Capitalism*, 288.

57. Andrew Carnegie, *The Gospel of Wealth and Other Timely Essays* (New York: Century Company, 1901), 2–3.

58. Carnegie, 12–13.

59. John Thomas, *Alternative America: Henry George, Edward Bellamy, Henry Demarest Lloyd, and the Adversary Tradition* (Cambridge, Mass.: Belknap Press of Harvard University Press, 1983).

60. Theodore Roosevelt, *The Winning of the West* (New York: G. P. Putnam's Sons, 1889), 1:92.

61. Mark Twain and Charles Dudley Warner, *The Gilded Age* (1873), in *Mark Twain: The Gilded Age and Later Novels* (New York: Library of America, 2002), 15.

62. Twain and Warner, 441.

63. Twain and Warner, 443.

64. George Peabody to Franklin Roosevelt, February 20, 1934, box 660, President's Personal Papers; Jane Farell to FDR, December 26, 1928, box 63, President's Papers as Governor, both Franklin D. Roosevelt Presidential Library, Hyde Park, N.Y.

65. Stanley Buder, *Visionaries and Planners: The Garden City Movement and the Modern Community* (New York: Oxford University Press, 1990), 20; Alex Wagner Lough, "The Last Tax: Henry George and the Social Politics of Land in the Gilded Age and Progressive Era" (PhD diss., Brandeis University, 2013), 113–115.

66. "Charles Frederick Adams," *The Public*, June 10, 1910, 532–535.

67. Stephen A. Barton, "'This Social Mother in Whose Household We All Live': Berkeley Mayor J. Stitt Wilson's Early-Twentieth-Century Socialist Feminism," *Journal of the Gilded Age and the Progressive Era* 13, no. 4 (September 2017): 532–563.

Chapter 2 • The Prophet of San Francisco

1. Thomas, *Alternative America*, 6–7.

2. Thomas, 4.

3. Henry George, "'Shall the Republic Live?': The Real Issue," *New York Journal*, November 2, 1896.

4. Sean Wilentz, *Chants Democratic: New York City and the Rise of the American Working Class, 1788–1850* (New York: Oxford University Press, 1984); Seth Rockman, *Scraping By: Wage Labor, Slavery, and Survival in Early Baltimore* (Baltimore: Johns Hopkins University Press, 2009); David R. Roediger, *The Wages of Whiteness: Race and the Making of the American Working Class* (London: Verso, 1999).

5. Richard George to Henry George, March 6, 1858, reel 1, HGP-NYPL.

6. George, *Life of Henry George*, 11–12.

7. George, *Life of Henry George*, 214.

8. Thomas, *Alternative America*, 10.

9. "Henry George, the Man from Rev Ignatius Horstman to Henry George Jr.," September 30, 1898, reel 13, HGP-NYPL; George, *Life of Henry George*, 17–18.

10. Henry George, *Progress and Poverty* (1879; reprinted, New York: Robert Schalkenbach Foundation, 2008), 491–492.

11. Linebaugh and Rediker, *Many-Headed Hydra*, 219; Jones, *Languages of Class*.

12. George, *Life of Henry George*, 31–32.

13. George, *Life of Henry* George, 34–26.

14. Mark Francis, *Herbert Spencer and the Invention of Modern Life* (Ithaca, N.Y.: Cornell University Press, 2007), 8.

15. Mark Lause, "Progress Impoverished: Origins of Henry George's Single Tax," *Historian* 52, no. 3 (May 1990): 399; Selig Perlman, *The Theory of the Labor Movement* (1928; reprinted, New York: Augustus M. Kelly, 1968).

16. Thomas, *Alternative America*, 10.

17. George, quoted in Thomas, 51.

18. Thomas, 59; Charles Albro Barker, *Henry George* (Oxford: Oxford University Press, 1955), 219.

19. George, *Life of Henry George*, 123.

20. George, *Life of Henry George*, 149.

21. Stephen Botein, "Printers and the American Revolution," in *The Press and the American Revolution*, ed. Bernard Bailyn and John B. Hench (Worchester, Mass.: American Antiquarian Society, 1980), 11–57.

22. Barker, *Henry George*, 67.

23. George, *Life of Henry George*, 166–167.

24. *Sacramento Bee*, October 26, 1883.

25. Tamara Venit Shelton, *A Squatter's Republic* (Berkeley: University of California Press, 2013), 37–74.

26. Jonathan Glickstein, *Concepts of Free Labor in Antebellum America* (New Haven, Conn.: Yale University Press, 1991), 13–19, 35–58; Rockman, *Scraping By*, 5–6; Huston, *The British Gentry, the Southern Planter, and the Northern Family Farmer*, 188.

27. Frank McCoppin to Henry George, April 10, 1868; Frank McCoppin to Henry George, July 23, 1868, both Reel 1, HGP-NYPL; Shelton, *Squatter's Republic*, 82.

28. Barker, *Henry George*, 115–119.

29. Christopher B. Daly, *Covering America: A Narrative History of a Nation's Journalism* (Amherst: University of Massachusetts Press, 2012), 121.

30. Edward C. Kemble, *A History of California Newspapers, 1846–1848* (Los Gatos, Calif.: Talisman Press, 1962), 130–131.

31. George, *Life of Henry George*, 241–246.

32. Barker, *Henry George*, 136; Stephan Thernstrom, *Poverty and Progress: Social Mobility in the Nineteenth Century City* (Cambridge, Mass.: Harvard University Press, 1964), 139; Roy Rosenzweig and Elizabeth Blackmar, *The Park and the People: A History of Central Park* (Ithaca, N.Y.: Cornell University Press, 1992), 59–91.

33. William Cronon, *Nature's Metropolis: Chicago and the Great West* (New York: W. W. Norton, 1991), 31–40.

34. Henry George, "What the Railroad Will Bring Us," *Overland Monthly*, October 1868, 297–306; William Deverell, *Railroad Crossing: Californians and the Railroad, 1850–1910* (Berkeley: University of California Press, 1994), 19–22.

35. Gwendolyn Mink, *Old Labor and New Immigrants* (Ithaca, N.Y.: Cornell University Press, 1982), 78.

36. Henry George, "The Chinese on the Pacific Coast," *New York Tribune*, May 1, 1869.

37. Dennis Kearney, *Speeches of Dennis Kearney* (New York: Jesse Haney, 1878), 29.

38. George, *Life of Henry George*, 298–300.

39. Henry George, "The Kearney Agitation in California," *Popular Science Monthly* 17 (August 1880): 433–453.

40. George, *Life of Henry George*, 195.

41. Shelton, *Squatter's Republic*, 96, 119; Henry George, "Chinese Immigration," in *Cyclopædia of Political Science, Political Economy, and of the Political History of the United States*, ed. John Joseph Lalor (Chicago: Rand McNally and Company, 1881), 1:409–414.

42. Henry George, *Our Land and Land Policy: National and State* (San Francisco: White and Bauer, 1871); Richard White, *Railroaded: The Transcontinentals and the Making of Modern America* (New York: W. W. Norton, 2011).

43. Charles A. Barker, "The Followers of Henry George," *Journal of Economics and Sociology* 12, no. 4 (July 1953): 380.

44. George, *Life of Henry George*, 278–281.

45. George, 249.

46. George, 301.

47. Thomas, *Alternative America*, 103.

48. George, *Life of Henry George*, 301–303.

49. Howe, *Confessions of a Reformer*, 136.

50. James Turner, *Philology: The Forgotten Origins of the Modern Humanities* (New York: Oxford University Press, 2013); Julie A. Reuben, *The Making of the Modern University: Intellectual Transformation and the Marginalization of Morality* (Chicago: University of Chicago Press, 1996); Eli Cook, "The Great Marginalization: Why Twentieth-Century Economists Neglected Inequality," *Real World Economics Review* 83 (2018): 20–34; Mason Gaffney and Fred Harrison, *The Corruption of Economics* (London: Shepheard-Walwyn, 1994), 29–164.

51. José Martí, "Schism of the Catholics in New York," in *Inside the Monster: Writings on the United States and American Imperialism*, ed. Philip S. Foner (New York: Monthly Review Press, 1975), 280.

52. David Bell, *Men on Horseback: The Power of Charisma in the Age of Revolution* (New York: Farrar, Straus and Giroux, 2020); Max Weber, *From Max Weber*, trans. H. H. Gerth (London: Routledge, 2009), 196–252.

53. George, *Life of Henry George*, 312.

54. Barker, *Henry George*, 312.

55. Arthur Power Dudden, *Joseph Fels and the Single-Tax Movement* (Philadelphia: Temple University Press, 1971), 138.

56. Angeline Loesch Graves, "By What Road?" *The Public*, September 27, 1912, 932; Newton Baker to Will Atkinson, September 17, 1927, box 32, NBP-LC.

Chapter 3 • The Truths of Smith and Proudhon

Epigraph. George, *Progress and Poverty*, xvi–xvii.

1. George, *Life of Henry George*, 328, 369; George, *Progress and Poverty*, 323; Francis, *Herbert Spencer and the Invention of Modern Life*, 113; Henry George, *A Perplexed Philosopher* (New York: Charles L. Webster and Company, 1893).

2. George, *Progress and Poverty*, 146.

3. George, *Progress and Poverty*, 141.

4. George, *Progress and Poverty*, 248–249.

5. Henry George, *Protection or Free Trade* (New York: privately printed, 1887), 286.

6. Henry George, *Social Problems* (New York: Doubleday and McClure, 1900), 273.

7. George, *Progress and Poverty*, 412.

8. George, *Progress and Poverty*, 264–265.

9. George, *Progress and Poverty*, 531.

10. George, *Progress and Poverty*, 534–535.

11. George, *Progress and Poverty*, 236–241.

12. George, *Social Problems*, 320; George, *Progress and Poverty*, 413–444.

13. George, *Progress and Poverty*, 236–237.

14. George, *Progress and Poverty*, 239.

15. George, *Progress and Poverty*, 235.

16. George, *Progress and Poverty*, 241–242.

17. George, *Progress and Poverty*, 241.

18. Mill, *Principles of Political Economy*, 244.

19. George, *Progress and Poverty*, 242.

20. Henry George, *The Science of Political Economy* (New York: Doubleday and McClure Co., 1898), 354.

21. Locke, *Two Treatises on Government*, 209; Mill, *Principles of Political Economy*, 173.

22. George, *Perplexed Philosopher*, 25.

23. George, *Progress and Poverty*, 334.

24. George, *Progress and Poverty*, 445–446.

25. George, *Progress and Poverty*, 453.

26. George, *Progress and Poverty*, 470.

27. George, *Progress and Poverty*, 462.

28. George, *Progress and Poverty*, 462, 468.

29. Stephen Kern, *The Culture of Time and Space, 1880–1918* (Cambridge, Mass.: Harvard University Press, 1983); Wiebe, *Search for Order*; White, *Railroaded*.

30. Spencer, *Study of Sociology*, 62, 253, 335.

31. George, *Progress and Poverty*, 503.

32. George, *Progress and Poverty*, 490; Spencer, *The Study of Sociology*, 199.

33. George, *Science of Political Economy*, 301–312.

34. Louis Post, *Ethics of Democracy: A Series of Optimistic Essays on the Natural Laws of Human Society* (1903; reprinted, Indianapolis: Bobbs-Merrill Company, 1916), 128.

35. Jonathan Levy, *Freaks of Fortune: The Emerging World of Capitalism and Risk in America* (Cambridge, Mass.: Harvard University Press, 2012), 265.

36. "Transcript of Interview with Debs Discussing Socialist Viewpoint," box 3, LSP-CU; Eugene Debs, "Prison Labor," in *Debs: His Life, Writings, and Speeches* (Chicago: Charles H. Kerr and Company, 1906), 354.

37. George, *Progress and Poverty*, 438.

38. George, *Progress and Poverty*, 468.

39. George, *Social Problems*, 12.

40. George, *Progress and Poverty*, 456.

41. George, *Protection or Free Trade*, 303.

42. Henry George, "To Destroy the Rum Power," in *Henry George: Collected Journalistic Writings*, ed. Kenneth Wenzer (London: M. E Sharpe: 2004), 3:159; Levy, *Ages of American Capitalism*, 94–125.

43. Spencer, *Social Statics*, 215–216.

44. George, *Progress and Poverty*, 564.

45. Donovan E. Smucker, *Origins of Walter Rauschenbusch's Social Ethics* (Quebec City: McGill-Queen's University Press, 1994), 103–108.

46. Walter Rauschenbusch, *Christianizing the Social Order* (New York: MacMillan Company, 1913), 394; Walter Rauschenbusch, *Christianity and the Social Crisis* (London: MacMillan and Company, 1913), 220–291.

47. Martin E. Marty, *Modern American Religion: The Irony of It All* (Chicago: University of Chicago Press, 1997), 286.

48. Henry George to Ms. Milne, August 14, 1889, reel 5, HGP-NYPL.

49. Henry George, *Moses / The Crime of Poverty* (New York: International Joseph Fels Commissions, 1918), 22.

50. George, *Moses / The Crime of Poverty*, 16; Thomas Spence, *The Rights of Man* (London, 1792), 22, 37.

51. George, *The Life of Henry George*, 312.

52. George, *Progress and Poverty*, 356.

53. George, *Progress and Poverty*, 563.

54. George, *Progress and Poverty*, 563.

55. George, *Science of Political Economy*, 54.

56. George, *Progress and Poverty*, 482.

57. George, *Progress and Poverty*, 524–525.

58. Mill, *Principles of Political Economy*, 109.

59. Francis A. Walker, *Land and Its Rent* (Boston: Little, Brown, and Company, 1891), 169–182; William Stanley Jevons, *The Coal Question* (London: Macmillan and Company, 1886); John M. Polimeni, Kozo Mayumi, Mario Giampietro, and Blake Alcott, *The Jevons Paradox and the Myth of Resource Efficiency Improvements* (London: Earthscan, 2008); Mill, *Principles of Political Economy*, 136, 434, 485.

60. George Stigler, "Alfred Marshall's Lectures on Progress and Poverty," in *Henry George, 1834–1897*, ed. Mark Blaug, Pioneers in Economics 34 (Aldershot, UK: Edward Elgar, 1992), 12.

61. Stigler, "Alfred Marshall's Lectures on Progress and Poverty," 14.

62. Alfred Marshall to Henry Foxwell, July 22, 1883, in *The Early Economic Writings of Alfred Marshall, 1867–90*, ed. J. K. Whitaker (New York: Free Press, 1975), 1:24–25.

63. Alfred Marshall, *Principles of Economics* (London: MacMillan and Company, 1890), vi; Fried, *Progressive Assault on Laissez Faire*, 160–205; Cook, "The Great Marginalization"; Gaffney and Harrison, *Corruption of Economics*, 29–164; Frank Fetter, "Clark's Reformulation of the Capital Concept," in *Capital, Interest, and Rent: Essays in the Theory of Distribution*, ed. Murray N. Rothbard (1927; reprinted, Menlo Park, Calif.: Institute of Humane Studies, 1977), 127; John Bates Clark, *The Distribution of Wealth* (New York: MacMillan Company, 1899), viii, 84.

64. Leonard, *Illiberal Reformers*, 28–29.

65. White, *The Republic for Which It Stands*, 290–294.

66. Ajay Mehrotra, *Making the Modern American Fiscal State: Law, Politics, and the Rise of Progressive Taxation, 1877–1929* (New York: Cambridge University Press, 2013), 10; McGerr, *Fierce Discontent*, 7–11.

67. John Stuart Mill, *John Stuart Mill's Social and Political Thought: Critical Assessments*, ed. G. W. Smith (London: Routledge, 1998), 271–310.

68. Francis, *Herbert Spencer and the Invention of Modern Life*, 315–316; John Offer, "Social Solidarity and Herbert Spencer: Not the Oxymoron That Might Be Assumed," *Frontiers in Sociology* 4, no. 1 (February 2019).

69. Herbert Spencer, *The Principles of Ethics* (New York: D. Appleton and Company, 1899), 2:83–84; D. Weinstein, *Equal Freedom and Utility: Herbert Spencer's Liberal Utilitarianism* (Cambridge: Cambridge University Press, 1998), 189–190.

70. Edward A. Ross, *Social Control: A Survey of the Foundations of Order* (1901; reprinted, New York: Macmillan Company, 1916), 1–6, 138, 247, 248, 251, 252.

71. Ross, 3.

72. Ross, 83.

73. Ross, 87–88.

74. Richard Hofstadter, *Social Darwinism in American Thought* (Boston: Beacon Press, 1944); Fried, *Progressive Assault on Laissez-Faire*, 33, 217; John Maurice Clark, *The Social Control of Business* (Chicago: University of Chicago Press, 1926); Rodgers, *Atlantic Crossings*, 280.

75. Gillis J. Harp, *Positivist Republic* (University Park: Pennsylvania State University Press, 1995), 46, 109–154; David W. Levy, *Herbert Croly of the New Republic* (Princeton, N.J.: Princeton University Press, 1985), 13, 30, 35, 38.

76. Herbert Croly, *The Promise of American Life* (New York: Macmillan Company, 1914), 191–192, 400.

77. Gabriel Kolko, *The Triumph of American Conservatism: A Reinterpretation of American History, 1900–1916* (New York: Free Press, 1977).

78. Roger Lowenstein, *America's Bank: The Epic Struggle to Create the Federal Reserve* (New York: Penguin Press, 2015); "Senator Aldrich's 'Democratized' Banking Scheme," *The Public*, November 17, 1911, 1169–1170.

79. James Kloppenberg, "The Virtues of Liberalism: Christianity, Republicanism, and Ethics in Early American Political Discourse," *Journal of American History* 74, no. 1 (June 1987): 9–33.

Chapter 4 • *Labor Omnia Vincit*

1. Horace White to Henry George, December 17, 1881, HGP-NYPL.

2. George, *Life of Henry George*, 347.

3. Henry George, *The Irish Land Question* (New York: D. Appleton and Company, 1881), 26–27.

4. George, *The Irish Land Question*, 45. George's use of "working classes" evokes an understanding of social class current in England at the time. See Jones, *Languages of Class*.

5. George, *Progress and Poverty*, 104; George, *Irish Land Question*, 8, 9.

6. George, *Progress and Poverty*, 362–366.

7. Michael Davitt, *The Fall of Feudalism in Ireland, or The Story of the Land League Revolution* (London: Harper & Brothers Publishing, 1904), 421–425; George, *Life of*

Henry George, 392–395; Louis F. Post, *The Prophet of San Francisco: Personal Memories and Interpretations of Henry George* (1930; reprinted, Honolulu: University Press of the Pacific, 2002), 40–42.

8. Moody, *Davitt and Irish Revolution*, 546–549; George, *Life of Henry George*, 383–385.

9. George, *Life of Henry George*, 387.

10. Henry George to Taylor, September 7, 1881, reel 2, HGP-NYPL.

11. George to Taylor, September 7, 1881; Lorein Foote, *Seeking the Great Remedy: Francis George Shaw and Nineteenth-Century Reform* (Athens: Ohio University Press, 2003).

12. Edward T. O'Donnell, "Henry George and the 'New Political Forces': Ethnic Nationalism, Labor Radicalism, and Politics in Gilded Age New York" (PhD diss., Columbia University, 1995), 138.

13. Henry George to James McClatchy, October 9, 1881, reel 2, HGP-NYPL.

14. O'Donnell, "Henry George and the 'New Political Forces,'" 313.

15. Post, *Prophet of San Francisco*, 27.

16. Robert La Follette, *La Follette's Autobiography: A Personal Narrative of Political Experiences* (Madison, Wisc.: Robert M. La Follette Co., 1919), 19.

17. Richard Schneirov, *Labor and Urban Politics: Class Conflict and the Origins of Modern Liberalism in Chicago, 1864–1887* (Urbana: University of Illinois Press, 1998), 133.

18. Samuel Gompers, *Seventy Years of Life and Labor: An Autobiography* (New York: E. P. Dutton & Co., 1925), 82.

19. George, *Life of Henry George*, 294–295.

20. Steven J. Ross, "The Culture of Political Economy: Henry George and the American Working Class," *Southern California Quarterly* 65, no. 2 (Summer 1983): 145–166.

21. Henry George to "Dear Doctor," April 28, 1883, reel 3, HGP-NYPL.

22. Henry George to August Lewis, May 24, 1894, reel 6, HGP-NYPL; *Voices for Reform* 1, no. 4 (April 2, 1887), box 32, TPP-CUA.

23. "Faithful over a Few Things," *The Public*, January 14, 1916, 31–32.

24. George, *Life of Henry George*, 423, 434; Peter d'A. Jones, "Henry George and British Socialism," *American Journal of Economics and Sociology* 47, no. 4 (October 1988), 477.

25. "Mr. Powderly's Position," *Portland (Ore.) Avant-Courier*, November 20, 1886.

26. Tom Johnson, *My Story* (New York: B. W. Huebsch, 1911), 49–52; Lincoln Steffens, "The Leader of the Leaders," box 19, LSP-CU.

27. Dan Beard to Henry George, October 11, 1890, reel 5, HGP-NYPL.

28. Henry George to Daniel Beard, October 12, 1890, box 53, DBP-LC.

29. Dan Beard to George Pratt, March 31, 1915, box 33, DBP-LC.

30. Cyril Clemens, *Uncle Dan* (New York: Thomas Y. Crowell Company, 1938), xi–xii.

31. George, *Life of Henry George*, 435.

32. Elwood P. Lawrence, "Henry George's Oxford Speech," *California Historical Society Quarterly* 30, no. 2 (1951): 118, 120–121; George, *Life of Henry George*, 434–437.

33. Henry George and George Douglas Campbell, *The Peer and Prophet* (Glasgow: William Reeves, 1885), 30, 33.

34. George and Campbell, 52.

35. George, *Life of Henry George*, 445.

36. George and Campbell, *Peer and Prophet*, 12–13.

37. William Lloyd Garrison, "The New Abolition," *The Standard* (New York), September 12, 1891, 1–8.

38. Garrison.

39. Rodgers, *Atlantic Crossings*, 70; Lough, "The Last Tax," 29.

40. Kevin Tierney, *Darrow: A Biography* (New York: Thomas Y. Crowell, 1979), 1–32; Brand Whitlock, *Forty Years of It* (New York: D. Appleton & Co. 1914); Mary Pilon, *The Monopolists: Obsession, Fury, and the Scandal behind the World's Favorite Board Game* (New York: Bloomsbury, 2015).

41. Henry George to Terence Powderly, July 25, 1883, box 8, TPP-CUA.

42. George, *Life of Henry George*, 447; Henry George to Terence Powderly, March 23, 1885, box 19, TPP-CUA.

43. George, *Progress and Poverty*, 310, 316.

44. *Records of the Proceedings of the Special Session of the General Assembly Held at Cleveland Ohio May 25 to June 3, 1886*, p. 70, box 113, TPP-CUA.

45. Thomas, *Alternative America*, 183–184.

46. Robert Weir, "A Fragile Alliance: Henry George and the Knights of Labor," *American Journal of Economics and Sociology* 56, no. 4 (October 1997): 423; "Mr. Powderly's Position," *Portland (Ore.) Avant-Courier*, November 20, 1886.

47. "The Mayor's Message," April 1–9, 1883, box 8, TPP-CUA; Vincent J. Falzone, "Terence V. Powderly: Politician and Progressive Mayor of Scranton, 1878–1884," *Pennsylvania History* 41, no. 3 (July 1974): 305–306.

48. Henry George to Terence Powderly, April 19, 1883, box 8; HG to Powderly, June 22, 1884, box 11, both in TPP-CUA.

49. *Proceedings: General Assembly, Knights of Labor, Hamilton, Ontario, 1885; Cleveland, Ohio, 1886; Richmond, Virginia, 1886*, p. 13, TPP-CUA.

50. *Proceedings: General Assembly, Knights of Labor*, 17.

51. *Proceedings: General Assembly, Knights of Labor*, 164–165; John Lewis to Terence Powderly, August 12, 1893, box 81, TPP-CUA; Charles Postel, *Equality: An American Dilemma, 1866–1896* (New York: Farrar, Straus and Giroux, 2019), 290.

52. *Proceedings: General Assembly Knights of Labor*, 40.

53. *Proceedings: General Assembly Knights of Labor*, 72–73.

54. O'Donnell, "Henry George and the 'New Political Forces,'" 416–430.

55. Philip S. Foner, *History of the Labor Movement in the United States: From the Founding of the American Federation of Labor to the Emergence of American Imperialism* (New York: International, 1955), 2:121

56. O'Donnell, "Henry George and the 'New Political Forces,'" 273.

57. Richard P. Hunt, "The First Labor Day," *American Heritage* 33 (August/September 1982), 109–122.

58. "Henry George and the 'New Political Forces,'" 326, 554; Jonathan Grossman, "Who Is the Father of Labor Day?" *Monthly Labor Review* 95, no. 9 (September 1971): 3–6.

59. Thomas, *Alternative America*, 222.

60. Thomas, *Alternative America*, 222.

61. Louis Post and Frederic Leubuscher, *Henry George's 1886 Campaign: An Account of the George-Hewitt Campaign in the New York Municipal Election of 1886* (1886; reprinted, New York: Henry George School, 1961), 28.

62. Post and Leubuscher, *Henry George's 1886 Campaign*, 27.

63. "The Mephistopheles of Today—Honest Labor's Temptation," *Puck*, October 20, 1886.

64. R. Wheatley, "New York Letter," *Zion's Herald* 63, no. 46 (November 17, 1886): 1.

65. Rosenzweig and Blackmar, *The Park and the People*, 15–372.

66. George, *Life of Henry George*, 338–339.

67. O'Donnell, "Henry George and the 'New Political Forces,'" 558–559; Gompers, *Seventy Years of Life and Labor*, 2:315–316; George, *Life of Henry George*, 338–9.

68. Jon Grinspan, *The Age of Acrimony* (New York: Bloomsbury, 2011); White, *Republic for Which It Stands*, 254.

69. Post and Leubuscher, *Account of the George-Hewitt Campaign*, 33.

70. Gompers, *Seventy Years of Life and Labor*, 2:318–319; Foner, *History of the Labor Movement*, 2:123.

71. Post and Leubuscher, *Henry George's 1886 Campaign*, 125.

72. Post and Leubuscher, 48.

73. Post and Leubuscher, 171.

74. Post and Leubuscher, 16.

75. Kazin, *American Dreamers*, 71.

76. *New York Freeman*, December 6, 1886.

77. Postel, *Equality*, 290.

78. Thomas Bender, *Intellect and Public Life: Essays on the Social History of Academic Intellectuals in the United States* (Baltimore: Johns Hopkins University Press, 1993), 49–77.

79. Lause, *Young America*, 132.

80. F. W. Evans, *Elder Evans to Henry George* (Mt. Lebanon, N.Y., 1885), Rare Book Collection, Library of Congress, Washington, D.C.

81. Post and Leubuscher, *Henry George's 1886 Campaign*, 12.

82. Leon Fink, *Workingmen's Democracy: The Knights of Labor and American Politics* (Urbana: University of Illinois Press, 1983), 131, 159.

83. "United Labor's Ticket: The First in the Field for Spring," *Chicago Daily Tribune*, February 27, 1887.

84. Fink, *Workingmen's Democracy*, 26, 98; Thomas R. Pegram, *Partisans and Progressives: Private Interest and Public Policy in Illinois, 1870–1922* (Urbana: University of Illinois Press, 1992), 65; Edward B. Mittelman, "Chicago Labor in Politics," *Journal of Political Economy* 28, no. 5 (May 1920): 407–427.

85. Post and Leubuscher, *Henry George's 1886 Campaign*, 118–120.

86. Richard Franklin Bensel, *The American Ballot Box in Mid-Nineteenth Century* (Cambridge: Cambridge University Press, 2004), 138–187.

87. Post and Leubuscher, *Henry George's 1886 Campaign*, 169.

88. Foner, *History of the Labor Movement*, 2:128.

89. Michael Davitt to Henry George, November 4, 1886, box 4, HGP-NYPL; Evans, *Elder Evans to Henry George*.

90. Foner, *History of the Labor Movement*, 2:145.

91. Post and Leubuscher, *Henry George's 1886 Campaign*, 172.

92. Post and Leubuscher, *Henry George's 1886 Campaign*, 171.

93. "Friedrich Engels to Friedrich Sorge, November 29, 1886," in *Karl Marx and Friedrich Engels' Correspondence, 1846–1895: A Selection with Commentary and Notes*, trans. Dona Torr (London: Martin Lawrence Ltd., 1934), 450–451.

94. "The New York Mayoralty," *Saturday Review of Politics, Literature, Science and Art*, November 6, 1886, 608–609; "A Flying Visit to the United States," *Nineteenth Century* (December 1886): 906.

95. "Cartoons and Comics," *Puck*, May 25, 1887, 206; "Cartoons and Comics," *Puck*, November 17, 1886, 186.

96. Sven Beckert, "Democracy and Its Discontents: Contesting Suffrage Rights in Gilded Age New York," *Past and Present* 174 (February 2002): 142–143.

97. Theodore Roosevelt, "Machine Politics in New York City," *Century Magazine* (November 1886): 75.

98. Roosevelt, 75.

99. Theodore Roosevelt to Lincoln Steffens, June 12, 1908, box 11, LSP-CU; Kathleen Dalton, *Theodore Roosevelt: A Strenuous Life* (New York: Alfred A. Knopf, 2002).

100. Henry Joseph Browne, *The Catholic Church and the Knights of Labor* (New York: Arno Press, 1976), 223–224.

101. Browne, 335.

102. Peter R. D'Agostino, *Rome in America: Transnational Catholic Ideology from the Risorgimento to Fascism* (Chapel Hill: University of North Carolina Press, 2004), 77.

103. *The Public*, October 12, 1901, 419.

104. Robert Emmett Curran, *Shaping American Catholicism: Maryland and New York, 1805–1915* (Washington D.C.: Catholic University Press of America, 2012).

105. *Proceedings of the General Assembly, Eleventh Regular Session, Oct. 4–19, Minneapolis, Minn., 1877*, p. 1494, box 113, TPP-CUA.

106. *Proceedings of the General Assembly, Eleventh Regular Session*, 1494, 1461; *Proceedings of General Assembly, 1888, Indianapolis, Nov. 13–17*, p 46, both box 113, TPP-CUA.

107. Browne, *Catholic Church and the Knights of Labor*, 320.

108. Michael Walsh, "The Myth of *Rerum Novarum*," *New Blackfriars* 93, no. 1044 (March 2012): 155–162.

109. Henry George, *The Condition of Labor: An Open Letter to Pope Leo XIII* (New York: United States Book Company, 1891), 23–24.

110. Henry George to Terence Powderly, January 31, 1889; Henry George to Terence Powderly, February 28, 1889, both box 51, TPP-CUA.

111. *Proceedings of the 13th General Assembly, 1889, Atlanta*, p. 43, box 114, TPP-CUA.

112. Browne, *Catholic Church and the Knights of Labor*, 339.

113. Henry George to Terence Powderly, November 24, 1889, box 57, TPP-CUA.

114. Browne, *Catholic Church and the Knights of Labor*, 275–276; Foner, *History of the Labor Movement*, 2:482.

115. Postel, *Equality*, 266–272.

116. Foner, *History of the Labor Movement*, 2:122–123.

117. *New York Leader*, July 25, 1887.

118. "America's Labor Party," *The Public*, January 25, 1919, 78–79; Lincoln Steffens to Ella Winer, December 16, 1919, box 15, LSP-CU; Daniel Kiefer to Lincoln Steffens, October 24, 1908, box 7, LSP-CU.

119. Henry George, "The New Party," *North American Review* 145 (July 1887): 1–8.

Chapter 5 • The Democracy of Henry George

1. "A Crowded Meeting Ratifies the Syracuse Platform," box 11, LPP-LC.

2. Post and Leubuscher, *Henry George's 1886 Campaign*, 171–174.

3. George, *Life of Henry George*, 483.

4. *The Nation*, February 4, 1892; Henry George, "Money in Elections," *North American Review* (March 1883): 201–212.

5. "By Men of All Parties," *New York Times*, December 5, 1889, 5.

6. L. E. Fredman, *The Australian Ballot: The Story of an American Reform* (East Lansing: Michigan State University Press, 1968), 62.

7. In Montana the Australian ballot was introduced into the state legislature by Will Kennedy, a single taxer and newspaper editor from Boulder, Colorado. Thomas A. Clinch, *Urban Populism and Free Silver in Montana: A Narrative of Ideology in Political Action* (Helena: University of Montana Press, 1970), 53; Keyssar, *The Right to Vote*, 143; Tracy Campbell, *Deliver the Vote: A History of Election Fraud, an American Political Tradition, 1742–2004* (New York: Carroll and Graf, 2006), 115–116; Eldon Cobb Evans, "The History of the Australian Ballot System in the United States" (PhD diss., University of Chicago, 1917); John Henry Wigmore, *The Australian Ballot System As Embodied in the Legislation of Various Countries* (Boston: Boston Book Company, 1889).

8. Barker, *Henry George*, 502.

9. Louis Post, "The United Labor Party," *The Public*, November 17, 1911, 1173–1179; John Commons et al., *History of Labour in the United States* (New York: Macmillan Co., 1918), 2:456–458; Alexander Speek, *The Singletax and the Labor Movement* (Madison: University of Wisconsin Press, 1917).

10. Harp, *Positivist Republic*, 94–95.

11. Thomas, *Alternative America*, 228–231.

12. Ronald Yanosky, "Seeing the Cat: Henry George and the Rise of the Single Tax Movement" (PhD diss., University of California, Berkeley, 1993), 325–325.

13. Post, "The United Labor Party."

14. Post, *Prophet of San Francisco*, 141.

15. Barker, *Henry George*, 508–520; Henry George to Mrs. Milne, August 14, 1889, reel 5, HGP-NYPL.

16. Johnston, *The Radical Middle Class*.

17. Clarence Darrow, "Clarence Darrow on Land and Labor: Address for the Single Tax League in LA, March 27, 1913," *Everyman* (June 1913): 19–20; Barker, *Henry George*, 539–541.

18. Yanosky, "Seeing the Cat," 338.

19. Post, *Prophet of San Francisco*, 121–125.

20. George, *Protection or Free Trade*, 344.

21. Louis Post, "Living a Long Life Over Again," p. 199 (a), box 4, LPP-LC.

22. George, *Protection or Free Trade*, 345–346.

23. Annie L. Diggs, *The Story of Jerry Simpson* (Wichita, Kans.: Jane Simpson, 1908), 196.

24. Henry George to Tom Johnson, August 11, 1893, reel 6, HGP-NYPL.

25. Henry George to August Lewis, May 24, 1894, reel 6, HGP-NYPL.

26. Johnson, *My Story*, 63.

27. Henry George to Tom Johnson, February 17, 1893, Reel 5, HGP-NYPL.

28. "Clearly a Blunder," *New York Times*, July 2, 1892, 4.

29. *Chicago Tribune*, May 9, 1892.

30. "An Address by McKinley," *New York Times*, August 3, 1892, 2.

31. Henry George to "Dr.," April 19, 1882, reel 5, HGP-NYPL; 23 Cong. Rec., 5395 (June 18, 1892); George, *Life of Henry George*, 571–573.

32. Johnson, *My Story*, 72–74.

33. "The Same Old Free-Trade Cry," *New York Times*, July 7, 1892, 4.

34. 26 Cong. Rec., 1330 (January 24, 1894).

35. 26 Cong. Rec., 1652 (January 30, 1894); 26 Cong. Rec., 5202 (May 24, 1894); 26 Cong. Rec., 1672–1673 (January 30, 1894); 26 Cong. Rec., 6687, 6714 (May 24, 1894); 26 Cong. Rec., 3561 (April 9, 1894).

36. Henry George to August Lewis, May 24, 1894, box 6, HGP-NYPL.

37. David Greenburg, *Republic of Spin: An Inside History of the American Presidency* (New York: W. W. Norton, 2016), 131.

38. "Not to Their Taste," *Chicago Tribune*, January 11, 1894, 5; "Tom Johnson's Brand of Politics," *Chicago Tribune*, July 30, 1894, 1.

39. Tom Johnson to Henry George, February 17, 1893, reel 5; Henry George (HG) to Tom Johnson, August 8, 1893, reel 6, both HGP-NYPL; 25 Cong. Rec., 446 (August 18, 1893).

40. Johnson, *My Story*, 63.

41. Paul M. Gaston, *Man and Mission: E. B. Gaston and the Origins of the Fairhope Single Tax Colony* (Montgomery, Ala.: Black Belt Press, 1993), 8–9.

42. Edwin S. Potter to Harold Ickes, November 24, 1920, box 31, Harold Ickes Papers, Library of Congress, Washington, D.C.

43. Pilon, *The Monopolists*, 39.

44. Mark Taylor, "Utopia by Taxation: Frank Stephens and the Single Tax Community of Arden, Delaware," *Pennsylvania Magazine of History and Biography* 126, no. 2 (April 2002): 305–325; Mark Taylor, *Arden* (Chicago: Arcadia, 2010).

45. Rhoda Hellman, *Henry George Reconsidered* (New York: Carlton Press, 1987), 109.

46. Post, *Prophet of San Francisco*, 53.

47. Henry George, *Social Problems* (New York: Doubleday and McClure, 1900), 242.

48. "Meeting of Single Taxers: Wary of Taking Sides with Any Political Party," *New York Times*, September 4, 1894, 4; Barker, *Henry George*, 588–589.

49. Robin Einhorn, *American Taxation, American Slavery* (Chicago: University of Chicago Press, 2006); Lawson Purdy, "The Best Method of Taxation and Assessment in Municipalities," *The Public*, January 5, 1901, 622–623.

50. *The Standard*, February 19, 1890, 1; Hellman, *Henry George Reconsidered*, 108.

51. Arthur Young, *The Single Tax Movement in the United States* (Princeton, N.J.: Princeton University Press, 1916), 137, 147–152.

52. "The New York Tax Reform Association," *The Public*, November 22, 1912, 1109–1114.

53. Henry Adams, *The Education of Henry Adams: An Autobiography* (Boston: Houghton Mifflin Company, 1918), 240–241.

54. Charles Francis Adams, Henry Adams, and Francis A. Walker, *Chapters of Erie and Other Essays* (1871; reprinted, Bedford, Mass.: Applewood Books, 2009), 5; Richard

Hofstadter, *The Age of Reform: From Bryan to F.D.R.* (New York: Knopf Doubleday, 1955); George Mowry, *The California Progressives* (Chicago: Quadrangle Books, 1963), 131–173.

55. Adams quoted in Yair Sagy, "The Legacy of Social Darwinism: From Railroads to the 'Reinvention' of Regulation," *Georgetown Journal of Law and Public Policy* 11, no. 2 (Summer 2013): 488.

56. Sagy, 518; Harp, *Positivist Republic*, 113.

57. "Death of Charles Francis Adams," *The Public*, April 2, 1915, 334; Thomas K. McCraw, *Prophets of Regulation: Charles Francis Adams, Louis D. Brandeis, James M. Landis, Alfred E. Kahn* (Cambridge, Mass.: Belknap Press of Harvard University Press, 1984), 1–56; "An Influential Convert to the Single Tax," *New York Outlook*, December 15, 1900.

58. Henry Carter Adams, "Relation of the State to Industrial Action," *Publication of the American Economic Association* 1, no. 6 (January 1887): 472–549.

59. Mill, *Principles of Political Economy*, 372; Christopher England, "Land Monopoly and Twentieth-Century American Utility Policy," *History of Intellectual Culture* 11, no. 1 (2014–2016): 1–19; Tom L. Johnson, "Tom L. Johnson's Program," *The Public*, April 21, 1911, 373–379.

60. Alan Richmond Prest, *The Taxation of Urban Land* (Manchester: Manchester University Press, 1981), 19.

61. *The Single Tax Discussion Held at Saratoga Sept. 5, 1890* (New York: American Social Science Association, 1890), 44; Robert V. Andelson, ed., *The Critics of Henry George*, vol. 1 (Malden, Mass.: Blackwell, 2003), 407–434.

62. *The Single Tax Discussion Held at Saratoga Sept. 5, 1890*, 84–85.

63. George, *Science of Political Economy*, 210.

64. George, *Science of Political Economy*, 204.

65. Mehrotra, *Making the Modern American Fiscal State*, 86–142.

66. Amanda Porerfield, *Corporate Spirit: Religion and the Rise of the Modern Corporation* (Oxford: Oxford University Press, 2018), 11–12, 131–135; Harp, *Positivist Republic*, 68.

67. Richard T. Ely, *Outlines of Economics* (New York: MacMillian Company, 1919), 468.

68. Richard T. Ely, "An American Industrial Experiment," *Harpers Monthly Magazine* (June 1902): 44.

69. Axel B. Shafer, *American Progressives and German Social Reform, 1875–1920* (Stuttgart: Franz Steiner Verlag, 2000), 86.

70. Richard T. Ely to John M. Glenn (forwarded to John Commons), November 19, 1909, box 1, John Commons Papers, Wisconsin Historical Society, Madison, Wisc.

71. Nancy Cohen, *The Reconstruction of American Liberalism, 1865–1914* (Chapel Hill: University of North Carolina Press, 2002), 288.

72. *New York Times*, February 25, 1892; Raymond Curtis, "The Populist Party in Kansas" (PhD diss., University of Chicago, 1928), 185–202; Diggs, *The Story of Jerry Simpson*, 248.

73. Louis Post, "The Single Tax and Politics," *The Standard*, August 31, 1892, 98–99.

74. Louis Post, "The Recent Contest in Kansas," *The Standard*, February 4, 1891.

75. *The Public*, April 1, 1899, 1; *The Public*, May 28, 1898, 3–4.

76. Ronald E. Seavoy, *An Economic History of the United States: From 1607 to the Present* (New York: Routledge, 2006), 229–231.

77. Michael Pierce, "The Populist President of the American Federation of Labor: The Career of John McBride, 1880–1895," *Labor History* 41, no. 1 (February 2000): 5–24.

78. Green, *Company Town*; Herbert Mitgang, *The Man Who Rode the Tiger: The Life and Times of Judge Samuel Seabury* (1963; reprinted, New York: Fordham University Press, 1996), 77–78.

79. Addams, "A Modern Lear."

80. "Transcript of Interview with Debs Discussing the Socialist Viewpoint," box 3, LSP-CU.

81. Nick Salvatore, *Eugene V. Debs: Citizen and Socialist* (Urbana: University of Illinois Press, 1984), 374; H. R. Starkweather to E. B. Gaston, November 12, 1894, Fairhope Single Tax Corporation Archives, Fairhope, Ala.

82. George, *Life of Henry George*, 577.

83. Post, *Prophet of San Francisco*, 126.

84. *New York Journal*, July 11, 1896.

85. Grinspan, *Age of Acrimony*, 217.

86. "Fighting against Bryan," *New York Times*, October 26, 1896, 2.

87. "Henry George on Election Issues," *St. Louis Post-Dispatch*, November 8, 1896.

88. George, *Life of Henry George*, 581–583.

89. Carl Schurz, "Mr. Henry George in the Municipal Campaign," *Harpers Weekly* 41 (October 23): 1897, 1047; Daniel De Leon, "Turpitudinous George," *The People* 7 (October 3, 1897): 1.

90. George, *The Life of Henry George*, 600.

91. Jacob Oser, *Henry George* (New York: Twayne, 1974), 11.

92. Willis Abbot to William Jennings Bryan, November 20, 1897; John Hirscher to William Jennings Bryan, October 15, 1897, both box 20, WJBP-LC.

93. Michael Kazin, *A Godly Hero: The Life of William Jennings Bryan* (2006; reprinted, New York: Anchor Books, 2007), 65.

94. Frank Campbell to William Jennings Bryan, October 14, 1897, box 20, WJBP-LC; William Riordon, *Plunkitt of Tammany Hall: A Series of Very Plain Talks on Very Practical Politics* (New York: McClure, Philips & Co., 1905), 70–76.

95. "Ask Bryan for Help," *Chicago Daily Tribune*, October 3, 1897.

96. John Altgeld to William Jennings Bryan, September 20, 1897, box 20, WJBP-LC.

97. "Bryan Makes a Stir," *Chicago Daily Tribune*, September 28, 1897.

98. George, *The Life of Henry George*, 597.

99. Daniel Carter Beard, *Hardly a Man Is Now Alive* (New York: Doubleday, Dolran & Company, Inc., 1939), 333.

100. Lyman Abbot, in *Addresses at the Funeral of Henry George, Sunday, October 31, 1897*, ed. Edmund Yardley (Chicago: Public Publishing Company, 1905), 23.

101. Abbot, 30.

102. Bryan quoted in "William Jennings Bryan: Henry George, One of the World's Foremost Thinkers," *New York Times*, October 30, 1897, 2.

103. "Henry George's Praise Sounded by Bryan," *New York Times*, January 25, 1905.

104. "Honor to Their Dead," *New York Sun*, November 1, 1897, 1.

105. George, *Science of Political Economy*, 203.

Chapter 6 • A Great and Glorious City

1. Riordon, *Plunkitt of Tammany Hall*, 8.

2. Mancur Olson, *The Logic of Collective Action: Public Goods and the Theory of Groups* (Cambridge, Mass.: Harvard University Press, 1965); Gordon Tullock, *Economics of Income Redistribution* (Boston: Kluwer-Nijhoff, 1983), 166.

3. "News," *The Public*, July 7, 1900, 200.

4. William Lloyd Garrison, "A Republic Means a Government of the Whole People," *The Public*, July 7, 1900, 204–205.

5. Dalton, *Theodore Roosevelt*, 221.

6. Louis Post, *Our Despotic Postal Censorship* (Chicago: Public Publishing Company, 1906).

7. *Johnstown (Pa.) Democrat*, reprinted in *The Public*, May 17, 1902, 82.

8. Franklin H. Giddings, *Democracy and Empire* (New York: Macmillian, 1900), 261.

9. Theodore Roosevelt, *The Strenuous Life: Essays and Addresses* (New York: Charles Scribner's Sons, 1906), 19.

10. Giddings, *Democracy and Empire*, 133.

11. Giddings, 104; Hofstadter, *Social Darwinism in American Thought*, 157.

12. George, *Protection or Free Trade*, 343.

13. *Assessment of Taxes in the District of Columbia*, 52nd Cong., 1st sess., H.R. Doc 1469 (1892); Department of Commerce and Labor, Bureau of the Census, *Wealth, Debt, and Taxation* (Washington, DC: Government Printing Office, 1907), 7.

14. Shelton Stromquist, "The Crucible of Class," in *Who Were the Progressives?* ed. Glenda Elizabeth Gilmore (New York: Palgrave, 2002), 158.

15. Harold F. Taggart, "The Election of 1898 in California," *Pacific Historical Review* 19, no. 4 (November 1950): 357–68.

16. Samuel Jones, *Letters of Love and Labor* (Toledo: Franklin Printing and Engraving Co., 1900), 67.

17. Whitlock, *Forty Years of It*, 113.

18. Samuel Jones, *The New Right* (New York: Eastern Book Concern 1899), 234–239.

19. Marnie Jones, *Holy Toledo: Religion and Politics in the Life of "Golden Rule" Jones* (Lexington: University Press of Kentucky, 1998), 169.

20. Jones, *Letters of Love and Labor*, 91.

21. Jones, *Holy Toledo*, 226.

22. Michael Pierce, *Striking with the Ballot: Ohio Labor and the Populist Party* (DeKalb: Northern Illinois University Press, 2010), 57–92.

23. Stromquist, "The Crucible of Class," 158.

24. Carl Wittke, "Peter Witt, Tribune of the People," *Ohio State Archaeological and Historical Quarterly* 58 (1949): 361–367.

25. Philip Porter, *Cleveland: A Confused City on a Seesaw* (Columbus: Ohio State University Press, 1976), 54–55; Hoyt Warner, *Progressivism in Ohio, 1897–1917* (Columbus: Ohio State University Press, 1964), 65.

26. "A Tom Johnson Movement," *Washington Post*, July 9, 1899, 1; Robert Bremner, "Reformed Businessman: Tom L. Johnson," *American Journal of Economics and Sociology* 8, no. 3 (April 1949): 299–309.

27. "The Street Car Question in Ohio," *The Public*, February 9, 1901, 692–695; "Johnson Was Turned Down Cold," *Akron Daily Democrat*, February 5, 1901, 5; "Tom Johnson Will Enter Politics," *Akron Daily Democrat*, January 28, 1901, 5.

28. "Tom Johnson Denies That He Is after Either the Governorship or Presidency," *Marietta (Ohio) Daily Leader*, April 20, 1901, 7.

29. *The Public*, April 13, 1901, 2.

30. "Mayor Johnson and Civil Service Reform," *The Public*, June 21, 1902, 174.

31. Cohen, *Reconstruction of American Liberalism*, 175; Kenneth Finegold, *Experts and Politicians: Reform Challenges to Machine Politics in New York, Cleveland, and Chicago* (Princeton, N.J.: Princeton University Press, 1995).

32. "Expertism in Government," *Public*, November 6, 1908, 747.

33. Richard T. Ely, "Social Observations in Germany," *Congregationalist* 77 (July 7, 1982): 246; Howe, *Confessions of a Reformer*, 7.

34. Kenneth Miller, *From Progressive to New Dealer: Frederic C. Howe and American Liberalism* (University Park: Pennsylvania State University Press, 2010), 69.

35. Frederic C. Howe, *Socialized Germany* (New York: Charles Scribner's Sons, 1915), 19, 332, 334.

36. Frederic C. Howe, *Denmark: A Cooperative Commonwealth* (New York: Harcourt, Brace and Company 1921).

37. Warner, *Progressivism in Ohio*, 64.

38. John T. McRoy, *Report of the Joseph Fels Fund and Single Tax Conference at Washington, D.C., January 15th, 16th, 17th, 1914* (n.p., 1914), 10.

39. Douglas B. Craig, *Progressives at War: William C. McAdoo and Newton D. Baker* (Baltimore: John Hopkins University Press, 2013).

40. C. H. Cramer, *Newton D. Baker: A Biography* (Cleveland: World Publishing Company, 1961), 186.

41. Willis Thornton, *Newton D. Baker and His Books* (Cleveland: Press of Western Reserve University, 1954), 4.

42. George Creel, "Newton D. Baker's Measure," *Colliers*, March 19, 1932.

43. Craig, *Progressives at War*, 23.

44. Thornton, *Newton D. Baker and His Books*, 44.

45. "Tom Johnson's Plans," *The Public*, June 15, 1901, 155–156.

46. "Melange," *Stark County Democrat*, May 14, 1901, 4; "The Suit Comes Up," *Stark County Democrat*, May 31, 1901, 2.

47. *The Public*, September 14, 1901, 356; Edward Bemis, "Report of Prof. Edward Bemis on the True Value of Ohio Railroads for the Purpose of Taxation; Prepared at the Request of Hon. Tom L. Johnson, Mayor of Cleveland" (Cleveland, n.p., n.d.); Eric J. Morser, *Hinterland Dreams: The Political Economy of a Midwestern City* (Philadelphia: University of Pennsylvania Press, 2011), 77–105.

48. *Proceedings of the Conference on Valuation Held in Philadelphia, no. 10th to 13th, 1916* (Philadelphia: Utilities Bureau, 1916); Christopher England, "'Land Monopoly' and Twentieth-Century American Utility Policy," *History of Intellectual Culture* 11, no. 1 (2014–2016): 1–29; Fried, *Progressive Assault on Laissez Faire*, 184.

49. Morris Llewellyn Cooke, *Snapping Cords: Comments on the Changing Attitudes of American Cities* (Philadelphia: n.p., 1915), 33–34.

50. "Proceedings of the Conference on Valuation held in Philadelphia November 10th to 13th," *Utilities Magazine* (January 1916): 36.

51. "Tom L. Johnson's Plans," *The Public*, June 15, 1901, 155–156.

52. *The Public*, August 31, 1901, 321.

53. Charles C. Williamson, *The Finances of Cleveland* (New York: Columbia University Press, 1907), 437.

54. "The Single Tax," *San Francisco Chronicle*, September 10, 1911.

55. Mitgang, *Man Who Rode the Tiger*, 103–105.

56. Wittke, "Peter Witt," 361–367.

57. Johnson, *My Story*, 122.

58. Carl Hovey, "The Police Question," *Metropolitan Magazine*, March 31, 1910.

59. Raymond Moley, Master's Thesis, Oberlin College, 1913, box 184, RMP-HL.

60. Raymond Moley, *Realities and Illusions, 1886–1931: The Autobiography of Raymond Moley* (New York: Garland, 1980), 70.

61. Harris R. Cooley, "Good Opportunities for Prison Labor," *Annals of the American Academy of Political and Social Science* 46 (March 1913): 96; Johnson, *My Story*, 173–174.

62. *Public*, November 23, 1901, 515–516.

63. Khalil Gibran Muhammad, *The Condemnation of Blackness* (Cambridge, Mass: Harvard University Press, 2010), 35–87.

64. Brian Donovan, *White Slave Crusades: Race, Gender, and Anti-vice Activism* (Champaign: University of Illinois Press, 2005); Barbara Antoniazzi, *The Wayward Woman: Progressivism, Prostitution, and Performance in the United States, 1888–1917* (Lanham, Md.: Rowman and Littlefield, 2014); Norman H. Clark, *Deliver Us from Evil: An Interpretation of American Prohibition* (New York: W. W. Norton, 1976).

65. Whitlock, *Forty Years of It*, 121.

66. Samuel Jones to Rev. Brooks Lawrence, October 15, 1903, box 10, BWP-LC.

67. Brand Whitlock, *On the Enforcement of Law in the Cities* (Indianapolis: Bobbs-Merrill Company, 1910), 84; Jones, *Holy Toledo*, 136–137.

68. "Parsons Rake Tom Johnson," *Atlanta Constitution*, February 13, 1906, 7.

69. *Singletax and Its Cleveland Champions: Letters and Answers Published in the Catholic Bulletin, Cleveland Ohio, May 1915 to May 1916* (Cleveland: L. G. Wey, 1916).

70. Johnson, *My Story*, 174.

71. Michael Pierce, "Farmers and the Failure of Populism in Ohio, 1890–1891," *Agricultural History* 74, no. 1 (Winter 2000), 58–85; R. Douglas Hurt, "The Farmers' Alliance and the People's Party in Ohio," *Old Northwest* 10, no. 4 (Winter 1984–1985), 439–62.

72. *The Public*, June 21, 1902, 164–165.

73. *The Public*, March 21, 1903, 791.

74. "Tom L. Johnson at Mr. Bryan's Fourth of July Celebration," *The Public*, July 11, 1903.

75. Frederic C. Howe, *The City: The Hope of Democracy* (New York: Charles Scribner's Sons, 1906), 157.

76. Howe, 164.

77. Howe, 282.

78. Howe, 265.

79. *The Public*, October 18, 1902, 435; *The Public*, October 25, 1902, 451.

80. Louis Post, "Editorial Correspondence," *The Public*, March 29, 1902, 805–808.

81. *The Public*, November 8, 1902, 481–482.

82. Johnson, *My Story*, 199.

83. "What Tom Johnson Aims At: Does Not Want Office, but to Control National Convention to Aid His Programme," *New York Times*, September 2, 1903, 1.

84. Howe, *Confessions of a Reformer*, 159.

85. "Where Are the Pre-war Radicals?" *Survey* (February 1926): 556–566.

86. Toledo municipal document, box 62, BWP-LC.

87. *New York Times*, August 4, 1906.

88. Warner, *Progressivism in Ohio*, 45; Oscar Crosby, "The Code of Principles," *Electric Railway Journal* 45, no. 8 (February 20, 1915): 370–373; John, *Network Nation*, 342; Hayes Robbins, "Public Ownership versus Public Control," *American Journal of Sociology* 10, no. 6 (May 1905): 787–813.

89. David Nord, "Experts versus Experts: Conflicting Philosophies of Municipal Utility Regulation in the Progressive Era," *Wisconsin Magazine of History* 58, no. 3 (Spring 1975): 219–236; Howe, *Confessions of a Reformer*, 132–133; Warner, *Progressivism in Ohio*, 147; *Cleveland Plain Dealer*, January 16, 1904.

90. "The Leader of the Leaders," box 19, LSP-CU; Master's Thesis, Oberlin College, box 184, RMP-HL; Melvin G. Holli, *The American Mayor: The Best and Worst Big-City Leaders* (University Park: Pennsylvania State University Press, 1999), 58.

91. "Mayor Johnson's Way," *The Public*, June 15, 1901, 155.

92. Thomas S. Hines, "The Paradox of 'Progressive' Architecture: Urban Planning and Public Building in Tom Johnson's Cleveland," *American Quarterly* 25, no. 4 (October 1973): 426–448.

93. Kevin Mattson, *Creating a Democratic Public: The Struggle for Urban Participatory Democracy during the Gilded Age* (University Park: Pennsylvania State University Press, 1997), 31–38.

94. "Tom Johnson to the Fore," *New York Times*, September 5, 1902, 8.

95. *Wall Street Journal* editorial reprinted as "'Ingenuous' Tom Johnson," in *Chicago Tribune*, October 3, 1902, 12.

96. Newton Baker, foreword, in *The Letters and Journal of Brand Whitlock*, ed. Allan Nevins (New York: D. Appleton–Century Company, 1936), vii–viii.

97. Brand Whitlock to Clarence Darrow, November 22, 1907, box 14, BWP-LC.

98. Louis Post to Brand Whitlock, June 6, 1907, box 13, BWP-LC; Brand Whitlock to H. E. Easly, March 27, 1907, box 12, BWP-LC; Brand Whitlock to Peter Witt, April 10, 1906, BWP-LC; Brand Whitlock to Marshall Sheppey, February 27, 1918, in *Letters and Journal of Brand Whitlock*, 255; Brand Whitlock, "Daniel Kiefer," *American Magazine* (September 1912): 549–553.

99. Whitlock, *Forty Years of It*, xi.

100. Robert Crunden, *A Hero in Spite of Himself: Brand Whitlock in Art Politics and War* (New York: Alfred A. Knopf, 1969), 77; W. D. Howells to Brand Whitlock, November 19, 1900; T. H. Dean to Brand Whitlock, June 27, 1901, both box 9, BWP-LC.

101. Brand Whitlock to William Bobbs, February 1, 1906, box 11, BWP-LC.

102. Brand Whitlock to William Bobbs, June 6, 1906, box 11, BWP-LC.

103. James D. Reid to [*The Public*?], March 11, 1907, box 12, BWP-LC.

104. David D. Anderson, *Brand Whitlock* (New York: Twayne, 1968), 48.

105. Brand Whitlock to Samuel Hopkins Adams, October 15, 1907, box 14, BWP-LC.

106. Upton Sinclair to Brand Whitlock, March 22, 1907, box 12; Jack London to Bobbs-Merrill Company, April 6, 1907, box 12; Brand Whitlock to Ben Lindsey, April 18, 1907, box 1; Thomas Mott Osborne to Brand Whitlock, April 26, 1907, box 12, all BWP-LC.

107. Whitlock, *On the Enforcement of Law in the Cities*, 39–41.

108. Whitlock, 93.

109. Whitlock, 39–41.

110. "William Allen White on Mr. Steffen's Book 'The Shame of the Cities,'" *McClure's Magazine* (June 1904): 220–221.

111. Lincoln Steffens, *The Struggle for Self-Government* (New York: McClure, Philips and Co., 1906), 244.

112. Steffens, *The Struggle for Self-Government*, 183.

113. Lincoln Steffens, "Tom L. Johnson's Victory," *The Public*, October 1, 1909, 941–2.

114. Warner, *Progressivism in Ohio*, 143–173.

115. Warner, *Progressivism in Ohio*, 200–201; Howe, *Confessions of a Reformer*, 163–164.

116. Warner, *Progressivism in Ohio*, 192–194.

117. "Transcript of Testimony by Tom Johnson," 1907, box 7, LSP-CU; "What Has Tom Johnson Done?" *The Public*, October 22, 1909, 1025–1026.

118. *Public*, August 16, 1902, 291–292.

119. Williamson, *Finances of Cleveland*, 227.

120. "What Has Tom Johnson Done?"

121. *Marion (Ohio) Daily Mirror*, September 11, 1907.

122. *Cleveland Press*, April 28, 1908; Holli, *American Mayor*, 56–57.

123. Lincoln Steffens, "The Leader of Leaders," box 19, LSP-CU.

124. "Mayor Johnson and the Traction Trust," *The Public*, September 4, 1908, 531–532.

125. Edward Bemis, "The Cleveland Referendum on Street Railways," *Quarterly Journal of Economics* 23, no. 1 (November 1908): 179–183; Brand Whitlock to William Allen White, January 16, 1909, box 17, BWP-LC.

126. Finegold, *Experts and Politicians*, 95–96.

127. Daniel Kiefer to Lincoln Steffens, October 24, 1908, box 7; Brand Whitlock to Lincoln Steffens, September 23, 1909, box 16, both LSP-CU.

128. Lincoln Steffens to Francis Heney, September 26, 1909, box 12, LSP-CU.

129. "Tom L. Johnson," *The Public*, April 7, 1911, 322.

130. *The Public*, July 21, 1911.

131. Edmund Vance Cooke, "A Man Is Passing," *The Public*, April 7, 1911, 325.

132. Lough, "The Last Tax," 278–279.

133. Herbert Bigelow to Brand Whitlock, October 18, 1906, box 11, BWP-LC.

134. Members and Officers of the Constitutional Convention of Ohio—1912, *Proceedings and Debates of the Constitutional Convention of the State of Ohio—1912* (Columbus, Ohio: F. J. Heer Printing Co., 1912), 2101–2113.

135. Warner, *Progressivism in Ohio*, 323–324.

136. *The Public*, November 17, 1911, 1167.

137. Morris Cooke, *Our Cities Awake: Notes on Municipal Activities and Administration* (New York: Doubleday, Page & Company, 1919), 248.

138. Craig, *Progressives at War*, 57–58.

139. Delos Wilcox, *Municipal Franchises: Transportation Franchise, Taxation, and Control of Public Utilities* (New York: Engineering News Publishing Company, 1911), 141–142.

140. Nord, "Experts versus Experts," 224.

141. "The Passing of Delos Wilcox," *Public Ownership* (May 1928): 84–87.

142. Steffens, *Struggle for Self-Government*, 193–194.

143. Wilcox, *Municipal Franchises*, 359–363.

144. *Marion (Ohio) Daily Mirror*, April 13, 1911.

145. Holli, *American Mayor*.

146. Tom Johnson to Brand Whitlock, February 23, 1907, box 12, BWP-LC.

Chapter 7 • Seeing the Cat

1. Quoted in Yanosky, "Seeing the Cat," 126–127; Post, *Prophet of San Francisco*, 15.

2. Jane Addams, *Twenty Years at Hull House* (New York: Macmillan Company, 1911), 179–181; Amos Pinchot to John Reed, November 22, 1916, box 67, APP-LC.

3. William C. Gorgas and Lewis J. Johnson, *Two Papers on Public Sanitation and the Single Tax* (Cincinnati: Joseph Fels Fund of America, 1915). See also Howe, *Confessions of a Reformer*, 136.

4. Hannah Arendt, "Ideology and Terror: A Novel Form of Government," *Review of Politics* 15, no. 3 (July 1953): 318.

5. Daniel Bell, *Marxian Socialism in the United States* (1952; reprinted, Princeton, N.J.: Princeton University Press, 1967).

6. "Henry George Jr. Memorial," *The Public*, April 6, 1917, 330–331.

7. Louis Post, "Living a Long Life Over Again," p. 12, box 4, LPP-LC.

8. Post, 48, 55.

9. Post, 66.

10. Dominic Candeloro, "Louis Post as a Carpetbagger in South Carolina: Reconstruction as a Forerunner of the Progressive Movement," *American Journal of Economics and Sociology* 75, no. 34 (October 1975), 423–424; Post, "Living a Long Life Over Again."

11. Post, "Living a Long Life Over Again," 140.

12. Louis Post, "A 'Carpetbagger' in South Carolina," *Journal of Negro History* 10, no. 1 (January 1925): 10–79; Candeloro, "Louis Post as a Carpetbagger," 423–432.

13. Post, "Democracy and the Negro," *The Public*, August 25, 1900, 310–312.

14. Dominic Candeloro, "Louis F. Post and the Single Tax Movement," *American Journal of Economics and Sociology* 35, no. 4 (October 1976): 415–430.

15. Post, *Prophet of San Francisco*, 25.

16. Post, 22.

17. Post, 26.

18. Post, 26.

19. Post, 47–49.

20. Post, 18.

21. Post, 40.

22. Candeloro, "Louis Post as a Carpetbagger," 430; Post, *Prophet of San Francisco*, 50; Louis F. Post, *Ethical Principles of Marriage and Divorce* (Chicago: Public Publishing Company, 1906); White, *The Republic for Which it Stands*; Amy Dur Stanley, *From*

Bondage to Contract: Wage Labor, Marriage, and the Market in the Age of Slave Emancipation (Cambridge: Cambridge University Press, 1998).

23. Louis Post, in "Where Are the Pre-war Radicals?" 560.

24. Homer Hoyt, *One Hundred Years of Land Values in Chicago* (Washington D.C.: Beard Books, 1933), 3.

25. Post, *Prophet of San Francisco*, 28; Cronon, *Nature's Metropolis*.

26. "Intelligent Newspaper Reading," box 6, LPP-LC.

27. "Democracy and the Negro," *Public*, August 25, 1900, 307–312.

28. Dominic Candeloro, "From the Narrow Single Tax to Broad Progressivism: The Intellectual Development of Louis F. Post, 1898–1913," *American Journal of Economics and Sociology* 37, no. 3 (July 1978): 325–336.

29. Elizabeth Hauser, "A. B. DuPont—An Appreciation," *The Public*, June 28, 1919, 684–686.

30. "Race Riots," *The Public*, August 9, 1919, 844–845.

31. Samuel Danziger, "Segregation and Land Monopoly," *The Public*, September 15, 1916, 891–892.

32. Francis A. Walker, *Discussions in Economics and Statistics* (New York: Henry Holt and Co., 1899), 2:422.

33. Leonard, *Illiberal Reformers*, 89–108; Fried, *Progressive Assault on Laissez-Faire*, 129; Jeffery Sklansky, *The Soul's Economy: Market Society and Selfhood in American Thought, 1820–1920* (Chapel Hill: University of North Carolina Press, 2002), 130–134; Muhammad, *Condemnation of Blackness*, 32.

34. Thomas C. Leonard, "Retrospectives: Eugenics and Economics in the Progressive Era," *Journal of Economic Perspectives* 19, no. 4 (Fall 2005): 207–224.

35. Post and Leubuscher, *Henry George's 1886 Campaign*, 89; George, *Social Problems*, 240.

36. Clarence Darrow, "Henry George Address at Henry George Anniversary Dinner of the Single Tax Club Chicago," *Everyman* (September–October 1913), 17. See also Whitlock, *Forty Years of It*, 292; and "No Medical Monopoly," *The Public*, April 30, 1898, 14.

37. Elizabeth Hauser, "A. B. DuPont—An Appreciation," *The Public*, June 28, 1919, 684–686; Candeloro, "Louis Post as a Carpetbagger," 431.

38. William Lloyd Garrison, "Olney and Tom L. Johnson," *The Public*, September 27, 1902, 394–395.

39. Steven Hahn, *A Nation under Our Feet* (Cambridge, Mass.: Belknap Press of Harvard University Press, 2003), 433.

40. Emma Lou Thornbrough, "T. Thomas Fortune: Militant Editor in the Age of Accommodation," in *Black Leaders of the Twentieth Century*, ed. John Hope Franklin and August Meier (Champaign: University of Illinois Press, 1982).

41. Hubert Harrison, "Socialism and the Negro," *Socialist Review* (July 1912); Mark Pittenger, *American Socialists and Economic Thought* (Madison: University of Wisconsin Press, 1993); Jeffery Perry, *Hubert Harrison: The Voice of Harlem Renaissance* (New York: Columbia University Press, 2009); "October 14–November 2, 1922," folder 1, box 9, Hubert Harrison Papers, Columbia University, New York.

42. Henry George Lecture Association, "W. E. B. Du Bois Lecture Tour Flyer," February 1913, box 162, W. E. B. Du Bois Papers, University of Massachusetts, Amherst;

W. E. B. Du Bois, "The Single Tax," *The Crisis* 22 (October 1921): 248; Manning Marable, *W. E. B. Du Bois: Black, Radical, Democrat* (Boston: Twayne, 1986), 88, 236.

43. George, "Chinese Immigration," 1:409.

44. William Eggleston to James Barry, May 12, 1926, box 4, JBP-BL.

45. William Lloyd Garrison to Henry George, December 4, 1893, reel 6, HGP-LC.

46. *The Public*, January 18, 1902, 644–645.

47. Shelton, *Squatter's Republic*, 37–75, 96–8.

48. *The Public*, September 20, 1919, 1031; "A Few Extracts from Letters Commending *The Public*," box 7, LPP-LC.

49. Post, "Living a Long Life Over Again," 219 (a).

50. "A Few Extracts from Letters Commending *The Public*."

51. George Knapp, "The Railway Maintenance of Way Employees Journal," box 7, LPP-LC.

52. Mark Twain to Louis Post, January 7, 1904, box 1, LPP-LC; "Mark Twain," *The Public*, April 29, 1910, 385–386.

53. William Bryan to Louis Post, December 20, 1901; William Bryan to Louis Post, October 9, 1901; William Bryan to Louis Post, July 14, 1903; Charles Bryan to Louis Post, September 28, 1905; Charles Bryan to Louis Post, July 5, 1912, all box 1, LPP-LC.

54. William Jennings Bryan to Louis Post, November 12, 1907; William Jennings Bryan to LP, September 2, 1919, both box 1, LPP-LC.

55. Kazin, *Godly Hero*, 126; Johnson, *My Story*, xvii.

56. William Jennings Bryan to Louis Post, February 10, 1902, box 1, LPP-LC.

57. *The Commoner*, February 21, 1902.

58. *Proceedings of the Constitutional Convention of the Proposed State of Oklahoma* (Muskogee, Okla.: Muskogee Ptg. Co., 1907), 395.

59. Dalton, *Theodore Roosevelt*, 217.

60. Howe, *Confessions of a Reformer*, 132–134.

61. Daniel Kiefer to Lincoln Steffens, November 5, 1908, box 7, LSP-CU.

62. "Circuit Court of Cook County, Chambers of Judge Murray Tuley," May 12, 1905, box 9, LPP-LC.

63. Edward Dunne, "Municipal Ownership, Delivered before the Henry George Association of Chicago, January 18, 1903," *The Public*, February 21, 1903, 732–734.

64. Richard Allan Morton, *Justice and Humanity: Edward P. Dunne* (Carbondale: Southern Illinois University Press, 1997), 38–40.

65. Kate Rousmaniere, *Citizen Teacher: The Life and Leadership of Margaret Haley* (Albany: State University of New York Press, 2005), 61–64.

66. Pegram, *Partisans and Progressives*, 121–150.

67. Pegram, 127.

68. Pegram, 128.

69. Rousmaniere, *Citizen Teacher*, 146.

70. Rousmaniere, 148–149.

71. Rousmaniere, 148; Pegram, *Partisans and Progressives*, 144–149.

72. Marietta Johnson, *Thirty Years with an Idea* (Tuscaloosa: University of Alabama Press, 1974), 40; John Dewey and Evelyn Dewey, *Schools of Tomorrow* (1915; reprinted, New York: E. P. Dunton and Co., 1962), xxviii.

73. Johnson, *Thirty Years with an Idea*, 33.

74. John Dewey, *Democracy and Education: An Introduction to the Philosophy of Education* (New York: MacMillan Company, 1916).

75. Henry George and John Dewey, *Significant Paragraphs from Henry George's Progress and Poverty*, ed. Harry Gunnison Brown (Garden City, N.Y.: Doubleday, Doran and Company, Inc., 1928), 1; Elizabeth Kent, *William Kent, Independent: A Biography* (n.p., privately printed, 1950), 87. For a discussion of Georgist philanthropists who saw their work through the single tax lens, see George Foster Peabody to Ralph Hayes, November 7, 1927, box 185, G. Peabody P-LC.

76. George Creel, *Rebel at Large: Recollections of Fifty Crowded Years* (New York: G. P. Putnam and Sons, 1947), 10.

77. Ivan Epperson, "Missourians Abroad: No. 3—George Creel," *Missouri Historical Review* 12, no. 2 (January 1948): 100–110.

78. Creel, *Rebel at Large*, 36.

79. Creel, 36.

80. Creel, 20, 93.

81. Creel, 42.

82. Creel, 44.

83. Creel, 45.

84. Creel, 47.

85. George Creel, *Wilson and the Issues* (New York: Century Company, 1916), 5–6, 51; "A Talk by Creel before the Wilmette Club of Chicago February 20," box 5; "On with Roosevelt by George Creel—address delivered at Barbecue, Ham Cotton Ranch, San Clemente, California, August 24, 1935," box 5; "Speech at the Conference on Government: International House, Berkeley, March 28 1934," box 5; "Address of George Creel Before Commonwealth Club of San Francisco August 30," 1935, box 5; "People's Institute Program, Sunday Evening, April 11, 1915," box 7, all GCP-LC.

86. J. J. Pastoriza, "The Doctrine Undefiled," *The Public*, April 6, 1917, 334.

87. Antonio Bastida, "Emasculated Single Tax or Common Property in Land," October 27, 1914, 3, 5–6, box 126, APP-LC.

88. Whitlock, "Daniel Kiefer"; William Eggleston to James Barry, June 9, 1907, box 4, JBP-BL.

89. Creel, *Rebel at Large*, 50.

90. Creel, 71.

91. "Mr. Creel Tells of Vice," *New York Herald*, oversized 5, GCP-LC.

92. Joseph Farris to Brand Whitlock, February 23, 1907, box 12; James Lyon to Brand Whitlock, July 5, 1907, box 13; Ben Lindsey to Brand Whitlock, March 26, 1907, box 12; Charles Ferguson to Brand Whitlock, December 5, 1907, box 14; George Landers to Brand Whitlock, June 13, 1908, box 15; Carl Noble to Brand Whitlock, June 25, 1908, box 15; George W. Webb to Brand Whitlock, June 8, 1908, box 15; C. W. Willard to Brand Whitlock, December 12, 1908, box 16; H. L. Fagan to Brand Whitlock, April 27, 1908, box 17, all BWP-LC.

93. John MacVicar to Brand Whitlock, January 29, 1908; Albert Graf to Brand Whitlock, February 24, 1908; Francis Bode to Brand Whitlock, April 1, 1908, all box 15, BWP-LC.

94. *Kansas City Star*, April 11, 1911.

95. Creel, *Rebel at Large*, 72; Robert Cuff, "Woodrow Wilson's Missionary to American Business, 1914–1915: A Note," *Business History Review* 43, no. 4 (Winter 1969): 545–551.

96. Charles Ferguson to Brand Whitlock, December 5, 1907, box 14, BWP-LC.

97. Creel, *Rebel at Large*, 74–75.

98. Creel, 85.

99. Ben Lindsey to Brand Whitlock, September 13, 1909; Brand Whitlock to Ben Lindsey, September 20, 1909; Ben Lindsey to Brand Whitlock, November 8, 1909, all box 18, BWP-LC.

100. Martin Kretzmann, "The Kid's Judge: Institutional Innovation in the Early Denver Juvenile Court under Judge Ben B. Lindsey" (PhD diss., University of Denver, 1977.

101. Franklin Roosevelt to Ben Lindsey, undated February 1913, container 13, PNSS-FRPL.

102. Charles Larsen, *The Good Fight: The Life and Times of Ben B. Lindsey* (Chicago: Quadrangle Books, 1972), 25, 66; "Address by Ben Lindsey at Citizens Mass Meeting," November 21, 1909, box 277, BLP-LC; *The Single Tax Conference, Held in New York City Nov. 19 and 20, 1910* (Cincinnati: Fels Fund Commission, 1911), 40; Ben Lindsey, *The Beast* (New York: Doubleday, Page, and Company, 1910).

103. Clarence Darrow, "Crime and Criminals: Delivered to Prisoners in a Chicago Jail," *The Everyman* (August 1913), 11–16; Clarence Darrow, *The Story of My Life* (Cambridge, Mass.: Da Capo Press, 1996), 39–53; Darrow, "Henry George Address at Henry George Anniversary Dinner of the Single Tax Club Chicago," 17–23.

104. Creel, *Rebel at Large*, 91.

105. "Creel Police Reforms Provide Pardon Board," oversized 4, GCP-LC.

106. "Total Abstainer Cops a 'Public Necessity,' " oversized 5, GCP-LC.

107. "Creel Pays I.W.W. Fine; Officer Is to Face Charges and Speech Free in Street," oversized 4, GCP-LC.

108. Robyn Muncy, *Relentless Reformer: Josephine Roche and Progressivism in Twentieth Century America* (Princeton, N.J.: Princeton University Press, 2015), 42–63.

109. "Changed Her Ideas of a Wife," oversized 4, GCP-LC.

110. Barker, *Henry George*, 588–589.

111. Howe, *Confessions of a Reformer*, 137–138. Marie Howe, a devoted feminist, had a similar impact on her husband. See Miller, *From Progressive to New Dealer*.

112. Brooke Kroeger, *The Suffragents: How Women Used Men to Get the Vote* (Albany: State University of New York Press, 2017), 25.

113. Pilon, *Monopolists*, 61, 67.

114. Alice Thacher Post, "Women as Managing Editors," *La Follette's* 1, no. 40 (October 9, 1909): 11.

115. Rebecca Edwards, *Angels in the Machinery: Gender in American Party Politics from the Civil War to the Progressive Era* (New York: Oxford University Press, 1997).

116. William Barry to William U'Ren, January 21, 1913, box 14, JBP-BL.

117. Holli, *American Mayor*, 61; Keyssar, *The Right to Vote*, 94–138.

118. William U'Ren to Joseph Fels and Daniel Kiefer, January 9, 1913, box 14, JBP-BL; Lincoln Steffens to Francis Heney, May 5, 1909, LSP-CUL.

119. William U'Ren to Joseph Fels and Daniel Kiefer, January 9, 1913.

120. James Barry to William U'Ren, January 21, 1913, box 14, JBP-BL.

121. "Extracts from the Henry George We Knew," n.d., box 1, JBP-BL.

122. Speed Mosby, "Recompense," *The Public*, November 17, 1900, 501–502.

123. Wiebe, *Search for Order*; Trachtenberg, *Incorporation of America*; Laurie, *Artisans into Workers*; T. J. Jackson Lears, *The Rebirth of a Nation: The Making of a Modern America* (New York: Harper, 2009).

124. Louis Menand, *The Metaphysical Club* (New York: Farrar, Straus, and Giroux, 2002); William James, *The Moral Equivalent of War* (1910; reprinted, London: Peace Pledge Union, 1943).

125. Darrow, "Henry George Address at Henry George Anniversary Dinner."

126. Herbert Bigelow, "The Greenwood Path," *The Public*, September 7, 1901, 346.

127. Alvin Saunders Johnson, "The Case against the Single Tax," *Atlantic Monthly* (January 1914): 27.

128. George Creel, "How 'Honest Harry' Sheared the Wolves," box 6, GCP-LC.

129. Mark Twain, *A Connecticut Yankee in King Arthur's Court* (1889; reprinted, Oxford: Oxford University Press, 1996), 326, 389.

130. Alfred Kazin, *On Native Grounds: An Interpretation of American Prose Literature* (New York: Harcourt Brace Jovanovich, 1970); Gene Adam Saraceni, "Herne and the Single Tax: An Early Plea for an Actor's Union," *Education Theatre Journal* 26, no. 3 (October 1974): 315–325; Herbert Edwards, "Herne, Garland, and Henry George," *American Literature* 28, no. 3 (November 1956): 359–367; John Perry, *James A. Herne: The American Ibsen* (Chicago: Nelson Hall, 1978); Leo G. Mazow, "George Inness: Henry George, the Single Tax, and the Future Poet," *American Art* 18, no. 1 (Spring 2004): 58–77; Edgar Lee Masters, "William Marion Reedy," *American Speech* 9, no. 2 (April 1934): 96–98; Max Putzel, *The Man in the Mirror: William Marion Reedy and His Magazine* (Columbia: University of Missouri Press, 1998).

131. Henry George to James Herne, April 22, 1893, reel 6, HGP-NYPL.

132. Quoted in Greenberg, *Republic of Spin*, 117.

133. Oswald Garrison Villard to Henry George Jr., December 25, 1904, box 14, HGP-NYPL.

134. "Henry George's Praise Sounded by Bryan," *New York Times*, January 25, 1905.

Chapter 8 • *The Good Ship Earth*

1. Peter Alexander Speek, "The Single Tax and the Labor Movement" (PhD diss., University of Wisconsin–Madison, 1915); Thomas, *Alternative America*.

2. Huston, *The British Gentry, the Southern Planter, and the Northern Family Farmer*, 35.

3. J. A. Hobson, "The Influence of Henry George in England," *Fortnightly Review*, January 1, 1897, 839, 841–843.

4. Hobson, 836.

5. Hobson, 841–843.

6. Fried, *Progressive Assault on Laissez Faire*, 94 (Hobson quoted), 146.

7. Mrs. Townshend, "The Case for School Nurseries," *Fabian Tract*, no. 145 (1909): 14; Freeden, *New Liberalism*; Jones, "Henry George and British Socialism"; Sydney Webb, "National Finance and a Levy on Capital: What the Labor Party Intends," *Fabian Tract*, no. 188 (1919): 19.

8. Quoted in Fried, *Progressive Assault on Laissez Faire*, 34.

9. Hobson, "Influence of Henry George in England," 841.

10. Hobson, 841.

11. Dudden, *Joseph Fels and the Single-Tax Movement*, 141; R. H. Gretton, *A Modern History of the English People, 1880–1898* (London: Grant Richards, 1913), 143.

12. George, *Life of Henry George*, 434.

13. Henry George Jr., "On the British Budget," *The Public*, July 23, 1909, 714–716.

14. Even the Georgists who fought alongside David Lloyd George distrusted him. Mary Fels to Newton Baker, September 15, 1929, box 95, NBP-LC.

15. Bentley Brinkerhoff Gilbert, "David Lloyd George: Land, the Budget, and Social Reform," *American Historical Review* 81, no. 5 (December 1976): 1058–1066.

16. "The American Federation of Labor," *The Public*, December 2, 1910, 1137.

17. William Allen White, *Emporia Gazette*, August 26, 1909.

18. Frederic C. Howe, "The British Budget," *The Public*, May 21, 1909, 486.

19. "Churchill's Land for the People Speech," *The Public*, August 6, 1909, 762–764; Winston Churchill, *The People's Rights: Selected from His Lancashire and Other Recent Speeches* (London: Daily News, 1909), 92.

20. Churchill, *The People's Rights*, 96–97.

21. "The Two Georges," *Boston Globe*, August 26, 1909, 6; Yardley, *Land Value Taxation and Rating*, ix.

22. William Allen White, *Emporia Gazette*, August 26, 1909.

23. Martin Robin, *Radical Politics and Labour, 1880–1930* (Kingston, Ontario: Industrial Relations Centre, Queens University, 1968), 23; Harry Gutkin and Mildred Gutkin, *Profiles in Dissent: The Shaping of Radical Thought in Western Canada* (Edmonton, Alberta: NeWest Publishers Ltd., 1997), 7–50.

24. Max Hirsch, *Land Values Taxation in Practice: A Record of the Progress in Legislation of the Principles of Land Values Taxation* (Melbourne: Renwick, Pride, Nuttal, 1910), 112–114.

25. F. J. Dixon, "The Progress of Land Value Taxation in Western Canada," *Proceedings of the Annual Conference on Taxation under the Auspices of the National Tax Association* 8 (1914): 405–415.

26. *Single Tax Review* 11 (May–June 1911): 15.

27. "Royal Commission on Taxation," series GR-0786, 1911, British Columbia Archives, Victoria.

28. "Vancouver Lesson for Lloyd George," *World*, February 20, 1911; Rees to "Dear Sir," September 11, 1910; Hallan to H. Hutchinson, November 14, 1910; James R. Hanna to L. D. Taylor, November 21, 1910, all file 7, LTP-VCA.

29. Albert Jay Nock, "The Things That Are Caesar's," *American Magazine* (July 1911): 336.

30. Frederic H. Fennis, *Property Assessment in Canada* (Toronto: Canadian Tax Foundation, 1970), 74.

31. Hirsch, *Land Values Taxation in Practice*, 48–87.

32. Melissa Bellanta, "Transcending Class? Australia's Single Taxers in the Early 1890s," *Labour History* 92, no. 1 (May 2007): 17–30; Andrew Dilley, "Labor, Capital, and Land: The Transnational Dimensions of the 1910 Federal Land Tax," *Labour History* 105 (2013): 1–14.

33. Frank Rogers, *The Single Tax Movement in New Zealand* (Auckland: Privately printed, 1953); Hirsch, *Land Values Taxation in Practice*, 7–46.

34. Bellanta, "Transcending Class?" 17–30; Dilley, "Labor, Capital, and Land," 1–14; *Joseph Fels Fund Bulletin* (July 1914).

35. Emil Schmied, "Unearned Increment Taxation in Germany," *The Public*, July 7, 1911, 643–644.

36. "Henry Georgism in Germany," *Boston Transcript*, April 13, 1910; "The Unearned Increment: Tax Is Popular in Germany, and Never Repealed," *New York Evening Post*, November 6, 1909, 3; "Germany Tries a Henry George Plan and Likes It," *New York Times*, May 1, 1910, SM8.

37. Grace Isabel Colbron, "The German Land Reform Association," *The Public*, October 12, 1901, 427; E. R. A. Seligman, *Essays in Taxation* (London: Macmillan Company, 1915), 505–515; R. Brunhuber, "Taxation of Unearned Increment in Germany," *Quarterly Journal of Economics* 22 (1907): 83–106; R. C. Brooks, "The Unearned Increment Taxes in Germany," *Yale Review* 16, no. 1 (1907): 236–261.

38. Howe, *Denmark*, 137–138.

39. "The George Movement in Scandinavia," *The Public*, June 9, 1911, 542–545; Ole Lefmann and Karsten K Larsen, "Denmark," in "Land Value Taxation around the World," ed. Robert Andelson, supplement, *American Journal of Economics and Sociology* 59, no. S5 (2000): 185–203; K. J. Kristensen, *Land Valuation in Denmark* (London: International Union for Land Value Taxation and Free Trade, 1946).

40. Signe Bjorner, "Taxation in Denmark," *The Public*, January 6, 1911.

41. Kristensen, *Land Valuation in Denmark*.

42. J. Rupert Mason, "Menneskerettigheder og samfundspligter," and A. W. Madsen, "Jordvardisberkatning I Storbritanien," in the *Eighth International Conference to Promote Land Value Taxation and Free Trade* (London, 1952), 2–6.

43. Martí, "Schism of the Catholics in New York," 280.

44. Martí, 281.

45. Martí, "Impressions of America (by a very fresh Spaniard)," in *José Martí: Selected Writings*, ed. and trans. Esther Allen (London: Penguin Books, 2002), 32.

46. Martí, "Schism of the Catholics in New York," 279.

47. Thomas W. Ganschow, "Sun Yat-sen and the United States: The Revolutionary Image before 1912," in *Sun Yat-Sen and China*, ed. Paul Kwang Tsien Sih (New York: St. John's University Press, 1974); "Sun Yat Sen's Economic Program for China," *The Public*, April 12, 1912, 349.

48. Marie-Claire Bergere, *Sun Yat-sen*, trans. Janet Lloyd (Stanford, Calif.: Stanford University Press, 1994), 167–170.

49. *The Independent*, June 13, 1912; Ramon H. Myers, "The Principle of People's Welfare: A Multidimensional Concept," in *Sun Yat Sen's Doctrine in the Modern World*, ed. Chu-yuan Cheng (Boulder, Colo.: Westview Press, 1989), 225–243.

50. "Sun Yat Sen's Economic Program for China," *The Public*, April 12, 1912, 349.

51. Joseph Fels to Louis Taylor, August 19, 1912, file 4, 940-3-B, LTP-VCA.

52. Milton I. Vanger, *The Model Country: José Batlle y Ordóñez of Uruguay, 1907–1915* (Hanover, N.H.: University Press of New England, 1980); James C. Knarr, *Uruguay and the United States: Diplomacy in the Progressive Era* (Kent, Ohio: Kent State University Press, 2012), 46–76.

53. C. N. Macintosh, "South American Progress," *The Public*, April 3, 1914, 321–322.

54. C. L. Logan, "Progressive Latin America," *The Public*, June 9, 1916, 535–537; C. N. Macintosh, "South American News," *The Public*, May 29, 1914, 511.

55. *Joseph Fels Fund Bulletin* (June 1914).

56. Carl Voss, ed., *Stephen Wise: Servant of the People* (Philadelphia: Jewish Publication Society of America, 1969), 173–174.

57. "Rebuilding Palestine," *The Public*, January 4, 1918, 9–10.

58. Louis Post, *Land Tenure in the Jewish Commonwealth* (New York: Zionist Organization of America, 1919).

59. "Endorses Zionist Tax Plan," *New York Times*, May 30, 1919, 14.

60. Raymond Russell, *Utopia in Zion: Israeli Experiences with Worker Cooperatives* (Albany: State University Press of New York, 1995), 226–227; Shilomo Sand, *The Invention of the Land of Israel* (Edinburgh: Verso Press, 2012); Gershon Shafir, *Land, Labor, and the Origins of the Israeli-Palestinian Conflict, 1882–1914* (Cambridge: Cambridge University Press, 1989), 150–151; S. N. Einsenstadt, *Israeli Society* (London: Weidenfield and Nicolson, 1967); Dan Horowitz and Moshe Lissak, *The Origins of the Israeli Policy: Palestine under the Mandate* (Chicago: University of Chicago Press, 1978); Yonathan Shapiro, *The Formative Years of the Israeli Labour Party: The Organization of Power* (London: Sage, 1976); Alfred Bonne, "Major Aspects of Land Tenure and the Rural Social Structure in Israel," in *Land Tenure*, ed. Kenneth H. Parson (Madison: University of Wisconsin Press, 1956), 112; Efraim Orni, *Agrarian Reform and Social Progress in Israel* (Jerusalem: JNF, 1972), 13–18; Jacob Metzer, *National Capital for a National Home* (Jerusalem: Yad Itzhak Ben Zvi, 1979), 49.

61. Mary Fels and Bernard A. Rosenblatt, "The Palestine Land Program," *The Public*, May 24, 1919, 542–543.

62. Louis Wallis, "Israel Nearing Home," *The Public*, September 27, 1919, 1047–1048; Mary Fels to Beatrice Webb, October 16, 1929, box 95, NBP-LC.

63. Bertrand Russell, *German Social Democracy* (London: Longmans, Greens, and Co., 1893), 19; Ray Monk, *Bertrand Russell: The Spirit of Solitude, 1872–1921* (New York: Free Press, 1996), 43–44.

64. Karl Marx and Frederic Engels, "Rent of Land," in *Collected Works* (New York: International, 1975), 265–266.

65. Henry George, *Progress and Poverty* (1879; reprinted, New York: Robert Schalkenbach Foundation, 2008), 237–253; J. A. Hobson, *The Science of Wealth* (New York: H. Holt and Company, 1911), 87–116.

66. J. A. Hobson, *Imperialism: A Study* (London: James Nisbet and Co., 1902), 103–104.

67. J. H. Dillard, "Imperialism and Social Problems," *The Public*, May 30, 1903, 118–9.

68. A. M. Eckstein, "Is There a 'Hobson-Lenin Thesis' on Late Nineteenth-Century Colonial Expansion?" *Economic History Review* 44, no. 2 (1991): 297–318.

69. Friedrich Engels, *The Origins of the Family, Private Property, and the State* (Chicago: C. H. Kerr and Company, 1902).

70. Gershon, *Land, Labor, and the Origins of the Israeli-Palestinian Conflict*, 150–151; Franz Oppenheimer, *The State* (Indianapolis: Bobbs-Merrill Company, 1914), 27–51.

71. Herbert Quick, *The Good Ship Earth: A Survey of World Problems* (Indianapolis: Bobbs-Merrill Company, 1913), 235.

72. Post and Leubuscher, *Henry George's 1886 Campaign*, 89; Hulliung, *Social Contract in America*, 71. William Lloyd Garrison II, Silvio Gesell, and Thomas Skidmore each concluded that natural rights to the earth included the right to immigrate freely. Silvio Gessell, *The Natural Economic Order: A Plan to Secure an Uninterrupted Exchange of the Products of Labor Free from Bureaucratic Interference* (San Antonio, Tex.: Free-Economy Publishing Co, 1934); Thomas Skidmore, *The Rights of Man to Property* (New York: Alexander Ming, 1829); William Lloyd Garrison II to Henry George, December 4, 1893, Reel 6, HGP-NYPL.

73. "Small Nationalities," *The Public*, July 6, 1917, 645.

74. Daniel B. Klein, *Knowledge and Coordination: A Liberal Interpretation* (Oxford: Oxford University Press, 2012), 75.

75. Craig, *Progressive at War*, 89.

76. Leo Tolstoy, *Resurrection* (London: Francis Riddell Henderson, 1900), 563.

77. "Tolstoy on Land Ownership," in *An Anthology of Tolstoy's Spiritual Economics*, ed. Kenneth C. Wenzer (Rochester: University of Rochester Press, 1997), 175.

78. Kalidasa Naga, *Tolstoy and Gandhi* (Patna: Pustak Bhandar, 1950); Martin Burgess Green, *Tolstoy and Gandhi: Men of Peace* (New York: Basic Books, 1983); Martin Burgess Green, *The Origins of Nonviolence: Tolstoy and Gandhi in their Historical Settings* (University Park: Pennsylvania State University Press, 1986).

79. Creel, *Rebel at Large*, 98–99.

80. "China," *The Public*, January 14, 1916, 36–37.

Chapter 9 • Justice, Not Charity

1. "*The Public*'s Annual Confession," *The Public*, January 5, 1912, 3–6.

2. Daniel Kiefer to Brand Whitlock, December 12, 1908, BWP-LC.

3. "Daniel Kiefer," *Single Tax Review* 10 (July–August 1910): 31–34; Brand Whitlock, "Dan Kiefer," *American Magazine* 74, September 1912, 549–553; W. E. Eggleston, A. D. Cridge, and W. W. U'Ren, "The Joseph Fels Fund of America," *The Public*, August 12, 1910, 761–763; "Editorial Confidences," *The Public*, January 6, 1911, 1–4.

4. Dudden, *Joseph Fels and the Single-Tax Movement*, 38, 194–195; *Single Tax Conference, Held in New York City, Nov. 19 and 20, 1910*, 16; Mary Fels, *Joseph Fels: His Life's Work* (New York: B. W. Huebsch, 1916), 185–187; Daniel Kiefer to Lincoln Steffens, November 5, 1908, box 1; Warren Worth Bailey to Lincoln Steffens, August 14, 1909, box 1; Joseph Fells to Lincoln Steffens, November 12, 1909, box 4, all LSP-CU.

5. "Germany's Increment Tax," *San Francisco Chronicle*, May 13, 1910, 6; "The 'Single Tax': It Must Not Be Confounded with Mere Non-taxation of Improvements," *San Francisco Chronicle*, September 10, 1911, 32.

6. George and Dewey, *Significant Paragraphs from Henry George's* Progress and Poverty, 77–80.

7. "The Two Georges," *Boston Daily Globe*, August 26, 1909, 6; "Far Reaching Influence: A Tribute to the Work and Writing of Henry George," *Boston Daily Globe*, October 10, 1909, 54.

8. "Mayor Fitzgerald and the Unearned Increment," *The Public*, February 24, 1911, 172–173.

9. "Mayor Takes Up Land Question," *Boston Daily Globe*, October 2, 1910, 16; "Explains New Taxation Phase," *Boston Daily Globe*, October 16, 1910, 24; "Boston Hall Meeting Sunday," *Boston Daily Globe*, October 13, 1910, 9.

10. "Boston and the Single Tax," *The Public*, February 16, 1912, 160.

11. "National Single Tax Conference at Boston," *The Public*, December 6, 1912, 1160–1164.

12. Rhode Island General Assembly, *Special Report of the Joint Special Committee on the Taxation Laws* (Providence, R.I.: E. L. Freeman Company, 1911), 50.

13. Albert Jay Nock, "Putting on the Screws," *American Magazine* (February 1911): 450–451.

14. Albert Jay Nock, "A Tax on Ignorance and Honesty," *American Magazine*, December 1910, 147–148.

15. Oscar Leser, Edwin R. A. Seligman, James C. Forman, Nils P. Haugen, and Frederick N. Judson, "Report of Committee on Causes of Failure of the General Property Tax," *State and Local Taxation: International Conference under the Auspices of the International Tax Association; Addresses and Proceedings* 4 (August 30–September 2, 1910), 301; Edwin R. A. Seligman, "The General Property Tax," *Political Science Quarterly* 5, no. 1 (March 1890): 24–64; J. H. T. McPherson, "The General Property Tax as a Source of State Revenue," *State and Local Taxation: National Conference under the Auspices of the National Tax Association; Addresses and Proceedings* 1 (November 1907): 475–484.

16. Walter William Pollock and Karl W. H. Scholz, *The Science and the Practice of Urban Land Valuation: An Exposition of the Somers Unit System* (Philadelphia: Manufacturers' Appraisal Company, 1926).

17. *Baltimore Sun*, July 3, 1913, and December 12, 1913.

18. Manufacturers' Appraisal Company, *The Somers Unit System of Realty Valuation* (Cleveland: privately printed, 1912), 16–22; "The Somers System of Tax Valuation," *The Public*, February 24, 1911, 173–179; E. W. Dotty, "The Somers System in Practice," *The Public*, March 10, 1911, 224–225.

19. "Urge Uniform Tax Plan," *Chicago Daily Tribune*, January 27, 1907, B7.

20. "Real Estate Men at Theater Party," *Chicago Daily Tribune*, June 12, 1910, J22; "Favors Somers Unit System, June 15, 1910, 16; "Assessment Values: Scientific Plan for Arriving at Basis on City Lots Explained by Expert," *Los Angeles Times*, December 2, 1913, II6.

21. "Somers System to Be Tried," *Los Angeles Times*, March 12, 1914, I13.

22. "Declines to Follow Henry George Plan," *Chicago Daily Tribune*, April 28, 1894, 9; Isaac Martin, *The Permanent Tax Revolt: How the Property Tax Transformed American Politics* (Stanford, Calif.: Stanford University Press, 2008); Mehrotra, *Making the Modern American Fiscal State*, 59–60, 204–206.

23. "News Notes," *The Public*, August 25, 1900, 314; "News Notes," *The Public*, April 7, 1906, 10.

24. "Lawson Purdy," *American Magazine* (July 1911): 310–313.

25. Mason Gaffney, *New Life in Old Cities* (New York: Robert Schalkenbach Foundation, 2006), 11.

26. Philip H. Cornick, "Lawson Purdy's Career in Property Tax Reform," *American Journal of Economics and Sociology* 9, no. 1 (October 1949): 7–24.

27. *The Public*, October 31, 1903, 467.

28. "Purdy Justifies Big Tax Increase," *New York Times*, January 11, 1911, 5; Daniel Hart London, "Indebted to Growth: Real Estate and the Political Economy of Public Finance in New York City, 1871–1943" (PhD diss., New York University, 2020), 63–64; Purdy's activism as assessor extended to counseling taxpayers to evade personal property taxes. "Purdy Aided W. W. Astor to Avoid Personal Tax," *New York Times*, January 20, 1907, 9.

29. These include Arkansas, California, Idaho, Maine, Minnesota, Nebraska, New Hampshire, New Jersey, Rhode Island, South Dakota, Utah, Wisconsin, and Wyoming. Young, *Single Tax Movement in the United States*, 241.

30. "Taxation in Piedmont," *The Public*, December 6, 1912, 1154–1155; "Tax Reform News," *The Public*, June 30, 1916, 612; *The Public*, October 27, 1916, 1012–1013; "Tax Situation in Los Angeles," and "Houstonizing Vermillion, South Dakota," *The Public*, July 14, 1916, 656–658, 661; "Henry George Taxation Hits Bayonne Realty," *New York Times*, December 8, 1906; Gaffney, *New Life in Old Cities*, 5.

31. Robert Murray Haig, *The Exemption of Improvements from Taxation in Canada and the United States: A Report Prepared for the Committee on Taxation of the City of New York* (New York: M. B. Brown, Printing and Binding Co., 1915), 261.

32. Mabel Newcomer, "The Decline of the General Property Tax," *National Tax Journal* 6, no. 1 (March 1953): 46.

33. Robin L. Einhorn, *Property Rules: Political Economy in Chicago, 1833–1872* (Chicago: University of Chicago Press, 1991).

34. Gail Radford, "From Municipal Socialism to Public Authorities: Institutional Factors in the Shaping of American Public Enterprise," *Journal of American History* 90, no. 3 (December 2003): 881; Morris A. Copeland, *Trends in Government Financing* (Princeton, N.J.: Princeton University Press, 1961), 94.

35. Wilcox, *American City*, 380; Edward White to Frank Walsh, March 15, 1929, box 16, FWP-NYPL.

36. Charles C. Williamson, *The Finances of Cleveland* (New York: Columbia University Press, 1907), 232–233.

37. George A. Schilling, "The Single Tax Mayor of Belleville," *The Public*, March 12, 1909, 247–249.

38. George Record, *How to Abolish Poverty* (Jersey City, N.J.: George L. Record Memorial Association, 1936), 11–21.

39. Lincoln Steffens, *Upbuilders* (New York: Doubleday, Page & Co., 1909), 25.

40. Ransom E. Noble Jr., "George L. Record's Struggle for Economic Democracy," *American Journal of Economics and Sociology* 10, no. 1 (October 1950): 71–83; Eugene M. Tobin, "In Pursuit of Equal Taxation: Jersey City's Struggle against Corporate Arrogance and Tax-Dodging by the Railroad Trust," *American Journal of Economics and Sociology* 34, no. 2 (April 1975): 213–224.

41. John T. McCartney, *Black Power Ideologies: An Essay in African-American Political Thought* (Philadelphia: Temple University Press, 1992), 30; McRoy, *Report of the Joseph Fels Fund and Single Tax Conference at Washington, D.C., January 15th, 16th, 17th, 1914*, 1, 3, 10.

42. *Single Tax Conference, Held in New York City, Nov. 19 and 20, 1910*, 6.

43. Thomas Goebel, *A Government by the People: Direct Democracy in America, 1890–1940* (Chapel Hill: University of North Carolina Press, 2002), 31.

44. Johnston, *Radical Middle Class*, 128–129.

45. Goebel, *Government by the People*, 80.

46. *Single Tax Conference, Held in New York City, Nov. 19 and 20, 1910*, 22.

47. Otis L. Graham, *The Great Campaigns: Reform and War in America, 1900–1928* (Englewood Cliffs, N.J.: Prentice-Hall, 1971), 158; William U'Ren to Daniel Kiefer, September 5, 1909, box 15, LSP-CU.

48. "The Oregon Fight for People's Power in Government," *The Public*, August 12, 1910, 40–42.

49. U'Ren to Joseph Fels and Daniel Kiefer, January 9, 1913, box, 14, JBP-BL.

50. Arthur Link, ed., *The Papers of Woodrow Wilson* (Princeton, N.J.: Princeton University Press, 1977), 24:175–176; Norman Hapgood, *The Changing Years: Reminiscences of Norman Hapgood* (New York: Farrar and Rinehart, 1930); "Wilson Urges Oregon System for New Jersey," *La Follette's Weekly Magazine*, January 28, 1911, 8; Goebel, *Government by the People*, 127.

51. Lawrence M. Limpin, *Workers and the Wild: Conservation, Consumerism, and Labor in Oregon, 1910–1930* (Urbana: University of Illinois Press, 2007).

52. "Land Values Taxation in Oregon," *The Public*, September 9, 1910, 843–844; William Eggleston to James Barry, June 21, 1910, box 4, JBP-BL.

53. James P. Cadman, "Oregon's Democracy in Action," *The Public*, January 13, 1911.

54. Young, *The Single Tax Movement in the United States*, 168–183.

55. Haig, *Exemption of Improvements from Taxation in Canada and the United States*, 261.

56. Reed Smoot, *Digest of the Report of British Board of Trade on Cost of Living in the Principal Industrial Towns of England and Wales, Germany, France, Belgium, and the United States* (Washington, D.C.: Government Printing Office, 1911).

57. Young, *Single Tax Movement in the United States*, 191–197; G. H. Moser to Frank Walsh, February 7, 1913, box 1, FWP-NYPL; *Joseph Fels Fund Bulletin* (June 1913).

58. *Joseph Fels Fund Bulletin* (January 1916).

59. 55 Cong. Rec. 5481 (July 26, 1917).

60. 56 Cong. Rec. 3776 (March 20, 1918).

61. G. J. Knapp to Peabody, January 8, 1933, box 46, G. Peabody P-LC; Young, *Single Tax Movement in the United States*, 202–208; *Joseph Fels Fund Bulletin* (October 1913).

62. Louis Wallis, "The Denver Fight and Its Lessons," *The Public*, May 28, 1915, 520–521; "Denver, Colorado, Adopts Single Tax," *The Public*, April 13, 1917, 361.

63. *Joseph Fels Fund Bulletin* (December 1915).

64. "J. J. Pastoriza," *The Public*, April 28, 1911, 400–401.

65. "Land-Value Taxation in Texas," *The Public*, August 11, 1911, 828–829.

66. Young, *Single Tax Movement in the United States*, 198; *Joseph Fels Fund Bulletin* (December 1914): 1.

67. Stephen Davis, "Joseph Jay Pastoriza and the Single Tax in Houston, 1911–1917," *Houston Review* 8 (1986): 57–78.

68. Young, *Single Tax Movement in the United States*, 201–202.

69. *Joseph Fels Fund Bulletin* (March 1914).

70. *Dallas Morning News*, February 21, 1915; United States Commission on Industrial Relations, *Final Report of the Commission on Industrial Relations*

(Washington D.C.: Banard & Miller Print, 1915), 127–133; *Joseph Fels Fund Bulletin* (March 1913).

71. *Joseph Fels Fund Bulletin* (December 1915).

72. Mary Fels, "Joe Pastoriza," *The Public*, July 13, 1917, 671.

73. Davis, "Joseph Jay Pastoriza and the Single Tax in Houston," 57–78.

74. "Joseph Fels Fund of America, Receipts and Disbursement, January 1 to December 31, 1914," box 6, JBP-BL.

75. *Joseph Fels Fund Bulletin* (September 1914).

76. "The SingleTax Forward Movement," *The Public*, November 15, 1912, 1084–1087.

77. William Eggleston to James Barry, September 15, 1922, box 4; William Eggleston to James Barry, September 13, 1922, box 4; James Barry to William Eggleston, August 14, 1922, box 4; Jackson Ralston to James Barry, September 7, 1923, box 11, all JBP-BL.

78. J. Stitt Wilson, "California Singletax Conference," *The Public*, January 19, 1917, 62–63.

79. J. J. Ryckman, "Land Reform in California," *The Public*, January 4, 1919, 15–16.

80. Samuel Danziger, "Reckless Misinterpretation," *The Public*, January 14, 1916, 26.

81. *Evening Mail*, November 14, 1916.

82. James Barry to Anna George De Mille, August 24, 1922, box 3, JBP-BL.

83. Young, *Single Tax Movement in the United States*, 217–218; Benjamin C. Marsh, "Land Value Taxation vs. Congestion," *Single Tax Review* (January–February 1914): 16–20.

84. *Joseph Fels Fund Bulletin* (August 1913).

85. *The Public*, November 2, 1901, 470; "A Century Ago, a Mayor Who Wrote Back," *New York Times*, January 1, 2013.

86. "An Effort to Save Life," *New York Tribune*, January 3, 1912, 6.

87. "Urge Sullivan-Shortt Bill," *New York Tribune*, July 10, 1911, 2.

88. "New Tax Bill Urged," *New York Sun*, October 27, 1911, 4.

89. William Jay Gaynor, *Some of Mayor Gaynor's Letters and Speeches* (New York: Greaves Publishing Company, 1913), 214–221.

90. *Joseph Fels Fund Bulletin* (August 1914).

91. *New York Tribune*, January 14, 1912.

92. Haig, *Exemption of Improvements from Taxation in Canada and the United States*, 277–278.

93. *Final Report of the Committee on Taxation of the City of New York* (New York: O'Connell Press, 1916), 34–35.

94. *Final Report of the Committee on Taxation of the City of New York*, 60.

95. Young, *Single Tax Movement in the United States*, 210–213; John Thomas Holdsworth, *Economic Survey of Pittsburgh* (Pittsburgh, Pa., 1912), 192, 207.

96. *New York Evening World*, August 4, 1920.

97. *New York Evening World*, October 1, 1920.

98. *New York Tribune*, April 2, 1920.

99. Charles Edward Russell, *The Story of the Nonpartisan League* (New York: Arno Press, 1975), 264–265.

100. *New York Times*, January 4, 1917.

101. McRoy, *Report of the Joseph Fels Fund and Single Tax Conference at Washington, D.C., January 15th, 16th, 17th, 1914*, 11.

102. *The Bulletin: Organ of the National Single Tax League* (January 1917).

103. Amy Chua, *World on Fire: How Exporting Free Market Democracy Breeds Ethnic Hatred and Global Instability* (New York: Doubleday, 2002).

104. Progressive Party, *A Contract with the People: Platform of the Progressive Party Adopted at Its First National Convention, Chicago, August 7th, 1912* (New York: Progressive National Committee, 1912); "A Charter of Democracy: Address by Theodore Roosevelt before the Ohio Constitutional Convention," February 21, 1912, box 1071, G. Pinchot P-LC.

105. Joseph Dixon, "Pre-election Statement Issued at National Progressive Headquarters," October 27, 1912, box 1071, G. Pinchot P-LC.

106. *Century Magazine* 86 (October 1913): 834.

Chapter 10 • Conservation for the People

1. Kenneth T. Gillingham and James H. Stock, "Federal Minerals Leasing Reform and Climate Policy," *Hamilton Project* (December 2016), https://www.hamiltonproject .org/assets/files/federal_minerals_leasing_reform_and_climate_policy_pp.pdf.

2. D. W. Bushyhead, "Fourth Annual Address," *Cherokee Advocate*, November 3, 1886.

3. Henry Dawes, "Address at the Third Lake Mohonk Indian Conference" (1885), quoted in Scott L. Malcomson, *One Drop of Blood: The American Misadventure of Race* (New York: Farrar, Straus and Giroux, 2000), 15; Henry George to Lewis, August 13, 1893, reel 6, HGP-NYPL; Alexandra Harmon, "American Indians and Land Monopolies in the Gilded Age," *Journal of American History* 90, no. 1 (June 2003): 106–133.

4. Alexandra Harmon, *Rich Indians: Native People and the Promise of Wealth in American History* (Chapel Hill: Univeristy of North Carolina Press, 2010), 176–177, 181.

5. Robert Baker, "Editorial Correspondence," *Public*, March 12, 1904, 774–775.

6. E. Louise Peffer, *The Closing of the Public Domain: Disposal and Reservation Policies, 1900–1950* (New York: Arno Press, 1972), 69.

7. Samuel Hays, *Conservation and the Gospel of Efficiency: The Progressive Conservation Movement, 1890–1920* (Pittsburgh: University of Pittsburgh Press, 1999).

8. Julian Simon, *The Ultimate Resource 2* (Princeton: Princeton University Press, 1996), 286.

9. George, *Progress and Poverty*, 110.

10. George, 401; Louis Post, "A Neglected Chapter," *The Standard*, July 27, 1889.

11. "Ballinger Controversy Notes," box 437, G. Pinchot P-LC.

12. "Address of Mr. Gifford Pinchot, Chief of the United States Forest Service before the People's Forum; For Release Dec. 27, 1909," box 437, G. Pinchot P-LC; Gifford Pinchot, *The Fight for Conservation* (1910; reprinted, Seattle: University of Washington Press, 1967), 113.

13. Amos Pinchot, "Untitled Campaign Speech, January 22, 1914," box 1071, G. Pinchot P-LC.

14. E. C. Branson to Harry Slattery, April 13, 1914, box 475; Harry Slattery to Angeline Graves, April 24, 1914, box 477, both G. Pinchot P-LC.

15. Harry Slattery to W. Tomlinson, October 17, 1913, box 475; James Barry to Gifford Pinchot, March 17, 1913, box 475; Harry Slattery to Herbert Quick, September 26, 1913, box 476; Gifford Pinchot to Ben Lindsey, March 8, 1917, box 492; Gifford Pinchot to Ben Lindsey, December 21, 1916, box 485, all G. Pinchot P-LC.

16. "Minutes of the Committee on Conservation of Forest and Wildlife of the Camp Fire Club of America," January 3, 1913, box 561, G. Pinchot P-LC.

17. Harold Ickes to William Kent, March 29, 1909, box 35, Harold Ickes Papers, Library of Congress, Washington, D.C.

18. Kent, *William Kent, Independent*.

19. William Kent to Rufus Wilson, November 18, 1913, box 6, JBP-BL.

20. William Kent, "A Candid and Welcome Criticism," *The Public*, May 14, 1909, 478.

21. Stoughton Cooley, "One Recourse Left," *The Public*, June 12, 1914, 556.

22. Kent, *William Kent, Independent*, 292–293.

23. Forestry Resolution Committee, "The Single Tax in Relation to Forestry," *The Public*, February 26, 1915, 223.

24. Forestry Resolution Committee, "The Single Tax in Relation to Forestry," *The Public*, February 26, 1915, 217–224; E. H. Prothingham to Daniel Kiefer, April 17, 1914; Louis Murphy to Stanley Bowmar, April 14, 1914, both box 126, G. Pinchot P-LC.

25. Henry George and David Dudley Field, "Land and Taxation: A Conversation," *North American Review* (July 1885): 1–14.

26. "A Plan for Publicity: A Brief Discussion of a Systematic Plan to Secure Publicity," box 492, G. Pinchot P-LC.

27. "Publicity Plans and Dates of Releases, Gifford Pinchot's Memorandums," box 492; Franklin K. Lane, "Development of Western Oil, Phosphate, Coal, and Potash Lands: Consideration of Proposed Legislation," box 613; Harry Slattery to Herbert Quick, September 26, 1913, box 476; William Kent to "Dear Congressman" (form letter), June 9, 1914, box 477; Gifford Pinchot to Col. House, November 19, 1915, box 485, all G. Pinchot P-LC.

28. Brand Whitlock to Marshall Sheppey, January 17, 1916, box 33, BWP-LC.

29. Keith W. Olson, *Biography of a Progressive: Franklin K. Lane, 1864–1921* (Westport, Conn.: Greenwood Press, 1979), 18; Anne Lane and Louis Wall, eds., *The Letters of Franklin K. Lane: Personal and Political* (Boston: Houghton Mifflin Company, 1922), 375; Unnamed to Daniel Kiefer, June 29, 1914, box 6, JBP-LC.

30. Olson, *Biography of a Progressive*, 45.

31. Lane and Wall, *Letters of Franklin K. Lane*, 23–27.

32. *The Public*, September 6, 1902, 345.

33. Olson, *Biography of a Progressive*, 29–30, 34–46.

34. *The Public*, May 28, 1898, 3–4.

35. Louis Post, "Franklin K. Lane for Interstate Commerce Commissioner," *The Public*, October 21, 1905, 449.

36. Olson, *Biography of a Progressive*, 86–8.

37. Franklin K. Lane, "Development of Western Oil, Phosphate, Coal, and Potash Lands: Consideration of Proposed Legislation," box 613, Franklin Lane Papers, Library of Congress, Washington, D.C.

38. Charles Ingersoll to Harry Slattery, February 2, 1914; Harry Slattery to Charles Ingersoll, February 6, 1914, both box 477, G. Pinchot P-LC.

39. William Kent to "Dear Congressman," June 8, 1914, box 477, G. Pinchot P-LC.

40. "Gifford Pinchot Warns against the Shield Bill, *The Public*, January 22, 1915, 84.

41. Harry Slattery to W. H. Cowles, April 28, 1914, box 476, G. Pinchot P-LC.

42. Kent, *William Kent, Independent*, 332.

43. Harry Slattery to William Kent, July 28, 1916; William Kent to Newton Baker, July 21, 1916, both box 485, G. Pinchot P-LC.

44. Woodrow Wilson to William Kent, March 9, 1916, box 485, G. Pinchot P-LC.

45. Olson, *Biography of a Progressive*, 104.

46. Peffer, *Closing of the Public Domain*, 182–190.

47. Kent, *William Kent, Independent*, 230–234.

48. Kent, *William Kent, Independent*, 230–234.

49. William Allen White, *The Man, His Times, and His Task* (Boston: Houghton Mifflin and Company, 1927), 264; Ronald J. Pestritto, *Woodrow Wilson and the Roots of Modern Liberalism* (Lanham: Rowman and Littlefield, 2005), 2; Sidney M. Milkis, *The President and the Parties* (New York: Oxford University Press, 1993), 22; Kendrick A. Clemens, *The Presidency of Woodrow Wilson* (Lawrence: Univeristy of Kansas Press, 1992), 27–28; John Milton Cooper Jr., *The Warrior and the Priest: Woodrow Wilson and Theodore Roosevelt* (Cambridge, Mass.: Belknap Press of Harvard University Press, 1983), 219; Foner, *Story of American Freedom*, 160–161; Elliot Brownlee, "Wilson's Reform of the Economic Structure: Progressive Liberalism and the Corporation," in *Reconsidering Woodrow Wilson: Progressivism, Internationalism, War, and Peace*, ed. John Milton Cooper (Washington, D.C.: Woodrow Wilson Center Press; Baltimore: Johns Hopkins University Press, 2008), 57–89.

Chapter 11 • *The Point of Least Resistance*

Epigraph: "Tom Johnson's Public Service," *The Public*, April 21, 1911.

1. Croly, *The Promise of American Life*, 141.

2. Croly, 202.

3. Croly, 165.

4. Croly, 81, 279–280.

5. Croly, 196.

6. Croly, 245.

7. Croly, 256.

8. Croly, 308.

9. Croly, 174–175.

10. Levy, *Herbert Croly of the New Republic*, 260–262.

11. John Patrick Diggins, *Mussolini and Fascism: The View from America* (Princeton, N.J.: Princeton University Press, 1972), 204, 231–234.

12. Joseph Dana Miller, "Natural Law in the Economic World," *The Public*, April 3, 1914, 319.

13. Levy, *Herbert Croly of the New Republic*, 134, 139–140, 257, 258.

14. Levy, *Freaks of Fortune*, 291, 302; Dalton, *Theodore Roosevelt*, 300–344, 376–377; Louis Post, "Roosevelt's Napoleonic Democracy," *The Public*, June 24, 1910, 577–579.

15. "The Democratic Party," *The Public*, August 16, 1912, 771.

16. "George Book in Campaign," *New York Times*, April 13, 1912, 2; Joseph Dana Miller, "Bi-monthly News Letter," *Land and Freedom* (November–December 1916): 350.

17. Eugene M. Tobin, *George L. Record and the Progressive Spirit* (Trenton: New Jersey Historical Commission, 1979), 19, 24; Ransom Noble, *New Jersey Progressivism before Wilson* (Princeton, N.J.: Princeton University Press, 1946); Joseph Patrick Tumulty, *Woodrow Wilson As I Know Him* (New York: Doubleday, Page and Co., 1921);

Maxine N. Lurie and Richard Veit, *New Jersey: A History of the Garden State* (New Brunswick, NJ: Rutgers University Press, 2012), 213; John M. Blum, *Joe Tumulty and the Wilson Era* (Boston: Houghton Mifflin, 1951), 23.

18. U'Ren to Joseph Fels and Daniel Kiefer, January 9, 1913, JBP-BL.

19. "Governor Wilson of New Jersey," *The Public*, January 20, 1911, 49.

20. Cramer, *Newton D. Baker*, 64–70; "Presidential Politics," *The Public*, June 14, 1912, 564.

21. Rudolph W. Chamberlain, *There Is No Truce: A Life of Thomas Mott Osborne* (New York: MacMillan, 1935), 177–178; David T. Beito, "Some Roads Taken, and Not Taken, from the Progressive Era to the New Deal," in *What Is Classical Liberal History?* ed. Michael J. Douma and Phillip W. Magness (Lanham, Md.: Lexington Books, 2009), 102.

22. Thomas J. Knock, *To End All Wars: Woodrow Wilson and the Quest for a New World Order* (Princeton, N.J.: Princeton University Press, 1995).

23. *Joseph Fels Fund Bulletin*, November 1914.

24. John, *Network Nation*, 365.

25. Foner, *History of the Labor Movement in the United States*, 2:177.

26. US Congress, House, *Assessment and Taxation of Real Estate in the District of Columbia*, 62nd Cong., 2nd sess. (1912), 2386, 394, 453–454.

27. Levy, *Herbert Croly of the New Republic*, 241.

28. Samuel Danzinger, "A Long-Needed Reform in Sight," *The Public*, June 12, 1914, 553.

29. Stoughton Cooley, "Democracy's Future," *The Public*, October 30, 1914, 1034.

30. Samuel Danzinger, "Herbert Quick on the Loan Board," *The Public*, April 14, 1916, 722.

31. Louis Post, Diary, 9; Louis Post, "Living a Long Life Over Again," 303–304, LPP-LC.

32. "Official Timidity—Or What?" *The Public*, June 8, 1917, 545; Frank Butler to James Barry, December 23, 1919, box 2, JBP-LC.

33. Brownlee, "Wilson's Reform of Economic Structure," 89.

34. Henry George, *Protection or Free Trade* (New York: Henry George, 1887), 341.

35. 55 Cong Rec., 2347 (January 31, 1917).

36. Miller, *From Progressive to New Dealer*, 210, 214, 222; Howe, *Confessions of a Reformer*, 263–265; *Baltimore Sun*, November 2, 1910; *New York Times*, November 6, 1910.

37. Unnamed to Daniel Kiefer, June 29, 1914; William Kent to James Barry, April 28, 1914, both box 6, JBP-BL.

38. "Lincoln Steffens to Allen Suggett, April 30, 1916," in *The Letters of Lincoln Steffens*, ed. Ella Winter and Granville Hicks (New York: Harcourt, Brace and Company, 1938), 1:371.

39. Michael Smith, "Carrancista Propaganda and the Print Media in the United States: An Overview of Institutions," *The Americas* 52, no. 2 (October 1995): 155–174.

40. M. C. Rolland, "The Trial of Socialism in Mexico," *The Forum* (July 1916): 81.

41. Mexican Bureau of Information, *Red Papers of Mexico* (New York: Mexican Bureau of Information, 1914), 8.

42. J. W. Slaughter, "A Visit to Mexico," *The Public*, June 30, 1916, 615–619; Harry Stein, "Lincoln Steffens and the Mexican Revolution," *American Journal of Economics and Sociology* 34, no. 2 (April 1975): 197–212.

43. Stein, "Lincoln Steffens and the Mexican Revolution," 203.

44. Mark Benbow, *Leading Them to the Promised Land: Woodrow Wilson, Covenant Theology, and the Mexican Revolution, 1913–1915* (Kent, Ohio: Kent State University Press, 2010), 58.

45. Benbow, 88; "Lincoln Steffens to Lou and Allen Suggett," July 16, 1916 in *Letters of Lincoln Steffens*, 1:377.

46. Miller, *From Progressive to New Dealer*, 250.

47. Dalton, *Theodore Roosevelt*, 445.

48. Stein, "Lincoln Steffens and the Mexican Revolution," 197–212.

49. "New Light on Colorado Shed by Labor Leader," May 14, 1914, oversized 5, GCP-LC.

50. Untitled to Samuel Danzinger, June 29, 1913, box 33, FWP-NYPL.

51. Frank Walsh to William Marion Reedy, April 17, 1915, box 33, FWP-NYPL.

52. Greenberg, *Republic of Spin*, 73–75.

53. Joseph A. McCartin, *Labor's Great War: The Struggle for Industrial Democracy and the Origins of Modern American Labor Relations, 1912–1921* (Chapel Hill: University of North Carolina Press, 1997), 26.

54. United States Commission on Industrial Relations, *Final Report*, 31.

55. United States Commission on Industrial Relations, 78–80, 113–116, 132.

56. Foner, *Story of American Freedom*, 164.

57. Thornton, *Newton D. Baker and His Books*, 55–56; Lincoln Steffens to Ella Winter, December 16, 1919, box 15, LSP-CU.

58. George P. West, "Labor and Fundamental Reform," *The Public*, March 23, 1917, 275–277.

59. "Land and Loan Measure in Missouri," *The Public*, September 29, 1916, 924–925; "Miners for Land Value Tax," *The Public*, April 27, 1917, 376–377.

60. "Speech delivered December 1, 1913, to the San Francisco League for Home Rule," *Joseph Fels Fund Bulletin* (January 1914): 3.

61. Daniel Kiefer to Alex Scott, February 14, 1916, box 34, FWP-NYPL.

62. Greenberg, *Republic of Spin*, 167–174.

63. Dante Barton to Frank Walsh, January 29, 1916; Frank Walsh to Dante Barton, February 1, 1916; Dante Barton to Frank Walsh, December 3, 1916, all box 34, FWP-NYPL.

64. "Walsh Endorses the Crosser Bill," *The Public*, March 17, 1916, 252.

65. Benton MacKaye, "The Lesson of Alaska," *The Public*, August 30, 1919, 930–932; "Conserving Natural Resources," *The Public*, September 27, 1919, 1037–1038.

66. Edward K. Spann, *Designing Modern America: The Regional Planning Association of America and Its Members* (Columbus: Ohio State University Press, 1996), 28.

67. Edwin R. A. Seligman, "The United States Federal Income Tax," *Economic Journal* 24, no. 93 (March 1914): 55–77; Cordell Hull, *The Memoirs of Cordell Hull* (New York: Macmillan, 1948), 48, 61. For evidence that Congress was not indebted to the ability-to-pay principle, see Senator Gilbert Hitchcock's proposal that the income tax be substituted for a tax on monopoly, with rates twenty times higher for industries that controlled more than half of their market. The vote failed narrowly—30 to 41—though the point of this tax, like the single tax, was precisely that the affected parties could not pay. Opponents largely complained that it was inexpedient or poorly designed, not that it violated ability to pay. 49 Cong. Rec., 3866–3858 (August 29, 1913).

68. Association for an Equitable Federal Income Tax, "Why the Federal Government Should Secure at Least Three Hundred Million Dollars by a Rapidly Progressive Individual Income Tax," box 561, WMP-LC.

69. Association for an Equitable Federal Income Tax.

70. *Hearings and Briefs before the Subcommittees of the Committee on Finance of the United States Senate, Sixty-fourth Congress, Second Session, on H. R. 20573* (Washington: Government Printing Office, 1917), 106–122.

71. 26 Cong. Rec., 1652 (January 30, 1894); "The Society to Lower Rents and Reduce Taxes on Homes to 'Dear Fellow Single-taxer,'" December 23, 1915, box 126, APP-LC.

72. "Single-Taxers and the Federal Income Tax," *Bulletin of the National Tax Association* 1, no.1 (February 1916): 1–2.

73. W. Elliot Brownlee, "Wilson and the Financing of the Modern State: The Revenue Act of 1916," *Proceedings of the American Philosophical Society* 129, no. 2 (June 1985): 173–210.

74. "Excess Profits Tax," box 561, WMP-LC.

75. Brownlee, "Wilson's Reform of Economic Structure," 82; "Excess Profits Tax—Discussion," *American Economic Review* 10, no. 1 (March 1920): 22; Mehrotra, *Making the Modern American Fiscal State*, 339; W. Elliot Brownlee, "Economists in the Formation of the Modern Tax System in the United States: The World War I Crisis," in *The State and Economic Knowledge*, ed. Mary Furner and Barry Supple (Cambridge: Cambridge University Press, 1990), 401–435.

76. Mehrotra, *Making the Modern American Fiscal State*, 293–348.

77. Arthur Link, *Woodrow Wilson and the Progressive Era* (London: H. Hamilton, 1954), 239–240.

78. Spencer C. Olin, "Hiram Johnson, the California Progressives, and the Hughes Campaign of 1916," *Pacific Historical Review* 31, no. 4 (1962): 403–412; Greenberg, *Republic of Spin*, 102–103.

79. Creel, *Rebel at Large*, 148–153.

80. *New York Times*, July 14 and 20, 1916.

81. Amos Pinchot to Stanley Isaacs, June 9, 1914, box 69, APP-LC.

82. Amos Pinchot to Henry Rickey, June 4, 1916, box 69, APP-LC.

83. John Allen Gable, *Adventures in Reform: Gifford Pinchot, Amos Pinchot, and the Progressive Party* (Millford, Pa.: Grey Towers Press, 1986); Lyman Abbot to Amos Pinchot, June 2, 1914, box 69, APP-LC.

84. Tobin, *George L. Record and the Progressive Spirit*, 22–23.

85. George Record to Amos Pinchot, May 23, 1914, box 69, APP-LC.

86. Ben Lindsey to Amos Pinchot, June 5, 1915; Edmund Osbourne to Amos Pinchot, June 10, 1914, both box 69, APP-LC.

87. Mitgang, *Man Who Rode the Tiger*, 105–114, 118.

88. Palmer Frederick, *Newton D. Baker: America at War* (New York: Dodd, Mead, and Company, 1931), 1:8.

89. Daniel Beaver, *Newton D. Baker and the American War Effort* (Lincoln: University of Nebraska Press, 1966), 26; Brand Whitlock to Marshall Sheppey, January 17, 1916, BWP-LC.

90. Frederick, *Newton D. Baker*, 1:81.

91. Newton Baker to Brand Whitlock, December 23, 1916, BWP-LC.

92. Edgar Eugene Robinson, *The Presidential Vote* (Stanford, Calif.: Stanford University Press, 1934), 292–299. Statistics are based on a comparison between the 1908 and the 1916 election because Roosevelt's third-party run in 1912 destabilized the two-party system. Although a shift in Socialist support for Wilson in 1916 has been credited with his victory in Ohio, the share of Socialist votes in two-party match-ups remained stable. From 1908 to 1916 the entire third-party vote declined only slightly from 46,519 to 46,177.

93. *St. Louis Republic*, November 9, 1916.

94. *Springfield (Mass.) Republican*, November 30, 1916.

95. 54 Cong. Rec., 2347 (January 31, 1917).

96. Ralph A. Hayes, "Making War," *The Public*, November 30, 1917, 1152–1155; Ralph A. Hayes, "Making War," *The Public*, December 7, 1917, 1173–1177.

97. "A War-Time Christmas Book," *The Public*, November 30, 1917, 1114.

98. *The Public*, October 12, 1917, 996.

99. Albert Nock to Brand Whitlock, May 27, 1917, BWP-LC.

100. Albert Jay Nock, "Democracy Here and Abroad," *New York Post*, January 30, 1918.

101. Clarence Darrow, "War Prisoners," speech delivered at the Garrick Theater, Chicago, November 9, 1919, box 14, Clarence Darrow Papers, Library of Congress, Washington, D.C.

102. McCartin, *Labor's Great War*, 67.

103. McCartin, 173–221; Lizabeth Cohen, *Making a New Deal: Industrial Workers in Chicago, 1919–1939* (1990; reprinted, Cambridge: Cambridge University Press, 2008), 172–205.

104. Frederick, *Newton D. Baker*, 1:48.

105. Newton D Baker to George Peabody, November 29, 1918, NBP-LC.

106. Frederic C. Howe, "The New Imperialism," *The Public* March 9, 1917, 225–227; Frederick, *Newton D. Baker*, 1:50; Knock, *To End All Wars*, 35; Kent, *William Kent, Independent*, 261–263.

107. *The National Defense Act, Approved June 3, as Amended by Act Approved August 29th, 1916* (Washington, D.C.: Government Printing Office: 1921), 44.

108. House Committee on Appropriations, *Nitrate Plants*, 65th Cong., 3rd sess., 1918–1919.

109. 56 Cong. Rec. 1441 (January 31, 1918).

110. Frederick, *Newton D. Baker*, 1:131; Robert Cuff, *The War Industries Board: Business-Government Relations during World War I* (Baltimore: Johns Hopkins University Press, 1973), 126; Craig, *Progressives at War*, 179–183.

111. Craig, *Progressives at War*.

112. *National Defense Act*, 45.

113. Newton Baker to Woodrow Wilson, November 3, 1917, NBP-LC.

114. "A Federal Land Tax," *The Public*, May 25, 1917, 499–500.

115. Woodrow Wilson to William McAdoo, May 6, 1917, box 522, WMP-LC.

116. T. W. Gregory to William McAdoo, March 1, 1917, box 175, WMP-LC; Brownlee, "Wilson's Reform of Economic Structure," 89.

117. Leffingworth to William McAdoo, March 18, 1918, box 199, WMP-LC.

118. *Joseph Fels Fund Bulletin* (August 1915).

119. Louis Post, "Living a Long Life Over Again," 321–330, box 4, LPP-LC.

120. Rodgers, *Atlantic Crossings* (Cambridge, Mass.: Belknap Press of Harvard University Press, 1998), 350.

121. "Lane and Mondell—Real Estate," *The Public*, August 2, 1919, 819–821.

122. Olson, *Franklin K. Lane*, 152; *New York Times*, August 4, 1919; National Catholic Welfare Conference, *Land Colonization: A General Review of the Problems and a Survey of Remedies* (Washington D.C.: National Catholic War Council, 1919).

123. Franklin K. Lane, "Work and Homes for Returning Soldiers, Sailors, and Marines," Report to the 65th Congress to accompany S. 5652, February 27, 1919.

124. Frederic C. Howe, *The Land and the Soldier* (New York: Charles Scribner's Sons, 1919), 90–92.

125. Howe, 190–192, 90.

126. John S. Codeman and James Heaton, "Secretary of Interior Lane's Plan of Land Reclamation," *The Public*, March 15, 1919, 262–264.

127. Glenn E. Plumb, "Plan of Organized Employees for Railroad Organization," *The Public*, April 26, 1919, 427–429.

128. Miller, *From Progressive to New Dealer*, 269; *New York Times*, September 7, 1919, and August 4, 1919; K. Austin Kerr, *American Railroad Politics, 1914–1920* (Pittsburgh: University of Pittsburgh Press, 1968), 166.

129. *New York Times*, April 19, 1920.

130. Matthew Woll, "American Labor Readjustment Proposals," and R. J. Coldman, "Collective Bargaining the Democracy of Industry," *Proceedings of the Academy of Political Science* 8, no. 4 (January 1920): 184–189, 213–217.

131. Bill G. Reid, "Agrarian Opposition to Franklin K. Lane's Proposal for Soldier Settlement, 1918–1921," *Agricultural History* 41, no. 2 (April 1967): 167–180.

132. Kerr, *American Railroad Politics*, 93–95.

133. Kerr, 114.

134. Kerr, 171–174.

135. Kerr, 28; Eric J. Moser, *Hinterland Dreams: The Political Economy of a Midwestern City* (Philadelphia: University of Pennsylvania Press, 2011), 77–105.

136. Kerr, *American Railroad Politics*, 124–126.

137. Kerr, 145–146; Homer Brews Vanderblue and Kenneth Farwell Burgess, *Railroads: Rates—Service—Management* (New York: Macmillan Company, 1923), 331–332; Fried, *Progressive Assault on Laissez-Faire*, 190–191, 196–198; Edgar Rich, "Transportation Act of 1920," *American Economic Review* 10 (September 1920): 507–527.

138. *New York Tribune*, April 21, 1919; Henry Guzda, "Labor Department's First Program to Assist Black Workers," *Monthly Labor Review* 105, no. 6 (June 1982): 39–44.

139. 55 Cong. Rec., 5481 (July 26, 1917).

140. Randolph Bourne, "Twilight of the Idols," in *The Radical Will: Selected Writings, 1911–1918* (New York: Urizen Books, 1977), 339.

141. Theodore Roosevelt, "Opposition Leaders in Wartime: The Case of Theodore Roosevelt and World War I," *Midwestern Quarterly* 9, no. 3 (Spring 1968): 225–242; Russell Buchanan, "Theodore Roosevelt and American Neutrality, 1914–1917," *American Historical Review* 43, no. 4 (July 1938): 775–790; Dalton, *Theodore Roosevelt*, 461, 484.

142. "Roosevelt Pledges All of His Aid to Wilson to Help Win War," *New York Times*, June 11, 1918, 5.

143. Newton Baker to Woodrow Wilson, September 6, 1917, reel 3, NBP-LC.

144. Newton Baker to John Sharp Williams, n.d., reel 3, NBP-LC.

145. Frederick, *Newton D. Baker*, 1:235–237; American Civil Liberties Bureau, *The Outrage on Hebert S. Bigelow of Cincinnati* (New York: National Civil Liberties Bureau, 1918). Upon Albert Nock's urging, Baker also argued for ending prosecution of the socialist journal *The Masses*. Albert Jay Nock to NB, May 28, 1918, reel 5, NBP-LC; Knock, *To End All Wars*, 227–246.

146. Miller, *From Progressive to New Dealer*, 292.

147. Louis Post, *The Deportations Delirium of Nineteen-Twenty* (Chicago: C. H. Kerr and Company, 1923); W. Anthony Gengarelly, "Secretary of Labor William B. Wilson and the Red Scare, 1990–1920," *Pennsylvania History* 47, no. 5 (October 1980), 325.

148. "Calls Post Factor in Revolution Plan," *New York Times*, June 2, 1920, 4.

149. "Small Nationalities," *The Public*, July 6, 1917, 644–645.

150. *New York Times*, October 29, 1917.

151. Similarly, Frederic C. Howe and Lincoln Steffens lobbied for independence for China and Mexico, respectively. Miller, *From Progressive to New Dealer*, 229; Lincoln Steffens to Allen Suggett, February 24, 1919, in *The Letters of Lincoln Steffens*, 1:422.

152. *The Public*, February 8, 1919, 123.

153. GC to the President, Robert Lansing, Newton Baker, and Josephus Daniels, n.d., box 1, GCP-LC.

154. Walton Bean, "George Creel and His Critics" (PhD diss.: University of California, Berkeley, 1941), 21–22.

155. George Creel, "Conference of the Press," box 5, GCP-LC.

156. Bean, "George Creel and His Critics," 200–201, 257; Greenberg, *Republic of Spin*, 95–100, 106.

157. Bean, "George Creel and His Critics," 132, 199; Greenberg, *Republic of Spin*, 111–112.

158. Eric Foner, *Give Me Liberty: An American History* (New York: W. W. Norton, 2017), 749; Foner, *The Story of American Freedom*, 169–170.

159. George Creel to Woodrow Wilson, September 25, 1918, and May 31, 1918, box 2, GCP-LC. Creel has been called "one of the movement's fiercest male gladiator's," though many single taxers played leading roles in the Men's League for women's suffrage, including Frederic C. Howe, Stephen Wise, Ben Lindsey, and George Peabody. Kroger, *Suffragents*, 25, 71, 206, 224, 242.

160. "Address of George Creel, Chairman of the Committee on Public Information, at the luncheon of the Chicago Association of Commerce, September 14, 1919, La Salle Hotel," box 5, GCP-LC; Bean, "George Creel and his Critics," 205, 248; George Creel, "Our Alien's, Were They Loyal or Disloyal?" *Everybody's Magazine* (March 1919): 71–72; George Creel to Woodrow Wilson, January 7, 1918, box 3, GCP-LC.

161. David F. Krugler, *1919: The Year of Racial Violence—How African-Americans Fought Back* (Cambridge: Cambridge University Press, 2014), 17, 275; Woodrow Wilson to George Creel, June 18, 1918; George Creel to Woodrow Wilson, June 18, 1918; George Creel to Woodrow Wilson, June 17, 1918; Woodrow Wilson to George Creel, July 21, 1918, all box 2, GCP-LC; George Creel, "Unite to Win," *The Independent*, April 6, 1918.

162. "Sections of New Jersey Democratic Platform Written by Creel at Wilson's request, 1918," box 1, GCP-LC.

163. Peter Novick, *That Noble Dream: The Objectivity Question and the American Historical Profession* (Cambridge: Cambridge University Press, 1988), 118–128.

164. Bean, "George Creel and His Critics," 31.

165. George Creel to Woodrow Wilson, February 19, 1918, box 3, GCP-LC.

166. "Report of the Committee on Public Information," 207–211, box 7, GCP-LC.

167. "Creel Comes back at Burnquist," oversized 8, GCP-LC; "Helping Brother Bates," oversized 6, GCP-LC; Lincoln Steffens to Laura Steffens, March 25, 1918, in, *Letters of Lincoln Steffens*, 1:425.

168. Untitled George Creel note, box 1, GCP-LC; "Hint Creel Inspired Fourteen Points," oversized 8, GCP-LC; Erez Manela, *The Wilsonian Moment: Self-Determination and the International Origins of Anticolonial Nationalism* (Oxford: Oxford University Press, 2007), 51.

169. Manela, *The Wilsonian Moment*, 103.

170. William Hobbs, "Wilson's Mental Dishonesty Seen," *Detroit Free Press*, oversized 2, GCP-LC.

171. Krugler, *1919*; Greenberg, *Republic of Spin*, 111–113.

172. Bean, "George Creel and His Critics," 200–201.

173. "Senators Attack Utility Seizures," p. 30, oversized 8, GCP-LC; 56 Cong. Rec., 5599 (April 25, 1918); Miller, *From Progressive to New Dealer*, 290.

174. "Accuse Wilson of Bad Faith in Cable Service," p. 33, oversized 8, GCP-LC.

175. "Speech—Woodrow Wilson Dinner, Los Angeles, December 28, 1935," box 5, GCP-LC.

176. Sun Yat-Sen, "International Development of China," *The Public*, December 6, 1919, 1134–1135.

177. "Speech—Woodrow Wilson Dinner, Los Angeles, December 28, 1935."

178. Manuel Carpio, "Much about Villa and Carranza, Little about the Mexican People," *The Public*, July 19, 1919, 766–768; Manuel Carpio, "Intervention: Mexican Side of It," *The Public*, August 23, 1919, 905–907.

179. "Purported Interview Creates a Sensation," *Atlanta Constitution*, October 23, 1919, 11; "Says Creel Advised the Mexican Senate," October 2, 1919, 141, oversized 8, GCP-LC.

180. "Says Creel Advised the Mexican Senate"; *New York Times*, November 15, 1919.

181. George Creel, "Woodrow Wilson's Last Years," *Saturday Evening Post*, January 10, 1931.

182. "Recognition of Mexico, Aim of Creel's Trip," *New-York Tribune*, October 16, 1920, 2; "Creel to Urge Recognition of Mexico by US," *San Francisco Chronicle*, October 16, 1920; "Says Creel Advised the Mexican Senate," 194–205; George Creel, "Scrambled Washington: Battle of the Bureaus," *Colliers*, June 11, 1921. Secretary of State Robert Lansing despised Creel and believed that he and Wilson shared some of his "socialistic tendencies." Robert Lansing, *War Memoirs* (New York: Bobbs-Merrill Company, 1935), 323.

183. Alexander Palmer to Woodrow Wilson, November 8, 1920, GCP-LC; "Creel Returning to Aid Mexicans," *New York Times*, October 16, 1920; "Says Creel Failed in Mexico 'Mission,'" *New York Times*, October 18, 1920, 1; "Mexico to Receive Recognition Soon," *New York Times*, October 20, 1920, 1; "Creel Made Denial in Mexico That He Had an Official Mission," *New-York Tribune*, October 18, 1920, 4; "Creel's Trip Cleared Up," *New York Times*, October 21, 1920, 11; "Says Creel Advised the Mexican Senate," 194–207.

184. "A Report to the Peoples of the World: Official Statement of President Obregon," June 26, 1921, box 8, GCP-LC.

185. "Embassy Uniformed of Obregon-Creel Relations," *New York Tribune*, August 14, 1921, 12; "American Aiding Obregon's Policy," *New York Herald*, July 7, 1921, 1; "U.S. Finds Creel in Note Writer for Obregon" and "Creel Is Personal Press Agent for General Obregon," oversize 9, GCP-LC.

186. "A Talk by Creel before the Wilmette Club of Chicago, February 20," box 5, GCP-LC.

187. "President Alvaro Obregon's Message to the American People," *Single Tax Review* (July–August 1921): 117–119.

Chapter 12 • *The Will to Believe*

1. Thorstein Veblen, *The Vested Interests and the Common Man* (New York: Viking Press, 1919), 172.

2. Rexford Tugwell, Thomas Murno, and Roy Stryker, *American Economic Life and the Means of Its Improvement* (1925; reprinted, New York: Harcourt, Brace and Company, 1930), 245.

3. Upton Sinclair, *The Book of Life: Mind and Body* (1921; reprinted, Long Beach, Calif.: privately printed, 1926), 1:188–191.

4. Robert S. Lynd and Helen Merrell Lynd, *Middletown: A Study in Contemporary American Culture* (New York: Harcourt: Brace and Company, 1929), 64–65, 106–107.

5. Lewis Mumford, "The Plan of New York," *New Republic*, June 15, 1932, 121–126, and June 22, 1932, 146–154.

6. Mabel Newcomer, "The Decline of the General Property Tax," *National Tax Journal* 6, no. 1 (March 1953): 46; Gail Radford, "New Building and Investment Patterns in 1920s Chicago," *Social Science History* 16, no. 1 (Spring 1992): 1–21; Leo Grebler, David M. Blank, and Louis Winnick, *Capital Trends in Real Estate: Trends and Prospects* (Princeton, N.J.: Princeton University Press, 1956).

7. Green, *Company Town*, 187–202.

8. *New York Times*, September 13, 1953.

9. Stoughton Cooley to James Barry, March 11, 1926, box 3, JBP-BL.

10. Committee of Manufactures and Merchants on Federal Taxation, *Sane Taxation* (Chicago, 1920).

11. 59 Cong. Rec., 8241–8243 (1920).

12. Haig, *Exemption of Improvements from Taxation in Canada and the United States*, 265, 268, 279.

13. Robert Murray Haig, *Taxation in the Urban Municipalities of Saskatchewan: A Report to the Government of the Province of Saskatchewan* (Regina, Saskatchewan: Regina King's Printer, 1917), 10.

14. Haig, *Taxation in the Urban Municipalities of Saskatchewan*, 28–31.

15. Haig, 41. Edwin R. A. Seligman similarly insisted that ability to pay meant that even the poor should have to contribute as much as they could. Seligman, *The Shifting and Incidence of Taxation* (London: MacMillan Company, 1899), 313.

16. "Report of the Municipal Taxation Committee, 1933," pp. 14, 80, GR802, British Columbia Archives, Victoria.

17. T. Bradshaw, "Survey of Financial Condition: Conducted at the Request of the City Council" (1935), pp. 6, 15, City of Vancouver Archives, Vancouver, British Columbia.

18. "Vancouver City Council Minutes," April 16, 1934, April 15, 1935, and June 5, 1935; "Comparative Statements," 112-B-1, all City of Vancouver Archives.

19. "Taxation and Financial Survey of the City of Vancouver" (1935), p. 6, City of Vancouver Archives.

20. Mark R. Bittner, *Over-All Tax Limitation for Real Estate in Pennsylvania* (Allentown, Pa.: Allentown Real Estate Board, 1936), 4.

21. William Anderson, "Are Our Taxes Too High?" *Better Roads* (June 1932).

22. Christopher England, "Land Value Taxation in Vancouver: Rent Seeking and the Tax Revolt," *American Journal of Economics and Sociology* 77, no. 1 (January 2018): 59–94.

23. Don Paarlberg. "Farm Real Estate Prices," *Journal of ASFMRA* 14, no. 2 (1950): 103–106; Ronald E. Seavoy, *An Economic History of the United States: From 1607 to the Present* (New York: Routledge 2006), 277.

24. John Dewey, *The Public and Its Problems: An Essay in Political Inquiry* (1927; reprinted, Chicago: Gateway Books, 1954), 129–130.

25. Franklin Roosevelt, "The Excessive Cost of Local Government—Address before Roundtable, University of Virginia, July 6, 1931," box 283, RMP-FRPL. This argument was echoed by memos written by Louis Faulkner and A. A. Berle Jr. "Memorandum of May 18, 1932," box 282, RMP-FRPL.

26. Levy, *Ages of American Capitalism*, 391–543.

27. Lincoln Steffens to Brand Whitlock, January 28, 1925, box 14, LSP-CU.

28. Lincoln Steffens to Daniel Kiefer, June 21, 1920, box 13, LSP-CU.

29. Lincoln Steffens to Frederic C. Howe, September 15, 1934, box 13, LSP-CU.

30. Darrow, *Story of My Life*, 52.

31. Albert Jay Nock, "The Jewish Problem in America," *Atlantic Monthly* (July 1941); Newton Baker to Theodore Roosevelt Jr., January 14, 1937, box 202, NBP-LC; "July 25, 1918," diaries, box 4, BWP-LC.

32. Clarence Darrow, "Shall We Abolish Capital Punishment?" box 14, Clarence Darrow Papers, Library of Congress, Washington, D.C.

33. Crunden, *Hero in Spite of Himself*, 390.

34. Albert Jay Nock, *Henry George: An Essay* (New York: William Morrow & Company, 1939).

35. Marjorie Hornbein, "The Story of Ben Lindsey," *Southern California Quarterly* 55, no. 4. (December 1973): 473.

36. David Max Chalmers, *Hooded Americanism: The History of the Ku Klux Klan* (Durham, N.C.: Duke University Press, 1981), 129–134; Ben B. Lindsey, "My Fight with the Klan," *Survey* 54 (June 1, 1925): 274.

37. "In Defense of Lindsey," *K. C. Star*, undated clipping, oversized 10; "Strategy Won for G. O. P. Says Creel; Demos Must Pit West vs. East, He Avers," undated clipping, oversized 9; "Creel Defends Ben Lindsey," oversized 10, all GCP-LC.

38. Katherine Benton-Cohen, *Inventing the Immigration Problem: The Dillingham Commission and Its Legacy* (Cambridge, Mass.: Harvard University Press, 2018).

39. Miller, *From Progressive to New Dealer*, 400.

40. Miller, *From Progressive to New Dealer*, 294.

41. Miller, *From Progressive to New Dealer*, 334–361.

42. Diary, box 10, LPP-LC.

43. David Williams, "The Bureau of Investigation and Its Critics, 1919–1921: The Origins of Federal Political Surveillance," *Journal of American History* 68, no. 3 (December 1981): 570.

44. Post, "Living a Long Life Over Again," p. 351, box 2, LPP-LC.

45. Bobbs Merrill Company to Alice Thatcher Post, May 31, 1935, box 10, LPP-LC.

46. Diary, p. 20, box 10, LPP-LC.

47. Post, *Deportations Delirium of Nineteen-Twenty*, 326.

48. Louis Post, *New Church Messenger*, January 11, 1928, container 6, LPP-LC.

49. Brandeis foreword, in Post, "Living a Long Life Over Again," p. iii, container 4, LPP-LC.

50. E. W. Morehouse, "The *O'Fallon* Opinions of the Supreme Court," *Journal of Land and Public Utility Economics* 5, no. 3 (August 1929): 329–334.

51. Fried, *Progressive Assault on Laissez Faire*, 187.

52. Foner, *Story of American* Freedom, 165.

53. Williams, "The Bureau of Investigation and Its Critics," 567.

54. Shawn M. Lynch, "'Red Riots' and the Origins of the Civil Liberties Union of Massachusetts, 1915–1930," *Historical Journal of Massachusetts* 38, no. 1 (Spring 2010): 76–78.

55. William Allen White, "The Red Scare is Un-American," *Emporia Gazette,* January 8, 1920.

56. Emma Goldman, *Living My Life* (1931; reprinted, New York: Cosmo Classics, 2011), 588–589.

57. Goldman, 452.

58. Margaret Sanger, *An Autobiography* (1938; reprinted, Elmsford, N.Y., Maxwell Reprint, 1970), 225, 229–234.

59. Weinrib, *The Taming of Free Speech*, 5, 47–52, 59, 96.

60. Goldman, *Living My Life*, 442.

61. William Marion Reedy, "The Daughter of the Dream," *St. Louis Mirror,* November 5, 1908.

62. Goldman, *Living My Life*, 462.

63. *St. Louis Mirror*, August 17, 1917; Robert Cottrell, *Roger Nash Baldwin and the American Civil Liberties Union* (New York: Columbia University Press, 2001), 30–32.

64. Laura M. Weinrib, "From Public Interest to Private Rights: Free Speech, Liberal Individualism, and the Making of Modern Tort Law," *Law and Social Inquiry* 34, no. 1 (Winter 2009): 187–223; Foner, *Story of American Freedom*, 163–184.

65. Greenberg, *Republic of Spin*, 138–144.

66. Walter Lippmann, *Public Opinion* (New York: Harcourt, Brace and Company, 1922), 369–410.

67. John Dewey, *The Public and Its Problems* (1927; reprinted, Athens, Ohio: Swallow Press, 2016), 71.

68. Dewey, 172.

69. Dewy, 223.

70. Dewey, 224.

71. Dewey, 27, 61, 144; George, *Progress and Poverty*, 236–241.

72. Dewey, *Public and Its Problems*, 20, 233.

73. Dewey, 232.

74. John Dewey, "Politics and Culture" (1932), in *John Dewey: The Later Works, 1925–1953*, vol. 6, ed. Jo Ann Boydston (Carbondale: Southern Illinois University Press, 1985), 45, 47.

75. John Dewey, *Art as Experience* (1934; New York: Perigee Books, 1980), 344.

76. John Dewey, *Liberalism and Social Action* (New York: G. P. Putnam, 1935), 67–68; John Dewey, "Socialization of Ground Rent," in *John Dewey: The Later Works, 1925–1953*, vol. 11, ed. Jo Ann Boydston (Carbondale: Southern Illinois University Press, 1987), 256–257.

77. Dewey, *Significant Paragraphs from Henry George's* Progress and Poverty, 2–3.

78. Robert B. Westbrook, *John Dewey and American Democracy* (Ithaca, N.Y.: Cornell University Press, 1991).

79. Ebenezer Howard, *Garden Cities of Tomorrow* (London: Swan Sonnenschein & Co., Ltd., 1902), 123.

80. Buder, *Visionaries and Planners*.

81. Carl Sussman, *Planning the Fourth Migration: The Neglected Vision of the Regional Planning Association of America* (Cambridge, Mass.: MIT Press, 1976), 10; Edward K. Spann, *Designing Modern America: The Regional Planning Association of America and Its Members* (Columbus: Ohio State University Press, 1996), 7.

82. Benton MacKaye, *Employment and Natural Resources: Possibilities of Making New Opportunities for Employment through the Settlement and Development of Agricultural and Forest Lands and Other Resources* (Washington, D.C.: Government Printing Office, 1919); Roy Lubove, *The Urban Community: Housing and Planning in the Progressive Era* (Westport, Conn.: Greenwood Press, 1967); Spann, *Designing Modern America*, 24–25.

83. *Second Annual Single Tax Conference, Held at Chicago, Nov. 24, 25, 26, 1911* (Cincinnati: Fels Fund Commission, 1912), 9.

84. Spencer Miller to George Peabody, April 14, 1933, box 42, George Peabody Papers, Library of Congress, Washington, D.C.

85. Stuart Chase, "Portrait of a Radical," *Century Magazine* (July 1924): 295–304.

86. Spann, *Designing Modern America*, 71.

87. Lewis Mumford, "Abandoned Roads," *Freeman*, April 12, 1922, 101–102.

88. Frederick L. Ackerman, "Our Stake in Congestion," *Survey Geographic* (May 1925): 141–142.

89. Newton Baker to Mrs. Fels, October 7, 1932, box 95, NBP-LC.

90. Quoted in Spann, *Designing Modern America*, 151.

91. Frederic A. Delano, "Zoning Laws and Their Relation to Taxation," *Annals of the American Academy of Political and Social Science* 155, no. 2 (May 1931): 40–42.

92. Buder, *Visionaries and Planners*, 177; Rexford Tugwell, "The Meaning of the Greenbelt Towns," *New Republic*, February 17, 1937.

93. Sussman, *Planning the Fourth Migration*, 13.

94. Spann, *Designing Modern America*, 127–128.

95. Jane Jacobs, *The Death and Life of Great American Cities* (New York: Random House, 1961).

96. George, *Social Problems*, 320.

97. Mitgang, *Man Who Rode the Tiger*, 31.

98. Mitgang, 110–111, 139–141.

99. Mitgang, 176.

100. Robert A. Caro, *Power Broker: Robert Moses and the Fall of New York* (New York: Alfred A. Knopf, 1974), 352.

101. Mitgang, *Man Who Rode the Tiger*, 342.

102. Cramer, *Newton D. Baker*, 199.

103. Walter Jackson, *Gunnar Myrdal and America's Conscience* (Chapel Hill: University of North Carolina Press, 1990), 16–22.

104. Cramer, *Newton D. Baker*, 209.

105. Cramer, 218, 219–220.

106. Douglas B. Craig, *Fireside Politics: Radio and Political Culture in the United States, 1920–1940* (Baltimore: Johns Hopkins University Press, 2000), 172–173.

107. "Puts Baker in the Race," *New York Times*, January 13, 1932, 4; Cramer, *Newton D. Baker*, 236.

108. Cramer, *Newton D. Baker*, 236, 238.

109. Newton Baker to Mary Fels, March 17, 1934, box 95, NBP-LC.

110. Newton Baker to Mary Fels, April 13, 1934, Box 95, NBP-LC.

111. Newton Baker to Mary Fels, April 13, 1934; Newton Baker to Mayo Fesler, September 26, 1930, both box 95, NBP-LC. See also Newton Baker to Mr. Broda, October 23, 1930, box 144; Newton Baker to Jerome Levy, October 13, 1933, box 144; Newton Baker to Stewart McDonald, May 2, 1935, box 153; Newton Baker to James W. Mellen, June 14, 1938, box 157, all NBP-LC.

112. Will Atkinson to James Barry, April 2, 1925, box 1, JBP-BL.

113. Newton Baker to Will Atkinson, June 26, 1925, box 32, NBP-LC.

114. Newton Baker to Mary Fels, October 7, 1932; Mary Fels to Newton Baker, September 25, 1932, both box 95, NBP-LC.

115. Newton Baker to Antenor Sala, April 16, 1932; Antenor Sala to Newton Baker, April 28, 1932; Newton Baker to Antenor Sala, February 16, 1932; Antenor Sala to Newton Baker, undated 1927, all box 202, NBP-LC.

116. Mary Fels to Newton Baker, July 30, 1931, box 95, NBP-LC.

117. George Creel, "Newton D. Baker's Measure," *Colliers*, March 19, 1932.

118. Mitgang, *Man Who Rode the Tiger*, 263–273.

119. Mitgang, 274.

120. George Peabody to Newton Baker, April 11, 1931; Newton Baker to George Peabody, October 17, 1931; George Peabody to Newton Baker, October 7, 1931; Newton Baker to George Peabody, March 17, 1936; George Peabody to Charles O'Connor Hennessey, December 22, 1931, all box 186, NBP-LC; Ellsworth Barnard, *Wendell Willkie: Fighter for Freedom* (Marquette: Northern Michigan University Press, 1966), 63; David Levering Lewis, *The Improbable Wendell Willkie* (New York: Liveright, 2018).

121. Mitgang, *Man Who Rode the Tiger*, 276.

122. Cramer, *Newton D. Baker*, 252.

123. Cramer, 253; Rexford G. Tugwell, *The Democratic Roosevelt* (Garden City, N.Y.: Doubleday, 1957), 226.

124. George Peabody to FDR, June 20, 1931, container 63, PG-FRPL; George Creel to FDR, July 7, 1932, 2340–2371, PPF-FRPL.

125. Newton Baker to Raymond Moley, October 28, 1929, box 158, NBP-LC.

Chapter 13 • Back to the Land

1. Franklin Roosevelt, "Governor Franklin D. Roosevelt's Address to State Forestry Association, 17th Annual Meeting, Albany, NY," in *Franklin D. Roosevelt and Conservation, 1911–1945*, ed. Edgar B. Nixon (Hyde Park, N.Y.: General Services Administration, 1957), 1:69–70; John F. Sears and John E. Auwaerter, *FDR and the Land* (Boston: Olmstead Center for Landscape Preservation, National Park Service, 2011); Tugwell, *The Democratic Roosevelt*, 85–87; "Democrats in Cayuga Fight Hearst Boom," *New York Times*, August 9, 1906, 3; "Single Tax League Formed," *New York Times*, July 5, 1913, 10; William [illegible] to Frank Walsh, April 21, 1916, box 34, FWP-LC.

2. Olson, *Biography of a Progressive*, 174; Franklin Roosevelt to George Peabody, December 31, 1913, box 69, G. Peabody P-LC.

3. Mitgang, *The Man Who Rode the Tiger*, 113–114.

4. "Report of the Committee of Conservation of Forest and Wild Life of the Campfire Club of America," January 14, 1913, box 217; "Conservationism Redefined: Address by Rexford Tugwell before the Fiftieth Anniversary of the Founding of New York's Forest Reserve," box 56, both RTP-FRPL; A. S. Houghton to Daniel Beard, January 12, 1912, box 62; William E. Coffin to Daniel Beard, August 15, 1911, box 33, both DBP-LC.

5. Dan Beard to Franklin Roosevelt, October 21, 1938, box 105, DBP-LC; Franklin Roosevelt to Daniel Beard, January 19, 1939, 1093–1124, PPF-FRPL; A. S. Houghton to Franklin Roosevelt, February 14, 1912, container 7, PNSS-FRPL; Cyril Clemens, "My Visit with Franklin D. Roosevelt," *Mark Twain Quarterly* 8, no. 3 (Winter–Spring 1949): 11–12.

6. Hellman, *Henry George Reconsidered*, 170.

7. Franklin Roosevelt, "The Excessive Cost of Local Government—Address before Roundtable, University of Virginia, July 6, 1931," box 283, RMP-HL.

8. Raymond Moley, *After Seven Years* (New York: Harper & Brothers Publishers, 1939), 12.

9. Moley, *Realities and Illusions*, 17.

10. Moley, *Realities and Illusions*, 173–175; Newton Baker to Charles Maphis, April 12, 1929, box 3, RMP-HL.

11. Moley, *After Seven Years*, 4.

12. Pilon, *The Monopolists*, 72.

13. Rexford Tugwell, *In Search of Roosevelt* (Cambridge, Mass.: Harvard University Press 1972), 69. Tugwell also argued that land values were socially created. Rexford Tugwell, Thomas Murno, and Roy Stryker, *American Economic Life and the Means of Its Improvement* (New York: Harcourt, Brace and Company, 1924), 428.

14. Rexford Tugwell, *To the Lesser Heights of Morningside: A Memoir* (Philadelphia: University of Pennsylvania Press, 1982), 25–32; Rexford Tugwell, *The Brains Trust* (New York: Viking Press, 1968), 37.

15. Tugwell, *In Search of Roosevelt*, 75, 91; "The Progressive Tradition: Address by Rexford Tugwell at Union College, Schenectady NY, Januáry 2," box 56, RTP-FRPL.

16. John Collier, "The Experiment in Milwaukee: What Socialism Has Accomplished and Where It Has Failed after a Year's Trial in Wisconsin's Chief City," *Harper's Weekly*, April 12, 1911, 11.

17. Tugwell, *In Search of Roosevelt*, 75, 91; "The Progressive Tradition: Address by Rexford Tugwell at Union College."

18. Raymond Moley, "The Men behind the New Deal," April 23, 1934, box 236, RMP-HL.

19. Raymond Moley, *27 Masters of Politics* (New York: Funk and Wagnalls Company, 1949), 7; Raymond Moley, *The American Century of John C. Lincoln* (New York: Duell, Sloan, and Pearce, 1962), 160.

20. Franklin D. Roosevelt, *Looking Forward* (New York: John Day Company, 1933), 219.

21. Roosevelt, *Looking Forward*, 109–124; Franklin Roosevelt, "The 'Forgotten Man' Speech," in *The Public Papers and Addresses of Franklin Roosevelt*, ed. Samuel Rosenman (New York: Random House, 1938), 2:625; Moley, *After Seven Years*, 173–175.

22. Gail Radford, "From Municipal Socialism to Public Authorities: Institutional Factors in the Shaping of American Public Enterprise," *Journal of American History* 90, no. 3 (December 2003): 886.

23. George Norris to Basil Manly, September 1, 1932, box 36, FWP-LC; Miller, *From Progressive to New Dealer*, 377–380.

24. "Judson King to Members of the Popular Government League," September 23, 1932, box 36, FWP-LC.

25. George Peabody to FDR, July 8, 1931; FDR to George Peabody, July 13, 1931, both container 63, PG-FRPL.

26. Preston J. Hubbard, *Origins of the TVA: The Muscles Shoals Controversy* (Nashville: Vanderbilt University Press, 1961), 1–27; *An Article by Hon. George W. Norris Printed in Congressional Record Dec. 19, 1927* (Washington, D.C.: Government Printing Office, 1927), 5–6.

27. Richard Lowitt, *George Norris: The Persistence of a Progressive* (Urbana: University of Illinois Press, 1971), 197–204.

28. Hubbard, *Origins of the TVA*, 64, 114.

29. Newton Baker to W. I. Drummond, March 29, 1924; Newton Baker to W. I. Drummond, March 17, 1924, both box 160, NBP-LC.

30. 63 Cong. Rec., 5176 (March 2, 1923); Newton Baker to Charles Mooney, December 7, 1923, box 157; Newton Baker to Ernest Greenwood, April 3, 1924, box 160, both NBP-LC.

31. "House Votes Favor Ford Shoals Bid," *New York Times*, March 8, 1924, 18.

32. 65 Cong. Rec., 3911 (March 10, 1924).

33. Judson King, *Twenty Years of It* (Washington, D.C.: National Popular Government League, 1933).

34. McRoy, *Report of the Joseph Fels Fund and Single Tax Conference at Washington, D.C., January 15th, 16th, 17th, 1914*, 15; Charles Dana Miller, "A Remembrance of Louis Post," *Land and Freedom* (January–February 1928).

35. Judson King, *The Hydroelectric War Goes On: Battle of the Underwood Bill* (Washington, D.C.: Popular Government League, 1924).

36. "The Ethics of Public Utility Valuation, for Release to the Morning Papers, Monday, January 7, 1929, by Judson King," box 69; "The Why and How of the REA:

Address before the Annual Meeting of the New Hampshire Electric Cooperative at Concord, New Hampshire, March 4, 1941, by Judson King, Special Consultant to the Rural Electrification Administration," pp. 4–5, box 719, both G. Pinchot P-LC.

37. Alfred Lief, *Democracy's Norris: The Biography of a Lonely Crusade* (New York: Octagon Books, 1977).

38. Lowitt, *George Norris*, 96–97.

39. Judson King to Frank Walsh, July 2, 1930, box 17, FWP-LC.

40. 71 Cong. Rec. 8190 (May 2, 1930).

41. Hubbard, *Origins of the TVA*, 145.

42. Newton Baker to George Norris, February 27, 1925; George Norris to Newton Baker, February 21, 1925, both box 177, NBP-LC.

43. 65 Cong. Rec. 767–769 (December 18, 1924); 69 Cong. Rec. 4407 (March 9, 1928); 66 Cong. Rec. 1506 (January 9, 1925); 65 Cong. Rec. 704 (December 17, 1924); 69 Cong. Rec. 3011–3018 (February 15, 1928); 69 Cong. Rec. 3759 (February 29, 1928).

44. 66 Cong. Rec. 1506 (January 9, 1925).

45. Newton Baker to George Norris, February 27, 1925; George Norris to Newton Baker, February 21, 1925, both box 177, NBP-LC; Judson King to Frank Walsh, July 20, 1929, box 16, FWP-LC; 65 Cong. Rec. 704 (December 17, 1924).

46. Jean Christine, "Giant Power: A Progressive Proposal of the 1920s," *Pennsylvania Magazine of History and Biography* 96, no. 4 (October 1972): 480–507.

47. Frank Walsh to Judson King, July 12, 1929, box 16, FWP-LC.

48. Daniel R. Fusfeld, *The Economic Thought of Franklin D. Roosevelt and the Origins of the New Deal* (New York: AMS Press, 1956), 148.

49. Tugwell acknowledged that "there had been hints of it in earlier works," likely a reference to George. In *American Economic Life*, Tugwell had quoted Hobson's theory of demand and juxtaposed it with George's dilemma of "progress and poverty." In his 1934 book, *Our Economic Society and Its Problems*, he dedicated two pages to an extended quote of *Progress and Poverty* in which he demonstrated that "production alone cannot raise levels of living," because the proceeds of progress accrued to a small elite. Tugwell, *The Brains Trust*, 43; Rexford Tugwell and Howard C. Hill, *Our Economic Society and Its Problems* (New York: Harcourt, Brace and Company, 1934), 246–248; Tugwell, Murno, and Stryker, *American Economic Life and the Means of Its Improvement*, 245.

50. Tugwell, *Democratic Roosevelt*, 234; Tugwell, Murno, and Stryker, *American Economic Life and the Means of its Improvement*, 706.

51. David Ekbladh, "'Mr. TVA': Grassroots Development, David Lilienthal, and the Rise and Fall of the Tennessee Valley Authority as a Symbol for U.S. Oversees Development," *Diplomatic History* 26, no. 3 (Summer 2002), 335.

52. Ekbladh, "'Mr. TVA,'" 363.

53. "The Why and How of the REA," 4–5.

54. Eugene Staley, *World Economic Development: Effects on Advanced Industrial Countries* (Montreal: International Labor Office, 1944), 5; David Ekbladh, "Meeting the Challenge from Totalitarianism: The Tennessee Valley Authority as a Global Model for Liberal Development, 1933–1945," *International History Review* 32, no. 1 (March 2010): 47–67.

55. Eugene Stanley, *History of the Illinois State Federation of Labor* (Chicago: University of Chicago Press, 1930), 23.

56. Spann, *Designing Modern America*, 146–147.

57. Spann, *Designing Modern America*, 157–159.

58. Albert Mayer, Henry Wright, and Lewis Mumford, "New Homes for a New Deal," *New Republic* 78, no. 1005 (March 7, 1934): 91–94.

59. Peter L. Laurence, *Becoming Jane Jacobs* (Philadelphia: University of Pennsylvania Press, 2016), 44–46.

60. Sarah Philips, *This Land, This Nation: Conservation, Rural America, and the New Deal* (New York: Cambridge University Press, 2007).

61. Harold Ickes to Harry Hopkins, November 22, 1934; Harry Hopkins to Harold Ickes, December 17, 1934, both box 364, Harold Ickes Papers, Manuscript Division, Library of Congress, Washington, D.C.; Frederic Delano to Franklin Roosevelt, June 26, 1934, 1091–1092, POF-FRPL.

62. Moley, *27 Masters of Politics*, 7.

63. Rexford Tugwell, *Letter from the Administrators of the Resettlement Administration* (Washington, D.C.: Government Printing Office, 1936), 20.

64. Tugwell, *Democratic Roosevelt*, 473.

65. Newton Baker to Raymond Moley, September 20, 1932, box 3, RMP-HL.

66. Frederic Howe to FDR, June 29, 1936, 3677–3713, PPP-FRPL.

67. London, "Indebted to Growth," 119–121, 134–135, 138–146.

68. George Peabody to William McAdoo, April 20, 1935; George Peabody to FDR, April 20, 1935, both box 660, PPF-FRPL; "Farm Tenancy—The Remedy: 20 Questions Asked & Answered," box 186, NBP-LC.

69. Benjamin Marsh to Jackson Gardner, April 20, 1935; "Jackson Gardner to the Senate Committee on Agriculture, May 1, 1935," both box 9, Jackson Gardner Papers, Franklin D. Roosevelt Presidential Library, Hyde Park, N.Y.

70. House Committee on Rivers and Harbors, *Regional Conservation and the Development of National Resources*, 75th Cong., 2nd sess. (1937), 481–484, 466, 781–785, 826, 827.

71. Upton Sinclair, *I Candidate for Governor and How I Got Licked* (Berkeley: University of California Press, 1934), 230.

72. "Radio Speech of George Creel over State-wide Hook up from Los Angeles, Friday Evening, July 13 at 7:30 o clock," box 5, GCP-LC.

73. George Creel, "Plan or Perish," *Colliers*, December 15, 1934.

74. Untitled clipping, 1934, box 5, GCP-LC.

75. "Speech of George Creel at Visalia," August 22, 1935, box 5, GCP-LC.

76. "Sinclair Modifies Some of His Plans," n.d., box 13, GCP-LC.

77. Kenneth T. Jackson, *Crabgrass Frontier: The Suburbanization of the United States* (Oxford: Oxford University Press, 1985), 190–218; London, "Indebted to Growth," 149–150.

78. Amy C. Offner, "Homeownership and Social Welfare in the Americas: Ciudad Kennedy as a Midcentury Crossroads," in *Making Cities Global: The Transnational Turn in Urban History*, ed. A. K. Sandoval-Strausz and Nancy H. Kwak (Philadelphia: University of Pennsylvania Press, 2018), 60–61.

79. Thomas Jefferson, *Notes on the State of Virginia* (1785; reprinted, Boston: Lilly and Wait, 1832), 172.

80. Lizabeth Cohen, *A Consumers' Republic: The Politics of Mass Production in Postwar America* (New York: Vintage Books, 2004); Lisa McGirr, *Suburban Warriors:*

The Origins of the New American Right (Princeton, N.J.: Princeton University Press, 2015); Levy, *Ages of American Capitalism*, 488–543.

81. George, *Progress and Poverty*, 351.

82. George, 294. See also Frederic C. Howe's critique of the homesteading tradition, in *The Land and the Soldier*, 159–162.

83. George, *Science of Political Economy*, 256.

84. Rexford Tugwell, *Industrial Discipline and the Governmental Arts* (1933; reprinted, New York: Arno Press, 1977), 64, 178; Tugwell, *To the Lesser Heights of Morningside*, 25–32; Tugwell, *Brains Trust*, 37.

85. David Kennedy, *Freedom from Fear: The American People in the Great Depression* (Oxford: Oxford University Press, 1999), 120; Charles Van Hise, *Concentration and Control: A Solution of the Trust Problem in the United States* (New York: MacMillian Company, 1912).

86. Levy, *Ages of American Capitalism*, 411.

87. Tugwell, *To the Lesser Heights of Morningside*, 25–32; Tugwell, *Brains Trust*, 37; Tugwell, *Industrial Discipline and the Governmental Arts*, 141–142.

88. Record, *How to Abolish Poverty*, 14–15.

89. Record, 18, 48.

90. Newton Baker to Henry Bates, July 5, 1934; Newton Baker to Henry Bates, June 22, 1934, both box 157, NBP-LC.

91. Newton Baker to E. A. Filene, May 22, 1934, box 95, NBP-LC.

92. Rexford Tugwell, *Roosevelt's Revolution: The First Year—A Personal Experience* (New York: Macmillan, 1977), 122.

93. Miller, *From Progressive to New Dealer*, 382–383.

94. Miller, 413.

95. Miller, 388.

96. Miller, 422.

97. Frederic C. Howe to LS, July 1938, box 6, LSP-LC.

98. Michael Vincent Namorato, ed., *The Diary of Rexford G. Tugwell* (New York: Greenwood Press, 1992), 204.

99. George Peabody to FDR April 3, 1933; George Peabody to FDR, February 20, 1934, both box 660, PPF-FRPL; *Saratogian* (N.Y.), July 18, 1936.

100. George Peabody to J. H. Dillard, March 5, 1934, George Peabody to FDR, February 12, 1934, both box 660, PPF-FRPL.

101. George Peabody to Eastman, June 27, 1934, box 660, PPF-FRPL.

102. George Peabody to FDR July 27, 1936, box 660, PPF-FRPL.

103. "Creel Names Committee to Aid Code Worker," *San Francisco Chronicle*, oversized 10, GCP-LC.

104. George Creel to Daniel Roper, September 5, 1933, box 4, GCP-LC.

105. George Creel to Roosevelt, September 23, 1933, box 4, GCP-LC.

106. "Businessmen, Labor Fight to Keep Creel," undated clipping, oversized 10; "Creel Won't Change Mind," undated clipping, oversized 11; "NRA Accept Resignation from Creel," undated clipping, oversized 11, all GCP-LC.

107. "Creel Decides to Keep Post as NRA Administrator," *San Francisco Chronicle*, October 12, 1933.

108. "Creel Takes Up Peach Row," undated clipping, oversized 10, GCP-LC.

109. Arthur Caylor, "Little NRA," undated clipping, oversized 10, GCP-LC.

110. "Speech at the Conference on Government, International House, Berkeley, March 28, 1934," box 5, GCP-LC.

111. "Speech at Trent Club, New York, February 11, 1936," box 5, GCP-LC.

112. Tierney, *Darrow*, 432.

113. "Special and Supplementary Report to the President by Clarence Darrow and William Thompson of the National Recovery Review Board," box 22, POF-FRPL 466.

114. Mordecai Lee, *The Philosopher-Lobbyist: John Dewey and the People's Lobby, 1928–1940* (Albany: State University of New York Press, 2015), 116, 126; "Inquiry into the NRA Sought in the House," *New York Times*, May 23, 1934, 5; Benjamin Marsh to FDR, May 21, 1934, box 22, POF-FRPL 466.

115. Barbara J. Alexander, "Failed Cooperation in Heterogeneous Industries under the National Recovery Administration," *Journal of Economic History* 57, no. 2 (June 1997): 322–344; Leverett S. Lyon, Paul T. Homan, Lewis L. Lorwin, George Terborgh, Charles L. Dearing, and Leon C. Marshall, *The National Recovery Administration: An Analysis and Appraisal Washington* (Washington D.C.: Brookings Institution, 1935), 871–885.

116. Alan Brinkley, *The End of Reform: New Deal Liberalism in Recession and War* (New York: Vintage Books, 1995), 175–200. For discussion of the limits of "control" in post-Depression liberalism, see Levy, *Ages of American Capitalism*, 399–543.

117. For more on the decline of expert governance after the New Deal, see Reuell Shiller, "Regulation and the Collapse of the New World Order, or, How I Learned to Stop Worrying and Love the Market," and Paul Sabin, "Environmental Law and the End of the New Deal Order," in *Beyond the New Deal Order: U.S. Politics from the Great Depression to the Great Recession*, ed. Gary Gerstle, Nelson Lichtenstein, and Alice O'Connor (Philadelphia: University of Pennsylvania Press, 2019), 168–203.

118. Albert Jay Nock, *Memoirs of a Superfluous Man* (New York: Ludwig Van Mises Institute, 2007), 63, 85.

119. Albert Jay Nock, "Current Comment," *The Freeman*, May 17, 1922, 217.

120. "The Failure of a Theory," *The Freeman*, October 25, 1922, 150.

121. Albert Jay Nock, "In the Vein of Intimacy," *The Freeman*, March 31, 1920, 52.

122. "Miscellany," *The Freeman*, September 26, 1923, 56.

123. "Current Comment," *The Freeman*, April 28, 1920, 147.

124. Jennifer Burns, *Goddess of the Market: Ayn Rand and the American Right* (Oxford: Oxford University Press, 2009), 48; H. L. Mencken, *The Letters of H. L. Mencken*, ed. Guy Forgue (New York: Alfred A. Knopf, 1961), xiii, 189; Albert Jay Nock and Frank Garrison, *The Letters of Albert Jay Nock, 1924–1945* (Caldwell, Idaho: Caxton, 1949), 40.

125. Diary, January 19, 1934, box 7, BWP-LC.

126. Albert Jay Nock, *Henry George: An Essay* (New York: William Morrow & Company, 1939), 203.

127. Nock, *Henry George*, 221–222.

128. Nock, *Our Enemy the State*, 36.

129. Nock, *Our Enemy the State*, 199

130. Nock, 195–196, 203.

131. Nock, 2.

132. Albert Jay Nock, "Officialism and Lawlessness," *Harpers* (January 1929): 11.

133. George Nash, *The Conservative Intellectual Movement in America* (1976; reprinted, Willington, Del.: ISI Books, 2006); Charles Nitsche, "Albert Jay Nock and Frank Chodorov: Case Studies in Recent American Individualist and Anti-statist Thought" (PhD diss., University of Maryland, 1981).

134. Nitsche, "Albert Jay Nock and Frank Chodorov"; Matt Zwolinski, "On Safety Nets, Political Authority, and Henry George: A Reply to Huemer," *Cato Unbound*, posted April 14, 2014, http://www.cato-unbound.org/2014/08/14/matt-zwolinski /safety-nets-political-authority-henry-george-reply-huemer; Stephen Moore, "How to Fight the Greed-and-Envy Lobby," *Cato Unbound*, posted August 12, 1999, http://www .cato.org/publications/commentary/how-fight-greedenvy-lobby; David S. D'Amato, "The Singular Henry George: Insights and Influence," *Libertarianism*, October 22, 2014, http://www.libertarianism.org/columns/singular-henry-george-insights-influence.

135. "In Depth with William Buckley," *C-Span Book Notes*, April 2, 2000.

136. Gilles Campagnolo, *Criticisms of Classical Political Economy: Menger, Austrian Economics, and the German Historical School* (London: Routledge, 2010), 267–279.

137. Sandye Gloria-Palmero, *The Evolution of Austrian Economics: From Menger to Lachman* (London: Routledge, 1999), 11–39, 90; David Young, "Austrian Views on Monopoly: Insights and Problems," *Review of Political Economy* 4, no. 2 (1992): 203–225.

138. Murray Rothbard, *Economic Controversies* (Auburn, Ala.: Ludwig Van Mises Institute, 2011), 575–586.

139. Rosanne Currarino, *The Labor Question in America* (Urbana: University of Illinois Press, 2011).

140. Cohen, *Making a New Deal*; Ellis Hawley, *The New Deal and the Problem of Monopoly: A Study in Economic Ambivalence* (Princeton: Princeton University Press, 1966); Brinkley, *End of Reform*; Ira Katznelson, *Fear Itself: The New Deal and the Origins of Our Time* (New York: Liveright, 2013); Levy, *Freaks of Fortune*, 231–263.

141. Moley, *Realities and Illusions*, 17.

142. Frank Freidel, foreword, in Raymond Moley, *The First New Deal* (New York: Harcourt, Brace and World, 1966), xiii.

143. Suzanna La Follette to Raymond Moley, March 26, 1954, box 30, RMP-LC.

144. Raymond Moley, *How to Keep Our Liberty* (New York: Alfred A. Knopf, 1952), 36.

145. Moley, *Realities and Illusions*, 195; Raymond Moley to Barry Goldwater, October 4, 1953, box 19, RMP-LC.

146. Raymond Moley, "Henry George and the Forgotten Man," *Henry George News* (July 1952): 1.

147. Moley, *How to Keep Our Liberty*, 229–230; "Henry George Address," August 31, 1964, box 142, RMP-LC.

148. Creel, *Rebel at Large*, 353–355.

149. George Creel to Henry, February 26, 1953, box 4, GCP-LC.

150. Richard Nixon to George Creel, August 30, 1952; Nixon to George Creel, November 28, 1952; George Creel to Nixon, December 23, 1952; Nixon to George Creel, September 27, 1952; Nixon to George Creel, December 20, 1952, all box 4, GCP-LC.

151. Creel, *Rebel at Large*, 47; George Creel to Jesse, January 25, 1952, box 4, GCP-LC.

152. Greenberg, *Republic of Spin*, 223–237.

153. "Address at People's Forum, March 3, 1912," container 1, PNSS-FRPL.

154. Gerald D. Nash, *A. P. Giannini and the Bank of America* (Norman: University of Oklahoma Press, 1992), 111–112.

155. Terry Golway, *Machine Made: Tammany Hall and the Creation of Modern American Politics* (New York: Liveright, 2014); Elliot Brownlee, *Federal Taxation in America: A Short History* (Cambridge: Cambridge University Press, 2004), 107–146.

156. Johnston, *Radical Middle Class*, 135.

157. C. Wright Mills, *The Power Elite* (1956; reprinted, Oxford: Oxford University Press, 2000); Kevin Mattson, *Intellectuals in Action: The Origins of the New Left and Radical Liberalism, 1945–1970* (University Station: Penn State University Press, 2010).

158. Alan Ryan, *Bertrand Russell: A Political Life* (New York: Hill and Wang, 1988), 1.

159. George Creel, "A Great Crisis—And Youth Is Asleep," October 27, 1941, oversized 15, GCP-LC.

160. Mitgang, *The Man Who Rode the Tiger*, 337.

161. Mitgang, 361; Samuel Seabury, *The New Federalism: An Inquiry into the Means by Which Social Power May Be So Distributed Between State and People as to Insure Prosperity and Progress* (New York: Dutton, 1950), 15, 26, 89–80, 89, 175, 210–11, 216.

162. Mitgang, *Man Who Rode the Tiger*, 359.

163. Eric Hobsbawm, *The Age of Extremes: A History of the World, 1914–1991* (New York: Pantheon Books, 1994), 112.

Conclusion

1. William Graham Sumner, *What Social Classes Owe to Each Other* (New York: Harper and Brothers, 1883), 123–152; Moley, *First New Deal*, 15.

2. "Where Are the Pre-war Radicals?" *Survey* (February 1926): 556.

3. Hofstadter, *Age of Reform*; James T. Kloppenberg, *Uncertain Victory: Social Democracy and Progressivism in European and American Thought* (New York: Oxford University Press, 1986).

4. Edward J. Larson, *Summer for the Gods: The Scopes Trial and America's Continuing Debate over Science and Religion* (New York: Basic Books, 2006), 37–39; Kazin, *A Godly Hero*, 254.

5. Adam Rome, *Bulldozers in the Countryside: Suburban Sprawl and the Rise of American Environmentalism* (New York: Cambridge University Press, 2001).

6. Matthew Lassiter, *The Silent Majority: Suburban Politics in the Sunbelt South* (Princeton, N.J.: Princeton University Press, 2007); Kevin Kruse, *White Flight: Atlanta and the Making of Modern Conservatism* (Princeton, N.J.: Princeton University Press, 2005); Thomas Sugrue, "Crabgrass-Roots Politics: Race, Rights, and the Reaction against Liberalism in the Urban North, 1940–1964," *Journal of American History* 82, no. 2 (September 1995): 551–578.

7. J. Eric Oliver, *Democracy in Suburbs* (Princeton, N.J.: Princeton University Press, 2001).

8. John Kenneth Galbraith, *American Capitalism: The Concept of Countervailing Power* (1952; reprinted, London: Transaction, 2011), x. Galbraith wrote a new introduction for the 1993 printing.

9. George, *Protection or Free Trade?* 285–295.

10. Thomas Piketty, *Capital in the Twenty-First Century* (Cambridge, Mass.: Belknap Press of Harvard University Press, 2013), 459.

11. David Harvey, *The Urban Experience* (Baltimore: Johns Hopkins University Press, 1985); John Friedman, "The World City Hypothesis," *Development and Change* 17, no. 1 (January 1986): 69–84; Saskia Sassen, *The Global City: New York, London, Tokyo* (Princeton, N.J.: Princeton University Press, 1991).

12. Matthew Rognlie, "A Note on Piketty and the Diminishing Returns to Capital," Northwestern University, June 15, 2014, mrognlie/piketty_diminishing_returns.pdf; Guillaume Allegre and Xavier Timbeau, "Does Housing Wealth Contribute to Wealth Inequality?" *OFCE* 9 (January 8, 2015).

13. Luke Murphy, "British Wealth Is Concentrated Not in Property but in the Land Underneath," *New Statesman*, August 29, 2018. https://www.newstatesman.com/politics /staggers/2018/08/british-wealth-concentrated-not-property-land-underneath; "Who Really Owns Britain?" *Country Life*, November 16, 2010, http://www.countrylife.co.uk /articles/who-really-owns-britain-20219.

14. Wendong Zhang, "2021 Farmland Value Survey, Iowa State University," Iowa State University Extension and Outreach: AG Decision Maker, accessed April 12, 2022, https://www.extension.iastate.edu/agdm/wholefarm/html/c2-70.html; Katy Keiffer, "Who Really Owns American Farmland?" *New Food Economy*, July 31, 2017.

15. Chrystia Freeland, "The Problem of Plutocrats: What a 19th-Century Economist Can Teach Us about Today's Capitalism," October 21, 2013, *Huffington Post*, http://www .huffingtonpost.com/chrystia-freeland/henry-george-capitalism_b_1997899.html.

16. Peter Orszag, "To Fight Inequality, Tax Land," *Bloomberg View*, March 3, 2015, http://www.bloombergview.com/articles/2015-03-03/to-fight-inequality-tax-land.

17. "A Tax Policy with San Francisco Roots," *New York Times*, July 30, 1911.

18. Edward L Glaeser, "Tax Land, Not Buildings, to Help Cities Thrive," *Boston Globe*, February 6, 2014.

19. "Tax Land Value, Close Loopholes to Solve Affordability Crisis," *Vancouver Sun*, October 17, 2017.

20. "Poor Land Use in the World's Greatest Cities Carries a Huge Cost," *The Economist*, April 4, 2015. For other examples, see Dan Reed, *Baltimore Sun*, June 1, 2015; Noah Smith, "Piketty's Three Big Mistakes," *Bloomberg View*, March 27, 2015; Eli Leherer, "The Right Way to Eliminate State Income Taxes," *Huffington Post*, posted on March 27, 2013; Scott Baker, "America Is Not Broke," *Huffington Post*, November 11, 2012; Tim Worstall, "Contra Piketty, It's Not a Wealth Tax We Need but a Land Tax," *Forbes*, March 27, 2015.

21. Michael Gibson, "San Francisco's Slow-Motion Suicide," *National Review*, April 8, 2019.

22. "Tony Blair Backs Labour's 'Land Value Tax' to Tackle Housing Crisis," *The Guardian*, December 2, 2017.

23. Sum Lok-kei, "Hong Kong Ranked World's Freest Economy for 25th Successive Year, Beating Singapore at 2nd Place and Mainland China in 100th," *South China Morning Post*, January 25, 2019; Anne Haila, *Urban Land Rent: Singapore as a Property State* (West Sussex, UK: John Wiley and Sons, 2016); Younghoon Ro, *Land Value Taxation in South Korea* (Boston: Lincoln Institute of Land Policy, 2001).

24. Joshua Vincent, "Neighborhood Revitalization and New Life: A Land Value Taxation Approach," *American Journal of Economics and Sociology* 71, no. 4 (October 2012): 1073–1094; Mark Allan Hughes, "Why So Little Georgism in America? Using the Pennsylvania Case Files to Understand the Slow, Uneven Progress of Land Value Taxation," Working Paper, July 20 (Cambridge: Lincoln Institute of Land Policy, 2007).

25. "GDP Per Capita," *World Bank*, accessed March 10, 2019, https://data.worldbank .org/indicator/NY.GDP.PCAP.PP.CD?end=2016&locations=LV-EE-LT-RU-UA-GE-BY -AM-AZ-MD-KZ-KG-UZ-TM-TJ&start=2016&view=bar.

26. Cameron K. Murray, "Unspoken Alternatives to Expensive Housing," *Australia Institute* (September 2018).

27. Anne Kristine Høj, Mads Rahbek Jørgensen, and Poul Schou, "Land Taxes and Housing Prices," Danish Economic Councils Working Paper 2017:1 (2017).

28. Matthew Keegan, "How Public Transportation Actually Turns a Profit in Hong Kong," *The Guardian*, March 19, 2019.

29. Matthew Feinberg and Matthew Willer, "From Gulf to Bridge: When Do Moral Arguments Facilitate Political Influence?" *Personality and Social Psychology Bulletin* 41, no. 12 (October 2015): 1–17.

30. Karl Marx, "Thesis on Feuerbach," *Marx/Engels Selected Works* (Moscow: Progress, 1969), 1:15.

31. George, *Social Problems*, 327.